Gospel Advocate Restoration Reprints

Seventh Day Adventism Renounced

D.M. Canright

Gospel Advocate Company
P.O. Box 150
Nashville, Tennessee 37202

Seventh-Day Adventism Renounced

AFTER AN EXPERIENCE OF TWENTY-EIGHT YEARS BY A PROMINENT MINISTER AND WRITER OF THAT FAITH

D.M. CANRIGHT

"Ye know not when the time is." Jesus, Mark 13:33.
"Beware of false prophets." Jesus, Matt. 7:15.
"Keep my commandments." Jesus, John 14:15

Seventh Day Adventism Renounced
Gospel Advocate Restoration Reprints, 2001

© 1914, D.M. Canright

Published by Gospel Advocate Co.
P.O. Box 150, Nashville, TN 37202
www.gospeladvocate.com

ISBN: 0-89225-163-8

Yours truly,
D. M. Canright.

PUBLISHER'S NOTE.

D. M. Canright died at Grand Rapids, Mich., May 12, 1919, in his eightieth year. Soon after his death his daughter wrote O. E. Payne, Hanna, Alta., Canada: "Father was more firm in his conviction of the error of their teaching the longer he lived, in spite of Adventist claims that he repudiated his writings against them. I tell you this in anticipation of your having such falsehoods to meet." (Quoted by Mr. Payne in The Christian Standard, October 16, 1920.)

The Publisher is glad to pass this information on to the defenders of the truth against the errors of Adventism. It will answer the oft-repeated, but wholly false, claim that Mr. Canright repudiated his writings against Adventism before he died. Again, the Publisher is gratified to be able to give to the public a book of such value that, although it has not been out of print a long time, yet it has sold at a premium. It has been so scarce that it was hardly available at any price.

If this volume serves to rescue one soul from the meshes of Adventism, the Publisher will be repaid.

B. C. GOODPASTURE.

Seventh-Day Adventism Renounced.

By ELDER D. M. CANRIGHT.

Testimonials.

THE work of a specialist is highly valued when his particular line is under investigation.

This work is the product of many years of careful study by a specialist on the history, methods and doctrines of Seventh-Day Adventists. For twenty-eight years I was intimately associated with that people, as member, minister, writer and author and aided much in building up that work. I joined them only fourteen years from their beginning, hence became well acquainted with all its founders, their early theories, and have all their first books published during the first forty years. Am perfectly familiar with every argument they use and the answer to it. I know their inside history and weak points as others could not. It is a complete text book on that subject. Here is what competent judges say who have read and used it:

"On some subjects there is one book that stands so far above all other books on the same subject that if a person has that one book he needs no other on that subject. Canright's 'Seventh-Day Adventism Renounced' is just such a book. It is a complete and perfect exposure of that delusion from beginning to end. Adventists have attempted no reply to it for the simple reason that **they** cannot, so they are trying to throw doubt on his character and standing, but that also is a hopeless task. If you are troubled with Adventism, get this book. Read it; study it; lend it; confront them with it; insist on them meeting it, and you will have no more trouble with them."—*Southland Evangelist*, Hartworth, Texas.

"It is the best book I have ever seen on the subject, after a study of it for twenty years."—Rev. Wm. Armstrong, Canton, Pa., Genessee Conf. of M. E. Church.

"It is a very full discussion of the question on which Adventists differ from us."—*Baptist Christian Herald*, Detroit, Mich.

"It is a thorough exposure of this modern delusion. How any system of error can survive such an exposure will be a mystery. This book ought to be circulated in every community where Adventism is preached."—*Christian Oracle* (Disciple) Des Moines, Iowa.

"I am delighted with it. It is kind, candid, careful, correct and comprehensive. I heartily commend the work as the best that has yet been published on that subject."—Prof. D. R. Dungan, President of Drake University, Des Moines, Iowa.

"He exposes with unsparing logic, but never with malice, the errors of Seventh-Day Adventism. This book is eminently fitted to do good."—

TESTIMONIALS.

Rev. Kendall Brooks, D. D., ex-President of Kalamazoo College, Mich.

"I did not know that it was possible to give so perfect an answer to the letter of Adventism. I have always felt that its spirit was contrary to the Gospel. Your exposure is doubtless the ablest and most comprehensive in existence." — Rev. Theodore Nelson, LL. D., late president of Kalamazoo Baptist College.

"I pronounce it simply overwhelming."—Rev. B. F. Whittemore, Principal of Lester Seminary, Holden, Mo.

"Your work is a book we have long needed, and now should be in the hands of every Christian."—Rev. J. Cairns, Colfax College, Wash.

"It is a grand book."—M. McLellan, Melbourne, Australia.

"No other book has fallen into our hands that is so well adapted to meet the sophistry and statements of Seventh-Day Adventists as this."—*Central Free Will Baptists*, Farmington, W. Va.

"The most effective work that has yet been published."—*Missionary Visitor*.

"It would be a good plan to place a copy of it in every circulating library in the land."—*Methodist Michigan Christian Advocate*, Detroit.

"A strong and vigorous book on Seventh-Dayism. The best thing published upon this subject."—*Chicago Standard*, Baptist.

"An interesting and valuable book."—*Central Baptist*.

"There is no other book in the market that can possibly fill its place." — *California Christian Advocate*, Methodist.

"It is complete and unanswerable."—*Northern Christian Advocate*.

"A very valuable book that exposes in a sharp and effective way the pretensions of modern Adventism."—*Arkansas Baptist*.

"A stalwart book which gives no uncertain sound. This is the first book which we have seen that ably and justly exposes to the world the true inwardness of the Seventh-Day Advent delusion."—Rev. G. J. Travis, Ph. D., Baptist.

"It is by far the most complete and satisfactory treatment of the subject that I have seen."—Rev. J. Sunderland, Baptist Cor. Sec. and Supt. of Missions, Minneapolis, Minn.

"The work is a trenchant and conclusive exposé and refutation of the doctrine in question." — Rev. John W. Haley, M. A., author of "Alleged Discrepancies of the Bible" and other works.

"A most crushing refutation of their sophistries."— *The Christian Pioneer*, Australia.

"A complete antidote to the fallacies of our Seventh-Day friends."— *Christian Colonist*, Australia.

President's Office, Little Rock University, Ark.: "'Adventism Renounced' is a most timely work, eminently fitted to combat the fallacies at which it aims."—Prof. W. F. Shedd.

"'Adventism Renounced' is like Webster's Dictionary or the sunshine, it needs no praise. No candid man can read the book and be an Adventist. Every preacher should have a copy."—J. V. Coombs, President of Indiana College, Covington, Ind.

"The book certainly surpasses in clearness, strength and adaptability to do the best work of any book which has ever appeared from the press on the Sabbath question and against Seventh-Day Adventists."— *Texas Baptist and Herald*.

"It is certainly an excellent book, pronounced very unanimously as the ablest treatise on the subject, and would do good service in the hands of pastors."—*Pacific Baptist*, Portland, Ore.

"It is the standard on Seventh-

TESTIMONIALS.

Day Adventism and no one who sends for it will be disappointed. We recommend it as simply and undeniably the best work on the question, as it deals with its errors from the experimental standpoint."—*The Standard*, Cincinnati, O.

"For an exhaustive discussion of the questions relating to the Seventh-Day and the first day, see 'Seventh-Day Adventism Renounced,' by Rev. D. M. Canright."—David C. Cook Pub. Co., Chicago, in the *New Adult Bible Class*, April, 1912.

"What books would you recommend to meet the advocates of S. D. Adventism?" Ans. "We would recommend you to read 'Seventh-Day Adventists Renounced,' by Eld. Canright."—*The Christian Workers' Magazine*, Oct., 1912, published by the Moody Bible Institute, Chicago. No better recommend could be given.

I close with three testimonies of men who were, like myself, long years in Adventism, but are now free in Christ:

"Your grand book is received. I do not think I ever appreciated a book any more than I do this one, it is so complete and unanswerable."—Prof. C. C. Ramsey, nine years Professor in their colleges, and now in Harvard University.

"I heartily commend Elder Canright's book as a faithful statement of the belief and practice of Seventh-Day Adventists, and the spirit and tendency of the system. Adventists can never meet these arguments."—Rev. D. B. Oviatt, seven years President of the Pennsylvania Conf. of S. D. Adventists.

"We were Seventh-Day Adventists for more than twenty years, believing the doctrine firmly. Were familiarly acquainted with Elder White and wife and the inside history of that people. We found it a yoke of bondage and obtained freedom and the blessing of God in renouncing it and uniting with the Methodists. We heartily endorse Elder Canright's book as correctly representing that people and their faith. It is an unanswerable refutation of that system."—Mr. and Mrs. C. A. Russell, Otsego, Mich.

I have selected only a few quotations from scores more like these, and have given only a few words from each of these, showing how this book is valued by good judges.

Preface to Fourteenth Edition.

"To criticise, expose and condemn others is not a pleasant task; but when religious teachers enthrone error, and mislead honest people, silence would be unkind and censurable."

Being profoundly convinced that Seventh-Day Adventism is a system of error, I feel it my duty to publish what I know of it. I do it in the fear of God. Knowing the sorrow it has brought to my heart and to thousands, I must warn others against it. I do not question the honesty of the Adventists, but their sincerity does not sanctify their errors. I have had to speak plainly, but, I trust, kindly. I have had to treat each subject briefly, and leave many untouched, but I have taken up the main pillars of that faith; if these fall, the whole must go down.

It is now nearly twenty-five years since this book was first published. This is the fourteenth edition. It has been translated into several languages, sold by numerous publishing houses, gone to the ends of the earth wherever Adventism has gone, and has been the greatest obstacle that work has ever had to meet. Yet Adventists have ventured no answer to it. Say what they may, it is evident that they would gladly answer it if they could do so safely.

"Replies to Eld. Canright," quoted in this work, is not an answer to this book, but to a few articles I wrote for a paper long before the book was published. The pamphlet itself proves this. The title page is dated "1888," while my book was not published till one year later, 1889. See my title page. Then on page eighty of their pamphlet I read this: "He promises a forthcoming book, by which we presume he designs to sweep away clean everything which his articles have left. It will receive due attention, if thought worthy of it, when it appears." This shows that this "Reply" was no answer to my book. One was promised but never appeared. The book discusses many topics not even mentioned in the articles, and, of course, is much more complete every way. Considering that Adventists are always so ready for debate, discussion and replies, how is it that this book, that has bothered them more than all others which have appeared against them, is so carefully let alone by them? The reason is manifest to all candid people.

And here is what my Advent brethren thought of me before I left them: "Battle Creek, Mich., July 13, 1881. Brother Canright: * * * I feel more interest in you than in any other man, because I know your worth when the Lord is with you, as a laborer. James White."

"Battle Creek, Mich., May 22, 1881. * * * It is time there was a change of the officers of the General Conference. I trust that if we are true and faithful the Lord will be pleased that we should constitute two of that Board. James White."

"Battle Creek, Mich., Aug. 6, 1884. * * * You have long been with us, and we all love you. G. I. Butler."

"Martinsburg, Neb., July 14, 1884. * * * You were a power in the world, and did a vast amount of good. * * * We need your help in the work greatly. Your precious talent, if humbly and fully consecrated to God, would be so *useful*. There are so many places where it would be a great help. G. I. Butler."

PREFACE TO FOURTEENTH EDITION. 7

Advent Review, March, 1887: "We have felt exceedingly sad to part in our religious connection with one whom we have long esteemed as a dear brother."

Advent Review, March 22, 1887: "In leaving us, he has taken a much more manly and commendable course than most of those who have withdrawn from us, coming voluntarily to our leading brethren, and frankly stating the condition of mind he was in. He did this before his own church, in our presence, and, so far as we know, has taken no unfair, underhanded means to injure us in any way. He goes from our midst with no immoral stain upon his character, chooses associations more pleasant to himself. This is every man's personal privilege if he chooses to take it."

The quotations in my book are from the Adventist books published up to the date when I wrote my book, 1889. Since then most of their books have been reprinted and paged differently. To conform to these books as now paged, I would need to change many of my references. To do this I would have to reprint my whole book, as it is in electrotype plates. A change of a few plates would necessitate a change of all. So it leaves them as they were. The quotations are all there, only some are on a different page in their present editions. I took great care to have every quotation exactly correct. They are reliable.

I design to be perfectly fair towards my Advent brethren. I was with them twenty-eight years, from the age of nineteen to forty-seven, the most active years of my life. I was dearly loved by them and I loved them. I love them now. I have thousands of dear friends among them still. It was a terrible trial to break away from all these tender ties. Even now the tears fall fast as I write these lines. But truth and duty were dearer to me than social ties.

Again I bear them record that they are a sincere, devoted, self-sacrificing people, thoroughly believing what they profess. They have many excellent qualities, and many lovely Christian people among them. Like all churches, they have their full share of undesirable members, not from any immoral teachings, but from human frailty, common in all churches. Daily I pray for them that the Lord may bless all that is good in them and forgive, and, in some way, overrule for good when they are in error. This is all I dare ask for myself.

D. M. CANRIGHT.

1914.

My Present Standing.

WHEN a prominent man leaves one church or party and joins an opposing one and gives his reasons for it he may expect that his old associates will reply to him. I expected no exception in my case when I renounced Adventism, so have not been disappointed. The great majority of my former brethren have been very friendly to me and treated me kindly. A few, a very few, have done otherwise. Their object has been to counteract my influence against what they regard as God's work. These few have started the report that I have been sorry I left Adventism, that I have said so, have tried to return to them, have confessed that my book was false, and some have said that I was very poor, a physical and mental wreck, with no hope of salvation, etc. These reports are accepted as facts by honest brethren and repeated till they are believed by many Adventists the world over. I have denied them in every possible way, but they are still believed and repeated, and doubtless always will be. I leave God to judge between us.

I now and here for the hundredth time solemnly affirm before God that I renounced Adventism because I believed it to be an error. I have never once regretted that I did so, have never intimated to any one that I have had the least desire to go back to that people. It would be impossible for me to do such a thing and be an honest man. I am now (1915) well in body and mind, have a good home worth $10,000 or $12,000, and have four grown children, of whom any man would be proud. On leaving the Adventists I joined the Baptist church at Otsego, Mich., and became its pastor till it was built up into a prosperous church. They have been my ardent friends to this day. Twenty years ago I moved to Grand Rapids, Mich., took a new mission and built this up, organized it into a church which has become one of the strong churches of the city, having several hundred members with a fine edifice. Have twice been its pastor, always an active member. At present I teach a large adult Bible class every Lord's day and often preach for them. Have always been in perfect harmony with the church. They honor me as their father, consult me on all important matters, and hotly resent the foolish reports which some circulate concerning me.

Out of scores of printed testimonies before me I select only a few which speak for themselves:

"*Grand Rapids, Mich., Nov. 1, 1907.*
"*To whom it may concern:*

"Having received many letters from all parts of the United States from those that have been informed by Adventists that Rev. D. M. Canright was not a member of a Baptist church and many other things pertaining to his character, we very emphatically denounce any such statements and will say that he is now and has been for many years an active member of the Berean Baptist church of this city and twice its pastor, a man above reproach and above all a noble Christian.

"Respectfully, W. H. Adrews, former clerk and charter member of the above named church. I hereby certify to the above.

"REV. ROBERT GRAY,
"Pastor of the Berean Church."

MY PRESENT STANDING. 11

"*Grand Rapids, Mich., April 9, 1910.*
"*To whom it may concern, world wide,*
"DEAR BRETHREN:
"This letter is to say that Rev. D. M. Canright has been known to the undersigned for many years as an earnest, consecrated Christian man, and a true minister of Jesus Christ. He has been 'a faithful and true witness' against the errors of the Seventh-Day Adventists in his books and tracts for many years.
"OLIVER W. VAN OSDEL,
"Moderator Grand River Valley Association.
"ALEXANDER DODDS,
"President City Baptist Mission Society.
"W. I. COBURN,
"President Baptist Ministers' Conference."

The Baptists are not the only people who think well of the Rev. Mr. Canright. A Congregational minister adds his word:

"This certifies that I have been acquainted with the Rev. D. M. Canright of this city for more than forty-five years. At least twenty years of that time he was an Adventist preacher, and during those years his reputation as a Christian man and as a preacher of rare ability was of the highest order. His name among the Adventist people of this state was of the highest order. His name among the Adventist people of this state was a household word for righteousness of character, and an able defender of their faith. And when he left the Adventist denomination, all who knew the man, if they were at all imbued with the Christian spirit, must admit that the change made by him was due to a candid, conscientious conviction of what he believed to be right. There could be no other motive in his case, for he was successful beyond many of his brethren, and honored by them in the highest degree. For at least twenty years he and his beloved family have lived in this city and he has maintained the same reputation that he had, as a Christian gentleman and respected citizen. What I have written is from personal knowledge of Rev. D. M. Canright and of the Adventist denomination in this state.

"J. T. HUSTED,
"Pastor of the Wallin Congregational Church.
"*Grand Rapids, Mich.,
April 12, 1910.*"

The Methodist pastors add their tribute as follows:

"Various inquiries having come to the different members of the Association concerning the character and standing of Rev. D. M. Canright, the regular monthly meeting of the Methodist Ministers' Association of Grand Rapids, Mich., did, by an unanimous vote, adopt the following expression of its confidence in and regard for the personal worth and ministerial usefulness of Brother Canright.

"Rev. D. M. Canright, formerly a minister in the Seventh-Day Adventist Association, more recently a minister in the Baptist Association of this city, has been known by some of our number in person for several years and by reputation by the rest, and all our knowledge and information concerning him are of the most favorable kind.

"Any reflections on his personal character as a man, a husband, a citizen, a son or a Christian are without foundation, in fact, are unwarranted by any facts known to his intimate acquaintances. He is honored among his brethren, respected in his own community, and is commended by us as being worthy of confidence and trust.

MY PRESENT STANDING. 13

He has had an honored and useful ministry, and in no sense is deserving of the attacks made on him.

"Done at Grand Rapids, Mich., this 11th day of April, 1910, by the authority of the Grand Rapids Methodist Ministers' Association, by
"JOHN R. T. LATHROP, District Supt.
"CHARLES NEASE, President.
"J. R. WOOTEN, Secretary."

"*Grand Rapids, Mich., April 11, 1910.*

"It is with sincere pleasure that I write concerning the character and integrity of the Rev. D. M. Canright. I have known him and his family a good many years, and do not hesitate to say that they are very estimable people, and have the confidence of their neighbors and friends in the community.

"I consider Mr. Canright a Christian gentleman in every sense of the word; a man of the highest integrity and one who desires, in every project with which he is connected, to make righteousness his guide to action.

"He has done business with our bank for a good many years and I have personally had reason to test his integrity and am unequivocal in my expression of confidence in him.

"Very truly yours,
"CHARLES W. GARFIELD."

(Mr. Garfield is president of a bank with $2,000,000.)

Adventists sometimes say I left them four or five times. I withdrew from that church just once, no more, that was final. Their church records at Battle Creek and Otsego will show that. For years I was troubled with doubts about some of their doctrines and three times stopped preaching for a short period, but remained a member in good standing. At a large camp-meeting I was persuaded to swallow my doubts, take up the work again, confess that I had been in the dark, and go on again. I yielded my judgment to the entreaties of my brethren and the love I had for old associates and said what I soon regretted. I found it a terrible struggle to break away from what had held me so long.

Since I left them they try to make it appear that I did not amount to much anyway. "Sour grapes," said the fox to the delicious fruit which he could not reach! As a refutation of their detractions, see Chapter II of my book. I will here state only a few facts briefly:

During two years, 1876, 1877, I was one of the general conference committee of three which had control of all their work in the world. There is no higher authority in the denomination. How did it happen that I was placed in that office if I was not one of their best men? Year after year I was elected on the boards having charge of their most important institutions, such as their Publishing House, College, Sanitarium, Sabbath School Association, etc., etc. For proof of this see their printed year books where my name appear constantly. I was made theological teacher in their college, president of a state conference, associate editor of a paper, etc. I selected and arranged the course of reading which all their ministers had to follow, and I was sent to their annual state conferences to examine these preachers in those studies, in their theology, and in their fitness for the ministry. Is such work usually committed to an inferior man?

But it was as a writer in their papers, as the author of numerous tracts, pamphlets and books covering nearly every controverted point of their faith, as a lecturer and debater in defense of their doctrines, that I was the best known during the last fifteen years I was with them. In

MY PRESENT STANDING.

these lines, not a man among them stood as prominent as I did. Every one at all familiar with their work during that period knows that I tell only the simple truth in the case. They know it, too. For my writings the office once paid me $500 in one check and many other times different sums. After twenty-seven years they still publish and use several of my tracts as being better than anything they have been able to produce since.

My long and thorough acquaintance with Adventism and all their arguments prepared me to answer them as no other could. Hundreds of ministers from all parts have written me their thanks for the aid my book has been to them in meeting Adventism. Did not God in his providence prepare me for this work? I humbly believe he did, and this reconciles me to the long and bitter experiences I had in that bondage. But if God and the truth is honored, I am content.

The only question is, do I know their doctrines well enough to state them clearly, and have I the ability to answer them plainly? Let my work be the answer.

Since I withdrew Adventists have published five or six different tracts to head off my influence. If I amount to so little, why all this effort? What they do refutes what they say. God has preserved me to outlive nearly all the Adventist ministers with whom I began laboring. At seventy-five am full of faith in God and the hope of eternal life through our Lord Jesus Christ.

I love those brethren still and know that most of them are honest Christian people, but in error on many of their views. I would be glad to help them if I could.

D. M. CANRIGHT,
Pastor Emeritus of the Berean Baptist Church.
Grand Rapids, Michigan.

Table of Contents.

	Page.
PREFACE TO FOURTEENTH EDITION, ...	5
MY PRESENT STANDING, ...	9
INTRODUCTION, ...	21

By Rev. Dr. Nelson.

CHAPTER I—DOCTRINES AND METHODS OF SEVENTH-DAY ADVENTISTS, ... 25

Their Doctrines—Extent of Their Work—Hostility to Others—Methods of Work—How to Meet It—Lack of Education.

CHAPTER II—AN EXPERIENCE OF TWENTY-EIGHT YEARS IN ADVENTISM, ... 37

Accepts Adventism—Ordained—First Doubts—Position of Elder White and Wife—Leading Men in Doubt—Extensive Labors—Elder White's Death—Doubts Increase—At Work Again—Renounces the Doctrine—Why?—Positions Held—False Reports—Joins the Baptists.

CHAPTER III—ADVENTISM A YOKE OF BONDAGE, . 59

Confessions of Ministers, Etc.—Ministers Who Have Renounced It—College Professors—Physicians—Leads to Infidelity—Church Backslidden.

CHAPTER IV—ORIGIN, HISTORY AND FAILURES OF ADVENTISM, ... 67

Time Set for the End of the World in the 2d Century, 10th Century, 17th Century, and Often Since—Seventh-Day Adventists' Origin—Miller—Fruit of Millerism—Time Setting—Miller's Confession—No Special Message—Eighteen Mistakes.

CHAPTER V—MY OBJECTIONS TO THE SEVENTH-DAY ADVENTIST SYSTEM, ... 81

Twenty-Six Objections—Their Position on the Prophecies—Ignorance of Many of Them.

18 TABLE OF CONTENTS.

Page.

CHAPTER VI—THE TWO-HORNED BEAST AND
THE MESSAGES, ... 89
   The Advent Theory—It is the Papacy—Arguments Answered—Image of the Beast—Deadly Wound—Mark of the Beast—Absurdities—Who Has the Mark of the Beast?—The Three Messages—God's Seal.

CHAPTER VII—THE SANCTUARY, ... 117
   Their Theory—The Shut Door—New Theories—Within the Vail—The Temple—Why They are Wrong—The Gospel Temple.

CHAPTER VIII—MRS. WHITE AND HER REVELATIONS, ... 129
   Warned Against False Prophets—Swedenborg—Ann Lee—Joanna Southcott—Joseph Smith—Mrs. White's Claims to Inspiration—Writes a New Bible—It is Their Guide—Not Inspired—Plagiarisms—Visions Suppressed—Her Mistakes—The Shut Door—False Predictions—Reform Dress—Philosophy of Her Trances—Harm She Does—Becomes Rich—The Result.

CHAPTER IX—THE NATURE OF THE SABBATH COMMANDMENT, ... 166
   Both Moral and Ceremonial—Benefit of—Days Do Not Differ Naturally—Must Be Made Holy—Ceremony Defined—Sabbath Chiefly Ceremonial—Temporal—On the Round Earth—Day Line—At the Poles—Lost Time.

CHAPTER X—WHY CHRISTIANS KEEP SUNDAY, 185
   Lord's Day Traced Back to the Apostles—Rev. 1:10—Testimony of Lexicons and Commentators—Jesus is Lord—A Fitting Day—Importance of the Resurrection Day—John 20:26—Pentecost—Acts 20:7—1 Cor. 16:1, 2.

CHAPTER XI—DID THE POPE CHANGE THE SABBATH? 210
   Advent Sayings—Catechisms—Catholic Testimony—Pliny—Barnabas—"Teaching of the Apostles"—Justin Martyr—Dionysius—Bardesanes—Clement—Tertullian—Origen—Apostolical Constitutions—Anatolius—Victorinus—Peter—Eusebius—Cyclopedias.

TABLE OF CONTENTS. 19

CHAPTER XII—SABBATARIAN POSITIONS ON THE
    HISTORY OF SUNDAY REFUTED, ... 234
    "Bible Only"—"Fathers Unreliable"—Sunday Not the
    Sabbath—Their Authors Examined—Pagans and Sun-
    day—Constantine and Sunday—Exact Date When the
    Sabbath Was Changed—Arguments Refuted.

CHAPTER XIII—THE SABBATH IN THE OLD TESTA-
    MENT, ... 249
    In Genesis—Ex. 16—"Jewish Sabbath"—Ex. 31:16, 17
    —In the Decalogue—Isa. 56, 58 and 66—Eze. 22.

CHAPTER XIV—THE SABBATH IN THE NEW TESTA-
    MENT, ... 264
    A Radical Change—New Testament Decalogue—
    Christ's Example—Mark 2:27, 28; Matt. 24:20; 28:1;
    Luke 23:56—The Time Table—In Acts—Paul's Ex-
    ample.

CHAPTER XV—THE JEWISH SABBATH ABOLISHED, 282
    Col. 2:14-17—Sabbath Days, the Seventh Day—The
    Greek Word for Sabbath—The Seventh Day Associ-
    ated with Meats, Drinks, Feast Days, Etc.—Comments
    by Others—No Annual Sabbaths—A Shadow—Types
    in Eden—Gal. 4:10; Rom. 14:5.

CHAPTER XVI—A HISTORY OF NUMEROUS EFFORTS
    TO REVIVE THE JEWISH SABBATH. ALL FAIL, . 298
    Why Not Found Out Before?—Efforts to Revive the
    Sabbath Fail—At the Reformation—In England—Sev-
    enth-Day Baptists—Adventist Effort—As a Test It
    Fails—Their "New Light"—Opposed by Luther, Bax-
    ter, Bunyan, Roger Williams, Etc.

CHAPTER XVII—THE LAW, ... 305
    Antinomianism—"The Law" Defined—The Two Laws
    —The Decalogue Alone Not the Law of God—The
    Law Was Given by Moses—Did Not Exist Until Moses
    —Was Given Only to Jews—Not for Gentiles, and
    Was Only Temporal—God's Higher Law Is Eternal—
    Object of the Law—Letter of the Law Abolished and
    the Law Changed—Law of Liberty.

CHAPTER XVIII—THE DECALOGUE EXAMINED, . . 338
    Shown to Apply Only to Israel—Catholic Division of
    —Eminent Authors on Its Abolition.

CHAPTER XIX—THE TWO COVENANTS, ... 350
  The Covenant Defined. It is the Decalogue—Is Found in Ex. 19 to 24—Extent of—Abolished—How the New Differs from the Old—Comments.

CHAPTER XX—WHAT LAW ARE CHRISTIANS UNDER? 360
  The Authority of Christ—He Gave Commandments—Apostles Gave Commandments—These are the Commandments of God.

CHAPTER XXI—FORTY-SEVEN PROMINENT TEXTS USED BY SABBATARIANS EXAMINED, ... 366
  This Includes in Order as They Come Every Important Text on the Sabbath or the Law from Gen. 2:1-3, to Rev. 22:14.

CHAPTER XXII—THE NATURE OF MAN, ... 395
  The Faith of All People—In the Apocrypha—Josephus—Faith of the Early Church—Soul Sleeping a Sickly Plant—Is No Cure for Infidelity—The Rational Argument—Bible Argument—Man's Spirit Is Deathless—The Body Only a Tabernacle—Their Texts Answered—Endless Punishment—Annihilation Texts Examined.

APPENDIXES 411

Introduction.

By Rev. Theo. Nelson, LL. D., late President of Kalamazoo College.

I MET for the first time the author of "Adventism Renounced" in the autumn of 1865. He was then a rising young minister in high favor with his people. Then, as now, I had entire confidence in his sincerity. Nor do I think it strange that, after more than twenty years devoted to Seventh-Day Adventist propagandism, he should finally renounce their doctrines, and return to the orthodox faith. It is not necessary to impute any sinister or unworthy motives. Rather, it is easy enough to believe that experience and study, or the evolution of intelligence, as well as the irresistible logic of events, would inevitably bring to pass this result. Seventh-Day Adventists have always made a great deal of the "signs of the times," of earthquakes and falling stars, of "wars and rumors of wars." Arguments which might profoundly impress the imagination of a youth during the troubled period of our great civil war, would naturally lose their hold upon the riper judgment of a man in these "piping times of peace."

Toward the Seventh-Day Adventists as a people I cherish none but feelings of kindness. Generally, their piety is undoubtedly genuine, though misanthropic and melancholy. They take a low view of human nature, and practically isolate themselves from their neighbors, and from those affairs which concern the well-being of society as a whole. They stand aloof from every movement which looks to human progress, because they believe that human progress is impossible, and that mankind are already doomed; that destruction is impending, "even at the door." In fact, their religious faith restrains, if it does not destroy, their sentiment of patriotism, and causes them to regard with suspicion, if not with feelings of hostility, the free government under which they live. Nothing can be more absurd than their interpretations of current events, and, especially, their belief that our general and state governments are about to be converted into engines of religious persecution and despotism. It cannot be otherwise than that many sincere Seventh-Day Adventists, who have been such by what they believed the imperative necessity of Scripture teaching, will be grateful to Mr. Canright for aiding them to put off a yoke which fetters their usefulness and galls their minds.

Seventh-Day Adventists believe and teach that before the second coming of Christ the United States will form a union of church and state, and, like France and Spain in the seventeenth century, will become a persecuting power. They hold that the prophetic Scriptures clearly foretell this extraordinary change in the form and spirit of our government. Touching the correctness of the interpretations of Scripture upon which their expectations are based, they admit no possibility of mistake. They assume to know that they have the right key to prophecy —that they have the "present truth." They believe and teach that the Seventh-Day Adventists are to be especially tried in this ordeal that is being prepared by the civil government; that they are to be the chief victims of the fiery persecutions that will be waged against the "Saints of the Most High"; that they are to suffer, at the hands of the secular power, imprisonments, tortures, "the spoiling of their goods," and perhaps death itself. Indeed, they stake their whole system of doctrine upon this meaning of the Word of God, and they regard these momentous events, which they claim the Bible forecasts, as much a reality as though those events had already transpired. Those events are a reality to them and have the same value in argument, and the same authority in action, as history itself. In their publications and sermons they often adopt the style of the confessor who is already brought to the scaffold, or bound to the stake; they speak out in a tone of defiant, heroic submission, as though the fagots were being kindled and the crown of martyrdom were in full view. To one who is familiar with the history of religious persecutions, and has studied the progress and development of religious freedom, especially in Anglo-Saxon nations; to one who is fairly acquainted with the spirit of the age and country in which we live, this ostentatious martyr-spirit of our Adventist friends seems quite absurd. Were it not for their well-known uprightness and probity of character, we should be disposed to challenge their belief, such is their eagerness to find its proof and confirmation in events which have no such meaning. Under our form of government would it be possible to achieve a more intimate and perfect union of "church and state" than is embodied in the government of monarchical English? Such a change would be a greater miracle than for God to grow a giant oak in an instant. The trend of our civilization, the most powerful currents of public opinion, are all in the opposite direction. Yet, even in England, Adventists are free to publish their peculiar doctrines, to establish churches, and to pursue their vocations like other men. Religious freedom is the spirit of the age, and, most of all, the spirit of the age in America. Hence, we say, there need be no fears for the grave forebodings of our Advent friends.

THEO. NELSON.

CHAPTER I.

DOCTRINES AND METHODS OF SEVENTH-DAY ADVENTISTS.

Seventh-Day Adventism originated about seventy-five years ago in the work of Mr. Miller, who set the time for the end of the world in 1843-4. Adding some doctrines to the original faith, Elder James White and wife in 1846 became the leaders of the Seventh-Day branch of Adventism. Their headquarters were at different times at Paris, Me., Saratoga, Oswego, and Rochester, N. Y. In 1855 they settled permanently at Battle Creek, Mich., which remained the center of the work till recently.

THEIR DOCTRINES.

In doctrine they differ radically from evangelical churches. The main points are these as taught in all their books: They hold to the materiality of all things; believe in the sonship of Christ; believe that they only have a correct understanding of the prophecies to which they give most of their attention; that the end of the world is to occur in this generation; that we are now in the Judgment which began in 1844; that the Seventh day, Saturday, must be kept; that keeping Sunday is the mark of the beast; that all should pay tithes; that Mrs. White is inspired as were the writers of the Bible; that the Bible must be interpreted to harmonize with her writings; that they are called of God to give the last warning to the world; that the dead are unconscious; that the wicked and the devil will be annihilated; that all churches but their own are Babylon and rejected of God; that everybody but themselves will soon become spiritualists;

that when Christ comes only 144,000 out of all then living on the earth will be saved, and all these will be Seventh-Day Adventists. Hence, they have no fellowship with other Christians; never work with them in any way, but zealously proselyte from all.

They believe in the Bible, in conversion, in purity of life, in rigid temperance, in strict morality, and in other good things common to all churches. There are many excellent persons among them. In character they are not be compared with the spiritualists, infidels, etc., as is sometimes unjustly done.

THE EXTENT OF THEIR WORK.

Their Year Book for 1912 reports the following:

Conferences, 129; mission fields, 87; organized churches, 2,769; membership, 90,808; unorganized, 15,758; total, 104,528. Ordained ministers, 828; licensed ministers, 458; missionaries, 1,234; book canvassers, 1,697; total laborers, 4,346; Sabbath Schools, 4,151; membership, 101,161; church schools, 594; students, 13,357; colleges and academies, 86; students, 7,169; publishing houses, 28; employees, 610; sanitariums, 74; employees, 1,989; tithes, $1,338,689.65; average per member, $12.81; contributions for missions, home church work, tithes and all funds by the denomination, $2,223,767.52.

They publish 121 periodicals in twenty-eight languages. Books and tracts published in ninety-one languages.

The above will give a fair idea of the strength of that church. However, their main efficiency is in the distribution of their literature. Every member, old and young, down to little children, is taught and urged to engage in every way possible in distributing these tracts, papers and books through every possible channel. Every one believes

DOCTRINES AND METHODS OF SEVENTH-DAY ADVENTISTS. 27

he is doing God's work when he does this. Hence every member is a missionary in some way. The result is their literature is coming to be widely scattered the world over. Yet the results of all this tremendous outlay of money and work are very meagre. In the last four years with 4,000 laborers in the field, they have only averaged a gain of 4,000 members per year, or one for every worker. They have been at work now for seventy-five years to get 104,-000 members. The Mormons, starting about the same date, now number 500,000, nearly five times as many. The Christian Scientists, only about half as old, have over a million members. There is very little real spiritual power in it. The work is done mostly by hard labor and argument, not by any such mighty power as attended the work of the Apostles, or Luther, or Wesley, or Moody and many others. Their work now extends to all parts of the civilized world and into many heathen lands.

The number of their actual converts does not tell the harm they do. Where they convert one they confuse a score, who after that have no settled faith in any church, and are useless for any Christian work. Other conscientious persons are bothered and worried over it for years, not knowing what to do.

THEIR HOSTILITY TO ALL OTHER CHURCHES.

One of the highly objectionable features of that system is the bitter hostility of its believers towards all other churches. Their theory is that all churches but their own were utterly rejected of God in 1844 for not embracing Miller's doctrine. Thus Mrs. White says: "I saw the state of the different churches since the second angel proclaimed their fall [in 1844]. They have been growing more and more corrupt. * * * Satan has taken full possession of the churches as a body. * * * The churches were left as were the Jews; and they have been filling up with every unclean and hateful bird. I saw great iniquity and vileness in the churches; yet they profess to be Christians. Their professions, their prayers and their exhortations are an abomination in the sight of God. Said the angel, God will not smell in their assemblies. Selfishness, fraud and deceit are practiced by them without the reprovings of conscience." Spiritual Gifts, Vol. I, pages 189, 190. She says it is the devil who answers their prayers. Thus: "I saw them look up to the throne and pray, Father give us thy spirit; Satan would then breathe upon them an unholy influence." Early Writings, page 47. Again: "The nominal churches are filled with fornication and adultery, crime and murder, the result of base, lustful passion; but these things are kept covered." Testimonies, Vol. II, page 449. All intelligent people know that such statements are a misrepresentation of the evangelical churches of to-day. Elder White says: "Babylon, the nominal church, is fallen; God's people have come out of her. She is now the synagogue of Satan." Present Truth. April, 1850.

Hence they say that the revivals and conversions in the churches are largely a deception, the work of the devil, not of God. Mrs. White says of them: "The converts are not renewed in heart or changed in character." "They will exult that God is working marvelously for them, when the work is that of another spirit. Under a religious guise, Satan will spread his influence over the land. *He hopes to deceive many by leading them to think that God is still with the churches.*" Great Controversy, pages 294, 296. On this the Review and Herald, May 3, 1887, says: "We are aware that to assume that this revival work, so unquestionably accepted by all the churches, is not genuine, will cause the hands of Christendom to be raised in holy horror. * * *

DOCTRINES AND METHODS OF SEVENTH-DAY ADVENTISTS. 29

If He [God] is with us, He has not been with the popular churches in any marked manner since they rejected the Advent message of 1843-4, and they are congratulating themselves over delusive appearances, and a prosperity which has no existence in fact. The hand of God cannot direct two movements so antagonistic in nature."

Believing this, they eagerly watch for evidence to prove it and shut their eyes to any facts against it. So they rejoice at any unfavorable thing they can hear against ministers, churches, or members. They report it, repeat it, publish it, mangnify it, and live on it. To weaken, divide, or break up a church, is their delight. They heartily join with worldlings, infidels and atheists in their opposition to churches, and thus strengthen their unbelief and help them to perdition. They have gathered up all the most unfavorable things possible to find against the churches and put it in a book occupying thirty pages, and this they hand out for all to read. It is sad to see honest men devoting their lives to such highly censurable work, which must please Satan well.

WHO IS DECEIVED?

Seventh-Day Adventists dwell much on how easy it is to be deceived, to be led by Satan, when we think it is the Lord—to believe a lie for the truth. It is amusing to see how innocently they apply all this to others, and never dream that it has any application to themselves! What, *they* deceived? *they* misled? Impossible! They *know* they are right. Exactly, and that is just the way all feel, whether they be Mormons, Shakers, Catholics, or what not. The Adventists themselves are an illustration of the ease with which people are misled.

THEIR METHODS OF WORK.

Tent Meetings. Largely they use tents to enter new fields. Being a novelty, they attract attention. At first they present subjects which will offend no one till they gain the confidence of the people. Gradually they introduce their peculiar dogmas, then come out more boldly, till at length they denounce all other churches as Babylon, and their pastors as hirelings and deceivers. They say these pastors cannot defend their doctrines; dare not try. They offer rewards to any who will prove so and so; boast how they have scared this one, defeated that one, and silenced another. If in sermons the least reference is made to them, they call it persecution, give out a review, and do everything to provoke controversy. When the resident pastors are compelled to defend themselves, the Adventists claim to be greatly abused.

If a doctor, lawyer, teacher, or business man should enter a town and denounce all others of his profession as quacks, fools, or deceivers, how would he be treated? All would combine against him as a common enemy.

This is the way the pastors and churches meet the attacks of the Adventists, because compelled to. Like Ishmael of old, the hand of the Adventist is against every man, and hence every man's hand is against them. Gen. 16: 12. It is useless for them to deny this, for all know it to be true. They all do it. I was taught that way and followed it, and taught others to do the same.

Camp-meetings. Adventists hold many camp-meetings yearly. Here their ablest speakers preach their doctrines to thousands, and distribute their literature widely. They hire the papers to print lengthy flattering reports of their meetings, which they write themselves. Their reporters are trained for this special work. They gain wide attention, and impress many in this way.

Bible Readings. Hundreds of their men, women, and even young girls, are trained with printed lessons which they learn by heart, to go from house to house and give Bible readings. At first they conceal their real object and name, till they get a foothold. Then they cautiously introduce their tenets, work against pastors and churches, and lead away many.

Book-selling. Hundreds also are employed to canvass for their doctrinal books. The real nature of the book is studiously concealed, and the subscriber is deceived into buying a radical Advent book.

Distribution of Tracts. In every possible way, publicly, privately, from tent or church, by book-agents, colporteurs, Bible-readers, or private individuals, in depots, on boats, in stores, or families, through the mails, by sale, loan or gift, their tracts are persistently crowded everywhere.

Missions. They have Missions in many of the large cities and in foreign lands; but they are largely proselyting agencies. They do little among the heathen, or for the destitute and fallen, but go into the best families to which they can gain access, and gather the converts whom other missionaries have made. Thus Mrs. White instructs them: "Mistakes have been made in not seeking to reach ministers and the higher classes with the truth. * * * Educate men and women to labor for these higher classes both here and in other countries." Testimony No. 33, pages 108, 109. Jesus sent his disciples into the highways and hedges for the poor, lame and blind, for publicans, harlots and sinners; but Mrs. White does not relish that kind. She wants them from "the ministers and higher classes," "the whole who need no physician," those who can bring talent and money into the cause.

Where They Work. Adventists have the best success in new fields, where they are least known. Hence the western States is where they are most numerous. In New England, where they started, they have had to struggle hard to hold their own. In some of the older fields they have lost in numbers, in others the gain is very small. In hundreds of places where there were fair sized, active churches in the past, now no church at all, or a straggling, discouraged handful. Battle Creek is a fair illustration. This was their headquarters for forty years. Once there were 2,000 Sabbath keepers here, all united. Now there are less than 1,000, divided into four opposing parties, their influence entirely gone. The same is true elsewhere. About all the converts they make are at the outset. After a few years' acquaintance, they have no influence and few or none join them. Their churches grow smaller, generally, till they are unnoticed. The average membership of their churches is 29—exceedingly small; how different from the evangelical churches! The longer these are in a town the stronger they grow, and the more influence they have generally. But Adventism does not wear.

HOW TO MEET ADVENTISM.

People are led into Adventism from lack of information. Hence, when Adventism enters a town the people should be told plainly what it is, what its effects are, and wherein it is unscriptural. Quite generally pastors make a mistake in letting it alone for weeks, till it has gained a foothold. I always noticed that where the pastors united and worked against us on the start, we could do but little. So I would advise churches and pastors to take right hold of the matter earnestly as soon as people are interested in it. Preach on it; visit those who are being led away; hold Bible-readings; furnish them with proper books and tracts. Sit down patiently and answer arguments. Visit them again and again. Adventists will work a whole year, will go a hundred times, will give them scores of tracts **to proselyte** one person. If we would work a tenth as hard, scarcely one would be led away. People love to be noticed. The very attention they receive from the Adventists often wins them more than their arguments.

WHAT WILL BE THEIR END?

Adventism is founded on *time*, and *time* will kill it. It began by setting a definite time, 1844, for the end of the world, and failed. Now they hold that it must come in *this generation* beginning in 1844. This is only another way of time setting. In time all this will fail and overthrow their system. Then will come doubt, discouragement, divisions, apostacies, infidelity, and ruin to souls. This end is inevitable. The wider their influence now, the more terrible the disaster then. These wild, enthusiastic, fanatical moves which end in failure are the delight of Satan, as they bring disgrace upon the cause of Christ and end in infidelity. That such will be the end of Adventism I have not a doubt.

LACK OF EDUCATION AND TALENT AMONG THE ADVENTIST LEADERS.

The men whom God has chosen to lead out in the great religious movements of the past have, with few exceptions, been men of high education, refinement, and great talents. Moses, the founder of Judaism, "was learned in all the wisdom of the Egyptians, and was mighty in words and in deeds." Acts 7:22. Nehemiah, who restored Jerusalem after the captivity, was cup-bearer to the king. Neh. 2. So Daniel, the great prophet, had "knowledge and skill in all learning and wisdom." Dan. 1:17. He was prime minister of a mighty empire for many years. Paul was so renowned for his learning, that the king said to him: "Much learning doth make thee mad." Acts 26:24. He did for Christianity ten times more than all the other apostles together. It is to him, and not to the other apostles, that the Gentile world is indebted for Christianity. Then the twelve, though uneducated, had the advantage over all other reformers, that they were taught directly by the Son of G. d, and could work miracles.

St. Augustine, A. D. 353-430, the father of Christian theology, to whom the church owes almost as much as to Paul, was highly educated. As is well known, Luther was a thorough scholar, educated in the best schools of his day, and filled a professor's chair in a university. So Calvin and Melanchthon were both profound scholars, occupying professors' chairs in halls of learning. Zwingle, the great Swiss reformer, was celebrated for his learning and scholarship. Wiclif, the "Morning Star of the Reformation," was a graduate of Oxford, England, and a doctor of divinity. Cranmer, the great English reformer, was a graduate, a doctor of divinity, archbishop, and regent of the kingdom. Wesley, the father of Methodism, was a graduate of Oxford, a man of vast reading, the author or editor of commentaries, grammars, dictionaries, etc. It is a false idea that God generally uses ignorant men as leaders in reform, as the above great names will show.

Now look at the founders of our heretical sects. Joanna Southcott was wholly illiterate, a mere washer-woman. Ann Lee, the foundress of the Shakers, received no education, worked in a cotton factory, and was cook in a hospital. Joseph Smith, the founder of Mormonism, received no education, and Brigham Young very little. Not one of these persons were of influence in the world, outside of their own deluded followers.

How is it with the leaders of Adventism? Wm. Miller, the founder, was reared in the backwoods, in poverty, and received only the poor advantages of a common district school. Except some general reading, this was the extent of his education.

Elder White, the leader of the Seventh-Day Adventists' party, only secured sufficient education to teach a common district school. He was no student of books. In all my travels with him, I seldom saw him read half an hour in any book. Of the languages or the sciences he knew nothing, and little even of common history. Mrs. White received no school education, except a few weeks when a child. She, like Joanna Southcott, Ann Lee, and Joseph Smith, was wholly illiterate, not knowing the simplest rules of grammar. Not one of the leading men in that work ever graduated from college or university, and many are illiterate as Mrs. White herself. Elder J. N. Andrews, Elder Smith, and one or two more, by diligent study and reading out of school, became well informed men in their line. After Elder White came Elders Butler and Haskell as leaders, neither of them educated men, nor of half the natural talent of Elder White. The present leaders are small men also. Such men are poorly prepared to lead out in a great reformation in this educated age. Not a man among them has now, or ever had, a particle of influence in the world, or any office or responsible position in state or nation. How different from the great reformers of the past, who often had extensive influence for good, not only with the masses, but with the great men and kings of earth. Hence, from whatsoever side we view Adventism, it has none of the marks of a genuine reformation sent of God to bless the world.

Elder A. A. Phelps, for years editor of a First-Day Adventist paper says:

"I watched, and waited, and worked, with patience, meekness and loyalty, in hearty co-operation, and with an earnest desire to see such unity, enterprise, breadth and moral power, as ought to characterize a scriptural and heaven-inspired movement. How slowly and reluctantly I yielded to the conviction—forced by sad facts and illustrations that I have not even dared to detail—that I was only throwing away my life in stemming such waves of discord, indolence, looseness, narrowness, dogmatism and spiritual death as I could not overcome."

Reader, if you are still outside of this spiritual Babylon, take warning from those who have been through the mill, and stay out.

Later, 1914. Already strong men among them admit that, (1) Mrs. White has made many mistakes in her inspired (?) writings; (2) Now contradicts what she once wrote; (3) Has copied from many other authors what she claims as revelations from God; (4) Has often been influenced by others to write what they wanted to help their projects. Time has proved this so clearly that it can no longer be denied. Hence her revelations are steadily losing influence with their able men. She is now eighty-seven years old and is reported as having largely lost her mind. The laity, specially in foreign lands, being ignorant of all these facts, still regard her as the voice of God to them.

CHAPTER II.

AN EXPERIENCE OF TWENTY-EIGHT YEARS IN ADVENTISM.

I long hesitated about bringing personal matters into this book, but could see no way to tell my story without it. My experience illustrates the power which error and superstition have over men. I am amazed at myself that I was held there so long, after my better judgment was convinced that it was an error. I propose to tell the simple facts, just as they were, hit whom they may. Public men become public property, and as such their conduct and work should be laid open and discussed. This is my reason for criticising the course of Elder White and wife, and others. They invite criticism by claiming to be reformers, better than other people.

I was born in Kinderhook, Branch county, Mich., Sept. 22, 1840. I had no religious training till I was sixteen. I was converted among the Methodists under the labors of Rev. Mr. Hazzard, and baptized by him in 1858. I soon went to Albion, N. Y., to attend school. Here, in 1859, I heard Elder and Mrs. White. He preached on the Sabbath question. I was uneducated, and knew but little about the Bible. I had no idea of the relation between the Old and New Testaments, the law and the gospel, or the difference between the Sabbath and the Lord's day. I thought he proved that the seventh day was still binding, and that there was no authority for keeping Sunday.

As I was anxious to be right, I began keeping Saturday,

but did not expect to believe any more of their doctrine. Of course I attended their meetings on Saturday and worked on Sunday. This separated me entirely from other Christians, and threw me wholly with the Adventists. I soon learned from them that all other churches were Babylon, in the dark and under the frown of God. Seventh-Day Adventists were the only true people of God. They had "the truth," the whole truth, and nothing but the truth. They defended Mr. Miller's work of 1844, believed in the visions of Mrs. White, the sleep of the dead, the annihilation of the wicked, feet washing, etc. At first these things staggered me, and I thought of drawing back; but they explained them plausibly and smoothed them over, and said they were no test anyway. Having no one to intelligently aid me, I began to see things as they did, and in a few weeks came to believe the whole system. I was again baptized, as their converts from other churches generally are, so as to get clean out of Babylon. Persuaded that time was too short, I gave up going to school, dropped the study of all else. listened to their preaching, devoured their books and studied my Bible day and night to sustain these new views. I was now an enthusiastic believer, and longed to convert everybody to the faith. I had not a doubt that it was the pure truth. This is about the experience of all who go with them, as I have since learned.

In May, 1864, I was licensed to preach. Soon began with Elder Van Horn at Ithaca, Mich. We had good success; raised up three companies that year. In 1865 worked in Tuscola county, and had excellent success. Was ordained by Elder White that year. Up to this date I had not had a doubt about the truthfulness of our faith. As I now began to see more of Elder White and wife, and the work at headquarters, I learned that there was much trouble with him. I saw that he ruled everything, and that all greatly feared him. I saw that he was often cross and unreasonable. This troubled me a little, but not seriously. In 1866 I was sent to Maine with Elder J. N. Andrews, the ablest man among them. This was a big thing for me. I threw myself into the work with great enthusiasm, and was very happy. Elder Andrews was strong in the faith and very radical, and I partook of his spirit. We had excellent success. By this time I had become quite a writer. I returned to Battle Creek in 1867. At that time there was great trouble with Elder White, and many church meetings were held to investigate the matter. It was clear to me that he was wrong, but Mrs. White sustained him in her "Testimonies" and severely blamed the church. Elder Andrews and a few others proposed to stand up for the right, and take the consequences. My sympathies were with them; but others feared, and finally all wilted and confessed that "we have been blinded by Satan." This was signed by the leading ministers, and humbly adopted by the whole church. See "Testimonies," Vol. 1, page 612. This shook my faith a good deal, and I began to question Mrs. White's inspiration. I saw that her revelations always favored Elder White and herself. If any dared question their course, they soon received a scathing revelation denouncing the wrath of God against them.

About this time several of our able ministers, with quite a party in the West, drew off from the body, in opposition to Elder White and the visions. They were denounced as "rebels," were doomed to perdition, and it was predicted that they would soon come to ruin! But they have continued their work for about fifty years, having several thousand believers. Their headquarters are at Stanberry, Missouri, where they publish two papers, books, etc. They have done a good work in exposing the fallacy of Mrs. White's inspiration.

But I dared not open my mind to a soul. I was only a youth, and had little experience. Older and stronger men had broken down and confessed. What could I do? I said nothing, but felt terribly. I wished I had never heard of the Adventists. Shortly I was back on my field in Maine. Busy with my work, preaching our doctrine, and surrounded with men who firmly believed it, I soon got over my doubts. I have since learned that scores of others have gone through a similar trial.

In 1868 I went to Massachusetts. Being away from the troubles at headquarters, I got on finely. But in May, 1869, I was in Battle Creek for a month. Things were in bad shape. Elder White was in trouble with most of the leading men, and they with him. I was well convinced that he was the real cause of it all, but Mrs. White sustained him, and that settled it. They were God's chosen leaders, and must not be criticised or meddled with. I felt sad. I was working hard to get men into "the truth," as we called it; to persuade them that this was a people free from the faults of other churches; then to see such a state of things among the leaders disheartened me greatly. So far, I myself had had no trouble with any one, and Elder White had been very cordial to me. But I saw then that if I ever came to be of any prominence in the work I should have to expect the same treatment from him that all of the others got. The more I saw of the work, the more objections I saw to it. I will not stop to give them here, as I will give them together in Chapter V.

I had been so thoroughly drilled in the Advent doctrines that I firmly believed the Bible taught them all. To give up the Advent faith was to give up the Bible. So all my brethren said, and so I thought. Hence I swallowed my doubts and went on. That year I went to Iowa to work, where I remained four years, laboring with Elder

Butler, who soon became president of their general conference. We had good success and raised up several churches. I finally opened my mind to Elder Butler, and told him my fears. I knew these things troubled him as well as myself, for we often spoke of them. He helped me some, and again I gathered courage and went on, feeling better. Still, I came to see each year more and more that somehow the thing did not work as I had supposed it would and ought. Wherever Elder White and wife went they were always in trouble with the brethren, and the best ones, too. I came to dread to meet them, or have them come where I was, for I knew there would be trouble with some one or something, and it never failed of so being. I saw church after church split up by them, the best brethren discouraged and maddened and driven off, while I was compelled to apologize for them continually. For years about this time, the main business at all our big meetings was to listen to the complaints of Elder White against his brethren. Not a leading man escaped—Andrews, Waggoner, Smith, Loughborough, Amadon, Cornell, Aldrich, Walker, and a host of others had to take their turn at being broken on the wheel. For hours at a time, and times without number, I have sat in meetings and heard Elder White and wife denounce these men, till I felt there was little manhood left in them. It violated all my ideas of right and justice, and stirred my indignation. Yet, whatever vote was asked by Elder White, we all voted it unanimously, I with the rest. Then I would go out alone and hate myself for my cowardice, and despise my brethren for their weakness.

Elder and Mrs. White ran and ruled everything with an iron hand. Not a nomination to office, not a resolution, not an item of business was ever acted upon in business meetings till all had been first submitted to Elder White for his approval. Till years later, we never saw an opposition vote on any question, for no one dared to do it. Hence, all official voting was only a farce. The will of Elder White settled everything. If any one dared to oppose anything, however humbly, Elder White or wife quickly squelched him. Long years of such training taught that people to let their leaders think for them; hence, they are under as complete subjection as are the Catholics.

These, with other things, threw me into doubt and discouragement, and tempted me to quit the work. I saw many an able minister and scores of valuable men leave us because they would not stand such treatment. I envied the faith and confidence of brethren who went on ignorant of all this, supposing that Battle Creek was a little heaven, when, in fact, it was as near purgatory as anything I could imagine. Many poor souls have gone there full of faith and hope, but have soon gone away infidels. In 1872 I went to Minnesota, where I had good success. By this time I had written much, and so was well known to all our people. In July, 1873, myself and wife went to Colorado to spend a few weeks with Elder White and wife, in the mountains. I soon found things very unpleasant living in the family. Now my turn had come to catch it, but instead of knuckling down, as most of the others had, I told the elder my mind freely. That brought us into an open rupture. Mrs. White heard it all, but said nothing. In a few days she had a long written "testimony" for wife and me. It justified her husband in everything, and placed us as rebels against God, with no hope of heaven only by a full surrender to them. Wife and I read it over many times with tears and prayers; but could see no way to reconcile it with truth. It contained many statements which we knew were false. We saw that it was dictated by a spirit of retaliation, a determination to break our wills or crush us. For awhile we were in great perplexity, but still my confidence in much of the doctrine and my fear of going wrong held me; but I was perfectly miserable for weeks, not knowing what to do. However, I preached awhile in Colorado and then went to California, where I worked with my hands for three months, trying to settle what to do. Elders Butler, Smith, White and others wrote to us, and tried to reconcile us to the work. Not knowing what else to do, I finally decided to forget all my objections, and go along as before. So we confessed to Elder White all we could possibly, and he generously forgave us! But from that on my faith in the inspiration of Mrs. White was weak. Elder White was very friendly to me again after that.

Now the Adventists say that I have left them five times, and this is one of the five. It is utterly untrue. I simply stopped preaching for a few weeks, but did not withdraw from the church nor renounce the faith. If this is leaving them, then most of their leading men have left them, too, for they all have had their periods of trial when they left their work awhile. About 1856, Elders J. N. Andrews and J. N. Loughborough, who were then the most prominent ministers among them, and several other persons, left the work and went into business at Waukon, Iowa. Mrs. White gave an account of this in "Experience and Views," pages 219-222. Elder White and wife went there, and, after a long effort, brought them back. Mrs. White says: "A dissatisfied party had settled in Waukon. * * * Brother J. N. Loughborough in discouragement had gone to work at his trade. He was just about to purchase land," etc., page 222. These men did just what I did.

Elder Uriah Smith, by far the ablest man then in their ranks, also had his seasons of doubt, when he ceased to work, and engaged in secular employments. Hear his own confession: "That I have had in my experience occasional periods of trial, I do not deny. There have been times when circumstances seemed very perplexing; when the way to harmonize apparently conflicting views did not at once appear, and under what have seemed for the time strong provocations to withdraw from the work, I have canvassed the question how far this could reasonably be done, or how much of this work could consistently be surrendered." Replies to Elder Canright, page 107. His own words show that he has doubted different parts of the theory, the same as I did. For years we were on intimate terms; often traveled and labored together. We freely talked over these matters. His doubts and trials were very similar to my own. This ran through a long period of years, till it was feared that he would quit them entirely. His wife was nearly driven to insanity over similar trials. Finally they broke down, "confessed" the same as I did once, and now profess to be satisfied. He wrote me that he had to indorse Mrs. White's visions out of policy. The thing is so unreasonable, that most of them at times are more or less troubled over it, just as I was. In the language of J. W. Morton, "I pity their delusions, and abominate the spiritual tyranny by which they and others are held to the most unscriptural dogmas. Even Mr. Smith, for whom, however he may denounce me, I entertain only the most kindly feelings, is in a position that calls for tender commiseration. He is expected, as the great man of the denomination (for he undoubtedly is by far the ablest man they have), to give a full and explicit endorsement to Mrs. White's claims of inspiration; and yet whoever scans his public utterances on this point—especially he who has skill to 'read between the lines'—can see that his endorsement is so feeble as to be no endorsement at all. Such a position is one in which I would not place my worst enemy. He is, in part at least, under the heel of a spiritual tyranny. Oh, that Uriah Smith had the courage, and the manliness, to assert, before God and man, his right to that 'soul liberty' which is the inheritance of every child of God!"

Elder Geo. I. Butler, who for many years took the place of Elder White as leader of the denomination, got into trial with his brethren, and, practically, out of the work. Till middle life he was a small farmer. Naturally he was a humble, good man, with a strong sense of fairness. Elder White became jealous of him. Later, Mrs. White also turned against him and required a servile submission which he would not make. Said when he could not be an Adventist, and be a man, then he would be a man, as others had decided. Disappointed and soured, under pretext of ill-health, he went off to Florida on a little farm—another example of the blighting effect of Adventism. He is now doing what I did two or three times, only from a different cause. Has he, then, left them?

In 1874 Elder White had arranged to have a big debate held at Napa City, Cal., between Elder Miles Grant, of Boston, Mass., and one of our ministers. Though Elder White and wife, Elder Cornell and Elder Loughborough, their ablest men, were there, they selected myself to defend our side, which I did for about a week, while the other ministers sat by. I mention this to show the confidence they had in me, though I had been in so great a trial but a few months before. In 1875 we returned to Michigan. Elder Butler was now out with Elder White, who took every possible opportunity to snub him; but I was in high favor, was sent to attend their state meetings in Vermont, Kansas, Ohio and Indiana. With Elder Smith, was sent as delegate to the Seventh-Day Baptist General Conference. In 1876 I was sent to Minnesota, then to Texas, and so on through most of the Southern States, to look after our interests there. Each year greater responsibilities were laid upon me. That year I raised up a large church at Rome,

New York, and labored over the State. Went with Elder White and wife to Indiana and Illinois, and was then sent to Kansas to hold a debate, and to Missouri for the same purpose. This year I was elected a member of the General Conference Committee of three, with Elder White and Elder Haskell, and continued on the committee two years. It is the highest official authority in the denomination.

In 1877 I went to New England, where I raised up two churches and did other work. I spent 1878 in general work in various States, as Massachusetts, Michigan, New York, Iowa, Wisconsin, Minnesota, Colorado, and Ohio. In the fall was president of the Ohio conference. In 1879 labored in Michigan, Ohio, Indiana, Kentucky, and Tennessee. At the general conference at Battle Creek in the fall, things were in a bad shape. Elder White was cross, and Mrs. White bore down heavy on several ministers. Harshness, fault-finding and trials were the order of the day. I felt that there was very little of the spirit of Christ present. I got away as quickly as possible. I saw more and more clearly that a spirit of oppression, criticism, distrust and dissension was the result of our work, instead of meekness, gentleness, and love among brethren. For the next whole year these feelings grew upon me, till I began to fear we were doing more harm than good. My work called me among old churches, where I could see the fruit of it. Generally they were cold and dead, backslidden, or in a quarrel, or nearly extinct, where once they had been large and flourishing churches. I lost heart to raise up more churches to go in the same way. One day I would decide to quit them entirely, and the next day I would resolve to go on and do the best I could. I never suffered more mental anguish in my life. I labored that year in New York, Pennsylvania, Illinois, Michigan and Ohio.

In the fall of 1880 I resolved to leave the Adventists, and, if I could, go with some other church. I was president of the Ohio conference. Our annual state meeting was at Clyde, Ohio. Elder and Mrs. White were there. My mind was made up to leave them as soon as the meeting was over. Against my protest they re-elected me president. Mrs. White urged it. Said I was just the man for the place; yet her special claim is to be able to reveal the hidden wrongs in the church. Here was an important matter. Why did she not have a revelation about it? No, I was all right so far as she knew. The next week I resigned, went east, and wrote Elder White that I would go with them no longer. Then she sent me a long written revelation, denouncing me as a child of hell, and one of the wickedest of men, though only two weeks before she thought me fit to be president of a conference!

For three months I taught elocution. I knew not what to do. I talked with ministers of other churches, but they did not seem to know how to help me. I could settle on nothing. I held on to my Christianity and love for Christ and the Bible, and preached and worked as I had opportunity. I was glad I had decided to leave the Adventists, and felt much better. Finally I met my present wife, who was an Adventist. Then I had a long talk with Elder Butler, Elder White, Mrs. White and others, and was persuaded that things were not as I had imagined. They said I was in the dark, led by Satan, and would go to ruin. All the influence of old friends, associations, habits and long cultivated ideas came up and were too strong for my better judgment. I yielded, and resolved again to live and die with them. In my judgment and conscience I was ashamed of the surrender I had made, yet I tried to feel right and go on.

DEATH OF ELDER WHITE.

Early in 1881 I went with Elder White to New York. By this time he had lost the leadership of the people.

Elders Butler and Haskell had taken his place, and hence he was very hostile to them, working against them, and planning all the while to get them out and get back in again himself. But the people had largely lost confidence in him as a leader. He wished me to work with him against them, saying that we would then be on the General Conference Committee together. He had good grounds to oppose Haskell, who was always a crafty, underhanded man. Elder White wrote me thus:—"February 11, 1881: I wish Elder Haskell were an open, frank man, so I need not watch him." Again:—"Battle Creek, Mich., May 24, 1881: * * * Elders Butler and Haskell have had an influence over her [his wife] that I hope to see broken. It has nearly ruined her. These men must not be suffered by our people to do as they have done. * * * I want you to unite with me. * * It is time there was a change in the offices of the General Conference. I trust that if we are true and faithful, the Lord will be pleased that we should constitute two of that board."

I could give much more to show how little confidence the leading men had in each other. I wrote Elder White that I could not unite with him nor work with him. July 13, 1881, he wrote me again: "I have repeatedly abused you, and if you go to destruction, where many, to say the least, are willing you should go, I should ever feel that I had taken a part in your destruction. * * * I do not see how any man can labor with me." Soon after this he died. I have no doubt that Elder White believed in the Advent doctrine, and persuaded himself that he was called of God to be a leader. He had some excellent qualities, and doubtless meant to be a Christian, but his strong desire to rule and run everything, together with an irritable temper, kept him always in trouble with some one. No one could work with him long in peace. Elder Butler told me that his death was providential to save the body from a rupture. Mrs. White was so offended at Butler, that she would have no communication with him for a long while. All these things helped me to see that I was being led by selfish, ambitious men, who were poor samples of religious reformers.

That year I labored in Canada, Vermont, Maine, New England, and Michigan, and was elected member of the State Executive Committee of Michigan that fall. I worked another year in Michigan. But I was unhappy; I could not get over my doubts; I had no heart in the work. Several leading ministers in the State felt about the same. I then decided to quietly drop out of the ministry and go to farming. This I did for two years, but retained my membership with the church and worked right along with them. But I was in purgatory all the time, trying to believe what I could not. Yet I was not settled on any other church, and feared I might go wrong, and so stood still. In the fall of 1884, Elder Butler, my old friend, and now at the head of the Advent work, made a great effort to get me reconciled and back at work again. He wrote me several times, to which I made no answer. Finally he telegraphed me, and paid my fare to a camp-meeting. Here I met old friends and associations, tried to see things as favorable as possible, heard explanations, etc., etc., till at last I yielded again. I was sick of an undecided position. I thought I could do some good here anyway; all my friends were here, I believed much of the doctrine still, and I might go to ruin if I left them, etc. Now I resolved to swallow all my doubts, believe the whole thing anyway, and stay with them for better or for worse. So I made a strong confession, of which I was ashamed before it was cold.

Was I satisfied? No. Deep in my heart I was ashamed of myself, but tried to feel that it was not so. But soon I felt better, because I had decided. Gradually my faith came back, till I again really felt strong in the whole doctrine, and had no idea I should ever leave it again. In a few weeks I was sent to attend large meetings in Pennsylvania, New York, Minnesota, Iowa, and New England; assisted in revival meetings in Battle Creek; was appointed with Elder Butler to lecture before the ministers on how to labor successfully; conducted a similar course in the Academy at South Lancaster, Mass.; was at the state meetings in New York, Michigan, Indiana and Ohio. In the spring of 1886 was appointed to lecture before the theological class in the Battle Creek College, and Associate Editor of the *Sickle*.

By my urgent appeal, an effort was made to bring up our ministers to some plan of study in which they are very deficient. I was on the committee to arrange this. I selected the course of studies and framed all the questions, by which they were to be examined. I was then furnished a shorthand reporter, and in the summer was sent to ten different states, namely, Ohio, Indiana, Illinois, Kansas, Colorado, Iowa, Wisconsin, Minnesota, Dakota, and Michigan, to attend their state conferences, examine their ministers, report their meetings for the daily press, etc., and this I did. In our conflict with the Disciples at Des Moines, Iowa, it was agreed that each side should select a representative man and hold a debate on the Sabbath question. They selected Professor D. R. Dungan, president of Drake University. Our people selected me. We expected a notable time, and I made every possible effort to be ready. That preparation did much to convince me of the unsoundness of some of our positions on the covenants, the two laws, etc. In our General Conference that fall, a sharp division occurred between our leading men over the law in Galatians. One party held it was the ceremonial law, the other the moral law—a square contradiction. After a long and warm discussion the conference closed, each party more confident than before.

There was also much disagreement over other points of doctrine, and a good deal of warm party feeling. This, with other things, brought up my old feelings of doubt, and decided me that it was time for me now to examine and think for myself, and not be led nor intimidated by men who could not agree among themselves.

I used every minute I could get for several weeks, carefully and prayerfully examining all the evidence on the Sabbath, the law, the sanctuary, the visions, etc., till I had not a doubt left that the Seventh-Day Advent faith was a delusion. Then I laid the matter before the leading men at Battle Creek, resigned all the positions I held, and asked to be dismissed from the church. This was granted February 17, 1887. That was the first and only time I ever withdrew from the church, nor was any charge ever made against me during the twenty-eight years I was with them. As soon as I took my stand firmly, to be a free man and think for myself, a great burden, which I had carried all these years, rolled off. I felt like a new man. At last I was out of bondage. I have never for a moment regretted the step I took.

They now report that I left them four or five times before, and then went back. This is entirely untrue. From the time I joined them, in 1859, till I withdrew, in 1887, I remained in good standing in that church. After I was licensed to preach in 1864, my credentials were renewed each year except one, when I was farming and did not ask for them. Till I left them, in 1887, I never preached nor wrote against them once; nor did I unite with any other church, nor teach any doctrine contrary to theirs. Let them deny any of these statements if they can. They say I may yet return to them. They know better. The moment I took my stand decidedly, that matter was settled forever. The fact that I remained with them under all these trials for twenty-eight years, shows I was not a vacillating man, as they now try to think.

WHY I DID NOT LEAVE THEM SOONER.

I am often asked why I did not leave them sooner? Why it took me so long to find that it was an error? Then the Adventists affirm that I must have been dishonest while with them, or I am dishonest now. They say I am an apostate now, because I left them and joined the Baptists. My answer is this: If to change one's opinion and join another church makes one an apostate, then more than half their members are apostates, for they have come from other churches to join the Adventists. Again, they circulate and commend highly a book called "Fifty Years in Rome," written by a man who was many years a learned priest in the Roman church. They say that his high standing and long experience in that church makes his book invaluable. But they say that the fact that I was with them in high standing so long, and now have left them, only proves that I am a hypocrite!

Any candid man can see the inconsistency of their positions. I united with the Adventists when I was a mere boy, uneducated, with no knowledge of the Bible, of history, or of other churches. I went into it through ignorance. For years my zeal for that faith, and my unbounded confidence in its leaders, blinded me to their errors. But, as I grew older, read my Bible more, read history, met with other churches, heard sermons and read books against Adventism, became better acquainted with our leaders, with the inside workings of the church, learned more about its unfavorable origin, the many mistakes we had made, saw the fruit of it in old churches, on families and society, got hold of the early writings of Mrs. White and others; gradually I began to see that Adventism was not just what I had first supposed it to be. When I embraced it in 1859, Seventh-Day Adventism was only fourteen years old, the believers were few, and it was comparatively untried. But when Adventism was twenty-five years older, ten times as large, and had fully developed its spirit and shown its fruits, when I had had the education, observation and experience of a quarter of a century, I think my judgment in the matter ought to be worth more than when I embraced it as a green boy.

Again, it was only during the last few years that I gained possession of early Advent documents, which show how they now deny and contradict what they once taught. These are now either suppressed or kept out of sight, so that not one in a thousand of them knows or will believe that they ever existed. My doubts of the system did not come to me all at once and clearly. It was well known that for the last dozen years I was with them, I was greatly troubled over these things. Gradually, year by year, the evidence accumulated, till at last it overbalanced the doctrine, and then reluctantly and sorrowfully I had to abandon and renounce it. God pity the soul that has to go through what I did to be honest to his convictions of right.

POSITIONS WHICH I HELD WHEN I LEFT THEM.

Notwithstanding it was well known to all that I frequently had serious doubts about their faith, yet, as soon as I took hold with them again, each time they immediately put me forward and set me at the most important work. Elder Butler says: "He doubtless would have been [elected to important office] had he not proved himself unreliable in so many instances. His ability would have justified it."—*Review and Herald Extra*, Nov. 22, 1887. Suppose, now, that I had been an office-seeking man, caring more for place and position than for truth and conscience, what would I have done? I would have gone right along, pretending to be full in faith and in harmony with them. But instead of this, time and again, I went directly to their influential men, Elders White, Butler, Haskell, etc., and told them my doubts. Let candid men judge of my motives.

The day I left them I held the following positions: Was teacher of theology in their college at Battle Creek, where I had a class of nearly two hundred of their best young people; was associate editor of the *Gospel Sickle;* was writing the lessons for all their Sabbath Schools throughout the world; had the charge of some eighteen churches in Michigan; was member of the Executive Committee of the International Sabbath School Association; member of the Executive Committee of the Michigan State Sabbath School Association; and at the last session of the general conference was chairman of the International Sabbath School Association, and was on nine different committees, several of them the most important in the conference, as the one on distribution of laborers over all the world, the theological committee, the one on camp meetings, on a special course of study in our college, on the improvement of the ministry, etc. This shows what they thought of my ability. I had just gotten out a new pamphlet, "Critical Notes," of which they printed an edition of 10,000 after I left them. Others of my works they have revised, left my name off, and use them still. Why reprint mine after I have left them and renounced what they teach? They now say that my writings are cheap and worthless. But while I was with them they published over twenty different productions of mine, and circulated hundreds of thousands of them, translated several of them into other languages, and paid me hundreds of dollars for them. Strange that all at once I have become so imbecile, and my writings so worthless. Any one can see the animus of all this.

Elder Smith, in Replies to Canright, page 25, says I left them at a time when my withdrawal embarrassed them more than it would have done at any other time. This confesses that I was becoming more and more useful to them, and all know that I was. At the time I left I was getting higher pay than ever before, and was on friendly terms with all. All the leading men, as Butler, Haskell, Smith, etc., were my warm personal friends, ready to do all in their power to assist me. Had I desired office, or better position, all I had to do was to go right along without wavering, and positions would come to me faster than I could fill them. But if I left them, where could I go? What could I do? How even make a living? I took this all in, and it required all the courage and faith in God I could master to take the risk.

It cost me a terrible struggle and a great sacrifice, for in doing it I had to leave all my life-long friends, the cherished hopes of my youth, the whole work of my life, all the means of my support, every honorable position I held, and bring upon myself reproach, hatred and persecution. I had to begin life anew, among strangers, with untried methods, uncertain where to go or what to do. No one who has not tried it can ever begin to realize the fearful struggle it requires. It is the dread of all this which holds many with them who are yet dissatisfied where they are. I know that this is so, for many have confessed it to me, and yet remained where they were. Anyone of candor and fairness can see readily that self-interest and personal ambition would have held me with them. Yet, as soon as I did leave them, though I went out quietly and peaceably, and let them entirely alone, and even spoke favorably of them, they immediately attributed to me all sorts of evil motives, base sins, and ambitious designs. They seemed to feel it a sacred duty to blast my reputation, and destroy my influence, if possible. "Apostate" was the epithet all applied to me. I was compared to Baalam, to Kora, Dathan and Abiram, to Judas, Demas, and a whole list of evil characters. Not one honest or worthy motive was granted me. The meanest and wickedest reports were circulated as to what I had done or said —things that I would despise even to think of. Yet all were eagerly accepted and believed as undoubted truth. But I expected it, for it is the way all are treated who dare to leave them and give a reason for it.

During the twenty years now since I left them, they have had spies constantly on my track, who have watched and reported the least thing I have said or done, to torture it into evil, if possible. This they circulate to the ends of the earth, and it comes back to me in newspapers and letters. They have issued four different publications against me, and Mrs. White, in her last "revelation," has devoted three articles to myself! Yet I don't amount to anything; never did! "Sour grapes," you see. It has been widely reported that I was smitten with a terrible disease, had broken up my church, been expelled from the denomination, and more yet, concerning all which the Lord judge between us. The pastors of all the churches here, and public men of the place have had to make written statements to meet these attacks in distant states. Sometimes this has seemed hard to bear, but knowing that I was right, I have had grace and patience to keep steadily at my work, and leave the rest with God and my friends.

I am in constant receipt of letters from all parts of the country, saying that the Adventists affirm that I have asked to be taken back among them! They will report it till I die, and long after. This book shall be my answer. They are so certain that the curse of God will follow all who leave them, or that they will become infidels, or return to them, that they cannot be reconciled to have it otherwise.

A SAMPLE LETTER.

"GLENWOOD SPRINGS, COLO., March 29, 1889.
D. M. CANRIGHT, Otsego, Mich.:

My Dear Friend and Brother:—If the lightning's shivering crash had torn my scalp loose from my head, I would not have been more surprised than I was to-day by having placed in my hands your pamphlet entitled "The Jewish Sabbath." I have read after you for years, sold your valuable works, and preached the "Third Angel's Message." Now, I wish to ask you, how do our people treat you? To my knowledge you were a great favorite, and quoted oftener than any standing near the head. Do they go back on you as hard as they did on Snook? I suppose that your great research and life-long study of the subject in hand goes for nothing with them, and that you are classed among the fallen angels. F. A. B."

ORDAINED A BAPTIST MINISTER.

April 19, 1887, at Otsego, Mich., where I had lived for eight years, I was ordained as a minister of the Regular Baptist Church, by an exceptionally large council, composed of several of the ablest ministers of the state. The *Otsego Union* of that date says: "Regularly appointed delegates were present from Baptist churches in Grand Rapids, Kalamazoo, Plainwell, Three Rivers, White Pigeon, Allegan, Battle Creek, Paw Paw, Hickory Corners, Prairieville and Otsego. Rev. A. E. Mather, D.D., of Battle Creek, was elected moderator of the council, and Rev. T. M. Shanafelt, D.D., of Three Rivers, secretary. The order of exercises was as follows: Reading of the Scriptures, by Rev. H. A. Rose, of Kalamazoo; prayer, by Rev. D. Mulhern, D.D., of Grand Rapids; ordination sermon, by Rev. Kendall Brooks, D.D., President of Kalamazoo College; prayer of ordination, by Rev. M. W. Haynes, of Kalamazoo, with laying on of hands by Rev. H. B. Taft, of White Pigeon, Rev. E. A. Gay, of Allegan, and Rev. H. A. Rose, of Kalamazoo; hand of fellowship, by Rev. T. F. Babcock, of Prairieville; charge to the pastor, by Rev. L. B. Fish, of Paw Paw; charge to the church, by Rev. I. Butterfield, of Grand Rapids.

"Rev. D. M. Canright has thus been fully recognized by a large and representative council as a regular Baptist minister, and pastor of the Baptist church in Otsego."

I have never regretted leaving the Adventists, nor for one moment had the slightest desire to return.

CHAPTER III.

ADVENTISM A YOKE OF BONDAGE.

Largely, people are drawn into the Seventh-Day doctrine through *fear*, fear of being damned if they refuse. Once in, they try to feel happy, but very few really are. With a large class, the more intelligent ones, there are so many doubts and fears, such a sensible want of something which they do not find, that they are unhappy. Many of their ministers have gone through the same trials that I have, and scores have left them, as I did, while others have fixed it up and remained with them. Elder White himself had doubts. Mrs. White says of him: "He should make it a rule not to talk unbelief or discouragement." "My husband has cherished this darkness so long by living over the unhappy past, that he has but little power to control his mind when dwelling upon these things." Testimonies, Vol. III, pages 96, 97. Mrs. White herself, as we might expect, is troubled with infidelity. She says: "In the night I have awakened my husband, saying, 'I am afraid that I shall become an infidel.'" Testimonies, Vol. I, page 597. Nearly all their prominent ministers had their times of trial, the same as I did, when they ceased preaching and went at other work, as we have seen.

I will quote a few words from letters received: "I have had many blue times in my experience because of these doubts. * * Once I decided that I must follow the convictions of my own judgment in these things; but when the time came the pressure was so strong that I tried to convince myself that I was wrong. * * The facts are, I am just miserable. * * It seems like a terrible thing to take a course that will cause all the cherished friends of this world to look upon you as one fallen from grace; and here I am, bound with these chains." Another writes: "It seems to me that the views held by Seventh-Day Adventists are so burdensome that they will crush me. They are a yoke of bondage which I cannot stand up under. Still I do want to be right." Another minister, D. H. Lamson, writes: "How am I straightened, while the fetters are being forged for most unwilling limbs! * * What distress we *are* in as a people! how miserable! and is there no relief?" And still another talented minister, W. C. Gage, writes me: "Our ministers, and people as well, are growing to be a denomination of hypocrites, by a slavish fear of expressing an honest belief. * * I am sick and disheartened. * * The basis of confidence is gone, and I shall only await the outcome of the matter." Still another, Uriah Smith, writes: "There is a fear, on the part of the powers that be, of free thought and free discussion. So far as this is the case, it is a shame and disgrace to us." And yet these brethren patch up the matter some way, and go right on as though nothing were wrong. I know how to pity them, for I myself have passed through precisely the same experience. And another writes: "I wish I had never heard the Advent doctrine preached. Previous to that, I know that I did enjoy the blessing of God. I was not troubled about doctrine. * * I think I then had some influence for good over others, but I fear my change of faith had a bad influence over my children." Strange to say, these are the very men who now denounce me the worst because I had the courage of my convictions, while they haven't.

These are fair samples of how scores among them feel, from men in leading positions, to the humblest in the church. Largely they keep it to themselves, but occasionally it will out. Many of them almost get out, and then fall back, to linger along in bondage all the rest of their lives. "But if these persons are in such bondage, why not break loose, and be free? Who would harm them?" Be it remembered that there is a bondage worse than African slavery—the bondage of religious tyranny and superstition. I was held there for years, and know its power.

Milton F. Gowell, Chicago, gives so true a picture of Advent experience, that I quote him in a letter to me. I was often at his father's house, in Portland, Me., when he was a boy. He says: "My recollections of those days are full of the terrors of law, prophetic charts, Mrs. White's visions, the Sabbath, Sabbath, Sabbath, health reform, bloomer dresses, and a great zeal for being industrious on Sunday, and little or nothing of Christ. All the *doing* was indelibly impressed on my mind as a boy, but the *believing* on Christ for salvation, and *resting* in his finished work, I have no remembrance of whatever. How many there are that join the Seventh-Day Adventists utterly unsaved, knowing nothing of the grace of God, hearing always barely the law. I joined them at the age of fourteen, under conviction, guilty before God, but unsaved, though I was baptized and received into the church as a *Sabbath keeper*. I received no peace, no rest, till I entered into rest by believing about three and a half years ago; saved from the borderland of infidelity." This is just the impression which all the children of that people are receiving—cold legalism. While this young man was finally saved from infidelity, hundreds of them are not, as I well know.

PROMINENT PERSONS WHO HAVE LEFT THE ADVENTISTS.

It is nothing new for men to leave a party, good or bad; but so large a number of prominent persons have left the Adventists as to excite surprise. It is clear that there must be something wrong in the system itself. First, according to the best of my judgment, from one-third to one-half of all who begin the observance of the Sabbath, sooner or later abandon it.

At different times large numbers have left them, mostly on account of Mrs. White's visions. We will name a few of the ministers who have departed from them: J. B Cook and T. M. Preble, the pioneers who started the movement, both renounced it; O. R. L. Crozier, Ann Arbor, Mich., has renounced the Sabbath; Elder B. F. Snook, the leading man in Iowa, is now a Universalist; Elder W. H. Brinkerhoof, of Iowa, has renounced the faith; Elder Moses Hull, the ablest speaker they ever had, is now a Spiritualist, and Elder Shortridge, a minister of much talent, has also gone the same way; Elders Hall and Stephenson, at the time very prominent in the work, went to the Age-to-Come party; C. B. Raynolds, of New York, has become a noted blasphemer; Elder H. C. Blanchard, Avilla, Mo., renounced the doctrine; ditto T. J. Butler, of the same State; Elder L. L. Howard, Maine, H. F. Haynes, New Hampshire, left them; Nathan Fuller, Wellsville, N. Y., became a libertine; M. B. Czechowski went to Europe and died in disgrace; H. F. Case, Elder Cranmer and Philip Strong, all of Michigan, left them.

Elder J. B. Frisbie, their pioneer and most efficient preacher for years in Michigan, finally left them. Dr. Lee, of Minnesota, who inaugurated the work among the Swedes, now opposes them. Elder A. B. Oyen, missionary to Europe, and editor of their Danish paper, has renounced the faith. Living right at the head of the work for many years, he had the best of opportunity to know all about its workings. Elder D. B. Oviatt, for many years president of the Pennsylvania Conference, renounced the faith, and is now a Baptist minister.

So Elder Rosquist and Elder Whitelaw, both of Minnesota, have recently left them and gone to the Baptists. Other ministers of the West have also gone over to the Baptists. C. A. Russell, Otsego, Mich., an excellent man, once preached that doctrine with me, but is now a Methodist. H. E. Carver, H. C. Blanchard, J. W. Cassady, A. C. Long, Jacob Brinkerhoof, J. C. Day, H. W. Ball, Goodenough, Bunch, and others, once members of that church, have written against it. Elder Hiram Edson and Elder S. W. Rhodes, noted pioneers in the work, died confirmed cranks, and a trial to the church. The sad example of several of their leading ministers who have been guilty of adultery, proves that their church has nothing to boast of over other churches in the puritv of its ministers and members.

THEIR COLLEGE PROFESSORS.

They have been very unfortunate in their college professors. Professor S. S. Brownsburger, the first Principal of their College at Battle Creek, Mich., which position he occupied for years, and then filled the same position in their college in California, is now wholly disconnected from the work. Elder W. H. Littlejohn, who next stood at the head of the college, was expelled from the church and fell into doubts. Next came Professor A. McLearn as head of the college. He has renounced the faith, and now opposes them strongly. Professor Vesey, a learned teacher in that college, has forsaken the faith. Professor C. C. Ramsy, born in that faith, was professor of mathematics in the Battle Creek college for three years; then filled the same place for three years in their college in California; then was called to take charge of their academy in the East, which he did for three years more. He was editor of their educational journal, prominent in Sabbath School work, and many other ways. He has renounced that faith, but remains an earnest

Christian. Others of their teachers of lesser note have also left them. What is the cause of such results? There must be something wrong.

THEIR PHYSICIANS.

They have been equally unfortunate with their physicians in their sanitarium at Battle Creek. Dr. H. S. Ley, an excellent man, was the first physician-in-chief. He left the institution in a trial, and was out of the work for years. Dr. Wm. Russell, a talented doctor, came next. What he there saw of Adventism made him an infidel, and he was dismissed. Next, I believe, came Dr. M. G. Kellogg. The treatment he received drove him into scepticism for years. Then came Dr. Sprague and Dr. Farfield, both of whom renounced the faith, and, I believe, are sceptical now. Mrs. Lamson and Miss Fellows, both matrons of the sanitarium, lost faith in the doctrine. Dr. Smith, brought up in the faith, renounced it. Here again we see that education unfits men for Adventism. I am not acquainted with another church which has lost so large a proportion of its most prominent men. Every year, nearly, so far, more or less have gone away from them, till they have lost more talent than now remains with them.

IT LEADS TO INFIDELITY.

A strong argument with Adventists is, that most of those who leave them become infidels, as all know. But, after long watching, I became satisfied that it is Adventism which has made them infidels. Look at Romanism. Wherever it has had sway a while, it filled the land with infidels. Go among the Mormons at Salt Lake. Large numbers of their children are becoming infidels. The natural rebound from fanaticism and superstition is into infidelity and scepticism. Right here in Otsego we have several infidels, the grown-up children of Adventists. I know them and meet them all over the country, and their numbers are increasing. I feel sure that the ripe fruit of Adventism in the years to come will be a generation of doubters.

THEIR CHURCH BACKSLIDING.

Seventh-Day Adventists claim to be raised up of God, to reform the church of to-day. They claim to be purer, more spiritual, and on a higher plane than other Christians. All other churches are Babylon and apostates, while they are the chosen saints. But now, after their church has had only fifty years trial, and hence is still small and young, and so ought to be better than older and larger churches, I can quote confessions from their own writers, proving that they are as worldly, backslidden and corrupt as they make out other churches to be. I will give a few.

Elder G. I. Butler, in the *Advent Review*, May 10, 1887, says: "A terrible stupor like that which enveloped the dis ciples in the Saviour's agony in the garden, seems to hang over the mass of our people." Mrs. White, in Testimonies, Vol. I, says: "The Spirit of the Lord has been dying away from the church," page 113; "The churches have nearly lost their spirituality and faith," page 119; "I saw the dreadful fact that God's people were conformed to the world with no distinction, except in name," page 133; "Covetousness, selfishness, love of money, and love of the world, are all through the ranks of Sabbath-keepers," page 140; "Vital godliness is lacking," page 153; "There is but little love for one another. A selfish spirit is manifest. Discouragement has come upon the church," page 166; "Spirituality and devotion are rare," page 469. Many of them are not even honest. She says: "As I saw the spirit of defrauding, of over-reaching, of meanness, even among some professed Sabbath-keepers, I cried out in anguish," page 480; "There is but little praying. In fact, prayer is almost obsolete," page 566; "Not one in twenty of those who have a good standing with Seventh-Day Adventists, is living out the self-sacrificing principles of the word of God," page 632. Of the Battle Creek church she says: "I can select family after family of children in this house, every one of whom is as corrupt as hell itself." "Right here in this church corruption is teeming on every hand," Vol. II, pages 360, 361; "Sin and vice exist in Sabbath-keeping families," page 391; "We have a dwarfed and defective ministry," Vol. IV, page 441. In Testimony, No. 33, just published, Mrs. White says: "There is a deplorable lack of spirituality among our people. * * There has been a spirit of self-sufficiency, and a disposition to strive for position and supremacy. I have seen that self-glorification was becoming common among Seventh-Day Adventists," pages 255, 256. Thus as they grow older, they have to confess to all the weaknesses and short-comings which they have so eagerly charged against other churches.

I could quote whole pages of such confessions as these from Mrs. White and their leading men. They are compelled to say it. It is common in their camp-meetings to see half their members forward as backsliders. Their preaching is largely scolding their members for their coldness. In fact, the thing is a practical failure in whatever way you look at it. Are they any better, any more spiritual, than the regular churches which they denounce so? No, as the above shows. After being well acquainted with both, I say confidently that there is as much devotion and spirituality among the Evangelical churches as among Adventists.

If, then, these things in the other churches prove that they are Babylon, they prove the same of the Advent church, too.[1]

[1] See Appendix A.

CHAPTER IV.

ORIGIN, HISTORY AND FAILURES OF ADVENTISM.

Every little while, from the days of Christ till now, individuals, and often large sects, have arisen, proclaiming the Second Advent at hand and themselves the God-appointed messengers to warn the world. Right on this point Jesus warned his church: "Take heed that no man deceive you. * * * The end is not yet." Matt. 24: 4-6. Yet right away it was said that Jesus would come before John should die. John 21: 23. The Thessalonians had to be corrected by Paul for expecting the Advent immediately at hand. II. Thess. 2: 1–8.

In the middle of the second century arose the Montanists. The Schaff-Herzog Encyclopedia says: "Ecstatic visions announcing the approach of the Second Advent of Christ * * * were set forth as divine revelations." Art. Montanism. Like Seventh-Day Adventists, they adopted a severe discipline—condemned the wearing of ornaments, intercourse with the world, etc. They created a great sensation, obtained a numerous following, and flourished for a century or more.

TENTH CENTURY ADVENTISM.

The following is from the "History of the Christian Church," by M. Reuter, D.D., Century 10, Chapter 2, pages 202, 203: "Among the numerous opinions, however, which disgraced the Latin church and produced from time to time such violent agitations, none occasioned such universal panic, nor such dreadful impressions of terror or dismay, as a notion that prevailed during this [tenth] century of the immediate approach of the day of judgment." "Public and private buildings were suffered to decay, and were even pulled down, from an opinion that they were no longer of any use, since the dissolution of all things was at hand."

The Fifth-Monarchy men of England, about 1660, "believed that the time was near at hand when, to the four great monarchies of Daniel's prophetic vision, was to succeed the fifth, which was to break in pieces all others, and to 'stand forever.'" Johnson's Encyclopedia, article Fifth-Monarchy Men. They undertook to set up the kingdom by overturning the English government.

The Irvingites of England "declare the speedy coming of Christ;" have "prophets," "revelations," "tongues," "gifts," etc. They have gathered large congregations and are spreading over the world.

Swedenborg, Ann Lee, Joanna Southcott, Joe Smith, etc., all made the speedy advent of Christ the ground-work of their systems, as is well known. Hence. movements of this kind are nothing new.

Seventh-Day Adventism originated in the well-known movement of William Miller, who set the time for the end of the world in 1843-4. They claim now that Mr. Miller's move was right, and in the providence of God. They claim to be simply carrying on the same work which he began. In all their books and sermons they point to 1844 as their origin, and endorse the work of the Millerites in 1843 and 1844. The following from Mrs. White will settle the point:

"I have seen that the 1843 chart was directed by the hand of the Lord, and that it should not be altered; that the figures were as he wanted them; that his hand was over and hid a mistake in some of the figures." Early Writings, page 64. God helped them make the mistake! "I saw that God was in the proclamation of the time in 1843." Spiritual Gifts, Vol. I., page 133. So God wanted them to set that time! " I saw that they were correct in their reckoning of the prophetic periods; prophetic time closed in 1844." Page 107. Again: "The Advent movement of 1840-44 was a glorious manifestation of the power of God." Great Controversy, Vol. IV., page 429. Elder White says: " We hold that the great movement upon the Second Advent question, which commenced with the writings and public lectures of William Miller, has been, in its leading features, in fulfillment of prophecy. Consistently with this view, we also hold that in the providence of God, Mr. Miller was raised up to do a specific work." Life of Miller, page 6. So it will be seen that Seventh-Day Adventists still believe in and defend the Millerite movements of 1843 and 1844. Indeed, they claim that all other churches who did not accept and endorse Miller's work were rejected of God on this account. Thus Mrs. White: "As the churches refused to receive the first angel's message [Miller's work], they rejected the light from heaven and fell from the favor of God." Early Writings, page 101.

Here, then, we have the origin of Seventh-Day Adventism, the fountain from which it flowed. As a stream will be like its fountain, let us examine it. Elder and Mrs. White, Elders Bates, Andrews, Rhodes, Holt, Edson, and all the founders of the Seventh-Day Adventist Church were in the movement of Miller, and helped in setting and preaching the time in 1843, 1844, and carried the Advent work right on afterwards.

The work of Mr. Miller is so well known, that I need but refer to the facts about it. William Miller was born at Pittsfield, Mass., 1782, but he was reared at Low Hampton, N. Y. He was a farmer, with only the poor advantages of a country school He united with the Baptist church. About 1831 he claimed that he had discovered by the prophecies the exact time, the very year, and, finally, the very day when Christ would appear and the end of the world would come. He succeeded in converting perhaps fifty thousand people to his views. The first date fixed was 1843. It failed. Then he fixed a day in October, 1844, and that failed. Many other times have since been fixed by Mr. Miller's followers, and all have failed. Over fifty years have come and gone, and the end has not come yet.

What was the one great burden of Miller, the one point on which he differed from the Evangelical churches? All these churches believed in the personal Second Advent of Christ just as strongly as Miller did. They loved Jesus and preached the Second Advent, even teaching that it was near at hand. But the Millerites said they knew the *time* when it was to be, and that time was 1843-4. They staked all upon this. The issue was plain and definite. All who did not endorse their *set time* were "opposers," "enemies," "in the dark," "evil servants," rejected of God and lost, just because they would not believe in setting a time for the end. Here are Miller's words: "I believe the time can be known by all who desire to understand. * * * Between March 21, 1840, and March 21, 1844, according to the Jewish mode of computation of time, Christ will come." Life of Miller, page 172. Jesus says: "Ye know not when the time is." Mark 13: 33. But the Millerites thought they knew better than Jesus Christ did. So they condemned all who did not agree with them. Here is a mild sample of what they said and the spirit that possessed them: "This is God's truth; it is as true as the Bible." "There is no possibility of a mistake in this time." "Those who reject this light will be lost." "Those who do not accept this argument are backsliders," etc. History of Advent Message, page 596. And this is the spirit that has followed them ever since—a harsh, denunciatory spirit against all who did not agree with their figures, interpretations and theories.

But their set times came and passed without the least regard to their figures and facts, proofs and demonstrations, prayers and predictions. Remorseless old Time, the true tester of every theory, marched right on and demolished them all. This demonstrated the folly and error of the Adventists. Miller's prediction was a wretched abortion. He preached and propagated a falsehood. All his work wherein he differed from evangelical churches was a falsehood. He preached that the world would end in 1843, and it didn't. He set 1844 for it to come, and it didn't. If ever a religious movement on earth was demonstrated to be a humbug and a failure, it was Millerism. But if Millerism was a failure, then Seventh-Day Adventism is also, for that was the fountain from which this has flowed; that was the foundation on which this is built. Deut. 18: 22: "When a prophet speaketh in the name of the Lord, if the thing follow not, nor come to pass, that is the thing which the Lord hath not spoken." This, surely, is a simple and fair test. By this rule the Lord was not in Miller's move.

"But were not the Adventists in 1843-4 very confident that they were right?" Confident is no name for it. They were *sure* that they were right, they *knew* they were right, for they proved it all by the Bible, every word of it, positively. The Bible said so; to deny it was to deny the Bible. But it failed all the same. It is just so with Seventh-Day Adventists now. They are the most positive people in the world, though they have made scores of terrible blunders.

That no one will know the *time* of the second advent is as plainly taught as words can teach. Read the following: "But of that day and hour knoweth no man, no, not the angels of heaven, but my Father only;" "Watch, therefore: for ye know not what hour your Lord doth come;" "Therefore be ye also ready: for in such an hour as ye think not the Son of man cometh;" "Watch therefore, for ye know neither the day nor the hour wherein the Son of man cometh." Matt. 24: 36, 42, 44; 25: 13. "Take ye heed, watch and pray: for ye know not when the time is." Mark 13: 33. "It is not for you to know the times or the seasons, which the Father hath put in his own power." Acts 1: 7. Jesus said, "Ye know not when the time is;" Miller said, "We know when the time is." Jesus said, "It is not for you to know the times or the seasons;" Miller said, "We know all about them." Jesus said, "No man knows the day;" Miller said, "We know the exact day." Which was right? The disappointments of the Adventists, time and again, during the past fifty years, in setting the date for the end of the world have clearly demonstrated their folly. The whole Advent move was conceived in error, born in a mistake, has grown up in folly, and must die in disgrace. "But were not the Millerites honest?" There is no doubt of it, but that proves nothing as to their correctness.

THE FRUIT OF MILLERISM.

"By their fruits ye shall know them." Millerism, for about four years, in a few states, created a great excitement. Churches were divided and broken up, pastors left their flocks to "lecture" on "time," while argument and strife were the order of the day. As the time set drew near, in thousands of cases, the Adventists not only left their work and their business, but gave away their property. Crops were left ungathered, goods were distributed freely, so that many who had been well to do were left penniless. After the time had passed, these were destitute and their families suffered. Many had to be arrested and put under guardians, to protect their families. Then the wildest fanaticism broke out here and there, which brought disgrace upon the very name of religion. Many said the Lord had come, probation was ended, it was sin to work, all property must be held in common, all the churches were apostate, Babylon, etc. Some Adventists had spiritual wives, some went to the Shakers, many went back into the churches, some into despair, and hundreds into doubt and infidelity—just what might have been expected. The glorious doctrine of the Second Advent was covered with shame, Satan rejoiced, while the cause of Christ was greatly injured. For proof of these facts, I refer to the testimony of thousands now living, and to the published works of the Adventists themselves. Thus Elder U. Smith is compelled to say: "The Advent body were a unit [in 1844] and their testimony shook the world. Suddenly their power was broken, their strength scattered, their ranks divided, and their testimony paralyzed. They passed the point of their expectation, and realized not their hope. That a mistake had been made somewhere, none could deny. From that point the history of a majority of that once happy, united people has been marked by discord, division, confusion, speculation, new mistakes, fresh disappointments, disintegration and apostasy." The Sanctuary, pages 13, 14.

Paul said, "God is not the author of confusion." I. Cor. 14: 33. Then surely he was not the author of Adventism, for the confusion it produced is unparalleled in religious history. Ten souls were ruined by it where one was saved. Immediately after 1844 they split up into numerous parties, each contradicting and condemning all the rest. Instead of renouncing the whole thing, as sane men ought to have done, each one set himself to find some "explanation" of their mistake. Hardly any two agreed, while each one was sure he had the true explanation. Their utter confusion is well illustrated by the following anecdote told by Mr. Miller himself: The first person in his own parish who fully embraced his views was an old woman, an humble Christian. Mr. Miller sent her his papers when he had read them. One week he received sixteen different sheets, all purporting to be Advent publications, but the most of them advocating contradictory sentiments. He sent them to the old woman. Soon she sent for him, and on his arrival began:

"Have you read all these papers?"

"I have looked them over."

"But are they all Advent papers?"

"They profess to be."

"Well, then," said she, "I am no longer an Adventist. I shall take the old Bible and stick to that."

"But," said Mr. Miller, "we have no confidence in one-half there is advocated in these papers."

"We?" exclaimed the old lady, "who is *we?*"

"Why," replied Mr. Miller, "*we* are those who do not fellowship these things."

"Well, but I want to know who *we* is."

"Why, all of us who stand on the old ground."

"But that ain't telling me who *we* is. I want to know who *we* is."

"Well," said Mr. Miller, in relating the story, "I was confounded, and was unable to give her any information who *we* were." History of Second Advent Message, pages 414, 415.

And so it has continued unto this day. What do Adventists believe? Go ask what language was spoken by the people after the Lord confused their tongues at Babel. Adventism is a second Babel. But Seventh-Day Adventists say, "We are united; we believe alike." Partly true, but they are only one branch of this Advent Babel. Such a brood of errors and heresies as has resulted from Adventism, cannot be found in the history of the church before. Time-setting, visions, miracles, fanatics, false prophets, sleep of

ORIGIN, HISTORY AND FAILURES OF ADVENTISM. 75

the dead, annihilation of the wicked, non-resurrection of the wicked, future probation, restoration, community of goods, denial of the divinity of Christ, no devil, no baptism, no organization, etc., etc. Gracious! And these are the people sent with a "message" to warn the church! They had better go back and learn and agree on what their "message" is, before they run to deliver it.

The other Adventists have set the time for the end of the world in 1843, 1844, 1847, 1850, 1852, 1854, 1855, 1863, 1866, 1867, 1868, 1877, and so on, till one is sick of counting. Learning nothing from the past, each time they are quite as confident as before.

This fanatical work has brought disgrace upon the doctrine of the Second Advent, so that it is not dwelt upon as much as formerly in other churches. The study of the prophecies has been brought into disrepute by the unwise course of the Adventists. No thoughtful man can fail to see this.

SEVENTH-DAY ADVENTISTS AND TIME-SETTING.

It is the one constant boast of the Seventh-Day Adventists that *they* never set time; *they* don't believe in it. But they deceive themselves and deceive others when they say so. Elder White, their leader, engaged in preaching three different set times for the Lord to come, viz., 1843, 1844, 1845. Here are his own statements on this: "I found myself happy in the faith that Christ would come about the year 1843." Life Incidents, page 72. Then he tells how he preached it. Of 1844, he says: "I stated my conviction that Christ would come on the tenth day of the seventh Jewish month of that year [1844]." Pages 166, 167. "It is well known that many were expecting the Lord to come at the seventh month, 1845. That Christ would then come we firmly believed. A few days before the time passed, I was at Fairhaven and Dartmouth, Mass., with a message on this point of time." "A Word to the Little Flock," by James White, page 22. So their leader was a time-setter. Mrs. White, their prophetess, was in the time-setting of 1843 and 1844. She herself says: "We were firm in the belief that the preaching of definite time was of God." Testimonies, Vol. I, page 56. Of the first date she says: "With carefulness and trembling we approached the time when our Saviour was expected to appear." Then she tells her disappointment. Testimonies, Vol. I, page 48. Again: "Our hopes now centered on the coming of the Lord in 1844." Page 53. She was a time-setter. Elders Bates, Andrews, Rhodes, and all the first crop of Seventh-Day Adventists were in the time-setting of 1843, 1844. They still endorse Miller's time-setting of 1843 and 1844 as right and approved of God. How much truth, then, is there in their assertions that they have never set time? But they say, "*We* did not keep the Seventh-Day when *we* set time; therefore *we* never set time!" That is too thin. The thief says, "*I* did not wear this coat when *I* stole the sheep, therefore *I* never stole him!" They say that they have given the *three* messages. Well, the first message was in 1844 when they set time. Are they the same people, or are they not?

Again they endorse Mr. Miller's work as of God. But Miller is responsible for all the time-setting done by the Adventists since his time, because they are the legitimate outgrowth of his work. He began setting time. He did it the second time. He taught them how to do it. He fathered the idea. He inculcated it in all his followers. They then simply took up and carried on what he had begun. Seventh-Day Adventists claim to be the original Adventists, and endorse Miller's work. In doing this they endorse time-setting, and should justly bear all the odium of that fanatical business.

But don't Seventh-Day Adventists rise to explain why

they were disappointed in 1843, and again in 1844, and for forty years since? O, yes; but we naturally become a little suspicious of the man who is compelled to be constantly explaining his conduct. Straight work needs no explanation. They say the Lord caused them to be disappointed in 1843, on purpose to test their faith, that was all! In 1844 they made just one little mistake, that was all! They then taught that the earth was the sanctuary. Come to find out, the sanctuary is up in heaven, and Jesus did really come, in a certain sense, that very year! So they were all right, after all. Don't you see? Clear as day. Now they have the whole matter removed from the troublesome facts of earth, where we can test them, to the beautiful theories of heaven, where no one can go to report on facts which might spoil their theories. Now they can speculate and argue in safety. But sober, thinking men see through all this. It is merely a make-shift to get out of a difficulty.

MILLER'S CONFESSION—HE OPPOSES SEVENTH-DAY ADVENTISM.

All the other Adventists long ago renounced the 1843-4 time-setting as an error. Thus: "The majority of Adventists took the position that the *time* was an error of human judgment." History of the Second Advent Message, page 383. Hear Mr. Miller himself: "On the passing of my published time, I frankly acknowledged my disappointment. * * * We expected the personal coming of Christ at that time; and now to contend that we were not mistaken, is dishonest. We should never be ashamed frankly to confess our errors. I have no confidence in any of the new theories that grew out of that movement, namely, that Christ then came as the Bridegroom, that the door of mercy was closed, that there is no salvation for sinners, that the seventh trumpet then sounded, *or that it was a fulfillment of proph-*

soy in any sense." History of the Advent Message, pages 410, 412.

From this we see: 1. That Miller, the founder and leader of that move, owned that it was an error. 2. He repudiated the idea that it was a fulfillment of prophecy in any sense. 3. He especially points out the Seventh-Day Advent positions as utterly wrong. He knew all about their arguments on the three messages, the sanctuary, the Sabbath, etc., and yet he not only rejected them, but earnestly warned his people against them, so that very few of the original Adventists ever accepted them. Hear Mrs. White herself on this point: "I saw leading men watching William Miller, fearing lest he should embrace the third angel's message and the commandments of God. As he would lean towards the light from heaven, these men would lay some plan to draw his mind away. I saw a human influence exerted to keep his mind in darkness, and to retain his influence among them. At length *William Miller raised his voice against the light from heaven.*" Spiritual Gifts, Vol. I, page 167.

Thus the father and founder of Adventism condemned and opposed the position which Seventh-Day Adventists took with regard to his own work. He had sense enough to see, and honesty enough to confess, that it was a mistake. But they will not have it so. They know better than he himself. They will have it that it was a wonderful fulfillment of Rev. 14: 6, 7. Miller denies it. Thus it will be seen that Seventh-Day Adventists give an interpretation to Miller's work which he himself condemned. Not a leading man in Miller's work ever embraced the views of the Seventh-Day Adventists, but have always opposed them as fanatical and as a side issue. None of the leaders of Seventh-Day Adventism, such as White, Andrews, Bates, Rhodes, etc., were ever of any note in Miller's work, though they were all in it; yet afterwards they claimed to be the only ones

ORIGIN, HISTORY AND FAILURES OF ADVENTISM. 79

who had the right view of it. All the rest were "in the dark," "foolish virgins," "apostates," etc. How modest!

MISTAKES OF ADVENTISTS.

A people who have made as many mistakes as Adventists have, ought to be very modest in their claims, and ought to see that they have been led by men and not by the Lord.

1. They set the time for the end of the world in 1843, and failed.
2. They set it again in 1844 and failed.
3. Elder White, the leader of the Seventh-Day Adventists, set 1845 for the end, and failed again.
4. They held in 1844 that the earth was the sanctuary, another mistake, as they admit now.
5. They all held for some time after 1844 that probation for sinners was ended—a fearful mistake. See pages 142-146 of this book.
6. For ten years Seventh-Day Adventists began the Sabbath at 6 P.M., instead of at sunset as now. Thus they broke the Sabbath every week!
7. They kept their children out of school for years, because time was so short they would need no education! Those children now have grand-children!
8. They gave away their goods in 1844, because they would not need them after that!
9. They would not vote, for that was like the fallen churches. Now they vote freely.
10. They held that it was wrong to take a church name, for that was Babylon. Now they have a name.
11. Church organization was wrong, for that was like Babylon. Now they organize.
12. For years they said it was denying their faith to set out trees, for they would never grow to bear fruit.

13. Led by a revelation from Mrs. White, the sisters put on the short dress with pants. None of them wear it now.

14. For thirty years they would not take up any collection on the Sabbath. Now they do it every week.

15. For fifty years they have been expecting the end of the world to come inside of five years, and it has not come yet.

16. They said Jesus would come to the earth in 1844. Now they say that was a mistake; he came to judgment in the sanctuary above. Thus: "The Adventists of 1844 * * thought the bridegroom would come; and *then he did come*—not to this earth, as they incorrectly supposed, but to the *marriage*." "They simply mistook the *kind* of coming referred to." U. Smith, in Parable of the Ten Virgins, pages 13, 14. He owns that, 1. They got the time wrong in 1843. 2. The place wrong. 3. The event wrong. Now let him add, 4. The whole thing wrong, and he will be right!

17. Then they said the door was shut, Matt. 25: 10; now they say that this was wrong; it is open yet. Thus: "There can be no other place for the shut door but at the autumn of 1844." Elder White, in Present Truth, May, 1850. "The door is still open, and other guests may come." U. Smith, in Parable of the Ten Virgins, page 17, February, 1889. These are the people who always *know* they are just right!

18. They once adopted a rigid vegetarian diet—no meat, no butter, only two meals per day, etc., but it was a failure. It killed many and ruined more, till they had to modify it and live like other people.

These are only samples out of numerous mistakes the Adventists have made; and this they have done with an inspired prophetess right at their head for forty-four years! These simple, undeniable facts alone should be enough to open the **eyes** of all to see that the Lord has not led them in their work.

CHAPTER V.

MY OBJECTIONS TO THE SEVENTH-DAY ADVENTIST SYSTEM.

1. It was born in a mistake. The origin of Adventism was in the Millerite time-setting of 1843 and 1844, which all know was a mistake.

2. That work produced great fanaticism, and wrought disaster to thousands of souls.

3. Out of that movement has grown a whole brood of errors, as they themselves will admit.

4. Seventh-Day Adventism is a system of popery—one man power. From the first, Elder White took this position, and molded the whole system to fit it. He would and did rule and dictate in everything in all the field. He would make it hot for one who dared to start anything which he had not bossed. He was head and president of everything. So now a few run everything. Their word is law. It is contrary to the Gospel, and has resulted in the mental degradation of the mass of that people. A few think for all.

5. The mere word of Mrs. White, an uneducated woman, is accepted as the voice of God to them dictating in everything. "As for my people, children are their oppressors, and women rule over them." Isa. 3: 12.

6. From the start, Elder and Mrs. White would take up publicly the faults, real or imaginary, of any one and every one, ministers, editors and all, and expose them before the whole congregation. If any objected, they were "rebels." All this was then printed in her "Testimonies" as inspired, and circulated for all to read. This has begotten in all a

habit of criticising and fault-finding, which is reprehensible to the last degree. Any one might have foreseen that it would result in this. Mrs. White herself now says: "There has been a picking at straws. And when there were no real difficulties in the church, trials have been manufactured." Testimonies, Vol. I, page 144. "Love for one another has disappeared, and a fault-finding, accusing spirit has prevailed. It has been considered a virtue to hunt up everything about one another that looked wrong, and make it appear fully as bad as it really was." Page 164. Mrs. White herself has set the example, and she is largely followed, till they are a denomination of fault-finders.

7. It is a fundamental doctrine with them that all the other churches are apostate and corrupt. Hence they are eagerly on the watch for every evil thing they can pick up against them. This is poor business, and it begets in themselves a hard, unlovely spirit.

8. They are constantly on the watch for all the evidence they can gather, showing that the world is rapidly growing worse. This again has a bad effect on themselves, tending to make them sour and gloomy.

9. Their ministers are mere lecturers, going from place to place, staying only a few weeks at a time, and repeating the same old sermons over and over. As a consequence they become narrow and small and dry. Their preaching is almost wholly doctrinal and argumentative. This makes them hard and combative, instead of tender and charitable.

10. Their churches are very small, generally numbering from fifteen to forty. They have no pastors, and seldom any preaching. Their meetings are held on Saturday, when others are at work, hence not a soul attends except themselves. So their meetings are small and dull and tiresome, especially to youth and children. Never mingling with other churches, they soon fall into a rut and become very dry.

The great mass of them are uncultured, and their local leaders are farmers or mechanics. The decorum seen in other churches is generally wanting in theirs. Their children are noisy, and often the members too. This is not good.

11. Their theory compels them to be narrow and uncharitable. They cannot work at all with other Christians in anything. This is another bad feature of that system. They condemn all Christian workers who do not follow them. See how Jesus rebuked that narrow, bigoted spirit: "And John answered him, saying, Master, we saw one casting out devils in thy name, and he followeth not us; and we forbade him because he followeth not us. But Jesus said, Forbid him not, for there is no man which shall do a miracle in my name, that can lightly speak evil of me; for he that is not against us is on our part." Mark 9: 38-40.

12. In a community they have no influence whatever over the irreligious. Not one of them attends their meetings; not a child outside of their own families attends their Sabbath schools. Other churches, by their public meetings, sermons and schools on Sundays, have a mighty influence for good over the unconverted.

13. Their work is largely proselyting. Truly, "they compass sea and land to make one proselyte." They will work just as hard to get a good old Christian out of another church as they will to convert a sinner. They tear down more than they build up.

14. They count all lost who reject their "message." Their missions of which they boast so much are the dread of all other missionaries, as they work as hard to proselyte members from churches as they do to convert raw heathen or sinners. Thus, of their " mission " in London, Elder Haskell says: "Thirteen have taken their stand on the Sabbath. * * These have come principally from the Church of

England." Review, April 10, 1888. Yes, their converts are always "principally" from other churches. I became sick of such work.

15. By their arguments they confuse the minds of many, so that they know not what to believe. They set them against other churches, and so they drift away from all and are entirely lost. Adventists have done a large amount of this work, and their influence in that line is fearful.

16. Many of their children grow up to keep neither Saturday nor Sunday, nor to attend any church, and hence they become irreligious.

17. Sunday-breakers who hunt, fish, sport or work that day, are encouraged in it by the arguments and examples of the Adventists. This certainly is evil. A community where Sabbatarians live has no quiet rest-day at all.

18. The power of God does not attend the Advent work as it should, if it is His special work. During my long experience with them, I was impressed with the fact that, as a rule, the work was exceedingly dry and powerless. This disheartened me greatly. I saw that it was so with all their ministers, from large to small. Their year book for 1888 shows that they did not average one convert to each minister!

19. In fields where they have been the longest and are the best known, they have the least success. As soon as it is well understood what it really is, they can do nothing.

20. The apostles, the reformers, and others whom God has sent, have built up large societies, and wielded a great influence for good in society. But the Adventists never do. They have no influence for good on society. This feature of the work often troubled me. Notice how the heretical and fanatical sects generally withdraw themselves from community, and build up a little exclusive society by themselves. See the Shakers, the Mormons, the Oneida Community, the followers of Mrs. Southcott, etc. Seventh-Day

Adventists become a little exclusive party in any community where they are. They go by themselves, and take part in almost nothing which interests others. Take my own town as an example. They have had a church here for thirty years, numbering from fifty to seventy-five. They take no part nor interest in any social, literary, moral, sanitary, temperance or religious work outside of their own. In these respects their influence is nothing. They are never thought of as helpers in any such necessary and noble work. They never attend a prayer meeting, a revival effort, or a Sabbath School except their own. The Young Men's Christian Association, which is wholly unsectarian, is doing a noble work to save the young men of the place. Not one Adventist attends or takes the least interest in it. On the contrary, the Adventist store is open for trade, and thus becomes a resort for idlers and Sunday breakers. In whatever way considered, their influence is detrimental to the best interests of religion and good society.

How different it was with the followers of the true reformers, Luther, Wesley, Calvin, etc. They stood with the people, worked for them, and made society generally better.

The moment a person becomes a thoroughly converted Seventh-Day Adventist, he is spoiled for any further usefulness in society. This is their record everywhere, as all will testify who know them. To convert men to their doctrine is the all-absorbing passion of their lives, leaving them neither interest, time nor means for anything else.

21. I came to see that the great burden of Adventists was about merely speculative theories concerning which they cannot *know* positively that they are correct after all. Such are their theories about the sleep of the dead, destruction of the wicked, the sanctuary in heaven, the time when Jesus will come, their interpretation of the image beast of Rev. 13: 11-18, the mark of the beast, etc. Do they *know* that

they are right about these? No, they think they are, and others equally honest, pious and intelligent, think differently. I came to feel that it was foolish for me to spend my life over what after all I did not know was really so. But we do know that it is right to evangelize the heathen and the vicious of our cities, to save the drunken and fallen, to preach Christ and convert sinners, and to work for everything that will improve the condition of men and society *now*. But with Adventists these things are secondary or neglected entirely, while they constantly put their pet theories first and dwell upon them most of the time.

22. All in their system that has been a blessing to them is held also by all evangelical churches, such as faith in God, in Jesus and the Bible, a pure heart, holy life, self-denial, etc. Nothing good has come to them or to the world by those doctrines which are peculiar to Adventists, as the *time* of the advent, the condition of the dead, the Sabbath, the visions, etc.

23. Having been disappointed so many times and so long, taking so gloomy a view of things generally, they are as a class a very discouraged and unhappy set of people.

24. It is "another gospel," Gal. 1: 6, which the apostles never preached. I was long impressed with the fact that we Adventists preached very differently from the apostles. For instance, we were always preaching and writing about the Sabbath, while Paul in all his fourteen epistles mentions it but *once*, Col. 2: 16, and then only to condemn it! "We find in the New Testament 'preach the gospel,' fifty times; 'preach Christ,' twenty-three times; 'preach the word,' seventeen times; 'preach the kingdom,' eight times; 'preach the law,' or 'the Sabbath,' not once!" Warner.

25. They are unpatriotic. Not a soul of them, man or woman, in field or hospital, lifted a finger to aid in putting down the rebellion or slavery. They staid at home and

found fault. See Mrs. White's Testimonies, Vol. I, pages 253-268. If a man had gone to the war he would have been expelled from the church, for Mrs. White forbade it. Hear her: "I was shown that God's people, who are his peculiar treasure, cannot engage in this perplexing war, for it is opposed to every principle of their faith." Testimonies, Vol. I, page 361. They hold that our nation is "the beast" of Rev. 13: 11-18, which will soon become a tyranny. Mrs. White says: "The nation will be on the side of the great rebel leader," the Devil. Testimony No. 31, page 132. So they all feel.

26. Their false ideas of Sunday leads them to join with infidels, atheists, Jews, saloon-keepers and the irreligious generally in opposing any restriction on Sunday desecration. It is one of the anomalies of the age to see a Christian church unite with the worst elements of society and the enemies of Christ, to oppose the best interests of society and the sacrificing work of the most devout and intelligent of the land. What is a religion good for, anyway, which spoils a person for all practical usefulness in society? what does it mean to "love your neighbor"?

THE ADVENTISTS AND THE PROPHECIES.

The Adventists claim great light above all others on the prophecies. The old women and the little children among them confidently believe that they know more about the prophecies than all the commentators and scholars in the world. They can tell exactly what every horn, and wing, head and tail, trumpet and vial, beast or angel in all the prophecies means! Any possibility of mistake? Not the slightest. And yet probably no people ever made as many mistakes in the same length of time as Adventists have.

Consider how little critical knowledge of exact historical dates and facts common people really possess. The great mass of intelligent business men, farmers, mechanics, mothers and housekeepers, would be poor judges in such matters. The most of them know nothing about it. They could not intelligently dispute any statement a lecturer might make on such points. These Advent preachers go before such an audience night after night for six or eight weeks, with their positive statements boldly made and often repeated, till their deluded hearers think them to be most wonderful historians, and accept their statements as undoubted truths! So of their Bible readers, who go from house to house to expound the deep things of God. I know them well, have taught many of them, and have been in their training schools. Many of them could not get a third grade certificate, nor have they ever read a volume of history. They simply learn by rote, parrot-like, a lesson which they repeat glibly to the astonished farmer or unread mother. Get them off this track and they are dumb. They are like those whom Paul rebuked, "Desiring to be teachers of the law; understanding neither what they say nor whereof they affirm." I Tim. 1: 7. This fits them exactly.[1]

[1] See Appendix B and C.

CHAPTER VI.

THE TWO-HORNED BEAST AND THE MESSAGES.

Seventh-Day Adventists lay great stress upon their interpretation of this symbol. Rev. 13: 11-18. Their theory of the mark of the beast, and his image, the seal of God, the Third Angel's Message, and all their special work about the Sabbath is built upon their assumption concerning that beast. If they are mistaken here, their whole system collapses. They claim that this beast is the United States, and that soon we shall have here church and state united, the image of the beast, the papacy. The mark of the beast is Sunday-keeping. A law will enforce this upon Seventh-Day Adventists. They won't obey. Then they will be outlawed, persecuted, and condemned to death! Of all the wild Advent speculations in the prophecies, this deserves to stand among the wildest.

1. Does the Bible *say* that this beast is the United States? Oh, no; they have to assume and argue out all this.
2. Do they *know* that their arguments on this are infallibly correct? No.
3. Were their leaders quite as sure in 1843, and then again in 1844, that they were right? Yes; and yet they failed both times.
4. Have they not made many mistakes in interpreting the prophecies? Yes; many of them.
5. Did not Elder White, their leader, set three different times for the end of the world, and fail in all? Yes. (P. 75.)
6. May they not then *possibly* be mistaken also in this?

Of course, as they must admit. So their system rests upon an uncertainty. Or are they infallible?

7. Do our hopes of Heaven depend upon such uncertainties as these? Would it not be safer to follow the plain precepts of Christ (Matt. 7 : 24, 25), than to run after these uncertain speculations? Better than to follow the lead of Adventists who have been making mistakes over and over again for eighty years? "Take heed that no man deceive you." Jesus. Matt. 24: 4. I will offer a few out of many facts showing that their application of this symbol is not correct.

While Seventh-Day Adventists largely quote and follow the leading commentators and Protestant churches in their application of the other beasts, here they take a wild leap into the dark, unsupported by one single biblical scholar. Evidently this lamb-like beast represents the Papacy, or the spiritual and ecclesiastical power of the Roman church, and is so applied by every commentator I have consulted. Thus: "This beast is the spiritual Latin empire, or, in other words, the Romish hierarchy." Clarke, on Rev. 13: 11. "It was, therefore, the emblem of the Roman hierarchy." Scott, on Rev. 13: 11. "The generality of interpreters confine this second beast to the papal power." Eclectic Commentary on Rev. 13: 11-18. "An exact description of the rise of the spiritual power of the Papacy." Notes on Rev. 13: 11, by the American Tract Society. "The beast with two horns like a lamb is the Roman hierarchy, or body of the clergy, regular and secular." Joseph Benson. "The two-horned beast or Romish church." Bishop Newton. Albert Barnes the same. Indeed, there is a perfect agreement among all commentators that this lamb-like beast represents the Papacy. For the argument on this I only need refer the readers to the commentaries.

Against this unanimous agreement of all Protestant

churches and authorities, you have the unsupported speculations of the Adventists, who have made so many mistakes before. The proofs that this lamb-like beast is the Papacy are many, clear, and easily seen; while the effort to apply it to the United States is labored, and the arguments strained, long, and far-fetched. Thus, in U. Smith's "Thoughts on Revelation," he devotes only *eleven* pages to the dragon of Chapter 12: 1-17, and only *eight* pages to the leopard beast of Chapter 13: 1-10, but wades heavily through *over one hundred pages* on the eight verses relating to the two-horned beast! This alone is proof of the desperate task he had on hand to prove that it was the United States.

Beginning with Rev. 11: 19, and ending with Rev. 14: 5, is a line of prophecy reaching from the First to the Second Advent—the dragon, the leopard beast, and the lamb-like beast. The dragon, Chapter 12: 1-17, is the pagan Roman empire. So all agree; Seventh-Day Adventists as well. The dragon had "seven heads and ten horns." Verse 3. This is succeeded, Chapter 13: 1-10, by the leopard beast with "seven heads and ten horns." What is this? Evidently the same Roman empire, the same ten kingdoms of Europe, with merely a change of religion from pagan to Catholic. Thus, Dr. Clarke: "The beast here described is the Latin empire, which supported the Romish or Latin church." On Rev. 13: 1. So Scott and all I have seen. This was the civil or political power of the ten kingdoms after professing Christianity. That this ten-horned leopard beast is not the Papacy nor the Catholic church, is shown by Rev. 17:1-5, where the same beast is again introduced with a woman riding on and ruling over it. The beast is the civil power, while the woman is the church. Even Elder Smith had to confess this. He says: "We here have the woman, the church, seated upon a scarlet-colored beast, the civil power by which she is upheld and which she controls and guides to her own ends as a rider controls a horse." On Rev. 17: 1-5. So, then, the leopard beast is the civil power. Just what it is in Rev. 17 is what it is in Rev. 13. Did the Papacy have ten horns? Did it have seven heads? No; but political Rome did.

That the lamb like beast of Rev. 13: 11-18 is not the United States at all, but is the Papacy, or ecclesiastical and spiritual power of the Romish church, is manifest.

1. Rev. 17: 1-5, where the woman, the church, is distinct from the ten-horned leopard beast and rules over it, shows that the beast is not the Papacy.

2. Just so; the lamb-like beast of Rev. 13 rules through the power of the leopard beast.

3. Whatever the woman is in Rev. 17, that is what the lamb-like beast is in Rev. 13. Hence, both are the papal power of Rome.

Notice the similarity of the two: a woman in one place, a lamb in the other, both having the appearance of gentleness and innocence. The church is represented by a pure woman, II. Cor. 11: 2, and by lambs, John 21: 15; false religious teachers are represented by bad women, Rev. 2: 18-23, and by beasts clothed like sheep, Matt. 7: 15. The woman and the beast work together in Chapter 17; so the lamb-like beast and the leopard beast work together in Rev. 13: 12, 14. The woman is drunk with the blood of saints, Rev. 17: 6; the lamb beast causes the saints to be killed, Rev. 13: 15. The woman is burned with fire, Rev. 18: 8; so is the lamb beast, Rev. 19: 20. The woman sits upon the beast, guiding and ruling it, Rev. 17: 3; so the lamb beast "exerciseth all the power of the first beast," Rev. 13: 12. It does not simply exercise *similar* power, or *as much* power, as the beast, but it uses the power of the beast itself, the same as the woman did. He does not himself kill anyone, but *causes* them to be killed, Rev. 13: 15. This is exactly

THE TWO-HORNED BEAST AND THE MESSAGES. 93

what the Papacy did. It ruled over the kings of earth, Rev. 17: 18, and "caused" heretics to be put to death by the secular power. "He exerciseth all the power of the first beast."

It has ever been the boast of the Roman church that *she* never puts heretics to death. She simply anathematizes them, turns them over to the civil powers, and by her influence with these, *causes* them to be killed by the secular powers. How exact is the language of the prophecy: he "causeth" it to be done; "he exerciseth [or useth] all the power of the first beast."

Seventh-Day Adventists argue that the leopard beast, Rev. 13: 1-10, is the papacy, because it does the same work as the little horn of Dan. 7: 8, 25, which is agreed by all to be the papacy. But they overlook the fact that the leopard beast does all its work simply as the agent of the church, the woman in Rev. 17, and the lamb-like beast in Chap. 13. Hence, of course, it does the same work that the little horn of Dan. 7 does.

Notice the inseparable connection between the leopard beast and the two-horned beast, the Roman civil government and the Papacy. 1. The lamb-like beast controls all the power of the first beast. Verse 12. 2. He does this in the presence and in the sight of the beast. Verses 12, 14. This shows that both occupy the same territory. 3. He causes men to worship the beast. Verse 12. 4. He causes men to make an image to the beast. Verse 14. 5. He causes men to receive the mark of the beast. Verses 16, 17. 6. The two beasts are working together when Christ comes. Rev. 19, 20. 7. Together they go into the fire. Verse 20. Evidently, then, these two beasts operate together in all their work. This is precisely what the Catholic church and the Catholic political powers of Europe have done for ages, as all know. Has the United States ever thus co-operated with the papacy? Emphatically, no. Is any man fanatical enough to believe that it ever will? The papacy has exactly fulfilled every specification of the lamb-like beast.

1. It came up in the right place "in his presence." Diaglott, Bible Union, Living Oracles, etc.

2. It came up at the right time after the wounding of the head. Rev. 13: 3. The interpretation adopted by Clarke, Scott, and the best authors, "refers it to the extinction of the old Roman Empire under the imperial form in the latter part of the fifth century, and its revival again under Charlemagne." Notes of Am. Tract Society.

3. The papacy came up in the right manner, peaceably and quietly.

4. It had the appearance of a lamb.

5. It has spoken like a dragon.

6. It has exercised all the power of civil Rome.

7. It brought the earth in subjection to Rome.

8. By its great signs and wonders it has deceived millions for ages.

9. It has made an image to the beast.

10. It has caused millions to be killed.

11. It has imposed its worship and mark upon all.

12. It has prohibited heretics from buying or selling. This is too well known to require proof.

The lamb-like beast is not the United States; because

1. "This two-horned beast symbolizes a religious or ecclesiastical government. The false prophet of Rev. 19: 20 performs the same work as this beast (see verse 14), and therefore must be identical with it. This is admitted by Seventh-Day Adventists. Now, as a prophet is a religious teacher, a false prophet must be a false religious teacher; and as this applies to a government, it must therefore apply to an ecclesiastical government. Such the United States is not, for its government is *purely* political; for one clause of

its constitution is as follows: 'Congress shall *make no law* respecting an establishment of *religion*, or prohibiting the free exercise thereof.'" The Two-Horned Beast, by A. C. Long.

2. The manner of its rise. The lamb-like beast comes up quietly and peaceably "out of the earth," Rev. 13: 11, while the other beasts come up out of the troubled sea. Rev. 13: 1. So the papacy came up quietly at first, with all the appearance of a lamb, but afterwards it spoke like a dragon. Witness its persecutions and tyranny. Not so with our nation. It was born in a terrible war of seven years. Then followed the war of 1812, the war with Mexico, the war of the Rebellion, and war with Indians almost every year. Not very peaceable.

3. It was to exercise *all* the power of the first beast. Seventh-Day Adventists say that the first beast is the Papacy, which put to death over fifty million people, ruled over other kings, and over the consciences of men. Even Adventists do not believe that the United States will do this.

4. "Church and state must be united. This is against one of the fundamental principles of our government. The constitution expressly forbids it, consequently it must first be changed. And will the intelligent voters of these United States, with the history of past ages before them, deliberrately change one of the main pillars of our government, and raise up the Inquisition, the block, the rack, etc., and thus put to death many persons, simply for their religious faith? It does not look reasonable." A. C. Long. Besides, all the tendency of the age is against a union of church and state.

ARGUMENTS ANSWERED.

1. "The two-horned beast must be the United States, because it can apply nowhere else." *Answer:* It applies admirably to the Papacy.

2. "There must be some symbol to represent this great nation." *Answer:* There is none for Russia, for Mexico, Brazil, Japan, China, and a dozen other nations, most of them professing Christianity too.

3. "The United States came up at the right time, about 1798, when the head received its deadly wound. Rev. 13: 3." *Answer:* This very point overthrows the argument for the United States; for that wound was given at the very rise of the leopard beast, more than 1,200 years before 1798. Look at verses 3–10; all the work of the beast comes *after* the wound and not *before*. This locates the rise of the lamb-like beast just when the Papacy rose.

4. "The United States came up in the right place." That is exactly what it *did not do*. The beast is located in Europe, and a whole ocean rolls between the two; whereas the two-horned beast was to come up "in his presence," in Europe, not America.

5. "Our government has 'come up' from small beginnings to a wonderful nation." *Answer:* The Papacy began much smaller, and has "come up" to be much larger.

6. "Our government is lamb-like." So was the Papacy in its rise and all its professions. A lamb in appearance, a dragon at heart, fits Rome much better. Our government does not put on sheep's clothes to hide wicked designs. It acts openly and boldly. But the Papacy professed outwardly to be a humble follower of the Lamb, while inwardly it was a dragon.

7. "No crowns on his horns. Hence, it must be a republic—the United States." *Answer:* The ten-horned beast of Dan. 7 had no crowns, yet all were kingly governments. So the dragon, Rev. 12: 3, had no crowns on his ten horns, yet all were kingly governments. So there were crowns upon his seven heads, yet several of these heads represented forms of government that had no crowns. So this argument fails.

8. "Spiritualism has wrought the miracles here." The miracles of spiritualism are a humbug, nor are they in any way recognized or used by our nation in making laws. But in the prophecy the miracles are wrought by official authority, and not by private individuals, wrought to secure and enforce laws for persecution. Verse 14. Spiritualism does not do this. And surely our nation will never lower itself to the working of miracles by official authority! But papal Rome has abounded in lying miracles, by which she deceived her followers for ages. Our nation is now over one hundred years old, and, according to Adventists, five or ten years more will end its work. But out of eight verses of the prophecy only *one* is yet fulfilled, if our nation.

1. The beast was to come up. Fulfilled.
2. He was to come out of the earth. Fulfilled.
3. Was to have two horns. Not fulfilled.
4. Was to look like a lamb. Fulfilled.

But all these specifications are much better fulfilled by the Papacy than by the United States.

5. Was to speak as a dragon. Not fulfilled.
6. Was to exercise all the power of the first beast. Not fulfilled.
7. Must cause the earth to worship the first beast. Not fulfilled.
8. Must do great wonders. Not fulfilled.
9. Must bring fire from Heaven. Not fulfilled.
10. Work miracles. Not fulfilled.
11. Is to make an image to the beast. Not fulfilled.
12. The image is to speak. Not fulfilled.
13. To cause all to be killed who do not worship the beast. Not fulfilled.
14. To cause all to receive the mark. Not fulfilled.
15. To prohibit all from buying or selling who do not have the mark. Not fulfilled.

Out of *fifteen* points only *four* have been fulfilled, and these relate simply to its rise. Of all the work it was to do, not a thing has been done yet. Adventists are always saying that the rest is just about to be done. But in the past forty years not one single point has been fulfilled, nor is there the least prospect that it ever will be. Unless God works a miracle, no such thing as they are looking for can be accomplished anyway.

The mark was to be enforced upon bondmen, verse 16; but slavery is abolished, and that can not be fulfilled here, but it was fulfilled under papal Rome. Souls were beheaded for not worshiping the beast. Rev. 20: 4. This was all fulfilled under the Papacy, but Seventh-Day Adventists themselves say no one will be killed here.

We have now proved conclusively that the two-horned beast is not the United States. This being so, then Seventh-Day Adventists are wrong on the image of the beast, the mark of the beast, the Third Angel's Message, and the Sunday question, and hence their whole theory collapses.

THE IMAGE OF THE BEAST. WHAT IS IT?

In Rev. 13: 14-17; 14: 9-11; 15: 2; 19: 20; 20: 4, great prominence is given to "the image of the beast." God's wrath is threatened against all who worship it. It must, then, be some very wicked thing. Seventh-Day Adventists claim that the image will be formed by a union of church and state in our nation. That will be an image to Catholicism, the beast, they say. See "Thoughts on the Revelation," page 581. Their great mission is to warn men of this coming image. Sunday-keeping, the Pope's Sabbath, is to be the chief feature of this image. After thorough investigation, I am satisfied that there is no truth in this claim.

1. If a union of church and state constitutes an image to he beast, then this image has been formed ages ago, and by

different nations, wherever there has been a union of church and state as in England, Scotland, Ireland, Germany, Switzerland, Russia, Norway and Sweden, Mexico, Brazil, Abyssinia, Puritan New England, etc. But this would overthrow the Seventh-Day Adventist theory that the image has never yet been formed.

2. They say that the Papacy is the beast to whom the image is formed. Elder Smith thus defines the Papacy: "The Papacy, then, was a church clothed with civil power." Thoughts on Revelations, page 585. Is this definition correct? No; it is utterly false, as every scholar knows. It was made to fit a theory as false as the definition. Look at any dictionary. "Papacy: 1. The office and dignity of the Pope. * * * 2. The Popes taken collectively." Web. The Papacy existed long before it was clothed with civil power. It has no civil power now, yet it is the Papacy still. So, then, an image to the Papacy does not necessarily include civil power or a union of church and state at all. On this false assumption is built the Advent theory of the image.

3. What is the Papacy? See Webster above. It is that ecclesiastical system of worship of which the Pope is head. Its distinguishing marks are these: 1. Popes. 2. Cardinals. 3. Monks. 4. Nuns. 5. Celibacy. 6. The mass. 7. Worship of the virgin. 8. Worship of saints. 9. Use of images. 10. Sign of the cross. 11. The confessional. 12. Use of incense. 13. Holy water. 14. Claim of infallibility. 15. A gorgeous worship, and the like. This is the Papacy, as known to everybody the world over. Now unite our Protestant churches with our state, pass a law and fine Sabbath-keepers, and how many of the above distinguishing features of the Papacy would you have? *Not one.* In order to have an *image* to the Papacy, you must have at least the main features of it, as above. But even Adventists do not expect to see any of the above items in their Sunday

law. Their idea of an image to the beast is a senseless, unscriptural affair from the first to last.

4. A stringent national Sunday law, such as Adventists expect, would by no means constitute an image to the Papacy; because the Catholics never had nor taught such a Sunday institution as that would be. Their Sunday is, and always has been, a loose holiday, a day for games, sports, beer gardens, saloons, dancing, voting, and even work, with a little church service and Mass in the morning. Look at the Sunday in any Catholic country or community. Such a strict Sunday as Adventists expect would be no more like that than a sheep is like an ox; hence, not an image to it. The Adventists themselves have shown that the doctrine of a strict Sunday did not originate with the Catholics, but with the Presbyterians and Puritans in the sixteenth century. History of the Sabbath, Chapter XXV. So, then, their Sunday law would constitute an image to the church of Scotland instead of the church of Rome!

So their theory breaks down on all sides.

5. All this on the supposition that the Papacy is the leopard beast to which the image is to be made. But we have proved that the leopard beast is not the Papacy, but the empire of Rome under the ten kingdoms after their adoption of Christianity. But their conversion was only nominal. They brought with them very largely their pagan doctrines, customs, religious rites, images, gods, shrines, temples, and pomp of worship. This became the model after which the Papacy was gradually but finally formed. The Papacy in its full and final development was an image of this half heathen, half Christian, worldly kingdom.

THE DEADLY WOUND, AND HOW IT WAS HEALED.

The utter fallacy of the Seventh-Day Adventist theory of these beasts is shown by the fact that they locate the deadly wound of Rev. 13: 3 in 1798, at the *end* of the forty-two months of verse 5, after nearly all the work of the beast is done. But in the prophecy it is distinctly located in the very *beginning* of the work of the leopard beast. Read Rev. 13: 1–10, and see where the wound was made, verse 3. The worship of the beast, his power, his blasphemies, his persecutions of the saints, his forty-two months, his 1260 years reign, the subjection of all the earth to him—all these come *after* the wound is healed, not before. On the overthrow of paganism, the breaking up of the empire by the northern barbarians, and the final extinction of the western empire, it looked as though the Roman empire was about to be entirely extinguished. But right here Christianity conquered those barbarians, and brought them under the rising influence of the Papacy. New life was infused into the old carcass, the empire was revived, the wound was healed. See Barnes, Clarke, Scott, etc.

THE MARK OF THE BEAST: WHAT IS IT?

1. *Seventh-Day Adventists* assert in the most positive manner that the Pope changed the Sabbath to Sunday. "The Pope has changed the day of rest from the seventh to the first day." Mrs. White, Early Writings, page 55.

2. Then they affirm that "Sunday-keeping must be the mark of the beast." The Marvel of Nations, by U. Smith, page 183. "The Sunday Sabbath is purely a child of the Papacy. It is the mark of the beast." Advent Review, Vol. I, No. 2, August, 1850. They thunder this into the ears of people, and threaten them with God's wrath if they keep Sunday, till they frighten ignorant souls to give it up.

3. This change in the Sabbath, they say, was made by the Popes at the Council of Laodicea, A. D. 364. Replies to Elder Canright, page 151. This was over 1500 years ago.

4. All who keep Sunday, they assert, worship the beast

and receive his mark. "Sunday-keeping is an institution of the first beast, and *all* who submit to obey this institution emphatically worship the first beast and receive his mark, 'the mark of the beast.' * * * Those who worship the beast and his image by observing the first day are certainly idolaters, as were the worshipers of the golden calf." Advent Review Extra, pages 10 and 11, August, 1850. This language is too plain to be mistaken. All who keep Sunday have the mark of the beast.

5. But, strange to tell, they now all deny that any one has ever had the mark of the beast. "We have never so held," says Smith, Marvel of Nations, page 184. All right, though this is a square denial of what they once taught, as above. It is a common thing for them to change their positions and then deny it. We proceed:

6. The United States will soon pass a strict Sunday law and unite church and state; then all who still keep Sunday will have the mark. Marvel of Nations, page 185.

ANSWER.

Does the Bible say that the mark of the beast is keeping Sunday? No, indeed. That is only another one of their assumptions. To establish this, they have to make a long, roundabout set of arguments, built upon inferences none of which are sound. Their theory is false, because:

1. The Jewish Sabbath was abolished at the cross. [Col. 2: 16.] Hence, it was not changed by the Pope.

2. Sunday is the Lord's day of Rev. 1: 18. See Chapter X of this book.

3. The Pope never changed the Sabbath. This point I have proved beyond all question in Chapter XI. This fact alone upsets their whole argument on the mark of the beast.

4. The Papacy is not the beast to whom the image is made, as they assume. Here again their whole theory is demolished.

THE TWO-HORNED BEAST AND THE MESSAGES. 103

5. Merely keeping Sunday would not be an image to the Papacy any way, as I have shown.

6. The two-horned beast is not the United States at all, but is the Papacy, as I have clearly proved.

7. The image to the beast was made ages ago by the Papacy. So every one of their arguments for the mark of the beast fails.

THE ABSURDITIES OF THEIR POSITION.

1. Sunday-keeping has been the mark of the beast for 1500 years. During all this long time millions have kept Sunday on the sole authority of the Roman church, and yet no one had the mark!

2. The keeping of Sunday has been time and again and in many countries enforced by law and severe penalties, just as they say it will be in the future here, and yet none of those who have kept it as thus enforced have had the mark of the beast!

3. Church and state have been united in various countries, and have enforced this institution of the Papacy, as they call it, and yet it was not enforcing the mark of the beast!

4. For over 1500 years, taking their own dates, all the pious of the earth, the martyrs, the reformers, the Luthers, Wesleys and Judsons, have observed Sunday and enjoyed the blessing of God, but now, all at once, the whole world, Christians and all, are to be damned and drink the wrath of God for doing just what all holy men have done for ages! Of Sunday-keeping in the future, Mrs. White says: "That must be a terrible sin which calls down the wrath of God unmingled with mercy." Great Controversy, page 282. This terrible sin is just what all the church of Christ has practiced for ages, and yet have had God's blessing! How absurd.

5. It is attempted to dodge this point by saying that those of other ages did not have the light on the Sabbath. I have shown the falsity of that on other pages. Luther, Bunyan, Baxter, Milton, all had the "light" on the Sabbath question, and rejected it and wrote against it. Then I can do it, too, and not have the mark of the beast, if they did not.

6. If it is worshiping the beast to rest from physical labor on Sunday after one knows that Sunday is the Pope's Sabbath, then many Seventh-Day Adventists are worshipers of the beast. Why? Because they often rest on Sunday. Book agents, colporters, teachers, drummers, persons visiting relatives, ministers in new places, etc., all frequently rest on Sunday, and even go to church all day! Are they worshipers of the beast? Why not? Do you say they only do it for convenience or from policy? Just so they can rest on Sunday for the same reason when the law shall require it, and not worship the beast any more than Adventists do now.

7. Deny it as they may, the Seventh-Day Adventist teachings do make all Sunday-keepers, both now and in past ages, worshipers of the beast, having the mark of the beast. Here is proof in their own words:

1. The Pope changed the Sabbath. Sunday is only the Pope's day. See above.

2. "The mark of the beast is the change the beast made in the law of God," in the Sabbath. Marvel of Nations, page 175. Then the mark of the beast existed as soon as the change was made, which they locate 1500 years ago. Is not this conclusion inevitable? If the mark of the beast is the change of the Sabbath which was made by the Papacy in the fourth century, then that mark has existed ever since. There is no escape from this conclusion.

3. All who have kept the law since that date, as changed

by the beast, have been keeping the law of the beast, not the law of God; have been worshipers of the beast, not worshipers of God. Here is their own argument for it: Referring to the prophesy that the Papacy should "change times and laws," Dan. 7: 25, which they claim the Pope fulfilled A. D. 364, by changing the Sabbath to Sunday, Elder Smith says: "When this is done [which is 1500 years ago], what do the people of the world have? They have two laws demanding obedience"—the law of God and the law of the Pope. If they keep the law of God, as given by Him, they worship and obey God. If they keep the law as changed by the Papacy, they worship that power. * * * For instance, if God says that the seventh day is the Sabbath, on which we must rest, but the Pope says that the first day is the Sabbath, and that we should keep this day, and not the seventh, *then whoever* observes that precept as originally given by God, is thereby distinguished as a worshiper of God; and he who keeps it as changed is *thereby marked* as a follower of the power that made the change. * * * From this conclusion no candid mind can dissent." Marvel of Nations, pages 174 and 175.

Then, for the past fifteen hundred years, all who have kept Sunday have been "marked" as followers of the beast and have worshiped him! From their own argument, does not this inevitably follow? Of course, it does When they try to deny and evade this abominable conclusion, they simply contradict and stultify themselves. Either their argument is a fallacy, or else this conclusion must follow. Look at this hideous Moloch which they have set up to frighten the ignorant. The Pope in the fourth century changed the law of God by changing the Sabbath to Sunday. This change is the mark of the beast; whoever after that keeps that law as thus changed, is keeping not the law of God, but the Pope's law; is worshiping, not God, but the Pope. But all Christians for fifteen hundred years have kept Sunday, the Pope's Sabbath, the mark of the beast, and, as Smith says, were "*thereby marked* as followers of the power that made the change." From this conclusion there is no escape. And so all Sunday-keepers have had the mark of the beast, and have it now.

But they say that they do not teach that anyone as yet has had the mark of the beast. This shows the absurdity of their argument. Sunday-keeping is the mark of the beast, yet Sunday-keepers have not got the mark of the beast! For instance: I have a hundred counterfeit bills; I pay them out to fifty men in Otsego, and they take and keep them, yet not a man of them has a counterfeit bill! Isn't that clear —as mud? But they don't know that they are counterfeit bills, and so are not guilty for having them. But have they not got counterfeit bills for all that? Certainly. So, if Sunday-keeping is the mark of the beast, then every man that keeps Sunday has the mark of the beast, whether he knows it or not. God may not hold them guilty for it, but they have it just the same. Now, as soon as these fifty men are informed that their bills are counterfeit, are they not guilty if they use them after that? Yes. So, as soon as a man is informed that Sunday is the mark of the beast, if he keeps it after that has he not the mark of the beast as truly as ever he can have it? And if he still keeps Sunday voluntarily is he not just as guilty before God as though the law compelled him to keep it? Yes, and more so; because now he has no excuse, while then he could plead that he was compelled to do it. So, then, it needs no Sunday law to give men the mark of the beast. All Sunday-keepers have it already, and as soon as they are informed that Sunday is the mark of the beast, then they are guilty as worshipers of the beast. But Seventh-Day Adventists have already informed thousands upon this point. Then if they have not the mark of the beast, why not? Surely *I* have been enlightened on it, and yet I keep Sunday, the Pope's Sabbath, the mark of the beast. Have I the mark of the beast? Let them answer if they dare. Remember that Luther, Milton, Baxter, Bunyan and Miller were all informed on the Sabbath question, and still wrote against it and kept Sunday. Reader, this Advent mark of the beast is an absurdity and only a scare-crow. Don't be frightened.

Even if the Pope did change the Sabbath to Sunday, that would not make Sunday *his* mark. The mark of any person was that which he used to mark things as belonging to him. In Bible times a master would put his mark on the right hand or forehead of his slaves. Heathen gods had their worshipers marked so. This custom is referred to and used here as an illustration. So the worshipers of the beast would be required to do something which would mark or distinguish them as his followers. But keeping Sunday does not distinguish a Catholic from members of other churches, for all churches keep Sunday—the Greek, Armenian, Lutheran, Episcopal, Methodist, etc. The Pope has never used Sunday to distinguish his followers from others, nor as proof of his authority as head of the church. He does point to the keys of St. Peter and his regular apostolic succession from him as proof of his authority. Says Dowling: "The Popes assert 'their *divine right* of supremacy in consequence of their claiming to be the successors of the Apostle Peter." History of Romanism, page 44. On this, not on Sunday-keeping, they base their claim of power. Some obscure catechism is quoted, claiming authority for the church to "command feasts and holy days," because that church has made Sunday holy. This falls infinitely short of making Sunday the proof of all their authority, the one "mark" of that church.

4. It is absurd to say that resting on Sunday is such a

fearful crime as Adventists affirm. Hear Elder Smith: "Sunday-keeping must be the mark of the beast." "The reception of his mark must be something that involves the greatest offense that can be committed against God." Marvel of Nations, pages 170, 183. So keeping Sunday is more wicked than lying, stealing, or even murder or idolatry! Such a statement is monstrous. In the mind of any candid, thinking man, it must break down under the weight of its own absurdity.

WHAT, THEN, IS THE MARK OF THE BEAST?[1]

Elder Smith himself has stated this as clearly as need be: "It will evidently be some act or acts by which men will be required to acknowledge the authority of that image and yield obedience to its mandates." "So the mark of the beast, or of the Papacy, must be some act or profession by which the authority of that power is acknowledged." Marvel of Nations, pages 169, 172. Exactly; any act or acts by which men show their reverence for the beast or his image, any form of worship by which they acknowledge his authority, that would be worshiping the beast and his image and receiving his mark. Dr. Clarke says: "The Latin [Catholic] worship is the universal badge of distinction of the Latin church from all other churches on the face of the earth, and is, therefore, the only infallible MARK by which a genuine papist can be distinguished from the rest of mankind." On Rev. 13: 16. This is the position taken by Protestants generally, and I believe it to be correct. A conformity to the system of worship set up by the Papacy, that great anti-Christian power, the image to the beast, would be worshiping the beast and his image and receiving his mark. To worship the beast is a great crime; but is it a crime to devote a day to God, even though the Bible has not required it? Surely not, for Paul says: "He that regardeth the day,

[1] See Appendix D.

regardeth it unto the Lord." Rom. 14: 6. About doing this he says: "Let every man be fully persuaded in his own mind." Verse 5. So we are at liberty to regard Sunday unto the Lord, if we so choose. Hence, it cannot be a sin as Adventists claim, and so cannot be the mark of the beast.

THE THREE MESSAGES, REV. 14: 6–12.

The one great claim of Seventh-Day Adventists is that they are preaching the three messages of Rev. 14: 6–12. This is their constant theme. So the Mormons claim that Joe Smith preached this message. But there is not a particle of foundation for the claim in either case. Read the first message, verses 6, 7. An angel is seen preaching the gospel to every nation, saying: "Fear God, and give glory to him, for the hour of his judgment is come; and worship him that made heaven, and earth, and the sea, and the fountains of waters." This was fulfilled by the apostles and early Christians, as they preached the gospel to all nations. Jesus said, "Go ye into all the world, and preach the gospel to every creature." Mark 16: 15. The angel in Rev. 14: 6, 7, is seen preaching the gospel to every nation, as Jesus commanded. Compare Paul's sermon to the idolatrous heathen at Lystra, Acts 14: 15, with the words of the first message, Rev. 14: 7, and they will be seen to be almost identical. Said Paul: We "preach unto you that ye should turn from these vanities unto the living God, which made heaven, and earth, and the sea, and all things that are therein." So Rev. 14: 7 says: "Worship him that made heaven, and earth, and the sea." This, then, was a message to idolators, announcing to them the living God who made all things, but of whom they had been ignorant. This is exactly what the early church preached to the heathen nations till idolatry was overthrown.

Paul says the gospel "was preached to every creature

which is under heaven," Col. 1: 23. This was before he died, and this exactly fulfilled Rev. 14: 6, 7. But the Advent work of 1844 was a small, local affair, limited to a few states; much less was it preached to all nations.

Adventists claim that Wm. Miller preached this message in 1840-4. He did no such thing. The burden of his preaching was that the end of the world would come in 1843 and then in 1844. But he preached what failed both times, as we know. Does God send men to make such blunders as that? Miller did not preach the hour of judgment come. That was an afterthought, an interpretation put upon his work which was not thought of at the time.

It is claimed that the apostles could not have preached this message, as the judgment did not come in their day. Let us see. Jesus preached thus: "*Now is* the judgment of this world." John 12: 31. Jesus said, "Now is the judgment." Who will contradict him and say it wasn't? Peter said: "For the time *is come* that judgment must begin at the house of God." I. Pet. 4: 17. Then the judgment did begin there. Here are two direct testimonies, and that is enough. So in exact harmony with these, the First Angel announces, "The hour of his judgment is come." Rev. 14: 7. If any one wants to see the truth, this is clear enough; if they don't want to, there is no use arguing with them further.

SECOND MESSAGE, VERSE 8.

"And there followed another angel, saying, Babylon is fallen, is fallen, that great city, because she made all nations drink of the wine of the wrath of her fornication." What is Babylon, that great city? It is fully described in Rev. 17 and 18, and is regarded by all Protestants as the Roman church. Adventists themselves agree with this, though endeavoring to make Babylon also include the Protestant churches. Even with their view Babylon, "the great," must refer primarily to

Rome, and only include other fallen churches as a secondary idea, as her daughters. Seventh-Day Adventists claim that this message was preached by the Millerites in 1844. When the churches refused to believe Miller that the end of the world would come in 1844, and that he could tell the very day, then and for this unbelief all these churches were rejected of God and fell. Mrs. White says: "Satan has taken full possession of the churches as a body. * * * Their profession, their prayers, and their exhortations are an abomination in the sight of God." Early Writings, page 135. What awful thing had they done to fall so? Why, Miller said the world would end in 1844, and they said it wouldn't. He was wrong and they were right, but God rejected them and blessed the Millerites! This is a fair illustration of the egotism and inconsistency of the Adventists. Did they preach what Rev. 14: 8 says? No! They said Babylon was fallen *because* she rejected Millerism, but the message gives a far different reason. Babylon fell "because she made all nations drink of the wine of her fornication." The Bible gives one reason, Adventists give another. Did the Protestant churches in America in the short space of about five years, during Miller's preaching, and by simply rejecting his time-theory—did they thus make all nations drunk? The idea is absurd. This message must have a far deeper and broader meaning than this. So they never preached this message. Just a few of the churches in the eastern states heard and rejected Millerism; for this all the tens of millions of church members throughout the whole world, who never even so much as heard of Miller, were rejected of God! What an unreasonable position. Again, Babylon must at least include Rome. Did the Catholic church fall in 1844? No, for she fell ages ago, as every Protestant knows. So, then, the fall of Babylon does not mean what Adventists say, nor did they preach what the message says.

A thousand times more probable is the application of this message to the work of Luther and the Reformation. Till the time of Luther the Papal church was supposed to be the true church, and as such it ruled over the kings of earth and the consciences of men. Luther startled the world with the bold proclamation that the Roman church was the "Mother of harlots," "Babylon the great," of Rev. 17: 1-6, and that she was fallen, as stated in Rev. 14: 8; 18: 1-4. October 6, 1520, he published his famous book on the "Babylonish Captivity of the Church."

I will quote from D'Aubigne's History of the Reformation, Vol. II.: "Luther had prepared a mine, the explosion of which shook the edifice of Rome to its lowest foundation. This was the publication of his famous book on the 'Babylonish Captivity of the Church,' which appeared on the 6th of October, 1520." Page 130. In it he said: "I know that the Papacy is none other than the kingdom of Babylon." Page 131. "Christians are God's true people, led captive to Babylon." Page 133. "All the evils that afflicted Christendom, he sincerely ascribed to Rome." Page 138. Says Luther: "It is true that I have attacked the court of Rome; but neither you nor any man on earth can deny that it is more corrupt than Sodom." Page 139. "This Babylon, which is confusion itself." "Rome for many years past has inundated the world with all that could destroy both body and soul. The church of Rome, once the foremost in sanctity, is become the most licentious den of robbers, the most shameless of all brothels, the kingdom of sin, of death, and of hell." Page 140.

Here was a proclamation of the fall of Babylon, which was worthy of the name. Truly, Rome had made all nations drunk with her wine. She had ruled over all nations; had become rich; had lived in splendor; had killed the saints; had become the habitation of every evil spirit. All this is exactly portrayed in Rev. 17: 1-6, where "Babylon the great," of Chapter 14: 8, is more fully described. Then in Rev. 18: 1-4 the announcement of the fall of Babylon, as noticed in Chapter 14: 8, is more fully explained, but it is the same message. This fits Luther's work exactly.

Luther's message was a mighty cry, which enlightened the earth, announced the fearful corruptions of Rome, and called out of her millions of people, and gave to the world that mighty power, Protestantism. In all the history of the world such a mighty religious move had never before been seen. This was worthy of a notice in prophecy.

Consider this fact: While Adventists find hundreds of prophecies, whole chapters of them, applying to their little work, they find none foretelling the great religious movement of the Reformation which revolutionized the world! It illustrates how they interpret everything to fit themselves. No; the second message of Rev. 14: 8, the fall of Babylon, applies to the Catholic church, not to Protestants, and was given three hundred and fifty years ago by Luther, not by the Millerites in 1844.

THE THIRD MESSAGE, REV. 14: 9-12.

This warning against the worship of the beast and his image, and his mark, has been given by all the Protestant churches for the last three hundred years. Look at the multitude of books against popery and the corruptions of Catholicism. From press and pulpit has been thundered one continual warning against apostate Rome. Never was a prophecy more plainly fulfilled than this.

Seventh-Day Adventists say that they are giving this message. Never was a claim more absurd.

1. They are mistaken entirely as to what the beast, image, and mark are, as I have shown.

2. According to their own showing, they have been

preaching for seventy years against a thing which does not exist—the image, which they say is yet to be made!

3. That part of the message about the torment of the wicked, their smoke going up for ever and ever, etc., they never preach, for it is just what they don't believe.

4. Their egotistical claim that they are the only ones who "keep the commandments of God," is shown to be false in Chapter XX.

5. There are six angels mentioned in Rev. 14. If the first three represent messages of warning, then the other three do also; and, hence, there are yet three messages more to come after the Third Angel's message! What do Adventists have to say about these? Nothing.

These few brief points are sufficient to show that their application of the three messages is entirely wrong.

IS THE SABBATH GOD'S SEAL?

Seventh-Day Adventists claim that "the seal of God is his Holy Sabbath." Thoughts on Revelation, page 452. They are now sent to "seal" the 144,000 of Rev. 7: 1-8 ready for translation. Not a soul living on earth when Jesus comes will be saved, unless he is thus sealed by keeping that day. Early Writings, page 11.

1. Does the Bible say that the Sabbath is the seal of God? No; this is another Adventist assumption which they claim to prove by a long, round-about, far-fetched set of inferences. It takes one of their ablest speakers an hour to make it appear even plausible when he has no opposition. Even then few can see through it.

2. The word "seal," as a noun and a verb, is used sixty-five times in the Bible, but not once is it said to be the Sabbath.

3. They argue that *sign* and *seal* are synonymous terms, meaning the same thing; and as the Sabbath is called a

sign (Ex. 31: 17), it is therefore a seal. To this I object, because (1) *Seal* is never defined by the word *sign*, nor *sign* by the word *seal;* nor is one term ever given as the synonym for the other. I have carefully examined fourteen different dictionaries, lexicons and cyclopedias, and find no exception to this statement. (2) The original term for seal (Hebrew, *chotham;* Greek, *sphragis*) is never rendered sign. (3) The original word for sign (Hebrew, *oth;* Greek, *semeion*) is never rendered seal. Hence they are not synonymous terms.

4. Rom. 4: 11 is used to prove that a sign is a seal; but it does not prove it. Anything may be put to two entirely different uses, as I may use my cane for a staff or for a pointer, but is therefore a staff and a pointer the same? No. So in Rom. 4: 11, circumcision was used as a sign and also as a seal; but this does not prove that a sign is a seal. So the Sabbath is a sign. Ex. 31: 17. Possibly God *might also* use it as a seal, but does he? Where is the proof? Nowhere.

5. The Sabbath was a sign between God and the children of Israel. Ex. 31: 17. So was circumcision. Rom. 4: 11. But neither is a sign to Christians.

6. The Sabbath was abolished at the cross. Col. 2: 16. Hence it cannot be God's seal now.

7. If the Sabbath is God's seal with which he seals his people for translation, then every one who has the Sabbath is sealed and ready for translation. When God puts his seal upon a man, that must settle it that he is God's. So in Rev. 7: 2-4, where the angel sealed a man with the seal of God, did he not thereby become one of the 144,000 who were "without fault?" Rev. 14: 1-5. Yes. Then, if the Sabbath is the seal, all who keep it are sealed and ready for Heaven. But (1) the old Pharisees all kept the Sabbath strictly; (2) millions of Jews keep it now; (3) all Seventh-

Day Baptists keep it; (4) the Marion party, who bitterly oppose Seventh-Day Adventists, all keep it; (5) many Seventh-Day Adventists keep it who have been expelled from their churches for their sins. Are all these sealed and ready for salvation? No. Then the Sabbath as a seal, as the proof of God's favor, as a test of character and fitness for Heaven, fails entirely. Hence, it cannot be God's seal.

What, then, is God's seal? It is plainly stated to be the Holy Spirit. Thus: "Who hath also sealed us, and given the earnest of the Spirit in our hearts." II. Cor. 1: 22. "In whom also, after that ye believed, ye were sealed with that Holy Spirit of promise." Eph. 1: 13. "And grieve not the Holy Spirit of God, whereby ye are sealed unto the day of redemption." Eph. 4: 30. These texts are plain enough as to what the seal of the Lord is. It is the Holy Spirit. Strange that men will set aside these plain texts, and try by long, uncertain arguments to make out that the old Jewish Sabbath is the seal, when the Bible never says a word about it.

Adventists argue that the Sabbath is the seal to the decalogue. They say there is nothing else in the Ten Commandments to tell who gave that law. The assertion is utterly false. The very first words of the decalogue tell who gave it: "I am the Lord thy God, which brought thee out of the land of Egypt, out of the house of bondage. Thou shalt have no other gods before me." Ex. 20: 2, 3. This tells us plainly as possible who gave that law, and cuts up by the roots the Advent argument on the seal. Now look at their "Law of God" chart. These words as God put them are left off! If left on they would clearly contradict the Advent argument.

CHAPTER VII.

THE SANCTUARY.

Seventh-Day Adventists make everything turn upon their view of the sanctuary. It is vital with them. If they are wrong on this, their whole theory breaks down. The reader should, therefore, study this subject carefully. They dwell upon it constantly, and affirm that they are the only ones in all Christendom who have the light on the subject. I will devote only a few pages to it, just enough to show the fallacy of their system.

They based their time of 1844 upon Dan. 8: 14. "Unto two thousand and three hundred days, then shall the sanctuary be cleansed." The sanctuary was the earth. It was to be cleansed by fire at the second advent. The 2300 days ended in 1844. Hence, Christ must come that year. They proved it all by the Bible; so there could be no mistake, they said. But Christ didn't come. Now what? Fanaticism dies hard, positive men don't like to yield. So they now find that the sanctuary does not mean the earth at all, as they had said, but a real building in heaven, just like the tabernacle which Moses built. That was a tent with two rooms, the holy place, containing the table, candlestick, and golden altar; the Most Holy, containing the ark, in which were the tables of stone, and over which was the mercy seat and cherubim. See Heb. 9: 1-7. The priests ministered in the first place every day in the year, but only the high priest went into the Most Holy, and he only on the last day of the year. Lev. 16. On that day he cleansed the sanctuary of the sins confessed there during the year. All this was a type of just such a building in heaven, where Christ ministers. Heb. 8: 1-5; 9: 1-9, 24. In 1844 he left the first place and entered the Most Holy to cleanse the heavenly sanctuary, which, really, is the judgment. This explains their disappointment. Jesus went into the Most Holy of the heavenly sanctuary to begin the judgment in 1844, instead of coming to the earth, as they first expected and preached! To prove all this they make long, inferential arguments, which are open to objections from all sides.

1. Do the Adventists *know* that they are right about this question? No.

2. If this subject is as plain and as important as they say it is, it is strange that nobody ever found it out before.

3. After being perfectly familiar with their view of it, and knowing all their arguments, I feel sure they are mistaken about it.

1. God sent the Adventists with a last solemn message to earth upon which the destiny of the church and the world depended. The very first thing they did was to get the wrong year, '43 instead of '44. Then, when they got that fixed up, instead of announcing the real event to take place, the change in Christ's work in the sanctuary in heaven, they said he was to come to earth, raise the dead, and burn the world, when nothing of the kind was to occur!

2. Not one in fifty of the original Adventists ever found out the real mistake they had made. Not even one of the leading Adventists, like Miller, Himes, Litch, etc., ever accepted this sanctuary explanation. Only a mere handful out of the great mass of 1844 Adventists found out the truth about the sanctuary, and these were men of no note in Miller's work.

3. Miller himself opposed the Seventh-Day Adventists' move, rejecting the idea of the sanctuary, the Sabbath, and the third angel's message. What a hopeless tangle that

Advent work was! No wonder people rejected it. What if Moses had opposed Joshua, and John the Baptist had opposed Christ? Miller was sent to do a work, got it wrong, and then opposed those who did finally get it right!

4. Instead of receiving the "light" on the sanctuary question from Mrs. White's visions, or from heaven, they got it from O. R. L. Crosier. But he soon gave it all up as an error, and has opposed the Seventh-Day Adventists for many years. It looks badly for a theory when its very authors renounce it.

5. Seventh-Day Adventists at first adopted the sanctuary theory to prove that the door of mercy was shut in 1844, a theory which Mrs. White and all of them held at that time. Here is my proof on this point:

ANN ARBOR, MICH., Dec. 1, 1887.

Elder D. M. Canright:—"I kept the seventh day nearly a year, about 1848. In 1846, I explained the idea of the sanctuary in an article in an extra double number of the Day Star, Cincinnati, O. The object of that article was to support the theory that the door of mercy was shut, a theory which I and nearly all Adventists who had adopted William Miller's views, held from 1844 to 1848. Yes, I *know* that Ellen G. Harmon—now Mrs. White—held the shut door theory at that time."

Truly yours,   O. R. L. CROSIER.

Now listen to Mrs. White: "Topsham, Me., April 21, 1847. * * * The Lord showed me in vision more than one year ago, that Brother Crosier had the true light on the cleansing of the sanctuary, etc., and that it was his will that Bro. C. should write out the view which he gave us in the Day Star (extra), Feb. 7, 1846. I feel fully authorized by the Lord to recommend that extra to every saint. * * *"
E. G. White, in "A Word to the Little Flock," pages 11,

12. Here you have the origin and object of that sanctuary theory. Before me lies "The Present Truth," Vol. I, No. 6, December, 1849, by James White. "The Shut Door Explained," is the leading article, in which it is argued from the type Lev. 16: 17, that when the high priest entered the Most Holy there could be no more pardon for sin. "On this day of atonement he is a high priest for *those only* whose names are inscribed on the breast-plate of judgment," page 44. No more salvation for sinners, is what their sanctuary theory was then used to prove. The whole volume is full of this idea.

6. Their argument from the type on this point was right; in the type no sin could be confessed and conveyed into the sanctuary after the high priest entered the Most Holy. Lev. 4: 1–7; 16: 17, 23, 24. So if this was a type of the entrance of Christ into the Most Holy in heaven in 1844, then truly the door of mercy did close there, and all sinners since are lost.

7. No work whatever was to be done on the day of atonement, or day when the sanctuary was cleansed. Lev. 23: 27-32. The law was very strict. If the Advent argument on the sanctuary is correct and the day of atonement began in 1844, then they ought not to have worked a day since. Hence, many Adventists after 1844 held that it was a sin to work; but time starved them out, and they had to go at it again.

8. Finally, being compelled to abandon the position that the door of mercy was entirely shut against sinners in 1844, they next taught that *only those* could be saved who *knew* of the change which Christ made in the sanctuary in Heaven in 1844. Thus Elder Smith, in "Objections to the Visions Answered," pages 24-26, says: "A knowledge of Christ's position and work is necessary to the enjoyment of the benefits of his mediation. * * * A general idea of his work was then (previous to 1844) sufficient to enable men

to approach unto God by him. * * * But when he changed his position (in 1844) to the most Holy place * * * that knowledge of his work which had up to that point been sufficient, was no longer sufficient. * * * Who can find salvation now? Those who go to the Saviour where he is and view him by faith in the most Holy place. * * * This is the door now open for salvation. But no man can understand this change without definite knowledge of the subject of the sanctuary and the relation of type and anti-type. Now they may seek the Saviour as they have before sought him, with no other ideas of his position and ministry than those which they entertained while he was in the first apartment; but will it avail them? They cannot find him there. That door is shut!" So Mrs. White: "They have no knowledge of the move made in Heaven, or the way into the most Holy, and they cannot be benefited by the intercession of Jesus there. * * * They offer up their useless prayers to the apartment which Jesus has left." Spiritual Gifts, Vol. I, pages 171, 172. What abominable doctrine! No one can be saved unless they know of the change which Christ made in Heaven in 1844. But no one except Seventh-Day Adventists has the slightest idea of that change. Reader, think of this.

9. But now they have abandoned this view of the sanctuary and hold that all who honestly seek God may be saved without any of this "light" on the sanctuary. Thus they have already held four different positions upon the sanctuary question: 1. It was the earth. 2. The door of mercy was shut to all sinners in 1844. 3. It was open only to those who learned about Christ's change in 1844. 4. It is now open to all. What will they hold next?

After thoroughly investigating the whole subject of the sanctuary, I feel sure that they are in a great error on that point.

1. God's throne was always in the most Holy place of the sanctuary, between the cherubim, over the ark, never once in the Holy place. For proof on this point see Lev. 16: 2; Num. 7: 89; I. Sam. 4: 4; II. Kings 19: 15. Smith argues that God's throne was sometimes in the holy place, and refers to Ex. 33: 9. But here the Lord appeared *outside* the tabernacle, and not in the Holy place at all. So his text fails him.

2. When Jesus ascended to Heaven, eighteen hundred years ago, he went directly to the right hand of God and sat down on his throne. Heb. 8: 1. Hence, he must have entered the most Holy then, instead of in 1844.

3. "Within the vail" is in the most Holy place. "And thou shalt hang up the vail under the taches, that thou mayest bring in thither within the vail the ark of the testimony: and the vail shall divide unto you between the Holy *place* and the most Holy." Ex. 26: 33. Also see Lev. 16: 2, 12, 13.

None can fail to see that "within the vail" is in the most Holy place where the ark was. This is just where Jesus went eighteen hundred years ago. Proof: "Which *hope* we have as an anchor of the soul, both sure and steadfast, and which entereth into that within the vail; whither the forerunner is for us entered, *even* Jesus made a high priest for ever." Heb. 6: 19, 20. As the high priest went "within the vail," so Jesus, our high priest, went "within the vail," into the most Holy place, to the right hand of God and sat down on his throne. Nothing could be more plainly stated. This upsets the whole Advent theory of 1844. For further proof see Ex. 27: 21; 30: 6; 40: 22-26; Lev. 4: 6, 17; 16: 15; 24: 3; Num. 18: 7; Matt. 27: 51.

4. "Before the throne," Rev. 8: 3. Elder Smith asserts that "the throne of God was in the first apartment of the sanctuary," because it is said that the seven lamps and the

golden altar were "before the throne," Rev. 4: 5; 8: 3. It is a desperate cause which seizes upon such proof. The same argument would prove that the ark and God's throne were always in the first apartment of the earthly sanctuary, which we know to be false. As there was only a vail which divided the holy from the most holy, where God's throne was, things in the holy place were said to be "before the Lord," as they were so near to the throne, which was just behind the curtain. Proof: Ex. 27: 20, 21; 30: 6-8; 40: 23-25; Lev. 4: 6, 15-18. Even outside of the tabernacle entirely, where the beasts were killed, was "before the Lord," as Lev. 4: 15 shows. Abraham walked "before the Lord," Gen. 24: 40, yet he was on earth, and the Lord was in heaven.

5. Not a single text can be found in all the Bible where the ark and cherubim and throne were in the holy place of the earthly sanctuary, the type; yet in the antitype they have the throne of God in the holy place, not on some special occasion, but all the time for 1800 years, just contrary to the type!

6. Adventists always assume and say that "the temple of God is the most Holy place." Sanctuary, page 234, by U. Smith. But this is false. The most Holy place, or the oracle, was a *room in the temple*, but it was not the temple itself. In fact the Scriptures carefully distinguish between the temple and the oracle or most Holy. See I. Kings 6: 5, 16, 17, 19, 23; 7: 50. The temple was the house, the whole building. I. Kings 7: 50; II. Kings 11: 13; I. Sam. 3: 3; Matt. 21: 12; Luke 1: 9; Rev. 11: 19.

7. When was the temple in heaven opened, Rev. 11: 19? Adventists use this text to prove that the most holy place in the heavenly sanctuary was not opened till 1844. But it fails them: 1. Because, as we have proved above, the temple is not the most holy place, but the whole building. 2.

Because the heavenly temple was opened when Christ began his ministry there, 1800 years ago. Heb. 8: 1, 2; 9: 8–12. 3. Because verse 19 of Rev. 11 properly belongs with Rev. 12, and begins that new line of prophecy, instead of closing the line in Chapter 11. The Syriac thus divides it. Clarke, Barnes, Scott, and every commentator I have consulted, connects this verse with Chapter 12 as the introduction. Says Scott: "V. 19.—This verse introduces a new subject, and should have been placed at the beginning of the next chapter." Certainly; for when was the temple in heaven opened? When Jesus went there to begin his ministry, of course, Heb. 9: 8–12. Thus fails the main pillar of the Adventists' sanctuary theory.

Thus far I have argued on their own grounds that there is a real building up in heaven, just like the sanctuary on earth. But that whole thing is extremely questionable.

1. As children are taught moral truths by object lessons, so God taught the Jews spiritual truths by the object lessons of the types of their worship. Hence, it does not follow that in Christian worship there must be just such material things used up in heaven. Rather the presumption is against it.

2. The whole temple service was for the Aaronic priesthood; but Christ is not a priest after the order of Aaron, but is after that of Melchisedic, Heb. 7: 11. Melchisedic had no temple nor temple service, so Christ should have none. From Adam till Moses there was no temple nor priestly service in heaven. Smith admits this. "There were no holy places laid open, and no priestly work was established in heaven." Sanctuary, page 238. Exactly; for that was under the Melchisedic priesthood, just as now. If no temple was needed there for 4000 years, none is needed there now.

3. Paul directly states that the types of the law were

"NOT the very image of the things" they represent, Heb. 10: 1. But Adventists make their argument on the assumption that they were exact images of things in heaven, thus ignoring Paul's statement.

4. Paul says that Christ is a minister of a greater and more perfect tabernacle, Heb. 9: 11. Then it must differ from the earthly one.

5. Paul says it is one "not made with hands," Heb. 9: 11. This shows that it is not a material building.

6. Paul says that Jesus' flesh is the vail, Heb. 10: 20. This shows that the temple was only figurative.

7. Scarcely one of the types had an antitype just like it. Thus lambs and oxen were the type of which Jesus was the antitype. But he was a *man* and they were *beasts*. The bodies of those beasts were *burned*, Heb. 13: 11, 12, but Christ, the antitype, was not burned. They were slain at the door of the sanctuary, Lev. 17: 3, 4, but Jesus was not slain at the door of any sanctuary. Their blood was carried into the temple and put on the altar, Lev. 4: 6, 7, but the blood of Christ was spilt on the ground. The Levitical priests made offerings daily, but Christ only once for all, Heb. 9: 25, 26, 28; 10: 10, 12, 14. "Elder Smith says: 'The fact that Moses made two apartments in his likeness of the heavenly temple is a *demonstration* that the latter has two apartments also.' Again: 'The Priests here on earth, in both apartments, served unto the example of a like service in heaven. Now Jesus is the only priest in heaven, and he must perform this 'like service.' The earthly priests offered, every day, the morning and evening sacrifice, sprinkling the blood of fresh-slain victims in the outer sanctuary. So for more than eighteen hundred years, Jesus, according to Mr. Smith, must have offered his own fresh-shed blood in the outer apartment of the heavenly sanctuary twice every day; that is more than *thirteen hundred thousand times* from his

ascension to 1844. This is the logical result of Mr. Smith's 'demonstration.' The apostle says, Heb. 7: 27: 'This he did once for all, when he offered up himself.' Thus the 'demonstration' flatly contradicts the scriptures." G. W. Morton. The law regulating the service of the priests and the temple was changed, Heb. 7: 12. Then certainly it is not carried out in heaven now. Adventists would have the whole Levitical law of the sanctuary service transferred to heaven and carried out there! This is the absurdity of their system. In Heb. 7: 11–28 Paul marks many points of difference between the types and the antitypes. The table of the Lord was in the temple in the Jewish age, Mal. 1: 7, but now the Lord's table is in the church, I. Cor. 10: 21; 11: 20. The seven lamps in the temple of heaven "are the seven spirits of God," Rev. 4: 5. Then they are not literal lamps. So it is more than probable that none of the things mentioned as being there are literal. In one place it is said that the saints in heaven are "clothed in white robes," Rev. 7: 9, but in another place this is explained to be the righteousness of saints, Rev. 19: 8.

In Rev. 8: 3 it is said that the prayers of all saints are offered upon the golden altar. Most evidently this is not to be taken literally, but only as a reference to the Jewish mode of worship. Col. 2: 16, 17, says that the meats, drinks, feast days, new moons and Sabbath days were a shadow of Christ. Reasoning as the Adventists do about the earthly sanctuary, Heb. 8: 5, we would expect to find something in the gospel exactly like them, meats, drinks, yearly feast days, monthly holy days, etc. But where are they? In the gospel there is nothing at all just like these types.

Paul says directly that the place into which Jesus went was "heaven itself, now to appear in the presence of God for us," Heb. 9: 24. The simple truth of the whole matter is that the age of types, object lessons, exact forms, set ceremonies, consecrated places and holy vessels—all this ended at the cross, Col. 2: 17. The answer of Jesus to the woman at the well is exactly to the point. She said: "Our fathers worshiped in this mountain; and ye say that in Jerusalem is the place where men ought to worship. Jesus saith unto her, Woman, believe me, the hour cometh, when ye shall neither in this mountain, nor yet at Jerusalem, worship the Father. * * * But the hour cometh, and now is, when the true worshipers shall worship the Father in spirit and in truth: for the Father seeketh such to worship him. God is a spirit; and they that worship him must worship him in spirit and in truth." John 4: 20-24. Under the gospel one place is no more holy than another. With the holy places went all the holy vessels, sacrifices, incense, tables of stone, and all. Peter states it all in a word: "Ye also, as lively stones, are built up a spiritual house, an holy priesthood, to offer up spiritual sacrifices, acceptable to God by Jesus Christ." I. Pet. 2: 5. To the same effect, Eph. 2: 20-22; I. Cor. 6: 19. Now we are under a new covenant; Heb. 8: 6-13, an high priest of a new order, Heb. 7: 11, we come to God by a new way, Heb. 10: 20, by new ordinances, Mark 15: 15-16; I. Cor. 11: 23-26, by a different temple, and a better sacrifice. Hence, there is no need of a temple in heaven just like the old Jewish one.

The Adventists idea of the sanctuary in heaven is an absurdity. In Early Writings, pages 114, 115, Mrs. White was taken to heaven and shown all about it. She saw the building exactly like the one on earth. In it was the candlestick, the table of show-bread, the altar, the curtains, the ark; and "in the ark were tables of stone containing the Ten Commandments." Think, now; what use for a literal candle in the immediate presence of God whose glory is above the light of the sun. "They need no candle, neither light of the sun, for the Lord God giveth them light." **Rev.**

22: 5. And what use for a literal table of show-bread there? Do the angels or the Lord eat the bread? Then real tables of stone in Heaven! and the Lord sitting on the ark over them! What puerile ideas. Hear Paul veto that idea: "Not in tables of stone, but in fleshy tables of the heart." II. Cor. 3: 3. Then think of the absurdity of having the Almighty God and all the "ten thousand times ten thousand" (one hundred million) angels around his throne, dwelling in a literal building with curtains, lamps, tables, walls, etc. It would need to be larger than a whole State. Let Adventists read this: "Howbeit, the Most High dwelleth not in temples made with hands." Acts 7: 48.

"But does not Paul say that the Jewish temple was a shadow, figure, a pattern of heavenly things, Heb. 8 and 9?" Yes; and so he says the offerings and holy days of the old covenant were shadows of Christ, Col. 2: 16, 17. But where are our feast days, new moons, meats, etc., under the gospel? Nowhere, only in a spiritual sense. So Paul says the earthly temple was only a *"figure"* of a "tabernacle not made with hands." Heb. 9: 9, 11. How could he say more plainly that the heavenly are not literal? Did Christ minister in a literal temple in heaven from Adam till the cross, four thousand years? No. Did Melchisedec have a temple? No. Gen. 14: 18-20. As Christ is a priest after his order, he needs no literal temple. According to the Adventists, the most Holy place of the heavenly sanctuary was entirely empty and unoccupied from the ascension of Jesus till 1844. Even Christ did not enter it once! Finally, their whole argument on the sanctuary depends upon proving that the seventy weeks of Dan. 9 are a part of the twenty-three hundred days of Dan. 8: 14. But does the Bible say they are? No; nor can they prove it. The very best they can claim is to make it plausible that **they are.**

CHAPTER VIII.

MRS. WHITE AND HER REVELATIONS.

Seventh-Day Adventists regard Mrs. White as a prophetess and her writings as inspired. They make long arguments from the Bible to prove that there should be gifts, miracles and prophets in the church. But these are the same arguments used by Mormons, Shakers, etc., in favor of their churches. They do not touch the case. The question is not, *Can* the Lord inspire men and women? but, *Has* he so inspired Mrs. White? The New Testament repeatedly warns us against accepting false prophets. "Beware of false prophets," Matt. 7: 15. "There shall arise false Christs and false prophets," Matt. 24: 24. "Believe not every spirit. * * * Many false prophets are gone out into the world." 1 John, 4: 1.

In every generation many have arisen claiming to be prophets. All have found followers more or less. All they have to do is to firmly believe in themselves and make extravagant claims and they will soon have followers. Let us notice a few prominent ones near our own times.

1. SWEDENBORG.

He was born in Stockholm, Sweden, 1688, and died in 1772. His father was a nobleman of high standing. Hence Swedenborg was highly educated and moved in the highest society. He traveled extensively, and conversed with the most learned men of the age. The king appointed him to a high office, which he filled with great acceptance for over thirty years. He rose to eminence in science and wrote seventy-seven books, covering every branch of science. He was a favorite with the king and royal family. He was of the purest character and devoutly religious.

SWEDENBORG'S RULES OF LIFE.

1. Often to read and meditate on the Word of God.
2. To submit in everything to the will of Divine Providence.
3. To observe in everything a propriety of behavior, and to keep the conscience clear.
4. To discharge with fidelity the functions of my employment, and the duties of my office, and to render myself in all things useful to society.

Not a stain rests upon his moral character.

At the age of fifty-five he began to have visions of heaven, hell, angels, and the spiritual world. He says: "I have been called to a holy office by the Lord himself, who most mercifully appeared to me, his servant, in the year 1743, when he opened my sight into the spiritual world and enabled me to converse with spirits and angels." Exactly like what Mrs. White claims. This work he continued for thirty years, and wrote about thirty inspired volumes. He made most remarkable predictions, which were exactly fulfilled it is claimed.

He founded a new religion based upon his revelations. The Bible is sacredly taught and holy living enjoined.

This church has steadily increased, till it has societies in all parts of the world and in the leading languages. They publish three weeklies, five monthly journals, and one quarterly, besides many books. He got the start of Mrs. White just one hundred years. His followers believe in him just as implicitly as hers do in her, and are very zealous in propagating their faith. In many respects both moves are much alike. The above is condensed from Schaff-Herzog's Encyclopedia.

2. ANN LEE AND THE SHAKERS.

These are so well known in America that I need say but little about them. Ann Lee, their leader, was born in England, in 1736; died, 1784. Like Mrs. White, "she received no education." She joined a society who were having remarkable religious exercises, and soon began "to have visions and make revelations," which, just like Mrs. White, she called "testimonies." "Henceforth she claimed to be directed by revelations and visions." Schaff-Herzog Encyclopedia, article "Ann Lee." She was accepted as leader and as "the second appearing of Christ." Like Mrs. White, she required a "peculiar kind of dress," "opposed war and the use of pork." Johnson's Cyclopedia, article "Shakers." They have no intercourse with other churches; are renowned for their purity and devotion. They number about 8,000. A careful comparison shows many points of similarity between Mrs. Lee and Mrs. White. The main evidence upon which Adventists rely for proof of Mrs. White's inspiration is the purity of her life and the high moral and religious tone of her writings. They say her revelations must either be of God or Satan. If of Satan they would not teach such purity and holiness. The same reasoning will prove Mrs. Lee also a true prophetess, for she exceeds Mrs. White in this line, so that "Shaker" has become a synonym for honesty. Adventists, please note this point.

3. MRS. JOANNA SOUTHCOTT.

She was born in England in 1750, of poor parents, and was wholly uneducated. She worked as a domestic servant till over forty years of age. She joined the Methodists in

1790. In 1792 she announced herself as a prophetess, and "published numerous [over sixty] pamphlets setting forth her revelations." Johnson's Cyclopedia, article "Southcott." She had trances the same as Mrs. White does, and announced the speedy advent of Christ. See Encyclopedia Americana, article "Southcott." She carried on a lucrative trade in the sale of her books as Mrs. White does. Strange as it may appear, many learned ministers believed in her, and thousands joined her followers, till in a few years they numbered upwards of *one hundred thousand!* She made many predictions, which her followers claimed were fulfilled. "The faith of her followers, among whom were several clergymen of the established church, rose to enthusiasm." Encyclopedia Americana, article "Southcott."

She "regarded herself as the bride of the Lamb, and declared herself, when sixty-four years of age, pregnant with the true Messiah, the 'second Shilo,' whom she would bear Oct. 19, 1814. * * * Joanna died in her self delusion Dec. 27, 1814; but her followers, who at one time numbered *a hundred thousand, continued till 1831 to observe the Jewish Sabbath.*" Schaff-Herzog Encyclopedia. "A post mortem examination showed that she had been suffering from dropsy." Johnson's Cyclopedia. "Death put an end to both her hopes and her fears. With her followers, however, it was otherwise; and, though for a time confounded by her decease, which they could scarcely believe to be real, her speedy resurrection was confidently anticipated. In this persuasion many lived and died, nor is her sect yet extinct." Encyclopedia Americana, article "Southcott."

Let candid people consider these facts. This movement occurring only thirty years before Mrs. White's work, was in several respects like the present Seventh-Day Adventist move. An illiterate woman is the leader. She has visions, writes numerous pamphlets and revelations and predicts the speedy advent of Christ. Her honesty is plainly manifested; her enthusiasm and that of her followers is great. In a short period one hundred thousand accept her "testimonies." The present Seventh-Day Adventist move is similar in many respects as has already been seen above.

And here notice the terrible tenacity of fanaticism when once started. When Joanna died we would have supposed that all sane persons would have given it up; but they fix it up some way and go right on, and there they are now. So with the followers of Mrs. White. No matter what blunders or failures she makes, they fix them up some way and go right on. They will do it after she is dead and gone.

4. JOSEPH SMITH AND THE MORMONS.

This prophet and his visions and revelations are so well-known that I mention them briefly. Smith was born in 1805, and died in 1844, the year before Mrs. White began her revelations. He came out in a great religious awakening, as Mrs. White did in the Advent move of 1843-4. In 1823 he also began to have "visions" and "revelations" and see angels. The second advent of Christ was at hand, he said, hence the name, "Latter day saints." His mission was to introduce "the new dispensation." They are the "saints," and all the other churches are "heathen," or Gentiles. Mrs. White's followers are the saints; all other churches are "Babylon" and apostate.

The proof of their inspiration outstrips Mrs. White. They work many miracles, as they strongly assert, have the gift of tongues, and can show many predictions strikingly fulfilled. I have met them frequently, seen Smith's son, and know them well. They also have a new Bible, a new revelation, have started a new sect, and will have nothing to do with others, but proselyte from all.

134   SEVENTH-DAY ADVENTISM RENOUNCED.

The Mormons began in 1831, about fifteen years before Seventh-Day Adventists did: but they number six hundred thousand, more than five times as many as Adventists. Adventists claim that they must be the true church because they are persecuted; but Mormons have been persecuted a thousand fold more. Smith and others were killed; many have been whipped, tarred and feathered, rotten-egged, stoned, mobbed, run out of town, and outlawed. So they must be the true church! Seventh-Day Adventists have suffered no persecution. Not one of them has ever been whipped, or stoned, or egged, or tarred and feathered, or mobbed, or killed. Persecution! They have no idea what it is and never will though they are anxious to pose as great martyrs.

THE VISIONS THEIR GUIDE.

Mrs. E. G. White, wife of the late Elder White, leader of the Seventh-Day Adventists, claims to be divinely inspired as were the prophets of the Bible. This claim is accepted by the whole denomination. They defend her inspiration as earnestly as they do that of the Bible. Year after year, in their State and General Conferences, ironclad resolutions have been unanimously adopted, endorsing her revelations in the strongest manner.

Time and again I have seen these resolutions adopted by a rising vote of the whole congregation, myself with them. "The visions of Mrs. E. G. White, a manifestation of spiritual Gifts according to the Scriptures," is a book of 144 pages published by them defending her inspiration.

They point to her and her visions as the sign and proof that they are the only true church. Rev. 12: 17. Hence it can be seen that this is a vital subject with them.

In my debate with the Adventists at Healdsburg, Cal., Feb. 21-28, 1889, they affirmed this proposition: "The visions of Mrs. E. G. White are revelations from God." Her writings are called "*Testimonies.*" In Testimony No. 33, just published, she makes this claim for her writings: "In ancient times God spoke to men by the mouth of prophets and apostles. In these days he speaks to them by the Testimonies of his spirit." Page 189. Again: "It is hardly possible for men to offer a greater insult to God than to despise and reject the instrumentalities [her Testimonies] that he has appointed to lead these." Page 208. Notice that her "*Testimonies*" are to *lead* God's people now. Of her inspiration Smith says: "It comes to us as a divine message; it is a ray of light from the throne; it is instruction by the Holy Spirit." Replies to Elder Canright, page 77.

In the Advent *Review*, July 2, 1889, are laid down these, "RULES: 1. We will not neglect the study of the Bible and the *Testimonies.*" This illustrates the place they assign her writings, viz., an appendix to the Bible. She occupies the same relation to her people that Mrs. Southcott did to hers, Ann Lee to the Shakers, and Joe Smith to the Mormons.

Among themselves they quote her as we do Paul. A text from her writings is an end of all controversy in doctrine and discipline. It is common to hear them say that when they give up her visions they will give up the Bible too, and they often do.

Her visions, or "testimonies," as they are called, are so inseparably connected with the whole Seventh-Day Adventist doctrine that a person cannot consistently accept the one without accepting the other. Besides, they are so constantly urged upon their people in every possible way, that a person cannot long feel comfortable among them unless he, too, accepts them. Any one who rejects or opposes them is branded as a rebel fighting against God. Thus Mrs. White herself says: "If you lessen the confidence of God's people in the testimonies he has sent them, you are rebelling against God as certainly as were Kora, Dathan and Abiram." Testimony No. 31, page 62. She claims that every line she writes, even in a private letter, is directly inspired by God—"the precious rays of light shining from the throne," page 63. Of her own words she says: "It is God, and not an erring mortal, that has spoken," Testimonies, Vol. III, page 257. She states over and over that those who doubt or oppose her are fighting against God, sinning against the Holy Ghost. Thus: "fighting the Spirit of God. Those * * * who would break down our testimony, I saw, are not fighting against *us*, but against God," page 260. I could quote scores of passages like these.

These inspired writings now embrace forty bound volumes. Thus they have another Bible, just the same as the Mormons have. They have to read our old Bible in the light of this new Bible. Any interpretation of the Bible found in these "testimonies" settles its meaning beyond further dispute. She says: "I took the precious Bible and surrounded it with the several testimonies to the church," vol. 2, page 605. Exactly; and by the light of these "testimonies" that old Bible must now be read. She continues: "God has, through the testimonies, simplified the great truths already given." Yes, we must now take the Bible as thus simplified by her! Swedenborg, Mrs. Southcott, Ann Lee, Joseph Smith and Mrs. White have each done the same thing—had a new revelation, written inspired books, and started a new sect with a new religion.

There is not a doctrine nor a practice of the church, from the observance of the Sabbath to the washing of feet, upon which she has not written. That settles it. No further investigation can be made on any of these matters, only to gather evidence and construe everything to sustain it. How, then, can their ministers or people be free to think and investigate for themselves? They can not, dare not, and do not. How often I have seen some intelligent thought extinguished with this remark: "That contradicts Sister White." This ends the matter. Everything she writes, whether in a private letter or newspaper article, is inspired. Thus: "God was speaking through clay. * * * In these letters which I write, in the testimonies I bear, I am presenting to you that which the Lord has presented to me. I do not write one article in the paper expressing merely my own ideas. They are what God has opened before me in vision—the precious rays of light shining from the throne." Testimony No. 31, page 63. There you have it, simon pure: every word she writes is a ray of light from the throne of God. Reject that, and you are rejected of God.

Thus it will be seen that Mrs. White claims the very highest inspiration, the voice of God speaking directly through her. Her followers contend that she must either be a true prophetess or else a hypocrite; but she is neither. Few are aware of what a powerful influence an excited religious imagination will have over a person. Enthusiasts and fanatics are generally honest people. Mrs. White is simply a religious enthusiast self-deceived. This I shall prove by stubborn facts.

I long studied Mrs. White to determine for myself her real character till her case is clear to my own mind. Naturally religious, young in years, uneducated, sickly, she was carried away in the Millerite excitement of 1840–44. Her fits she accepted as the power of God. Encouraged and sustained by her husband, this thought grew to be a reality to her. A careful study of her writings shows that each year she has become a little stronger in her claims of inspiration till now she asserts that all her utterances, even in a letter, or in a sermon, are inspired. She claims that her dreams, her impressions of mind are all the voice of God to her. She devotes 38 pages of her Testimony No. 33 to vindicating her own high inspiration. Probably she has some way of fixing up her mistakes, contradictions and deceptions satisfactory to herself. So now anything she can learn in any way, any impression of mind, any thought clear to herself, is the Spirit speaking to her. I have no doubt that she believes it. She is more deceived than her followers, for many of them privately doubt her inspiration while publicly defending it.

That she is not inspired is plainly shown by many facts. She has never wrought a single miracle. The old prophets and the apostles wrought miracles freely, to prove that God had sent them. In all these seventy years, in all her forty volumes, not a single prediction has she ever made that has come to pass. This is astonishing, considering that she dwells almost wholly in predictions. It seems as though she ought to have blundered into many things which could afterward be construed into a fulfilled prophecy. But not one can be found. This shows how wild and utterly wrong her theories have been.

She says in "Spiritual Gifts," Vol. II, page 293: "I am just as dependent upon the Spirit of the Lord in relating or writing a vision as in having a vision." Here she claims that the very words in which her visions are recorded are of divine inspiration. But I know that the words in her written "testimonies" are not inspired; for—

1. When writing them out she will often change what she has written, and write it very differently. I have seen her scratch out a whole page, or a line, or a sentence, and write it over differently. If God gave her the words, why did she scratch them out and alter them?

2. I have repeatedly seen her sit with pen in hand and read her manuscript to her husband for hours, while he suggested many changes, which she made. She would scratch

out her own words and put in his, somtimes whole sentences. Was he inspired, too?

3. As she is ignorant of grammar, of late years she has employed an accomplished writer to take her manuscript and correct it, improve its wording, polish it up, and put it in popular style, so her books will sell better. Thousands of words, not her own, are thus put in by these other persons, some of whom were not even Christians. Are their words inspired, too?

4. She often copies her subject matter without credit or sign of quotation, from other authors. Indeed her last book, "Great Controversy," which they laud so highly as her greatest work, is largely a compilation from Andrew's History of the Sabbath, History of the Waldenses by Wylie, Life of Miller by White, Thoughts on Revelation by Smith, and other books.

This she pretends was all revealed to her directly from heaven. It is not something she has heard or read or studied out, but it is what God has revealed to her by the Holy Ghost. Stubborn facts shows that her claim is utterly false and her book a deception the same as the Book of Mormon, which Smith stole from Spaulding.

The Pastor's Union of Healdsburg, Cal., investigated the matter and published many examples out of hundreds where she had copied her matter directly from other authors without anything to show it was copied. They went through several works and scores of pages finding the same thing all through her book. This proves her guilty of stealing her ideas and matter from other authors and putting them off on her followers as a revelation from God!

5. PASSAGES SUPPRESSED.

Several important passages in the first edition of her visions have been suppressed in all later ones as they contradict what Adventists now believe. For thirty years they have chafed under this charge of suppression. They have denied it, made light of it; and finally the pressure was so hard that in 1882, they republished her first visions, claiming to give them all and word for word. They say: "No changes from the original work have been made." Preface to Early Writings, page 4. They also say the work was printed "under the author's own eye and with her full approval." Page 4. They denounce it as a wicked slander to say that anything has been suppressed.

But I have before me the original work entitled, "A Word to the Little Flock," published by Jas. White, 1847; also "The Present Truth," August, 1849, containing her original visions. Comparing the present edition with the original, I find seven different places where from *five* to *thirty* lines in a place have been cut right out with no sign of omission! The suppressed passages are very damaging to her inspiration. I will give one short one as an illustration. It teaches what they now deny, viz., that no one could be converted after 1844. The suppressed lines are in brackets.

AS ORIGINALLY PUBLISHED.

"I saw that the mysterious signs and wonders, and false reformations would increase and spread. The reformations that were shown me were not reformations from error to truth [but from bad to worse, for those who professed a change of heart had only wrapped about them a religious garb, which covered up the iniquity of a wicked heart. Some appeared to have been really converted, so as to deceive God's people, but if their hearts could be seen they would appear as black as ever]. My accompanying angel bade me to look for the travail of soul for sinners as used to be. I looked, but could not see it, for the time for their salvation is past." Present Truth, page 22, published August, 1849.

AS NOW PUBLISHED.

"I saw that the mysterious signs and wonders, and false reformations would increase and spread. The reformations that were shown me were not reformations from error to truth.

"My accompanying angel bade me look for the travail of soul for sinners as used to be. I looked, but could not see it, for the time for their salvation is past." Page 37, edition of 1882.

Now if they mean to be honest and dare publish these suppressed passages, why don't they? They know very well what they are; Mrs. White knows what they are; yet the book is republished "under her own eye" and all these passages left out when it is stated that "no changes from the original work have been made." I have both books before me now and know the statement to be untrue and so do they; yet they keep right on sending it out.

6. In 1885 all her "testimonies" were republished in four volumes, under the eye of her own son and a critical editor. Opening hap-hazard to four different pages in Vol. I., I read and compared them with the original publication which I have. I found on an average *twenty-four changes of the words on each page!* Her words were thrown out and other words put in and other changes made, in some cases so many that it was difficult to read the two together. At the same rate in the four volumes, there would be 63,720 changes.

Taking, then, the words which were put in by her husband, by her copyist, by her son, by her editors, and those copied from other authors, probably they comprise from one-tenth to one quarter of all her books. Fine inspiration that is! The common reader knows nothing about these damaging facts, but I could not avoid knowing them, for I have been where I saw it myself.

MRS. WHITE'S MISTAKES.

I could fill a volume with proof of her mistakes, for all of her books are full of them. I will select but a few.

The shut door. For several years after 1844, Mrs. White had visions saying that probation ended in that year, that there was no more salvation for sinners. Of course she has to deny this now, but the proof is overwhelmingly against her.

1. Seventh-Day Adventists are compelled to admit that for some time after 1844 Adventists did hold that probation was ended. Even Mrs. White admits it. She says: "After the passing of the time of expectation, in 1844, Adventists still believed the Saviour's coming to be very near; they held that * * * the work of Christ as man's intercessor before God had ceased. Having given the warning of the judgment near, they felt that their work for the world was done, and they lost their burden of soul for the salvation of sinners. * * * All this confirmed them in the belief that probation had ended, or, as they then expressed it, 'the door of mercy was shut.'" Great Controversy, page 268. This statement of Mrs. White herself is enough to settle the point that the Adventists believed "the door of mercy was shut" in 1844. Notice here that the "shut door" means the end of probation, the close of mercy for sinners.

Mr. Miller for a while advocated the shut door in 1844. He says:

"We have done our work in warning sinners and in trying to awake a formal church. God in his providence has SHUT THE DOOR; we can only stir one another up to be patient." Advent *Herald*, Dec. 11, 1844.

Then in the Voice of Truth Feb. 19, 1845, he says: "I have not seen a genuine conversion since."

Elder G. I. Butler, in the *Review and Herald*, March 3, 1885, says: "As the time passed there was a general feeling among all the earnest believers that their work for the world was done." "There can be no question that for months after the time passed it was the general sentiment that their work of warning the world was over." "Their burden was gone, and they thought their work was done." Yes; that is just what they did believe, probation was ended.

2. I have conversed with several individuals who affirm positively that they heard her teach this repeatedly. There are many now living who will swear that they heard her teach it.

3. *Written testimony.* John Megquier, Saco, Me., a man noted for his integrity, writes: "We well know the course of Ellen G. White, the visionist, while in the state of Maine. About the first visions she had were at my house in Poland. She said that God had told her in vision that the door of mercy had closed, and there was no more chance for the world." The True Sabbath, by Miles Grant, page 70. Mrs. L. S. Burdick, San Francisco, California, was well acquainted with Mrs. White. She writes: "I became acquainted with James White and Ellen Harmon (now Mrs White) early in 1845. At the time of my first acquaintance with them they were in wild fanaticism, used to sit on the floor instead of chairs, and creep around the floor like little children. Such freaks were considered a mark of humility. They were not married, but traveling together. Ellen was having what was called visions: said God had shown her in vision that Jesus Christ arose on the tenth day of the seventh month, 1844, and shut the door of mercy; had left forever the mediatorial throne; the whole world was doomed and lost and there never could be another sinner saved." L. S. Burdick, "True Sabbath," page 72. O. R. L. Crosier kept the Sabbath with them in 1848. He

writes: "Ann Arbor, Mich., Dec. 1, 1887. Yes, I *know* that Ellen G. Harmon, now Mrs. White, held the shut door theory at that date." Then he gives his proof. These persons knew the facts and have put their testimony on record.

4. *The Present Truth*, James White, editor, Oswego, N. Y., May, 1850, has an article by the editor on the "Sanctuary, 2300 Days, and the Shut Door." Elder White says: "At that point of time [1844] the midnight cry was given, the work for the world was closed up, and Jesus passed into the most holy place. * * * When we came up to that point of time, all our sympathy, burden and prayers for sinners ceased, and the unanimous feeling and testimony was that our work for the world was finished forever. * * * He [Jesus] is still merciful to his saints, and ever will be; and Jesus is still *their* advocate and priest; but the sinner, to whom Jesus has stretched out his arms all the day long, and who had rejected the offers of salvation, was *left without an advocate* when Jesus passed from the holy place and shut that door in 1844." Any honest man can see that the shut door meant no salvation for sinners, and this is what Elder White taught in 1850. In a report of labor in the *Advent Review*, May 15, 1850, Elder White, in noticing the death of a sister Hastings, says: "She embraced the Sabbath in 1846, and has ever believed that the work of warning the world closed in 1844."

Again: "Many will point us to one who is said to be converted, for positive proof that the door is not shut, thus yielding the word of God for the feelings of an individual." Present Truth, Dec. 1849. This shows that they held to the shut door idea for years after 1844. What a fanatical and abominable doctrine that was for Christians to teach! Mrs. White was right with them and in full harmony with them on this all these years. She had revelations almost daily.

If they were of God, why did she not correct them in this fearful error? Even if she had said nothing confirming this delusion, yet the simple fact that she had no revelation contradicting it during all those years, is enough to destroy her claim to inspiration. But the fact is, she taught this error as strongly in her visions as the brethren did in their arguments.

Here are her own words: "March 24, 1849. * * * I was shown that the commandments of God and the testimony of Jesus Christ, relating to the shut door, could not be separated. * * * I saw that the mysterious signs and wonders and false reformations would increase and spread. The reformations that were shown me were not reformations from error to truth, but from bad to worse, for those who professed a change of heart had only wrapped about them a religious garb, which covered up the iniquity of a wicked heart. Some appeared to have been really converted, so as to deceive God's people, but if their hearts could be seen they would appear as black as ever. My accompanying angel bade me look for the travail of soul for sinners as used to be. I looked, but could not see it, for the time for their salvation is past." "Present Truth," pages 21-22, published August, 1849.

Here you have the shut door and no mercy for sinners just as clear as language can make it. Every candid reader knows what it teaches. It is pitiable to see the shifts and turns, evasions, dodges, quibbles, if not something worse, resorted to on this passage to save Mrs. White's visions. But there it stands, to mock at all their efforts. Here is another passage teaching the same doctrine: "It was just as impossible for them to get on the path again and go to the city, as all the wicked world which God had rejected." "A Word to the Little Flock," page 14, published in 1847. At this time, then, God had rejected the wicked world—shut door, you see.

Here is another vision in which she teaches the doctrine of the shut door in its very worst form, that is that after 1844 not one ray of light comes from Jesus to the wicked but they are all turned over to the devil to whom they now pray instead of to God. After Jesus left the holy place she says: "I did not see one ray of light pass from Jesus to the careless multitude after he arose and they were left in perfect darkness. * * * Satan appeared to be by the throne trying to carry on the work of God. I saw them look up to the throne and pray, Father give us thy spirit; then Satan would breathe upon them an unholy influence."—Early Writings, page 46–47. Not one ray of light comes to sinners since 1844 but all are left to the Devil! What is the use of their denying that she taught this doctrine? She certainly did and she knows it. This fact and the bold denial of it now, brand her as a false teacher.

I will briefly notice some other mistakes she has made, enough to show that she is wholly unreliable.

1. For over forty years she, herself, has been constantly expecting the end of the world, and it has not come yet. This alone ought to open the eyes of all to see that she has no knowledge of the future.

2. Slaves. In 1849 she foretold what would happen when Jesus comes, and said: "I saw the pious slave rise in triumph and victory and shake off the chains that bound him, while his wicked master was in confusion." Early Writings, page 28. But now there are no slaves. She had not then dreamed of the abolition of slavery.

3. Nations angry. "The nations are *now* getting angry." Early Writings, page 29. That was thirty-eight years ago. It takes a long time for them to get fighting mad!

4. Another mistake. "Some are looking too far off for the coming of the Lord." Page 49. That was thirty-eight years ago, and no Adventist then looked for time to last ten years.

5. Another blunder. "The time for Jesus to be in the most holy place was nearly finished." Page 49. Jesus went there in 1844. Hence, he had then been there six years. She saw that the time for him to be there was nearly finished, but it has continued sixty years since. A false prediction, as any one can see.

6. A few months only in 1849. "Now time is almost finished, and what we have been [six] years learning, they [new converts] will have to learn in a few months." Page 57. But instead of a few months, they have had sixty years!

7. She broke the Sabbath for eleven years. Though she had vision after vision about the Sabbath, yet for eleven years they all began it at six P. M. instead of at sunset as the law requires. Lev. 23:32. When they found their mistake, she saw it, too, in vision. She says: "I inquired why it had been thus that at this late date we must change."
Testimony No. 1, page 13. A poor leader she.

8. HER PREDICTIONS ABOUT THE REBELLION A FAILURE.

"Jan. 4, 1862, I was shown some things in regard to our nation." Testimonies, Vol. I, page 253. All will remember the great anxiety and uncertainty of those days. How would the war end? Specially were her people anxious, as they were non-combatants and liable to the draft. Here was an inspired prophetess right in their midst, having abundant revelations about the length of women's dresses, what people should eat, etc. What relief to all would have been a few short words from heaven about the results of the war. The pressure upon her for light was so great that she had to say something. So she took her pen and scribbled away through thirty-two long pages about the war. At this date it is amusing to read it. This "revelation" alone is enough to show that she knows absolutely nothing of the future. All she wrote was merely a restatement of the popular view of the matter at that time. I shall quote a few sentences as samples. "The system of slavery, which has ruined our nation, is left to live and stir up another rebellion." Was slavery left to stir up another rebellion? Now we know that statement was utterly untrue.

Again. "It seemed impossible to have the war conducted successfully," page 256. Another failure, for it was conducted successfully. All can see that her ideas were just those generally rife at the time. I have long watched and studied her carefully, till I have become satisfied that this is always true of her prophesyings—they are wholly moulded by the sentiment around her at the time. Here is another: "This nation will yet be humbled into the dust" page 259. Was it? No. Again: "When England does declare war, all nations will have an interest of their own to serve, and there will be general war," page 259. Did anything of this kind happen? No; but it is just what all then expected. Once more: "Had our nation remained united, it would have had strength; but divided, it *must fall*," page 260. How it did fall! "I was shown distress and perplexity and famine in the land," page 260. Just what all expected then; but where was the famine? "It looked to me like an impossibility now for slavery to be done away," page 266. Of course it did, for that was just the way it looked to all others then. But did it look that way to God? That was the question. Was he telling her?

She claims that what she writes is not merely her own ideas but the mind of God himself. Thus: "I do not write one article in the paper expressing merely my own ideas. They are what God has opened before me in vision." Testimony, No. 31, page 63. This, then, was the way the thing looked to God at that time! Again: "Blood has been poured out like water, and for naught." Testimony for the Church, Vol. I, page 367. Was it for naught, ye brave soldiers? Ye liberated slaves? Ye freed nation? I could give scores of such quotations all through her writings, showing how they have failed always and everywhere.

THE REFORM DRESS.

One of the worst blunders Mrs. White ever made, one which plainly showed her fanaticism and that God had nothing to do with her work, was the move she made on dress. First she wrote: "God would not have his people adopt the so-called reform dress," "Testimonies," Vol. I, page 421. "If women would wear their dresses so as to clear the filth of the streets an inch or two," it would be in harmony with their faith, page 424. Four years pass, and she again writes: "God would now have his people adopt the reform dress," page 525. "Nine inches as nearly accords with my views of the matter as I am able to express it in inches," page 521. Here are two revelations exactly opposite as to the style of dress and the length, an inch or two, and then nine inches, from the ground is the length. What occasioned this change in the mind of the Lord? The answer is easy: In the time between the two revelations Mrs. White had spent some time at Dr. Jackson's "Home," Dansville, N. Y. Here a short dress with pants was worn, and she fell in with the idea and soon had a vision requiring its adoption as above. That is the whole of it. But the dress was a shame and a disgrace and an utter failure. Think of a modest woman on the streets with pants on, and her dress cut off half way up to the knees! But for about eight years Mrs. White pushed that dress with all her power, put it on herself as an example, till most of the sisters put it on. But it created a terrible commotion. Husbands swore, brothers refused to walk with their sisters, men sneered and boys hooted. Some of the sisters argued, some cried, some rebelled, but most submitted. I know, for my own wife wore it for eight years—had to. Finally, Mrs. White quietly dropped it off herself, and now no one wears it. Here they are all living in direct violation of a plain revelation from God! Common sense came out ahead of fanaticism.

If God ever spoke through Mrs. White about anything, he did about the dress, requiring the women to wear it. I was there and know how she urged it, heard her many times. Her Testimonies at the time were full of it. She said: "I have done my duty; I have borne my testimony, and those who have heard me and read that which I have written, must now bear the responsibility of receiving or rejecting the light given. If they choose to venture to be forgetful hearers, and not doers of the work, they run their own risk, and will be accountable to God!" Testimonies, Vol. I, page 525. Yet they have all run the risk and laid off the dress, Mrs. White with the rest. How does she get out of it? By all sorts of dodges, by blaming everybody but herself. It has been a great stumbling block to them.

HER REVELATIONS INFLUENCED BY OTHERS.

Mrs. White originates nothing. In her vision she always sees just what she and her friends at the time happen to believe and be interested in. Her husband and other leading men first accept or study out a theory and talk it till her mind is full of it. Then when she is in her trance that is just what she sees. One who has been all through the Advent work and well knows, says: "The visions have brought out no points of faith held by Seventh-Day Adventists."

Mrs. White herself confesses that she is influenced by others in writing her "Testimonies." Thus: pages 138-139. "What appeared in Testimony No. 11, concerning the Health Institute should not have been given until I was able to write out all I had seen in regard to it. * * * I yielded my judgment to that of others and wrote what appeared in No. 11. * * I In this I did wrong." Testimonies, Vol. I, page 563. She here "lets the cat out of the bag." She made such a blunder that she was compelled to blame some one else for it and so to tell the truth that she was influenced by others to do it! Fine inspiration.

Elder White was well aware of how she was influenced by others to see and write as they impressed her to do. Hence he was very jealous of having leading men talk anything to her alone opposing his views, for he feared she would then have a revelation favoring them and opposing him as indeed she did towards the last. Thus he wrote me: "The pressure has been terribly hard on my poor wife. She has been impressed very much by Elders Butler and Haskell." Again: "I think my wife has been more severe than the Lord really required her to be in some cases. Satan has taken great advantage. * * * Elders Butler and Haskel have had an influence over her that I hope to see broken. It has nearly ruined her. These men must not be supported by our people to do as they have done." James White, Battle Creek, May 25, 1881. That shows the confidence which her own husband had in her revelations.

THE PHILOSOPHY OF MRS. WHITE'S VISIONS.

The proof is abundant that Mrs. White's visions are merely the result of nervous disease, a complication of hysteria, catalepsy and ecstacy. That she honestly believes in them herself, I do not doubt. I have personally known four other women, all Seventh-Day Adventists, who likewise had visions. All were sincere Christians, and fully believed in their own visions. But all were sickly, nervous females, and hysterical. Not being encouraged in them, but opposed by their ministers, they finally gave them up. In every age such cases have been numerous, of whom a few, like Mrs. Southcott, Mrs. Ann Lee and Mrs. White, have become noted for awhile.

Medical books and cyclopedias, under the words "hysteria," "catalepsy" and "ecstacy," give a complete description of Mrs. White's case, as stated by herself and husband. This anyone may see by one day's study. My space will allow me to give but a few points.

1. The sex—a female. "The vast preponderance of hysteria in the female sex has given rise to its name." Raynold's System of Medicine, article, "Hysteria." So say all the authorities. This fits Mrs. White, a female.

2. The age. "Hysteria is infinitely more common among females, beginning usually from fifteen to eighteen or twenty years of age." Theory and Practice of Medicine, by Roberts, page 399. "In the female sex, hysteria usually commences at or about the time of puberty, *i. e.*, between twelve and eighteen years of age." Raynold's System of Medicine, article, Hysteria. Here again it exactly fits the case of Mrs White. She had her first vision at the age of seventeen. See Testimonies, Vol. I, page 62. "Notwithstanding this mode of life, their health does not materially deteriorate." Johnson's Cyclopedia, article, Hysteria. So with Mrs. White. She has gradually improved in health and her visions have as gradually ceased. At first she had visions almost daily, but they have grown less frequent as she grew older and healthier, till after about forty-five years of age, since which time she has not averaged one in five years, and even these are short and light, till now she has ceased entirely to have them. Now read this: "Hysteria generally attacks women from the age of

puberty to the decline of the peculiar functions of her sex." Johnson's Cyclopedia article, Hysteria. Mrs. White's case again, exactly.

3. The cause. Hysteria, catalepsy, epilepsy and ecstacy are all nervous diseases, which sometimes co-exist or alternate or blend together so it is difficult to distinguish them. The causes noted are: "1. Mental disturbance, especially emotional; for example, a sudden fright, prolonged grief or anxiety. *2. Physical influences affecting the brain, as a *blow* or *fall on the head.*" Theory and Practice of Medicine, Roberts, page 393. "In ten of my cases the disease was due to reflex causes, which consisted in six cases of injuries to the head." Fundamental Nervous Disease, Putzel, page 66. This is Mrs. White again, exactly. At the age of nine she received a terrible blow on the face, which broke her nose and nearly killed her. She was unconscious for three weeks. See her life in Testimony, Vol. I, pages 9–10. This shock to her nervous system was the real cause of all the visions she afterwards had.

4. Always weakly and sickly. "Most hysterical persons are out of health." Theory and Practice of Medicine, Roberts, page 404. "Fainting fits, palpitation of the heart appear very frequently and are sometimes so severe that persons affected with them seem to be dying." Encyclopedia Americana, article, Hysteria. Now read the life of Mrs. White, and she tells it over and over, times without number, about fainting frequently, pain at the heart, and about being so sick that she expected to die. And it is remarkable that most of her visions were immediately preceded by one of these fainting death spells. This shows plainly that they are the result of nervous weakness. She says: "My feelings were unusually sensitive." Testimonies Vol. I, page 12. Now read this: "Women * * * whose nervous system is extremely sensitive, are the most

subject to hysterical affections," Encyclopedia Americana, article, Hysteria. An exact fit.

MRS. WHITE'S PHYSICAL CONDITION AS WRITTEN BY HERSELF IN TESTIMONY, VOL. I.

When nine years old a girl hit her on the nose with a stone, broke her nose, and nearly killed her. Page 9. "I lay in a stupor for three weeks." Page 10. "I was reduced almost to a skeleton." Page 11. "My health seemed to be hopelessly impaired." Page 12. "My nervous system was prostrated." Page 13. Here was the origin of her hysteria of after years. In this condition she "listened to the startling announcement that Christ was coming in 1843." Page 14. "These words kept ringing in my ears; 'the great day of the Lord is at hand.'" Page 15. "I frequently attended the meetings and believed that Jesus was soon to come." Page 22. Of her impression of hell she says: "My imagination would be so wrought upon that the perspiration would start." Page 24. "I feared that I would lose my reason." Page 25. At one time she did become insane for two weeks as she writes herself. Spiritual Gifts, Vol. II, page 51. She continues: "My health was very poor." Testimonies, Vol. I, page 55. It was thought that she could live but a few days. Then it was she had her first vision, really a fit. Page 58. "I was but seventeen years of age, small and frail." Page 62. "My strength was taken away," and angels talk with her. Page 64. "My friends thought I could not live. * * * Immediately taken off in vision." Page 67. Notice that her visions happen when she is very sick! This tells the story; they are the result of her physical weakness. If it was the power of the Holy Ghost, why didn't God send it when she was well? Why not?

"I often fainted like one dead." The next day she was

MRS. WHITE AND HER REVELATIONS. 155

well and "rode thirty-eight miles." Page 80. This is characteristic of hysterical females, as all know who have seen them. They are just dying one hour and all well the next. Mrs. White has gone through that a thousand times. She is just dying, is prayed for, is healed by God, and all well in a few minutes. In a few days she goes right over it again. But if God heals her, why don't she stay healed? This used to bother me. When Jesus healed a man, did he have to go back and be healed over again every few days? She goes on: "I fainted under the burden. Some feared I was dying. * * * I was soon lost to earthly things"— had a vision. Page 86. Again: "I fainted. Prayer was offered for me and I was blessed and taken off in vision." Page 88. There you have it, the same old story. It is simply her hysterical imagination, nothing more. Next page. "I fainted * * * taken off in vision." So she goes on all through her book. Says the Encyclopedia Americana, article, Hysteria: "Fainting fits, palpitation of the heart appear very frequently and are sometimes so severe that persons afflicted with them seem to be dying." Mrs. White exactly.

On page after page the same story is repeated by herself. In the account of her last vision, Jan. 3, 1875, she was very sick till it ended in a vision. Testimonies, Vol. III, page 570. Dreadful sick, almost dead, then a vision—this is the story, times without number, from her own pen. That tells the story. The vision is the result of her physical weakness.

5. Visions in public. "As a rule a fit of hysteria occurs when other persons are present, and never comes on during sleep." Theory and Practice of Medicine, by Roberts, page 401. Most of her visions occur in public, and generally while she is very sick, or when praying or speaking earnestly. This was the case with her first vision. Spiritual Gifts, Vol. I, page 30. So, again, on pages 37, 48, 51, 62,

83, and many more, she has her visions in the presence of many. I do not know that she ever had a vision while alone.

INCLINATION TO EXAGGERATE AND DECEIVE.

6. All medical books state that hysterical persons are given to exaggeration and deception. The inclination is irresistible. Nothing can break them of it. Gurnsey's Obstetrics, article Hysteria, says: "Such persons entertain their hearers with marvelous tales of the greatness and exploits of their past lives. * * * These accounts are uttered with an air of sincerity well calculated to deceive the honest listener, and such unbridled license of the imagination and total obliviousness in regard to the truth, which are vulgarly attributed to an entire want of principle and the most inordinate vanity, are in reality due to that morbid condition of the female organism which is designated by the comprehensive term hysteria."

Mrs. White is always telling what great things she has done. The deception which she so often practices, and which I have witnessed in her myself, is here accounted for on principles which do not impeach the moral character, and I am glad to accept the explanation.

7. Does not breathe. "Stoppage of respiration usually complete." "Generally appears to hold his breath." Roberts' Theory and Practice of Medicine, page 393-394. Elder White, describing her condition in vision, says: "She does not breathe." Life Incidents, page 272. They always refer to this fact with great confidence as proof of the supernatural in her visions; but it will be seen that it is common in these diseases.

8. Importance of self. "There is a prevailing belief in the importance of self, and the patient thinks that she differs from every other human being." Raynold's System of

Medicine, article Hysteria. Mrs. White to a hair. Hear her laud herself: "It is God, and not an erring mortal, who has spoken." "God has laid upon my husband and myself a special work." "God has appointed us to a more trying work than he has others." Testimonies, Vol. III, pages 257, 258, 260. I have known her nearly thirty years, and I never knew her to make confession of a single sin or evil in all that time, not she. Seventh-Day Adventists ridicule the Pope's claim to infallibility but they themselves are bowing to the authority of a woman who makes higher claims to infallibility than ever pope or prophet did. Space will not allow me to fill out every particular of her experience by quotations from medical works compared with her own statements; but even these given above are sufficient to show the nature and philosophy of her attacks. They are the result of nervous disease, precisely the same as has been often seen in the case of thousands of other sickly females.

TESTIMONY OF THREE PHYSICIANS.

9. Dr. Fairfield was brought up a Seventh-Day Adventist; was for years a physician in their Sanitarium at Battle Creek. He has had the best opportunity to observe Mrs. White. He writes: "Battle Creek, Mich., Dec. 28, 1887. Dear Sir:—You are undoubtedly right in ascribing Mrs. E. G. White's so-called visions to disease. It has been my opportunity to observe her case a good deal, covering quite a period of years, which, with a full knowledge of her history from the beginning, gave me no chance to doubt her ("divine") attacks to be simply hysterical trances. Age itself has almost cured her.

W. J. FAIRFIELD, M. D."

Dr. Wm. Russell, long a Seventh-Day Adventist, and a chief physician in the Sanitarium, wrote July 12th, 1869, that he had made up his mind some time in the past, "that

Mrs. White's visions were the result of a diseased organization or condition of the brain or nervous system." "When giving to a conference at Pilot Grove, Iowa, 1865, an account of her visit at Dr. Jackson's health institute, she stated that the doctor, upon a medical examination, pronounced her a subject of hysteria." Mrs. White's Claims Examined, page 76.

Here is the testimony of three physicians, who have personally examined Mrs. White. She joined the Millerites in their great excitement of 1843–44. In their meetings she often fainted from excitement. In the enthusiasm and fanaticism of the time many had various "gifts," visions, trances, etc. She drank deeply of their spirit. The grief and disappointment of the passing of the set time were too much for her feeble condition. Says Dr. Roberts: "The exciting cause of the first hysterical fit is generally some powerful and sudden emotional disturbance." "Sometimes the attack is preceded by disappointment, fear, violent, exciting, or even religious emotions." Library of Universal Knowledge, article Catalepsy. Just her case in 1844, in the great excitement and disappointment she then met.

HAS VISIONS OF HEAVEN, ANGELS, ETC.

Dr. George B. Wood's "Practice of Medicine," page 721 of Vol. II, in treating of mental disorders, and explaining the cause and phenomena of trances, says:

"Ecstacy is an affection in which, with a loss of consciousness of existing circumstances, and insensibility to impression from without, there is an apparent exaltation of the intellectual or emotional functions, as if the individual were raised into a different nature, or different sphere of existence. The patient appears wrapped up in some engrossing thought or feeling, with an expression upon his countenance as of lofty contemplations or ineffable delight. * * *

Upon recovering from the spell, the patient generally remembers his thoughts and feelings more or less accurately, and sometimes tells of wonderful visions that he has seen, of visits to the regions of the blessed, of ravishing harmony and splendor, of inexpressible enjoyment of the senses or affections."

A person perfectly familiar with Mrs. White could not have described her visions more accurately. Another high medical authority, in describing ecstacy and catalepsy, says: "It often happens that the two diseases alternate or co-exist. In ecstacy the limbs are motionless, but not rigid. The eyes are open, the pupils fixed, the livid lips parted in smiles, and the arms extended to embrace the beloved vision. The body is erect and raised to its utmost height, or else is extended at full length in recumbent posture. A peculiar radiant smile illuminates the countenance, and the whole aspect and attitude is that of intense mental exaltation. Sometimes the patient is silent, the mind being apparently absorbed in meditation, or in the contemplation of some beatific vision. Sometimes there is mystical speaking or prophesying, or singing, or the lips may be moved without any sound escaping. * * * Usually there is complete insensibility to external impressions. Ecstacy is often associated with religious monomania. It was formerly quite common among the inmates of convents, and is now not unfrequently met with at camp-meetings and other gatherings of a similar nature. Many truly devout people are extatics." G. Durant, M. D., Ph. D., member of the American Medical Association, Fellow of the New York Academy of Medicine, etc., etc., recipient of several medals, etc.

This is Mrs. White's case very clearly. Hundreds of similar ones have occurred in every age and are constantly occurring now. The sad part of it is that so many honest souls are deluded into receiving all this as a divine revelation.

WHAT HARM DOES SHE DO?

Much in many ways:

1. It is an error and a deception.
2. She deceives herself and others.
3. She teaches false doctrines.
4. She has a harsh, uncharitable spirit, and begets this in all her followers.
5. She builds up an isolated sect, and thus destroys all their influence for good.
6. Her teachings make her people narrow, bigoted, and gloomy. Thus she blasts the peace of thousands of souls.
7. It leads her advocates to deceive. Being afraid that it will hurt them in new places, if it is known in what light they really hold her visions, they keep them back as long as they can and then they deny that it is a matter of importance with them. This is false and deceptive, for they hold faith in her visions to be as important as keeping the Sabbath, and they hold her visions to be as sacred as the Bible.
8. To defend her mistakes and errors, both she and her apologists have to deny the plainest facts and resort to arguments very questionable.
9. To defend her errors, they compare them to supposed errors in the Bible, and thus destroy faith in that book.
10. She rules her whole people with a rod of iron, and dictates to them in everything, even the smallest and most private affairs of family life. She boasts that her work "is to come down to the minutiæ of life." Testimonies, Vol. II, page 608. With this idea she meddles with everything public and private, and all the affairs of families, till it becomes, to a man of spirit, an intolerable bore. She meddles between husband and wife, parents and children, breaks up marriage engagements which do not suit her, dictates to all her followers what they shall eat, how, and when; the cut

and color of their dress; their business, the disposition of their means, etc., etc. In proof of this let a person read any of her "Testimonies," for they are all full of it.

11. Her severity and harshness have driven many to despair, others to back-slide, and others out of the church. I can name many individuals and families whose happiness she has blasted. She broke the heart and darkened the life of my first wife by her cruel words to her. Any one who dares to get in her way must either succumb, be crushed, or driven out. The effort to bind her visions as inspired upon the faith and consciences of the whole denomination has produced continual wrangling, division, and much bitter feeling, right among themselves for the last sixty years. Families, churches and conferences have been divided over them, while hundreds, yes, thousands, have been driven from them because they would not accept Mrs. White's visions as inspired.

12. They produce doubts and infidelity. When those who have been led to firmly believe them finally come to see that they have been deceived, then they are in danger of losing faith in everything and so becoming out and out infidels, or at least skeptical. Large numbers have gone to ruin that way whom I have personally known. Some have gone to the Spiritualists, some to the Free Thinkers, some to the Shakers, some to the Mormons, and some to the world. They have nearly driven Mrs. White herself into infidelity. Here are her own words: "In the night I have awakened my husband, saying, 'I am afraid that I shall become an infidel.'" Testimonies, Vol. I, page 597. How unlike the apostles that sounds.

MRS. WHITE BECOMES RICH.

There is no example in the Bible where a prophet took advantage of his inspiration to enrich himself. They generally worked hard, had little, and died poor. But Mrs. White began poverty poor. She says: "We entered upon our work penniless." Testimonies, Vol. I, page 75. But as soon as they became leaders, they managed to supply themselves well. Since I knew them, thirty years ago, they have had an abundance, and have used means for themselves lavishly. They would always have the best and plenty of it. Everywhere they went they required to be waited upon in the most slavish manner. Mrs. White dresses very richly, often is furnished women to wait on her, and all their time and expenses are paid by the conference.

When Elder White died he left a large fortune. He was a sharp business man, and took advantage of his position to benefit himself and family, and she aided him in it by her revelations. How different from Mr. Moody! Mrs. White is eighty years old, is worth thousands, has a large income, has not a single soul dependent upon her, says that time is about to end, urges all to cut down their possessions, yet takes large royalty on all her numerous books and seems as eager for money as others. How is this?

The last year I was with them she received $18 per week, was furnished two women to wait on her and all traveling expenses paid. The same year they sold 20,000 copies of Great Controversy on which she received a royalty of $2,500 besides an income from all her other works. Her inspiration has paid her well financially.

Take an example or two of how she used her revelations to make money: In 1868 Elder White had on hand several thousand dollars' worth of old books which were dead property, as they were not selling and were growing out of date. He hit on a plan to raise a "book fund" for the free distribution of books and tracts. This fund he used to buy out his and her old books! When the money did not come fast enough, she had a revelation about it thus: "Why do not our brethren send in their pledges on the book and tract fund more liberally? And why do not our ministers take hold of this work in earnest? * * * We shall not hold our peace upon this subject. Our people will come up to the work. The means will come. And we would say to those who are poor and want books, send in your orders. * * * We will send you a package of books containing four volumes of Spiritual Gifts, How to Live, Appeal to Youth, Appeal to Mothers, Sabbath Readings and the two large charts, with key of explanation, * * * and charge the fund four dollars." Testimonies, Vol. I, page 689. Every one of these books was their own. The money came and they pocketed it all. I was there and know.

Mrs. White now has forty inspired books. To sell these, every possible effort is made through every channel. She is constantly urging it by all her inspired authority. Hear her: "The volumes of Spirit of Prophecy and also the Testimonies should be introduced into every Sabbath keeping family. * * * Let them be worn out in being read by all the neighbors. * * * Prevail upon them to buy copies. * * * Light so precious, coming from the throne of God, is hid under a bushel. God will make his people responsible for this neglect." Testimonies, Vol. IV, pages 390, 391. So, of course, her books must be pushed and sold while she makes money. It pays to be inspired!

WHY I ONCE BELIEVED MRS. WHITE INSPIRED.

I once accepted Mrs. White's claim to inspiration for the same reason that most of her followers do. I first accepted the Sabbath and then other points of the faith till I came to believe it all.

2. Once among and of them I found all stating in strong terms that Mrs. White was inspired of God. I supposed they knew, and so took their word for it; and that is what all the others do as they come in, deny it as they may.

3. I soon found that her revelations were so connected with the whole history and belief of that church that I could not consistently separate them any more than a person could be a Mormon and not believe in Joseph Smith. I believed the other doctrines so firmly that I swallowed the visions with the rest, and that is what all do.

4. When I began to have suspicions about the visions I found the pressure so strong that I feared to express them, or even to admit them to myself. All said such doubts were of the Devil and would lead to a rejection of the truth and then to ruin. So I dared not entertain them nor investigate the matter; and this is the way it is with others.

5. I saw that all who expressed any doubts about the visions were immediately branded as "rebels," as "in the dark," "led by Satan," "infidels," etc.

6. Having no faith in any other doctrine or people, I did not know what to do nor where to go. So I tried to believe the visions and go along just as thousands of them do when really they are in doubt about them all the time.

Her last Testimony just out reveals the fact that there is a wide-spread effort among her people to modify her high claims. She protests vehemently and warns them to keep their hands off. Sooner or later there must be a revolt against her high claims.

The following from Chambers' Encyclopedia, Article Southcott, is also applicable to Mrs. White and her followers: "The history of Joanna Southcott herself has not much in it that is marvelous; but the influence which she exercised over others may well may be deemed so, and the infatuation of her followers is hard to be understood, particularly when it is considered that some of them were men of some intelligence and of cultivated mind. Probably the secret of her influence lay in the fact that the poor creature was in earnest about her own delusions. So few people in the world are really so that they are always liable to be enslaved by others who have convictions of any kind, however grotesque. On her death-bed Joanna said: 'If I have been misled, it has been by some spirit, good or evil.' * * * Poor Joanna never suspected that the spirit which played such vagaries was her own."

Just so of Mrs. White. It is marvelous that with all the proof of her failures intelligent men are still led by her. But the case of Joanna, of Ann Lee, and others, helps us to solve this one. All have earnestly believed in their own inspiration, and this alone has convinced others.

The Adventists' Addition to the Bible

"The Bible and the Bible Only, as a Rule of Faith and Practice," is the Protestant watchword for which saints have fought and martyrs died.

The Catholic church has the Bible and—and—something else—an infallible Pope to interpret it.

The Swedenborg church has the Bible and—and—something else—Swedenborg's revelation to interpret it.

The Shakers have the Bible and—and—something else—Mother Ann Lee's revelation to interpret it.

The Mormons have the Bible and—and—something else—Joe Smith's revelations to interpret it.

Christian Scientists have the Bible and—and—something else—Mrs. Eddy's Science and Health to tell what it means.

Seventh Day Adventists have the Bible and—and—something else—Mrs. White's revelations to interpret it.

Each of the above churches has done exactly the same thing, namely, has put right along with the good old Bible another interpreter to tell what that old Bible really means. Whatever these new interpreters say it means, all their members must accept as true without further question. Dare a Catholic dispute the Pope's interpretation, or a Mormon dispute Smith's, or an Adventist dispute Mrs. White's interpretation? No, indeed.

CHAPTER IX.

THE NATURE OF THE SABBATH COMMANDMENT.

That the Sabbath of the decalogue was partly moral and partly ceremonial, or positive, in its nature has been the doctrine of the church as taught by its best theologians in all ages. Take a few examples out of scores that could be given. Watson's Theological Institutes, the great Methodist standard, says: "But as the command is partly positive and partly moral, it may have circumstances which are capable of being altered in perfect accordance with the moral principles on which it rests." Vol. II, page 511. So Scott's Commentary on Ex. 20: 8-10 says: "The separation of a portion of our time to the immediate service of God is doubtless of moral obligation. * * * But the exact proportion, as well as the particular day, may be considered as a positive institution."

The moral basis of the Sabbath is readily manifest. That man should devote some part of his time to the special service and worship of God is reasonable, and we would naturally expect that the Lord would, in some way, designate such time, just as he did do in the Sabbath precept.

Experience proves that man's physical nature requires a day of rest about as often as one in seven. Many experiments have been tried and careful observations made, all showing that both men and beasts will accomplish more work in a given time, do it in a better manner and preserve better health by resting every seventh day than they will by laboring continuously. This is the testimony of business men and of eminent physicians. Hence the Sabbath rest had its foundation in nature itself. The mind also requires a day of rest as regularly as the body. Constant thought and mental application is ruinous to the mind. This has been proved in the case of students, lawyers, business men, etc. Socially and religiously, the weekly rest day is of the ut-utmost importance to man's highest good. All other means combined can hardly equal the observance of the Lord's day for the purpose.

Then as to the influence of the church and its power for good, its hold upon its own members and upon community, its opportunity to teach and preach the gospel, the regular weekly rest day is its strong hold as all well know. Hence, if ever a law of God had a moral basis, the Sabbath commandment has. * * * "The Sabbath was made for man" because he needed it physically, mentally, socially, morally and religiously. Mr. Gladstone says: "Sunday is a necessity for the retention of man's mind and of a man's frame in a condition to discharge his duties."

All experience shows that a Sabbathless community is a godless, immoral, and, generally, a thriftless community. Hence he is an enemy of society and of religion who would break down the restraints of such a weekly rest in the community. So we say that the Sabbath law rested upon a moral basis in providing a weekly Sabbath for the nation of Israel.

THE CEREMONIAL SIDE OF THE SABBATH.

But when we come to the definite day, which it shall be, nature does not indicate that. All the benefits above mentioned would be secured by keeping one day as well as another. There would not be a particle of difference whichever day was selected. Suppose that all the churches would change in one week and keep Saturday instead of Sunday, what practical difference would it make? None at all. Physical rest, mental rest, social and religious privileges, a quiet day, —all that can be secured by one day can by another, so far as the day itself is concerned. But to secure the greatest good from the day, all should rest the same day. Where this is not done confusion and evil follows. Hence, the law provided that all must rest the same day. Ex. 20: 8-11.

God has marked no difference in the nature of days in themselves. All nature goes right on just the same every day alike. We see nothing in one day of the week which differs from another, and there is no difference. No day is holy in and of itself and by its own nature. The learned Dr. Edwards says: "No identical period of duration is, in itself, intrinsically holy." Sabbath Manual, page 92. In every case God had to make the day holy by a special appointment. The same appointment of some other day would have made it just as holy.

Nor does nature indicate clearly just the proportion of time to be used. Hence God's example of six days' work and the seventh of rest was doubtless given as a model for man to follow. To this the Lord pointed in giving the Sabbath law. Ex. 20. And this divine model all Christians now follow in resting on the Lord's day after six days' work.

Another fact which Sabbatarians overlook is that God's act of resting on the day did not confer any holiness upon it. Gen. 2:3, says: "God blessed the seventh day and sanctified it because that in it *he had rested*." So Ex. 20: 11. He "rested the seventh day, wherefore the Lord blessed the Sabbath day and hallowed it." First, God rested on the day, but that did not make it holy. After that he blessed it but still it was not holy time. Third, he hallowed it, made it holy. So the day was not holy in itself nor did God's resting on it make it holy.

The Lord has made other days holy, days on which he

never rested. The day of atonement was as holy as the weekly Sabbath. Thus: "It shall be an holy convocation unto you. * * * And whatsoever soul *it be* that doeth any work in that same day, the same soul will I destroy from among his people. Ye shall do no manner of work: * * * It shall be unto you a Sabbath of rest." Lev. 23: 27-32. So there were seven of these yearly holy days. Elder Smith, Adventist, says: "The word *Sabbath* means *rest*. That is the one sole idea it conveys, first, last, and all the way between,—cessation from labor, rest. Here were seven annual days on which there was to be an entire suspension of labor. Were these days Sabbaths, or were they not? If they were not, can any one tell us why they were not?" What Was Nailed to the Cross, page 11.

So, then, according to the Bible and the arguments of the Adventists themselves, different days may become holy Sabbath days without the Lord's resting on them or even blessing them, for he did neither to these days. Further, a day which was once a holy Sabbath day, so holy that it was death to work on it, as in the case of the day of atonement, Lev. 23: 27-32, may cease to be so and become a common working day. See Col. 2: 16. Even Adventists do not keep those old holy days. So, then, holiness can be put upon a day, taken from it, or changed to another day. It is not necessarily a permanent, unchangeable affair. Let Sabbatarians meditate here awhile. More still: A day once appointed, and made a holy Sabbath day by God himself, may cease to be such and become even hateful to God. Thus: Isa. 1: 13-14, "The new moons and Sabbaths, the calling of assemblies, I cannot away with; *it is* iniquity, even the solemn meeting. Your new moons and your appointed feasts my soul hateth; they are a trouble unto me; I am weary to bear *them*." All these holy days God himself had appointed, but see how he hates them now.

Is it any proof, then, that a particular day is holy now because it was once holy? None whatever.

Notice also how many other things were made holy by God's appointment. Under the *law* we read of "the holy temple," "the holy hill," "the holy ark," "the holy instruments," "the holy vessels," "the holy water," "the holy perfume," "the holy altar," "the holy veil," "the holy linen coat," "the holy ointment," "the holy nation," "the holy Sabbath," etc. Those pertained to the worship and service of God in his *holy temple*, which was "only a shadow," "figure" or "type of the *true* temple"—the "spiritual house" of Christ, "his body, the church." While they stood as *types* they were "holy," and no longer. They had no inherent holiness, but were made holy by the command of God. Law and Gospel, page 43, by S. C. Adams.

Like all the above holy things, the seventh day had no holiness in itself. It had to be "made" so. Mark 2: 27. But moral duties are not made. They exist in the very nature of things. For instance, it is morally wrong to murder. It would have been wrong even if God had given no command against it. But it never would have been wrong to work on the seventh day unless God had given a commandment to keep it. So, then, the sanctity of the day does not rest upon the nature of the day itself, but, like a hundred other hallowed things, simply upon God's appointment, which may be altered any time at his will.

All must admit that this commandment does differ from those which are admitted to be wholly moral. No one could all his lifetime live in open violation of the commandments against idolatry, blasphemy, murder, adultery, stealing, etc., and yet have the least hope of heaven. Yet the most zealous Sabbatarian will admit that millions of devout Christians have lived holy lives who never kept the seventh day, but rested on Sunday instead. And Sunday-keepers will admit that those who keep Saturday instead of Sunday are Christian people. Now, certainly, one or the other of these classes does not keep the Sabbath commandment, if the essential thing is to keep the particular day. Would any seventh-day man recognize as a Christian any person who would every week violate the letter of any other commandment? No, nor would he excuse him on any plea of ignorance either. Yet they will freely admit that thousands right around them who do not keep the Sabbath commandment as they read it, are yet good people and Christians. So, they themselves being judges, this commandment does differ from the others in some way.

WHAT IS A CEREMONY?

Adventists claim that there was nothing ceremonial in the decalogue or about the Sabbath. But let us consider what a *ceremony* is. Webster says: "Ceremony. Outward rite; external form in religion." That is exactly what the observance of the Sabbath was in Jewish worship. Do not Adventists class the keeping of all the other holy days as ceremonial? Yes; but they were all "holy convocations," Lev. 23: 2, like the seventh day. Read Elder Smith's own arguments on this point. He says: "Were these other days which were *exactly like that*,—days of rest and convocation,—were these days also Sabbaths, or were they not?" What Was Nailed to the Cross, page 11. Then he argues that they were all Sabbaths like the seventh day. Well, then if the keeping of these was a ceremony, and a part of the "ceremonial" law, then the same is true of the seventh day.

The observance of the Sabbath on a particular day was a ceremonial service, the very first and chief of all their "outward rites and external forms." Thus, Smith's Dictionary of the Bible, article, Law of Moses, under the term "Ceremonial Law," says: "(3). Holiness of Times. (*a*) The Sabbath. Ex. 20: 8–11. (*b*) The Sabbatical Year. (*c*) Year of Jubilee. (*d*) The Passover. (*e*) The Feast of Weeks. (*f*) Feast of Tabernacles. (*g*) Feast of Trumpets. (*h*) Day of Atonement." Thus the Sabbath stands at the head of all the ceremonial seasons. God himself so places it. Lev. 23: 1–44. "These are my feasts: Six days shall work be done, but the seventh day is the Sabbath." Then follow in order all the holy days of the year, the Sabbath standing first. It is arranged that way time and again, showing it is so designed. Again, Dr. Smith says: "The Sabbath was the keynote to a scale of Sabbatical observance consisting of itself, the seventh month, the seventh year, and the year of Jubilee."

Adventists argue that the decalogue covers all sins. The greater embraces the lesser, they say. The sixth command prohibits murder, the highest crime of the kind, and that embraces and so forbids all lesser sins of the kind, as anger, quarreling, malice, hatred, etc. Well, now, let them try that on the fourth command and they will hit a truth which ought to open their eyes, viz.: the weekly Sabbath, as chief and head of all holy seasons and ceremonials, was placed there to represent all that class in the Jewish law. Rev. Dr. Potts, Methodist, says: "The law under the Mosaic dispensation was formulated into nine moral precepts, with a Sabbath commandment added." The Lord's Day our Sabbath, page 10.

THE SABBATH ON A ROUND EARTH.

In their very nature all purely moral laws are universal and eternal in their application, are binding in heaven, in Eden, on Jews or Gentiles, saints or sinners, now or hereafter. Test the particular seventh day, Saturday, by that

THE NATURE OF THE SABBATH COMMANDMENT. 173

rule, and it fails everywhere. Go to Venus, where the days are about twenty-three hours long; to Jupiter, where they are only about ten hours long; to Saturn, where they are about twelve hours long, or to some of the larger planets, where their days are much longer than ours. How could the inhabitants of those worlds keep our seventh day? They could keep *a* seventh day, their own, but that would not be of the same length of ours, nor come at the same time of ours. Their seventh day would not be our Saturday, nor would the seventh day of any two planets be alike, nor come at the same time. All the universe can keep a seventh part of time, but not the same seventh part. Not knowing this, see what a blunder Mrs. White made. She says: "I saw that the Sabbath would never be done away, but the redeemed saints, *and all the angelic host*, will observe it in honor of the great Creator to all eternity." Spiritual Gifts, Vol. I, page 113. Elder U. Smith, Biblical Institute, page 145, says: "We infer that the higher orders of his intelligences keep the Sabbath also. * * * The Sabbath of each of his creatures will be the Sabbath of all the rest, so that all will observe *the same period together* for the same purpose."

Here you have your definite seventh-day theory with a vengeance. Look at the utter absurdity and impossibility of the theory. All intelligent beings in heaven and earth and on all the planets, keep "the same period together." So the Sabbath day on this little planet of ours regulates the Sabbath days of all the planets in the universe! I wonder how they manage it in Jupiter, where their days are only ten hours long, or in Venus, where they are twenty-three hours long, or in some of the planets where they are as long as several of our days? As the Sabbath must be kept from sunset to sunset (Lev. 23: 32), I wonder how they find out, on all those planets, just when it is sunset down here!

The stubborn facts nearer home show that God's children do not, and cannot, all "observe the same period together." Everybody knows that it is Saturday in India some twelve hours sooner than it is here, and that it is Saturday here twelve hours after it has ceased to be Saturday there. In Australia the day begins eighteen hours sooner than it does in California. So the Seventh-Day brethren in California are working nearly the whole time that their brethren in Australia are keeping Sabbath! Come even nearer home than that. The sun sets about three hours later in California than it does in Maine. So when the Seventh-day Adventists in Maine begin to keep the Sabbath at sunset Friday evening, their own brethren in California, where the sun is yet three hours high, will still be at work for three hours! So, very few of them on this earth, "observe the same period together." While some of them are keeping Sabbath on one part of the earth, others of them are at work on another part of the earth. How much less, then, do all the heavenly hosts keep the same period with men on earth.

Now, if, as Mrs. White and Bro. Smith say, the angels keep our Sabbath, the question is, with which party do they keep it? With those in Australia, or those in America? If the angels keep the Sabbath at the same time the Sabbatarians keep it in Australia, then the Sabbatarians in America are working while the angels keep Sabbath, and so, of course, the angels work while those here rest. So we see how absolutely false and absurd is the theory that all can keep the Sabbath at the same time.

I have to confess that for many years I was so stupid as to suppose that the Lord himself kept the Sabbath at the same time I did here. I supposed that when the sun set Friday evening and I began keeping the Sabbath, the Lord and the angels began keeping it too. But now I see how utterly impossible that is; for if the Lord keeps the Sabbath at the same time I do here, then he does not keep it with the brethren on the other side of the globe, because they begin the Sabbath at least twelve hours earlier than we do here. In fact, it takes just forty-eight hours, or the time of two whole days, from the time any one day begins in the extreme east till it ends at the furthest place in the west. Will the reader stop and think carefully, sharply, on this point, for it is an important one? It takes twenty-four hours for the *first end* of a day to go clear around the earth. Then, as the *last end* of the day is twenty-four hours behind the *first end*, it must also have twenty-four hours more to go clear around the earth, and that makes forty-eight hours in all that each day is on the earth somewhere.

I am quite certain that the average Sabbatarian feels when he keeps the seventh day that he is now keeping holy time with the Lord himself, and with the angels, and with all his brethren. I used to feel that way I know, and the above quotations from Mrs. White and Elder Smith show plainly that even they think so, too. But it will be seen that this cannot be so unless the Lord keeps the time of two whole days each week. And in that case, those on this side of the earth would be working while the Lord was keeping the Sabbath with those on the other side of the earth. Then those on the opposite of the earth would be working while the Lord kept Sabbath with those on this side. And so none of them would keep the Sabbath with the Lord after all! In fact, taking it all around the earth, there is not a single hour in the whole week, when there is not some Sabbatarian at work on some part of the earth!

But, further, does the Lord keep our seventh day with us, or does he keep the seventh day with the people on other planets? Our days and weeks are not at all in harmony with theirs, nor can one of them be like another. Now, if the Lord rests only on our Saturday, then he could not rest on the seventh day of Venus or Mars or Jupiter, etc., as the seventh day of each planet differs in length and comes at a different time, from that of our earth or any other planet. How, then, could God rest on all these days? If he did he must keep Sabbath all the time, and then nobody, angels or men, could keep the Sabbath with the Lord if they worked at all!

What, then, becomes of Mrs. White's statement that "all the angelic hosts" keep our Sabbath? or Elder Smith's hypothesis that all the universe "will observe the same period together?" Both are utterly absurd. The same definite seventh day cannot be kept by all the universe; even on this earth alone it cannot be kept by all at the same time; but all can keep a seventh part of the time. This principle upon which the fourth commandment was based, may be of universal application in earth and in heaven, in time or eternity. But just which day that shall be, is a matter of minor consequence to be determined by the circumstances in the case, which may and must differ at different times and different places. To the Jewish people it certainly was the seventh day, or Saturday, and no other day would have met the commandment. All the rigorous limitations and exactions of the Sabbath day, as under the Jewish law, could be carried out by a small people in a limited territory where the church bore rule. A particular day, the seventh, Deut. 5: 12-13; definite hours, sunset to sunset, Lev. 23: 32; no fires in all their houses, Ex. 35: 3; stoning to death for picking up a stick, Num. 15: 32-36—this was the Jewish law. But we are not Jews nor under the Jewish law. Under the new dispensation of the gospel, other circumstances have arisen plainly and grandly marking another day as the all important day in Christian memory—the resurrection day. When the gospel was to go to all nations, to all climates, and around the earth, the Christian rest day was necessarily and wisely left upon a far different basis.

THE NATURE OF THE SABBATH COMMANDMENT. 177

WHERE SHALL WE BEGIN THE DAY?

If a man's salvation depends upon keeping the same day to a minute that God kept at creation, then it is infinitely important that we know exactly to a rod where his day began so as to begin ours there too. But the Lord has not said a word about it nor given the least clue as to where to begin the day. Nor do Sabbatarians *know* anything about it, but have to guess at the whole thing. The day is now generally reckoned to begin at a certain line 180 degrees west from Greenwich, England. It runs north and south through the Pacific Ocean about 4,000 miles west of America. I wrote Prof. E. S. Holden of Lick Observatory asking, "1. Have we the date when the day line was established there? 2. Who did it, and why? 3. When? 4. Has it been reckoned from other places than Greenwich?" He answered: "1. There was no one date. 2. No one For convenience. 3. During the last hundred years. 4. Yes. Canary Islands, Tenereffe, Ferro, Paris, Berlin, Jerusalem, Washington, etc." So we see: 1. It is only within the last hundred years that the day line has been fixed where it now is. 2. This was done merely for convenience, not because there was anything in nature requiring it. 3. At different times the day line has been counted from at least seven different places, from Jerusalem in the east to Washington in the west, about 8,000 miles difference, or one-third the way around the earth. Hence, the beginning of the seventh day has varied that much at different dates. 4. In another century it may be changed again. 5. There is just as much authority for one place as the other, and no divine authority for either, as it is all man's work and done at hap-hazard. 6. Hence, so far as duty to God is concerned, any nation, church or society is at liberty to begin the day wherever they please. One place will be just as apt to be in harmony with God's day line as another.

Sabbatarians in America can fix their day line in the Atlantic instead of in the Pacific and then our Sunday will be Saturday, and they will be all right and convert a nation in a day! Could any one prove that this would not be in harmony with God's day line at creation? Certainly not. It would be just as apt to be right as the present day line. Then why not do it? Indeed, this is exactly parallel to what Seventh-Day Adventists have done within the past few years in the case of a whole colony in the Pacific Ocean. Pitcairn Island, in the Pacific, was settled one hundred years ago by persons who brought their reckoning eastward from Asia. But it happens to be on the American side of the present day line; hence their Sunday was our Saturday, and they all kept it one hundred years as Sunday. According to Adventists, this was an awful thing, for Sunday is the Pope's Sabbath, the mark of the beast! So, a few years ago, Adventists went there and converted them all to keeping Saturday. How? They simply induced them to change their reckoning of the day line a few miles and lo! their Sunday was Saturday! Now they are all pious Sabbath-keepers while before they were all keeping Sunday, the mark of the beast! And yet they are keeping exactly the same day they always kept! If this is not hair-splitting, tell me what is. It illustrates the childishness of the whole Sabbatarian business. Now let the Adventists just shift their day line a little further east to include America and they can keep our day with us.

If the day began in the traditional place where Eden is said to have been located, then the day line would be away west of the present location some 7,000 miles, west even of Australia; and then the Seventh-Day people in Australia are not keeping the Sabbath at all. In that case the Sunday-keepers of New Zealand and Australia are now actually keeping the original seventh day, and Sabbatarians there are keeping the sixth day! Do they know, and can they prove, that this is not so? No; they simply have to take the reckoning just as it happened to be, right or wrong, without knowing which it is. And yet, at great expense, they have sent missionaries there to convert the people over to keep another day, when actually they do not know but what those people are really keeping the seventh day, and they themselves are wrong! None, not even themselves, pretend to know where God began to reckon that day; yet they draw the line to a hair, and say that all will be damned who do not toe that line and count from that spot! Does the salvation of a man's soul depend upon such mathematical niceties and such uncertainties as these? If it does, we may well despair of heaven.

The very fact that God has never revealed just where the true day line is, or where the seventh day began, shows that it is of no consequence for us to know. Alaska, the northwest point of America, was settled by Russians ages ago, before the present day line existed. Of course they brought their reckoning with them and hence their Sunday was on Saturday. In 1867 we bought Alaska and it became a part of the United States. The day we took possession our laws changed their Sunday to Saturday, all by human authority. Did that change the Edenic Sabbath for that people? Again, in going around the earth one way we lose a day and going the other way we gain a day. Hence, in one case we must add a day and in the other drop a day. All have to do this to keep in harmony with the world. Adventists do this, but by what authority, and where? The Bible says keep the seventh day and from sunset to sunset. Ex. 20: 8-11; Lev. 23: 32. Let two Adventists start from Chicago, one going east, the other west, around the earth. Each keeps carefully the seventh day as the sun sets. When they meet again at Chicago they will be two days apart! One will be keeping Sunday and the other Friday. How do they manage it! Each gives up his seventh day and both take that of the world. So they only have a worldly day after all!

Look also at the difficulty in crossing this supposed day line in the Pacific Ocean. I have personally conversed with Sabbatarians who have crossed this line both ways, east and west. Going west, a day is *added*, going east it is dropped, and this is done at *noon* of the day which finds them nearest the supposed line. On the vessel, a man going west sits down to dinner 11:50 a. m. Friday. While he is eating the time is changed and he rises from dinner Saturday noon! Then he has only six hours of Sabbath till sunset; or coming east, he sits down to dinner Saturday noon and rises from dinner Friday noon! He has kept eighteen hours Sabbath; then it is gone in a second at high noon, and he has six hours to work till sunset. Now he must begin Sabbath once more and keep it over again—twenty-four hours! In one case he only kept six hours Sabbath, and in the other case he kept forty-two hours!

These stubborn facts demonstrate the utter absurdity of the Sabbatarian view. They claim that these things do not bother them any; but I know that they do, and badly, too. They have written much on it, devised all sorts of diagrams, illustrations and arguments to meet the difficulty; but none are satisfactory, even to themselves. Hence new methods are constantly being devised to dodge the difficulty. The latest discovery is that adopted by the Seventh-Day Adventist ministers of the New York conference. It is that the earth is absolutely *flat* and *stationary*, with sun, moon and stars much smaller than the earth and revolving around it! "The sun, he do move," the old darkey said, and they say, Amen.

THE SABBATH AT THE NORTH POLE.

Now test the definite Seventh-Day theory in the frozen regions of the north. The day must be kept from sunset to sunset. Lev. 23:32. But in the winter there are months when the sun is not seen there at all, so they have no sunset. And again, in summer there are months when the sun is above the horizon all the time, when there is no sunset. Here the theory breaks down entirely, and the day must be reckoned by artificial means. They can keep one-seventh of the time, and that is absolutely all that can be done. Seventh-Day Adventists have argued that there was no real difficulty here; it was all imaginary. They try to bluff it off with a laugh; but that does not answer the facts. I know that they themselves have got into serious trouble right here. So great was their difficulty, even in northern Sweden and Norway, that in 1886 it was seriously discussed as to whether they must not change and reckon the day not from sunset as now, but from 6 P. M. Mrs. White and son were there and favored the change.[1] I was on a committee of the General Conference to investigate the matter. We decided against the change and it was abandoned. What endless and needless difficulties people get themselves into trying to keep a law which was only designed for the Jews in a limited locality. How contrary to the freedom and simplicity of the gospel!

In reply to all these facts, which cannot be denied, Seventh-Day people say: Is not the first day of the week, or Sunday, just as definite a day as the seventh day, or Saturday? Is it not just as difficult to keep Sunday all around the world as it is to keep Saturday? Do you not claim that you should keep the first day in honor of the resurrection? and will it do, then, to keep some other day? The answer to these questions is not hard to give. The essential idea is that we should devote one day in seven to religious duties. To secure the highest good, all should unite in observing the same day. From the days of the apostles the Christian church has, with one consent, observed the day on which Jesus rose from the dead, the first day of the week, or Sunday. But it is not claimed that it is absolutely essential that exactly the same minutes and hours, or even the same definite day, must be kept anyway and under all circumstances, whether or no. That would be legalism, and contrary to the very nature and freedom of the gospel. Suppose the Jewish day on which Jesus arose was reckoned from sunset to sunset, as doubtless it was, must we also reckon it that way? As it is found more convenient to reckon the day from midnight to midnight, and as all are united in doing so, it is for the best interests of religion to conform to this custom. If, in traveling around the world, men should mistake their longitude, as in case of Alaska and Pitcairn's Island, and call Saturday Sunday, it is not material. They had better all unite on that than to quarrel over it.

If, in the long period of darkness at the north pole, men should lose the time, and then select some other period than that which exactly corresponds to our Sunday, hour for hour, the difference would not be material. Or, if in locating the day line from which to reckon the beginning of the day, that line had happened to be located 5,000 miles further east or 10,000 further west, it would not have made a particle of difference. And as to whether we now begin the day just where God did in Eden or not, is a matter of no consequence. And whether our brethren in China rest at the same time we do or not, is of little account. And whether the Sabbath of Jupiter and Mars and Neptune, and of heaven itself, comes when ours does or not, is of little interest to us. It will be time enough to settle that matter when we go to live with them. So, while traveling around the earth, east or west, or crossing the day line, whether or not we are able to keep exactly the same time, or even exactly one-seventh part of time to a minute, is of little importance. We do the best we can under the circumstances, and conform to the time as reckoned by those where we go. To "strain at a gnat and swallow a camel," is not a good practice in any cause. But with the strict Sabbatarian all this is entirely different. A certain day, beginning at precisely such a line to a hair, and at such a minute to a second, is holy time. If you don't hit that exact time just right, you might as well keep no day at all! That may do for Judaism, but it certainly is not according to the spirit and freedom of the gospel.

I believe this is a fair statement of the position held by the great body of the intelligent observers of Sunday. It harmonizes exactly with the statement of our Savior, that "the Sabbath was made for man, and not man for the Sabbath." Mark 2:27. Man and his highest good are first; the Sabbath is secondary and subservient to these. Practically, the Sabbatarian exactly reverses this order. The Sabbath is the all-important thing, a rigid, iron rule, unbending and inflexible. Man and his necessities and his good are of little or no account in comparison with the supremely great duty to keep the Sabbath. "Man was made for the Sabbath, and not the Sabbath for man," would much better express their idea of the relative importance of the two. It is well for the people and the world that such pharisaical ideas have found few advocates in the church of Christ.

LOST TIME.

Then how do Sabbatarians know that our Saturday is the exact seventh day from creation down? Says Rev. J. H. Potts, D. D., editor of the Michigan (Methodist) Christian Advocate: "That in selecting the Jewish Sabbath day, Moses selected the regular successive seventh day of human time from Adam down cannot be proved by any authority, human or divine." The Lord's Day our Sabbath, page 12. This is endorsed by Bishop Harris and several other eminent divines. So Rev. Geo. Elliott, in his "Abiding Sabbath," says: "There is no possible means of fixing the day of the original Sabbath." So say all unbiased writers.

During the long period before the flood; during the patriarchal age when they had no records; during their slavery in Egypt when even traditional knowledge was largely lost; during the anarchy under the judges, and all down the ages since, are they sure that no mistake has been made, not even of one day? Of course they are not. The only possible way they can tell is by human tradition. In answer to my inquiry upon the point, Rabbi Isaac M. Wise, Cincinnati, O., the most learned Jew of the land, wrote me: "The Jewish Sabbath is, in point of the particular time, a matter of tradition." So after all, their Sabbath-keeping rests upon tradition of men, the very thing Adventists condemn.

But it is said that if the day had been lost, God knew which it was and would have pointed it out at the giving of the manna. Or if it had been lost before Christ's time, he would have known it and would have corrected them. But this assumes the very thing to be proved, viz.: that God cares as much about special hours and minutes as they do. This they can not prove. Evidently from the slight importance which he attached to keeping the Jewish Sabbath Jesus would have kept any day which he found observed by the nation.

CHAPTER X.

WHY CHRISTIANS KEEP SUNDAY.

Almost universally Christians regard Sunday as a sacred day. Do they offer for this any adequate reasons? Yes, indeed, and those which have been satisfactory to all the best and ablest Christians the church has ever had. After keeping the seventh day and extensively advocating it for over a quarter of a century, I became satisfied that it was an error, and that the blessing of God did not go with the keeping of it. Like thousands of others, when I embraced the Seventh-Day Sabbath I thought that the argument was all on one side, so plain that one hour's reading ought to settle it, so clear that no man could reject the Sabbath and be honest. The only marvel to me was that everybody did not see and embrace it.

But after keeping it twenty-eight years; after having persuaded more than a thousand others to keep it; after having read my Bible through, verse by verse, more than twenty times; after having scrutinized, to the very best of my ability, every text, line and word in the Bible having the remotest bearing upon the Sabbath question; after having looked up all these, both in the original and in many translations; after having searched in lexicons, concordances, commentaries and dictionaries; after having read armfuls of books on both sides of the question; after having read every line in all the early church fathers upon this point; and having written several works in favor of the Seventh-Day, which were satisfactory to my brethren; after having debated the question for more than a dozen times; after seeing the fruits of keeping it, and weighing all the evidence in the fear of God, I am fully settled in my own mind and conscience that the evidence is against the keeping of the Seventh-Day.

Those who observe Sunday say that they do it in honor of the resurrection of Christ upon that day, and that this practice was derived from the apostles and has been continued in the church ever since. Let us see. "The Lord's Day" is a term now commonly applied to the first day of the week, in honor of the Lord's resurrection on that day. Thus: "We believe the Scriptures teach that the first day of the week is the Lord's day." Baptist Church Directory, page 171. Excepting a few Sabbatarians of late date, all christendom, numbering four hundred and sixteen million people, of all sects and all nations, regard Sunday as a sacred day and agree in applying the term "Lord's Day" to Sunday. So every dictionary, lexicon and cyclopedia applies that term to the first day. Here is a grand, undeniable fact of to day. When did this stream begin? Let us trace it up to its head through all the centuries.

18th century, A. D. 1760. Rev. A. H. Lewis, D. D., Seventh-Day Baptist, is the author of "Critical History of Sunday Legislation." From page 181 I quote: "The profanation of the Lord's Day is highly offensive to Almighty God." Laws of Massachusetts, A. D. 1760.

17th century, A. D. 1676. The Laws of Charles II of England say: "For the better observation and keeping holy the Lord's Day, commonly called Sunday, be it enacted," etc. Critical History of Sunday Legislation, page 108.

16th century, A. D. 1536. Going back over 300 years ago to the reformers, we find all Christians calling Sunday the "Lord's Day." Calvin, voicing the universal sentiment of his time, says: "The ancients have, not without sufficient reason, substituted what we call the Lord's

Day in the room of the Sabbath." Calvin's Institute, Book 2, chapter VIII, section 34. Luther, Zwingle, Beza, Bucer, Cranmer, Tyndale, etc., likewise speak of the Lord's Day as the first day of the week. Here is another great fact as to the Lord's Day. It was in existence and universally observed 300 years ago.

15th century, A. D. 1409. "He that playeth at unlawful games on Sundays * * * shall be six days imprisoned." Statute of Henry IV of England. Critical History of Sunday Legislation, page 90.

14th century, A. D. 1359. "It is provided by sanctions of law and canon that all Lord's Days be venerably observed." Archbishop of Canterbury. Critical History of Sunday Legislation, page 82.

13th century, A. D. 1281. "The obligation to observe the legal Sabbath according to the form of the Old Testament is at an end * * * to which in the New Testament hath succeeded the custom of spending the Lord's Day * * * in the worship of God." Archbishop of Canterbury. Critical History of Sunday Legislation, page 81.

12th century, A. D. 1174. "We do ordain that these days following be exempt from labor: * * * All Sundays in the year," etc. Emperor of Constantinople. History of Sabbath and Sunday, page 191.

11th century, A. D. 1025. "Sunday marketing we also strictly forbid." Laws of Denmark. Critical History of Sunday Legislation, page 77.

10th century, A. D. 975. "Sunday is very solemnly to be reverenced." Saxon Laws. Critical History of Sunday Legislation, page 75.

9th century, A. D. 813. "All Lord's Days shall be observed with all due veneration and all servile work shall be abstained from." Council of Mayence.

8th century. In the year 747, an English council said:

"It is ordered that the Lord's Day be celebrated with due veneration, and wholly devoted to the worship of God." Andrew's History of the Sabbath, page 377.

7th century, A. D. 695. "If a slave work on Sunday by his lord's command, let him be free." Saxon Laws. Critical History of Sunday Legislation, page 71.

6th century, A. D. 578. "On the Lord's Day it is not permitted to yoke oxen or to perform any other work except for appointed reasons." Council of Auxerre.

5th century. Passing back to about A. D. 450, we come to the history of the church written by Sozomen. In book 2, Chapter VIII, page 22, of Constantine, he says: "He honored the Lord's Day, because on it he arose from the dead." This shows what was meant by Lord's Day in those early times.

Stepping back once more to about A. D. 400, we reach the great theologian of the early church, St. Augustine. He says: "The day now known as the Lord's Day, the eighth, namely, which is also the first day of the week." Letters of St. Augustine, letter 55, Chapter XIII. He says the first day of the week was known as the Lord's Day in his times.

4th century. In A. D. 386, the Emperors of Rome decreed as follows: "On the day of the sun, properly called the Lord's Day, by our ancestors, let there be a cessation of lawsuits, business, and indictments." Critical History of Sunday Legislation, page 36. Even the civil law at that early date recognized Sunday as the Lord's Day.

Going back again to the era of Constantine the Great, the first Christian Emperor, we reach Eusebius, the "Father of Church History," A. D. 324. He constantly and familiarly uses the term "Lord's Day" for the first day of the week. One passage: "They (the Jewish Christians) also observe the Sabbath, and other discipline of the Jews, just like them; but, on the other hand, they also celebrate the Lord's Days very much like us in commemoration of his resurrection."

Eccl. History, book 3, Chapter XXVII. Here Lord's Day is distinguished from the Jewish Sabbath, and is said to be kept on account of the resurrection.

This brings us to the era of the Early Christian Fathers. I quote them as translated in the "Ante-Nicene Christian Library."

A. D. 306. Peter, Bishop of Alexandria in Egypt: "But the Lord's Day we celebrate as a day of joy, because on it, he rose again." Canon 15.

3d century, A. D. 270. Anatolius, Bishop of Laodicea, in Asia Minor: "Our regard for the Lord's resurrection which took place on the Lord's Day will lead us to celebrate it." Chapter X.

About A. D. 250. The Apostolical Constitution: "On the day of our Lord's resurrection, which is the Lord's Day, meet more diligently." Book 2, section 7.

A. D. 250, Cyprian, Bishop of Carthage in Africa: "The eighth day, that is, the first day after the Sabbath and the Lord's Day." Epistle 58, section 4.

A. D. 200. Tertullian in Africa: "We solemnize the day after Saturday in contradiction to those who call this day their Sabbath." Apology, Chapter XVI. "We however, just as we have received, only on the day of the Lord's resurrection, ought to guard not only against kneeling, but every posture and office of solicitude, deferring even our business." On Prayer, Chapter XXIII.

2nd century, A. D. 194. Clement of Alexandria, Egypt: "He, in fulfillment of the precept, according to the gospel, keeps the Lord's Day, when he abandons an evil disposition, and assumes that of the Gnostic, glorifying the Lord's resurrection in himself." Book 7, Chapter XII.

A. D. 180. Bardesanes, Edessa, Asia: "On one day, the first of the week, we assemble ourselves together." Book of the Laws of Countries.

A. D. 140. Justin Martyr: "But Sunday is the day on which we all hold our common assembly, because Jesus Christ, our Savior, on the same day rose from the dead." Apology, Chapter LXVII.

A. D. 120. Barnabas. "We keep the eighth day with joyfulness, the day also on which Jesus rose again from the dead." Chapter XVII.

A. D 96. St. John on Patmos: "I was in the spirit on the Lord's Day." Rev. 1: 10.

A. D. 60. Luke, Asia Minor: "And upon the first day of the week, when the disciples came together to break bread, Paul preached unto them." Acts. 20: 7.

Thus we have traced the Lord's Day or Sunday as a sacred day among Christians from our time back through all the centuries up to the New Testament itself.

Who can fail to see that the "Lord's Day" and the "first day of the week" are spoken of in the same manner both by the apostles and down through all the fathers and reformers to our day? To every unbiased mind the evidence must be conclusive that the Lord's Day of Rev. 1: 10, written A. D. 96, is the resurrection day the same as it is in every instance where it is used by all the Christian fathers immediately following John. Mark this fact: *In not one single instance either in the Bible or in all history* can a passage be found where the term the *Lord's Day is applied to* the seventh day, the *Jewish Sabbath*. This fact should be, and is decisive as to the meaning in Rev. 1: 10. Even Sabbatarians themselves do not call the seventh day the Lord's Day, but always say "Sabbath day."

TESTIMONY OF LEXICONS AND CYCLOPEDIAS.

Webster: "Sunday, the first day of the week; the Christian Sabbath; the Lord's Day."

Smith's Dictionary of the Bible: "Lord's Day. The

first day of the week, or Sunday, of every age of the church."

Schaff-Herzog Encyclopedia: "Lord's Day, the oldest and best designation of the Christian Sabbath, first used by St. John." Rev. 1: 10.

Buck's Theological Dictionary, article Sabbath. "It (the first day of the week) is called the Lord's Day." Rev. 1: 10.

Johnson's New Universal Cyclopedia: "Lord's Day, a name for the first day of the week, derived from Rev. 1: 10."

The Greek words rendered "Lord's Day," [Rev. 1: 10,] are *Kuriake hemera*. *Kuriake*, the adjective, is from the noun *kurious*, and is thus defined:

"*Kuriakos*—Of, or pertaining to the Lord, *i. e.*, the Messiah; the Lord's. 1 Cor. 11: 20; Rev. 1: 10."—*Greenfield*.

"*Kuriakos*—Pertaining to the Lord, to the Lord Jesus Christ: e. g., *kuriakos deipnon*, the Lord's supper. [1 Cor. 11: 20;] *kuriake hemera*, the Lord's Day [Rev. 1: 10."]—*Robinson*.

"*Kurikos*—Of, belonging to, concerning a lord or master, especially belonging to the Lord (Christ); hence *kuriake hemera*, the Lord's Day."—*Liddell & Scott*.

"This is the usual name of Sunday with the subsequent Greek fathers."—*Parkhurst*.

"*Kuriakos*—Pertaining to the Lord Jesus Christ; the Lord [1 Cor. 11: 20; Rev. 1: 10."]—*Bagster's Analytical Greek Lexicon*.

So we might go all through the lexicons, finding the same definitions in all. Not a single one refers this term to God the Father, but without an exception all refer it to the Lord Jesus. There must be some good reason for this universal agreement.

So the commentators. "The Lord's Day. **The first day of the week.**" Dr. Clark on Rev. 1: 10.

"On the Lord's Day, which can be meant of no other than the day on which the Lord Jesus arose from the dead, even the first day of the week." Scott on Rev. 1: 10.

Dr. Barnes says: "This was a day particularly devoted to the Lord Jesus, for (a) that is the natural meaning of the word Lord as used in the New Testament; and (b) if the Jewish Sabbath was intended to be designated, the word Sabbath would have been used."

Prof. Hacket, in his comments on Acts 1: 24, says: "*Kuriakos*, when taken absolutely in the New Testament, refers generally to Christ."

"Lord's Day, namely, the first day of the week."—*Burkett's Notes on the N. T.*

"The Lord's Day, the Christian Sabbath, the first day of the week."—*Eclectic Commentary on Rev. 1: 10.*

"The Lord's Day. The first day of the week, commemorating the Lord's resurrection." Family Bible with notes, on Rev. 1: 10. Go through the whole list of commentaries, and all say the same thing. Have they no ground for this? Yes, good enough to be conclusive.

1. In all the Bible, the seventh day is never once called the Lord's Day.

2. "The Sabbath" was the term invariably used for the Jewish seventh day. John himself always used that term when speaking of the seventh day. See John 5: 9, 10, 16, 18; 7: 22, 23; 9: 14, 16; 19: 31. Had he meant that day in Rev. 1: 10, he certainly would have said "Sabbath Day," not Lord's Day.

3. The Greek word *kuriakos*, is a new word originating in the New Testament and found only in one other place, 1 Cor. 11: 20, "the Lord's supper." Beyond dispute it here applies to the Lord Jesus. "The adjective *kuriake* was 'formed by the apostles themselves.' [Winer, N. T. Gram., page 226.] To the same effect testify Liddell and

Scott. Of the mode of dealing with words in their lexicon, they say. 'We have always sought to give the earliest authority for its use first. Then, if no change was introduced by later writers, we have left it with that early authority alone.' (Pref. page 20.) When we turn to the word *kuriakos*, they give as their first citation, and therefore, as its earliest authority, the New Testament. The question now arises why form a new word to express a sacred institution, if the institution itself be not new? Winer says: 'Entirely new words and phrases were constructed mainly by composition, and for the most part to meet some sensible want.' (Gram. page 25.) What conceivable sensible want respecting the Sabbath did the Old Testament leave unexpressed? Clearly the new want arose from a new institution. This position receives additional strength from the fact that the only other New Testament use of *kuriakos* is found in 1 Cor. 11: 20, designating 'the Lord's supper,' which is certainly a new institution." Peter Vogel in debate with Waggoner, page 110. This is a strong point and should be decisive.

4. As the gospel was a new institution, it necessitated the use of new terms. So we have "Christians," Acts 11: 26, as the new name for God's people; "apostles," "evangelists," and "deacons" as the officers of the new church; "baptism" as the initiatory rite into the church, the "Lord's supper," 1 Cor. 11: 20, and the "Lord's Day," as institutions of that church. Rev. 1: 10. The new relations as originated by the gospel could not be expressed by the old terms of the law; hence new words and new terms had to be used. For 1,500 years "Sabbath" had been the established name of the weekly rest day of the law and was still used by all for the seventh day. Hence if Christians were to have a new weekly rest day commemorating gospel facts, they must find a new term for it. Hence we have "Lord's Day."

UNDER THE GOSPEL JESUS IS LORD.

There is a good reason why in the gospel the "Lord's Day" is Christ's day. Officially and emphatically he is the one Lord in this dispensation.

The term Lord applies to Christ about four hundred and fifty times in the New Testament. Hence in the gospel all things are commonly spoken of as belonging to Jesus as, "the disciples of the Lord," etc. Acts 9: 1. Now read together "The Lord's body," 1 Cor. 11: 29, "this cup of the Lord," "blood of the Lord," Verse 27, "Lord's death," Verse 26, "the Lord's table," 1 Cor. 10: 21. "The Lord's supper." 1 Cor. 11: 20, "the Lord's Day," Rev. 1: 10. Do not all refer to the same Lord? Of course they do, and who can fail to admit it? Under the official jurisdiction of Jesus the Lord, come of necessity all the institutions now obligatory. Hence Lord's Day is Christ's Day, and that is the way it is always used in the early fathers as we have seen.

Objections answered: The seventh day is called the "Sabbath of the Lord," Ex. 20: 10; "my holy day," Isa. 58: 13; and Jesus says he was "Lord of the Sabbath day," Mark 2: 28. Isn't that the Lord's Day? No; for: 1. The word Sabbath is used in each of these three texts but is not in Rev. 1: 10. 2. All three texts were spoken before the cross and under the law, but Rev. 1: 10, is under the gospel. 3. The Jewish Sabbath was abolished at the cross, Col. 2: 16; Rom. 14: 5; Gal. 4: 10, sixty years before John wrote on Patmos, hence that could not have been the Lord's day when John wrote. 5. The fact that the term "Lord's day" immediately after the time of John, whenever used by the early church, was always applied to Sunday, and never to the Sabbath, settles its meaning in Rev. 1: 10.

But it is objected that John and all the other evangelists in the gospels call Sunday simply "the first day of the week," instead of the Lord's day. Hence if John, in Rev.

1: 10, had meant that day he would have said "first day of the week," as he did in the gospel. The answer is easy. Jesus predicted that he would be put to death and rise the third day. Each evangelist is careful to show that the prediction was fulfilled. Hence they were particular to give the names of those three days as they were called by the Jews; that is, "preparation day," "Sabbath day," and "first day of the week." This is a sufficient answer. Moreover, it is probable that the resurrection day was not immediately called the Lord's day; but by the time John wrote the Revelation, A. D. 96, it had come to be the well known name for that day, as we have shown.

WHY IT IS FITTING THAT THE FIRST DAY OF THE WEEK SHOULD BE THE MEMORIAL DAY OF THE GOSPEL.

Why do people keep any day? Always because of what occurred on that day. Why were the Sabbath, the passover, and other days kept? Because of what occurred on those days. Why do we observe the 4th of July, Christmas, the days of our birth, marriage, etc? It is important, then, to inquire if anything occurred on Sunday to make it worthy of being observed by Christians.

Of all things used to commemorate past events, a memorial day is the best. A monument, a statute, a college, and the like are local and only seen by the few; but a day comes to all and regularly. Hence with what enthusiasm every nation celebrates its memorial days, as our own 4th of July. So religion has consecrated memorial days, as the Sabbath, the Passover, Pentecost, and others of the Jewish age. And shall the grandest of all institutions, the gospel, have no memorial day? If so it would be the one only exception among all the religions of the world and a great loss to the church. If the material creation merited a memorial day, how much more the spiritual redemption of the race?

But why theorize? It is the grandest and best known fact in all the earth to-day that the Christian church has a memorial day, the day of the Lord's resurrection, the Lord's day. It is regularly observed in every nation under Heaven. We have already shown how this day has always from the very days of the apostles, been regarded as a memorial day. It only remains to inquire, if it was the one day best adapted to this purpose. Study the life of Jesus, scan every noted day in it, in the year, in the month, in the week, and it must be admitted by all that no other than the resurrection day could be thought of for a moment. Think over the days of the week. How meager are the events of any other day compared with those of the resurrection day. Monday what? Tuesday? Wednesday? Thursday his betrayal; Friday his death; Saturday in the grave. Would we select any of these days as a memorial day for a rejoicing church? Surely not.

"On the Jewish Sabbath the Saviour lay under the power of death. It was to his disciples a day of restlessness and gloom. The remembrance of that day would always be to them grievous. The thought of the agony, the cross, the bitter cry, the expiring groan, and the mournful sepulcher could only create a feeling of sorrow. Forevermore the Jewish Sabbath day was despoiled of its gladness to the Christian heart." The Lord's Day Our Sabbath, page 21.

It was the resurrection day on which every thing turned. Jesus might have lived the pure life he did, might have wrought all the miracles he did, might have died on the cross as he did, might have been buried as he was, yet all this would not have saved a soul if he had not risen from the dead. "If Christ be not raised, your faith is vain; ye are yet in your sins. Then they also which are fallen asleep in Christ are perished." 1 Cor. 15: 17-18. The resurrection completed the work which made Jesus the Saviour of the world. Jesus himself when asked for the evidence of his authority, pointed to his resurrection on the third day as the proof of it. John 2: 18-21; Matt. 12: 38-40; 16: 21. This test of his divinity was well known to all, for the Pharisees said to Pilate. "Sir, we remember that that deceiver said, while he was yet alive, After three days I will rise again." Matt. 27: 63.

When Jesus died, the hope of his disciples was buried with him, Luke 24: 17, 21, and the holy women were heartbroken. But the wicked Jews rejoiced and Satan triumphed while the angels mourned. If ever the devil had hope it was while Jesus was dead during that Sabbath day. But as Sunday begins to dawn, a mighty angel like lightning descends, the earth quakes, the grave opens and Christ arises a conqueror over Death, Hell, and the Grave. Matt. 28: 1-4. Satan's last hope is gone; the wicked Jews are dismayed; the holy women are glad; the hope of the disciples is revived; angels rejoice; the salvation of a world is secured; the sufferings and humiliation of the Son of God are ended; and he walks forth the Almighty Saviour, the Lord of all. Never such a morning dawned on this lost world before. No wonder it became the memorial day of the church. It was impossible to be otherwise.

Paul says that Jesus was "declared to be the Son of God with power, according to the Spirit of holiness, by the resurrection from the dead," Rom. 1: 4. It was this that proved his divinity. So that there will be a day of Judgment God "hath given assurance unto all men, in that he hath raised them from the dead." Acts 17: 31.

1. On Sunday Jesus rose from the dead. Mark 16: 9.
2. On this day he first appeared to his disciples.
3. On this day he met them at different places and repeatedly. Mark 16: 9-11; Matt. 28: 8-10; Luke 24: 34; Mark 16: 12-13; John 20: 19-23.

4. On this day Jesus blessed them, John 20: 19.

5. On this day he imparted to them the gift of the Holy Ghost. John 20: 22.

6. Here he first commissioned them to preach the gospel to all the world. John 20: 21; with Mark 16: 9–15.

7. Here he gave his apostles authority to legislate for and guide his church. John 20: 23.

8. Peter says God "hath begotten us again unto a lively hope by the resurrection of Jesus Christ from the dead." 1 Pet. 1: 3.

9. On this day Jesus ascended to his father, was seated at his right hand and made head over all. John 20: 17; Eph. 1: 20.

10. On that day many of the dead saints arose from the grave. Matt. 27: 52–53.

11. Here this day became the day of joy and rejoicing to the disciples. "Then were the disciples glad when they saw the Lord." John 20: 20. "While they yet believed not for joy." Luke 24: 41.

12. On that day the gospel of a risen Christ was first preached, saying: "The Lord is risen indeed." Luke 24: 34.

13. On that Sunday Jesus himself set the example of preaching the gospel of his resurrection by explaining all the scriptures on that subject and by opening the minds of the disciples to understand it.

"Then opened he their understanding, that they might understand the Scriptures." Luke 24: 27, 45.

14. Finally on this day the purchase of our redemption was completed.

With all these thrilling events of gospel facts crowded into that one resurrection day, making it memorable above all days in the history of the world, how could it but become the great day in the memory of the church? The facts of that one day became the theme of the church ever since. The great battle between the apostles and the unbelieving Jews was concerning the events of that day; did Jesus rise, or did he not? The Jews "gave large money" to disprove it, Matt. 28: 12, while the apostles built the church and staked their lives upon it. Thus in God's own providence, the Jewish Sabbath was thrown into the shade, while all the hopes and thoughts and arguments and songs of the new church were necessarily turned to another day, the resurrection day.

Memorable day, one that should stir the heart of every Christian and move sinners to repentance as indeed it has done every week from that day on. "The Lord's Day," how appropriate the title for that grand day on which our Lord triumphed over all and laid deep and secure the foundation of the Christian church. Most appropriately, then, has it become the one memorial day of the gospel, the day of gladness and rejoicing. Shall we, then, call it a pagan day? the pope's day? the mark of the beast? a day hateful to God and an abomination to Christ? God forbid. It was said of Jesus, "What evil hath he done?" So we ask, "What evil has the observance of the Lord's Day ever done?" What man, or church, or nation, has ever been made worse by it? Nay, verily, this is not its character nor its record.

THE EIGHTH DAY OF JOHN 20: 26.

I have become satisfied myself that the meeting of Christ with his disciples "after eight days," John 20: 26, was on Sunday. He had met with them the previous Sunday evening. Verse 19. Here "after eight days" he meets them again. Sabbatarians count up and satisfy themselves that this occurred on Monday or Tuesday. But compare this with the expression "after three days." The number of the day after his death on which Christ was to rise is given in three ways. 1. "In three days," Matt. 26: 61; 27: 40. 2. "The third day," Matt. 16: 21; 20: 19. 3. "After three days," Mark 8: 31. All these expressions mean the same. He died Friday and rose Sunday; hence Sunday was "three days," "the third day" and "after three days" in their common way of speaking. In the same way, "In eight days," "on the eighth day" and "after eight days" would all be the same, that is the next Sunday, or eighth day.

What strengthens this position is the well known fact that the term, "the eighth day," became a common term for the resurrection day among all the early Christian fathers. Thus Eld. Andrews, the seventh-day historian, writing of Dionysius, A. D. 170, says of Sunday, "Every writer who precedes Dionysius calls it first day of the week, 'eighth day,' or Sunday." Testimony of the Fathers, page 52. Thus Barnabas, A. D. 120 says: "We keep the eighth day with joyfulness, the day also, on which Jesus rose again from the dead." Epistle of Barnabas, Chapter XV. Justin Martyr, A. D. 140 says: "The first day after the Sabbath, remaining the first of all the days, is called however, the eighth, according to the number of all the days of the cycle, and [yet] remains the first." Dialogue with Trypho, Chapter XLI. And Cyprian, A. D. 250, says "the eighth day, that is the first day after the Sabbath, and the Lord's day." Epistle 58, Section 4. Where did the early church get the idea that the eighth day was the Lord's day, if not from the apostles? Evidently, then, the meeting in John 20: 26, was on Sunday. The only visits of Jesus with his disciples which the Holy Spirit saw fit to date carefully are those occurring on Sunday.

PENTECOST, ACTS 2.

That the day of Pentecost, Acts 2, fell on Sunday has been believed and maintained by Christians in all ages.

1. The time of Pentecost was thus stated: "Ye shall

count unto you from the morrow after the Sabbath from the day that ye brought the sheaf of the wave offering, seven Sabbaths shall be complete, even unto the morrow after the seventh Sabbath shall ye number fifty days." Lev. 23:15, 16. The day after the seventh Sabbath would certainly be the first day of the week.

2. The Karaite Jews held that Pentecost according to the law must always be on Sunday.

3. *Pentecost* means *fiftieth*, the fiftieth day after the first Sabbath where they began to count, hence it must fall on the first day of the week.

4. Dr. Scott's commentary says: "As Jesus arose on the first day of the week, so the Holy Spirit descended on the same, seven weeks, or on the fiftieth day afterwards." On Acts 2:1.

5. So plain is the point that even the Seventh-Day Adventists themselves have admitted it. Thus Elder U. Smith: "The sheaf of first fruits was waved on the sixteenth day of the first month. This met its antitype in the resurrection of our Lord, the first fruits of them that slept, the sixteenth of the first month. * * * The feast of weeks, or Pentecost, occurred on the *fiftieth day* from the offering of the first fruits. The antitype of this feast, the Pentecost of Acts 2, was fulfilled on that very day, *fifty days from the resurrection of Christ*, in the outpouring of the Holy Ghost upon the disciples." The Sanctuary, page 283, 284. Fifty days from the resurrection of Christ would be on the first day of the week. This is just what God directed; it was to be on the morrow after the seventh Sabbath and on the fiftieth day. Lev. 23:15, 16.

6. So the Eclectic Commentary: "It happened on the first day of the week." On Acts 2.

7. "Pentecost in that year must have fallen on the first day of the week." The Bible Commentary on Acts 1.

8. "That the day of Pentecost fell on Sunday is undeniable, because the resurrection of Christ was upon a Sunday, and Pentecost was the fiftieth day from the resurrection." Bramhall's Works, V. 51.

9. "It consequently occurred in the year in which Christ died on the first day of the week, or our Sunday." Lange on Acts 2:1.

10. "The Pentecost day was Sunday." Wheadon's Commentary on Acts 2:1.

Notice now the importance of that day. Jesus told the disciples to tarry in Jerusalem till endued with power from on high. Luke 24:49. They must begin their preaching there. Verse 47. On that Pentecost they were to be baptized with the Holy Ghost. Acts 1:5. In the last days of Judah and Jerusalem the law was to go forth out of Zion and the word of the Lord from Jerusalem while all nations were gathered to it. Isa 2: 1-4. All this was fulfilled on Pentecost. The Holy Ghost came on the disciples in mighty power; then they began preaching the gospel and thousands were converted. This was only the first fruits of what has occurred, in fact, on succeeding Sundays ever since. It has been the great day of power and of conversions in the church from that day on. Thus God signally honored Sunday at the very opening of the gospel as he has continued to do ever since.

ACTS 20: 6, 7.

All agree that the disciples had some regular day for meetings. Paul said: "Not forsaking the assembling of ourselves together." Heb. 10:25. This implies a regular time and a stated place for meetings. Reproving them for making the Lord's supper a feast, Paul says: "When ye come together therefore into one place, this is not to eat the Lord's supper," but rather to feast, 1 Cor. 11:20. This indicates that they had a place and a time to come together for the supper. There is not the slightest evidence that the Christians ever had the Lord's supper or held distinctively Christian worship on the Jewish Sabbath. In every case where meetings on the Sabbath are mentioned it is in connection with the regular Jewish worship. There is no record that Christians ever met alone for worship on that day. They certainly could not have had the Lord's supper in the synagogues on the Sabbath with the Jews. Nor is there the least intimation that it was ever tried. They must, therefore, have met by themselves in some other place than the synagogue and on some other day. Turning to Acts 20: 6, 7, we read: "And we sailed away from Phillippi after the days of unleavened bread, and came unto them to Troas in five days; where we abode seven days. And upon the first day of the week, when the disciples came together to break bread, Paul preached unto them, ready to depart on the morrow."

Here they met by themselves, and in an upper room, for the Lord's supper. The time is the first day of the week. The incidental manner in which it is mentioned shows that what they did was a well understood custom among them— "*When* they came together to break bread upon the first day of the week." Three things are mentioned: 1. They came together. It is mentioned as though all knew it was common for them to do this. 2. To break bread. This again is stated as though all knew that this, too, was a common practice with Christians. 3. Upon the first day of the week. Like the other two items, this is mentioned as a well understood practice among them; hence no explanation is given of it. It is said that the disciples "came together," or assembled themselves together, a common phrase for their church meetings. Thus Peter "went in and found many that were come together." Acts 10:27. "Ye *come together* not for the better. * * * When ye *come together* in the church." 1 Cor. 11:17, 18. "If therefore the whole church be *come together* into one place." "When ye *come together* every one of you hath a psalm." 1 Cor. 14:23, 26. "Not forsaking the *assembling* of yourselves together." Heb. 10:25. This indicates, therefore, their customary meeting.

Notice the further fact, verse 6, that Paul was there seven days, yet no notice whatever is taken of the Sabbath Day, not even to name it, while the first day is prominently noticed. The breaking of bread and the assembling on the first day of the week, it will be noticed, are connected together. Notice further, that though Paul was there a whole week and over the Jewish Sabbath, yet the Lord's supper is not administered until Sunday. This shows that for some reason Sunday was regarded by them as the only proper day for it. "It shows further, that Paul tarried there several days waiting for the regular day of worship to come, the first day of the week." "And the reason assigned for their coming together was to *break bread*, and not because Paul was there."

Sabbatarians argue that this meeting at Troas was on Saturday evening and hence Paul went on his journey Sunday morning. Even if this were so, it would not prove that Paul did not regard Sunday, for, hastening if possible to be at Jerusalem on Pentecost, verse 16, he had to go when the vessel went whether he liked to or not, for he was only a passenger. See verse 13, and chapter 21: 1, 2. But it is more probable that Luke reckoned time after the Roman method, from midnight to midnight, as John did in John 20:19. "The same day at evening, being the first day of the week." Here Sunday evening is reckoned as belonging to the first day. Luke wrote for the Gentiles, was a learned man himself, and wrote Acts long after the resurrection, when Roman ways were coming more to be adopted. Moreover the meeting at Troas was on the first day of the week and they departed "on the morrow," verse 7, which surely could not have been on the same day.

Prof. A. Rauschenbush, of Roschester Theological Seminary, says: "These events did not occur in the time of the Old Testament, but of the New; not in Palestine, but upon the west coast of Asia Minor, nearly a thousand miles away. Furthermore, this was the time of Roman rule, and upon every land and people that the Romans conquered they imposed, not only their laws, but also their mode of reckoning time. Now, from their earliest history, the Romans began the day at midnight. At this visit of Paul to Troas the west coast of Asia Minor had been in their possession for one hundred and eighty years." Saturday or Sunday, page 14. Prof. Hachett, on Acts 20:7, says: "As Luke had mingled so much with foreign nations and was writing for Gentile readers, he would be very apt to designate the time in accordance with their practice; so that his evening or night of the first day of the week would be the end of the Christian Sabbath and the morning of his departure that of Monday."

This is rendered almost certain by the fact that Acts is addressed to "Theophilus," who was not a Jew, but a Roman living in Italy. That the early Christians partook of the Lord's supper every Sunday, is acknowledged on all hands.

Dr Scott, on Acts 20:7, says: "This ordinance seems to have been constantly administered every Lord's Day."

Shaff-Herzog Encyclopedia, Art. "Lord's Supper" says: "Originally the communion was administered every day, then every Sunday."

"It is well known that the primitive Christians administered the Eucharist every Lord's Day."—*Doddridge.*

"In the primitive times it was the custom of many

churches to receive the Lord's supper every Lord's Day."—*Matthew Henry.*

"Every first day of the week."—*Carson.*

"All antiquity concurs in evincing that, for the first three centuries, all the churches broke bread once a week."—*Alex. Campbell, in "Christian System," page 325.* Dr. Albert Barnes on this verse says: "It is probable that the apostles and early Christians celebrated the Lord's supper on every Lord's Day."

The Apostolic Constitutions, about A. D. 250, says that on "the Lord's Day meet more diligently * * * [partaking of] the oblation the sacrifice, the gift of the holy food." Book II, section 7, paragraph 55. Again, "We solemnly assemble to celebrate the feast of the resurrection on the Lord's Day." Book VII, section 2, paragraph 36.

Fabian, bishop of Rome, A. D. 250: "On each Lord's Day the oblation of the altar should be made by all men and women in bread and wine." Decrees of Fabian, book V, chapter 7.

These testimonies throw great light upon the passages in the New Testament where the first day of the week, the Lord's Day, is referred to. They show that a weekly celebration of that day was established in all churches by the apostles themselves. If Adventists could find anywhere after the resurrection a gathering of Christians only for worship on the Sabbath, it would be used by them as evidence of a custom in favor of Saturday. Let them make the same deduction now in favor of Sunday.

1 COR. 16: 1–2.

With Acts 20 let us read 1 Cor. 16:1-2: "Now concerning the collection for the saints, as I have given order to the churches of Galatia, even so do ye. Upon the first day of the week let every one of you lay by him in store, as God hath prospered him, that there be no gatherings when I come." What Paul here directs the Corinthians to do he had also established among the churches at Galatia, verse 1. And this letter is addressed to "all that in every place call upon the name of Jesus Christ our Lord." Chapter 1: 2. He also says that what he writes must be received as "the commandments of the Lord." Chapter 14: 37. Here, then, is an inspired commandment of the Lord Jesus touching the first day of the week and it is to all that call upon his name. This requires a definite act of religious duty to be performed regularly upon each recurring Sunday, for this did not relate to simply one first day, but to each one as it came. They are to lay apart on that day a portion for the poor out of what God gives them. This implies that it would be with them a day of lesiure and devotion when they would be at home, have the time, and be in a proper frame of mind to do this benevolent act—an act of worship, "a sacrifice acceptable, well pleasing to God." Phil. 4: 18. Of old God had said none "shall appear before the Lord empty." Deut. 16: 16. On 1 Cor. 16: 1-2, Dr. Clark remarks: "The apostle follows here the rule of the synagogue; it was the regular custom among the Jews to make their collections for the poor on the Sabbath day." For this purpose they had " 'The purse of the alms,' or what we would term the *poor's box.* This is what the apostle seems to mean when he says, let him lay by him in store; let him put it in the alms purse or in the poor's box." On this text Dr. Barnes truthfully remarks: "There can have been no reason why this day should have been designated except that it was a day set apart to religion and therefore deemed a proper day for the exercise of benevolence towards others." Why did Paul name Sunday rather than any other day in the week if it was not a religious day ?

Adventists say that this does not imply any meeting that

day. They were only to lay by at home. But this would defeat the very object Paul had in view. Paul said he hasted to be at Jerusalem. He could not be delayed to gather up collections when he came. So they were to have them all collected and ready when he came. But if these gifts were all at their homes then the collection would have to be made after he came, just the thing he commanded to avoid, "that there be no collections when I come." Verse 2. Dr. Machnight renders it: "On the first day of every week, let each of you lay somewhat by itself according as he may be prospered, putting it into the treasury, that when I come, there may be no collections."

We have now found four things which the disciples did on Sunday.

1. They assembled together. 2. They had a sermon. 3. They had the Lord's supper. 4. They gave for the poor. Opening to the very first of the early Christian fathers we find it was the custom of all Christians to do just these things every Sunday. Thus Justin Martyr, A. D. 140, in his Apology, Chapter LXVII, says: "And on the day called Sunday, all who live in cities or in the country gather together in one place, and the memories of the apostles or the writings of the prophets are read, * * * bread and wine and water are brought, and the president in like manner offers prayers and thanksgiving, according to his ability, and the people assent, saying, Amen; and there is a distribution to each, and a participation of that over which thanks have been given, and to those who are absent a portion is sent by the deacons. And they who are well to do, and willing, give what each thinks fit; and what is collected is deposited with the president, who succors the orphans and widows."

This shows that our conclusion from the above texts was correct. Thus as we see on opening to the early apostolical fathers immediately following the apostles, we find all Christians of all sects in all parts of the world holding their meetings on Sunday in remembrance of the resurrection, just as we do now. This shows beyond all reasonable doubt that the custom was established by the apostles themselves, and that by the authority of Christ. John 20 : 21–23.

Consider this important fact witnessed the world over to-day. We have five abiding witnesses that Christ lived, all mentioned in the New Testament. 1st. *The Church.* "I will build my church." Matt. 16:18. 2nd. *New Testament.* John "wrote these things." John 21 : 24. 3d. *Baptism.* "Go baptizing them." Matt. 28 : 19. 4th. *Lord's Supper.* 1 Cor. 11 : 20; "Eat the Lord's Supper." 5th. *Lord's Day.* "On the Lord's Day." Rev. 1 : 10. There are now about 500,000,000 people professing faith in Christ, scattered among all nations differing in doctrine almost endlessly. This difference extends back almost to the days of the apostles. Yet all these differing sects hold in common these five memorials of Christ's life—the Church, the New Testament, Baptism, the Lord's Supper, and the Lord's Day. The Eastern Church, the Armenian, Syrian, Roman Catholic, Episcopal, Lutheran, Methodist, Baptist, and hundreds more, all hold sacredly these five things in some form. All agree that all five began back with the apostles and came from their hands. There is perfect agreement on this, viz., that one is as old as the other, that all have come down hand in hand together. These 500,000,000 all firmly believe and teach this. This unanimous agreement must be accounted for in some reasonable way. It cannot be ignored nor bluffed off lightly. There can be only one truthful answer—all must have started together at the beginning and have kept together till this day. And all history confirms it.

CHAPTER XI.

DID THE POPE CHANGE THE SABBATH?

The one great point in the Sabbath question upon which Seventh-Day Adventists stake the most, upon which they insist the strongest, which they repeat the most frequently and the most confidently, is that the pope of Rome did change the Sabbath from the seventh day to the first day. They assert that this is all the authority Sunday-keepers have for observing that day. Sunday is the pope's Sabbath, and Sunday-keeping is the mark of the beast, Rev. 14: 9-12, a terrible sin in the sight of God. See almost any work on the Sabbath published by them.

They claim that Sunday keeping came from the pagans through the pope into the church. Thus: "The name, origin, authority, and sacredness of the Sunday institution are altogether and only pagan." Replies to Elder Canright, page 133. Then the pope changed the Sabbath into the Sunday. Mrs. White says: "The pope had changed it [the Sabbath] from the seventh to the first day of the week." Again: "The pope has changed the day of rest from the seventh to first day." Early Writings, pages 26, 55. Again: "Here we find the mark of the beast. The very act of changing the Sabbath into Sunday, on the part of the Catholic church, without any authority from the Bible." The Mark of the Beast, page 23. "Sunday keeping must be the 'mark of the beast.'" The Marvel of Nations, by U. Smith, page 183. To this claim Mrs. White has set the seal of divine inspiration. She says: "The change of the Sabbath is the sign or mark of the authority of the Romish church." "The keeping of the counterfeit Sabbath is the reception of the mark." Great Controversy, Vol. 4, page 281.

This settles it with every Seventh-Day Adventist. My experience is that a belief of this as a fact induces more persons to give up Sunday for Saturday than all other arguments made by the seventh-day people. Convince a man that Sunday-keeping is only a Catholic institution, a rival to the Lord's Sabbath and hateful to God, and of course, if he has any conscience, he will keep it no longer. Every one of them accepts this as a historical fact in fulfillment of Daniel 7: 25. Indeed, this is the *one main pillar* in their whole system, upon which all the rest depends. If their position upon this point is false, then their whole system is also false, as they will readily admit. On this Elder Waggoner says: "Elder Canright did not exaggerate when he said that we consider this a material question. We do indeed so consider it." Replies to Elder Canright, page 165. Then they should be able to prove the point very plainly. They claim to be raised up to preach against this change of the Sabbath by the pope.

The unmingled wrath of God is soon to be poured out upon all who continue to keep Sunday, the Pope's Sabbath. It would seem that such a radical position should be supported by the clearest evidence. They claim that it is a historical fact that somewhere during the first five centuries after Christ, the pope did change the Sabbath to Sunday. If this be so, they should be able to produce reliable historical proof for it, giving the *time, manner, place, persons,* facts and reasons for so remarkable an occurrence. I have before me two books written expressly to prove this assertion. They are: "Who Changed the Sabbath?" 24 pages, and "Marvel of Nations," 282 pages. But the only direct proof offered is simply quotations from *Catholic Catechisms,* which claim that their church made the change! And is this all the historical (?) proof they can present on this point? Yes, for all that the Sabbatarian writers and scholars for the last 200 years have been able to find is just this and nothing more. Not one single historian in all the annals of the world has ever stated that the pope changed the Sabbath. For twenty-eight years I myself quoted these catechisms as proof positive on that subject.

Goaded by my call for proof on this point, the Adventists selected Elder Waggoner to answer it, to find some author who says that the pope changed the Sabbath. The elder made a desperate attempt, covering forty-nine closely printed pages. He searched the libraries of America and Europe. What did he find? If he had a passage to the point, he could have quoted it in a few lines. But he had none. Not a single author did he quote saying that the pope changed the Sabbath. So it rests merely on the claim of just these Catholic Catechisms. Then if we admit on their mere assertion the boastful claim of the Catholics that they changed the Sabbath, why not also admit their claim that the pope is infallible, that he has the keys of St. Peter, the chair of the apostle, the only true apostolic succession, etc.? Seventh-Day people quickly repudiate all these other claims of the Catholics, but eagerly admit their claim that they changed the Sabbath, simply because this suits their theory, for which they can find no other proof. They denounce Catholic writers as forgers, cheats, deceivers and liars, then, when it suits their purpose, turn around and quote their mere assertions as unquestionable truth!

Moreover, even the claims of the Catechism are misrepresented. The theory is that some hundreds of years after Christ the pope, by his own authority, changed the Sabbath, and the Catechisms are explained to teach this idea. But not one of them make such a claim or anything like it.

Every one of these Catholic quotations states distinctly that the change in the Sabbath was made, not by the pope, but "by the church" in the days of Christ and the apostles, not several hundred years afterward. Thus:

"Question. What are the days which the church commands to be kept holy?

"Answer. 1. The Sunday, or our Lord's day, which we observe by apostolic tradition, instead of the Sabbath." Catholic Christian Instructed, page 209.

From the same work, we take the following:

"Question. What warrant have you for keeping the Sunday, preferable to the ancient Sabbath, which was the Saturday?"

"Answer. We have for it the authority of the Catholic church, and apostolic tradition."

Catholics claim that their "church" originated in the days of the apostles, and any change made by the apostolic church was made by the Catholic church. Hence they claim that the "Catholic church" changed the Sabbath in the days of the apostles. Adventists in using these quotations from the Catechisms explain them as saying that the change was made by the apostate popes hundreds of years after the apostles. But the Catechisms claim no such thing, as is seen in the above quotations. Thus even the Catechisms, when fairly read, teach that Sunday observance originated with the Christian church in the days of the apostles, just the truth exactly.

That Adventists do misrepresent the teachings of the Catholics is shown by the following:

TESTIMONY OF A CATHOLIC PRIEST.

"Having lived for years among the Seventh-Day Adventists, I am familiar with their claims that the Pope of Rome changed the Sabbath from the seventh to the first day of the week. Such assertions are wholly unfounded. Catholics

claim no such thing; but maintain that the apostles themselves established the observance of Sunday and that we received it by tradition from them. The councils and popes afterwards simply confirmed the keeping of the day as received from the apostles.   JOHN MEILER,
   Rector of St. John's Church, Healdsburg, Cal."

The "Catholic Dictionary," by Addis and Arnold, after quoting Rev. 1:10; Acts 20:7; 1 Cor. 16:1, 2 says: These texts "seem to indicate that Sunday was already a sacred day on which deeds of love were specially suitable. Heb. 10:25 shows this much: that the Christians, when the epistle was written, had regular days of assembly. The scriptural references given above show that the observance of Sunday had begun in the apostolic age; but even were Scripture silent tradition would put this point beyond all doubt."

John Ankatell, A. M., priest of the diocese of New York, writing in the Outlook, July, 1889, says of Sunday, the Lord's Day: "We *think* it was given by our Lord to the apostles during the great forty days after his resurrection, but we cannot *prove* this." He states the Catholic doctrine exactly, viz: That the change was made by Christ and the apostles, but that the scriptures are not plain enough on this point to prove it; hence we have to rely upon Catholic authority which says it was made in New Testament times. All Catholics and all their catechisms say the same. But this is entirely different from saying that the pope made the change several hundred years after Christ. This is a sample of how Adventists pervert the testimony they use.[1]

We will now present historical evidence, proving that the observance of the first day of the week as a day of worship was universal among Christians in the days immediately following the apostles. If Sunday worship originated here, then it did not originate with the papacy, which came up several hundred years later.

[1] See Appendix E.

PLINY'S LETTER, A. D. 107.

Pliny was governor of Bithynia, Asia Minor, A. D. 106–108. He wrote A. D. 107 to Trajan, the emperor, concerning the Christians, thus: "They were wont to meet together, on a *stated day* before it was light, and sing among themselves alternately a hymn to Christ as God. * * * When these things were performed, it was their custom to separate and then to come together again to a meal which they ate in common without any disorder." Horne's Introduction, Vol. I, chapter 3, section 2, page 84. That this was Sunday is evident. 1. They came together to worship Christ. 2. They assembled to eat a meal together, the Lord's supper. We have already proved that the "stated day" for this was Sunday. "Upon the first day of the week when the disciples came together to break bread." Acts 20:7. This is exactly parallel to Pliny.

Eusebius, the historian, A. D. 324, says: "I think that he [the Psalmist] describes the morning assemblies in which we are accustomed to assemble throughout the world." "By this is prophetically signified the service which is performed very early and every morning of the resurrection day throughout the whole world." Sabbath Manual, page 125. This is exactly what Pliny says: They met together "on a stated day before it was light;" they assembled to eat together a meal. Eusebius says it was the custom of all Christians "to meet very early and every morning of the resurrection day." This ought to settle it and does. Pliny's stated day was Sunday. This was in the very region where the apostles labored, and only *eleven* years after St. John died. Elder Andrews, Sabbatarian, says: "This testimony of Pliny was written a few years subsequent to the time of the apostles. It relates to a church which probably had been founded by the apostle Peter." Hist. Sab., page 237. It shows that the apostles taught Sunday keeping.

BARNABAS, A. D. 120.

This epistle was highly prized in the earliest churches, read in some of them as part of scripture, and is found in the oldest manuscript of the scriptures, *namely the Sinaitic*. That it was written by a pious man of learning and influence cannot be doubted. Elder Andrews, Seventh-Day Adventist, admits that the epistle of Barnabas "was in existence as early as the middle of the second century, and, like the 'Apostolical Constitutions,' is of value to us in that it gives some clue to the opinions which prevailed in the region where the writer lived." Testimony of the Fathers, page 21.

The Schaff-Herzog Encyclopedia says: "The epistle was probaly written in Alexandria at the beginning of the second century and by a Gentile Christian." The Encyclopedia Brittanica, the highest critical authority, says: "This work is unanimously ascribed to Barnabas, the companion of St. Paul, by early Christian writers. * * * But the great majority of critics assign it to the reign of Hadrian sometime between 119 and 126 A. D." Smith's Dictionary of the Bible says: "The epistle is believed to have been written early in the second century." Johnson's New Universal Cyclopedia says: It "is supposed by Hefele to have been written between 107-120 A. D. * * * It is frequently cited by the Fathers, and was by many regarded as being of authority in the church; some even claiming for it a place in the sacred canon."

This is a summary of the best modern criticism as to the date, character and authority of the epistle of Barnabas. Read and reverenced in the church as next to the gospels themselves as early as A. D. 120, or within twenty-four years of the death of St. John, it shows what Christians believed and practiced immediately after the apostles. In this epistle we read: "Incense is a vain abomination unto me, and your new moons and Sabbaths I cannot endure.

He has, therefore, abolished these things." Chapter II. Elder Andrews admits that "he presently asserts the abolition of the Sabbath of the Lord." "Testimony," etc., page 22. Coming to the first day of the week, Barnabas says: "Wherefore, also, we keep the eighth day with joyfulness, the day, also, on which Jesus rose again from the dead." Chapter 15.

What does Elder Andrews say to this testimony? He admits that it teaches the abolition of the Jewish Sabbath and the keeping of Sunday. But he argues that such a doctrine is contrary to the Bible; that is, to *his* ideas of the Bible. While I was yet a firm believer in the seventh day, when reading this book, I was struck with the fact that Elder Andrews, all through his book, had to oppose and combat the teachings of all these early fathers! The reason is manifest: he held one doctrine and they held another. He believed in the seventh day, and they believed in the first day. Some of them lived early enough to have conversed with the apostles themselves, while he lived eighteen hundred years later! Which would be apt to know the best?

In his "History of the Sabbath," page 308, he says: "The reasons offered by the early fathers for neglecting the observance of the Sabbath show conclusively that they had no special light on the subject by reason of living in the first centuries, which we in this latter age do not possess." What a confession that is from the ablest historian the seventh day ever had! He admits that "the early fathers" "in the first centuries" neglected "the observance of the Sabbath." What further need have we for witness to prove that the seventh day was not observed in the first centuries? But how does this harmonize with the theory that the Sabbath was changed to Sunday by the pope several hundred years afterwards? Suppose those early fathers were not good theologians, nor able reasoners; could they not testify to a simple *fact?* Could they not state whether they did or did not keep Saturday? Surely they knew enough for that, and this is all we wish to ask.

We do not quote these fathers to prove a doctrine; for that we go only to the Bible. We quote them to prove a simple, historical *fact*, viz: that the early Christians did keep Sunday, hence it could not have started with the popes centuries later.

THE TEACHING OF THE APOSTLES, A. D. 125.

This was not written by the apostles; yet its date is very early. Some place it as early as A. D. 80. Professor Harnack, of Berlin, says many place it between A. D. 90, and A. D. 120. This is the date most favored. It can not be much later. The New York Independent says of it: "By all odds the most important writing exterior to New Testament." Professor D. R. Dungan, President of Drake University, says: "It is evident that it is not far on this side of the death of the apostle John." The noted scholar, Rev. Wilbur F. Crafts, in his Sabbath for Man, page 383, says: It was "written, as the best scholars almost unanimously agree, not later than forty years after the death of the last of the apostles, and during the lifetime of many who had heard John's teaching." In the preface to this important document, the editors, Profs. Hitchcock and Brown in the Union Theological Seminary, N. Y., say: "The genuineness of the document can hardly be doubted." "The document belongs undoubtedly to the second century; possibly as far back as 120 A. D.; hardly later than 160." Introduction.

Chapter fourteen of the Teaching of the Apostles says: "But every Lord's day do ye gather yourselves together, and break bread, and give thanksgiving," etc. This testimony is clear and decisive that the Lord's day was the established day of worship, at that early day.

JUSTIN MARTYR, A. D. 140.

I quote from "The Complete Testimony of the Fathers," by Elder Andrews: "Justin's 'Apology' was written at Rome about the year 140," "and this at a distance of only forty-four years from the date of John's vision upon Patmos." "It does not appear that Justin, and those at Rome who held with him in doctrine, paid the slightest regard to the ancient Sabbath. He speaks of it as abolished, and treats it with contempt." Page 33.

This is the confession which even the historian of the Seventh-Day Adventists is compelled to make. The Jewish Sabbath was wholly disregarded by Christians within forty-four years of the death of the last apostle. And this is proven by the testimony of a man who lived right there.

Hear Elder A. again: "We must, therefore, pronounce Justin a man who held to the abrogation of the ten commandments, and that the Sabbath was a Jewish institution which was unknown before Moses, and of no authority since Christ. He held Sunday to be the most suitable day for public worship." Page 44. This is the doctrine that the early church and fathers held. Justin in his "Apology" for them to the emperor fairly represented what Christians generally held then, just as he should have done. Elder Andrews conveys the impression that Justin represented only a small party of apostate Christians at Rome and that he is quite unreliable. But the facts are just the reverse. He was a Greek, born in Palestine and held his "Dialogue with Trypho," at Ephesus, Asia Minor, in the church where St. John lived and died, the very center of the Eastern church, and only forty-four years after John's death. Of Justin the the Encyclopedia Americana says: "One of the earliest and most learned writers of the Christian church. * * * He was also equally zealous in opposing alleged heritics." Schaff-Herzog Encyclopedia says: "In these works

Justin professes to present the system of doctrine held by all Christians and seeks to be orthodox on all points. The only difference he knows of as existing between Christians concerned the millennium. Thus Justin is an incontrovertible witness for the unity of the faith in the church of his day, and to the fact that the Gentile type of Christianity prevailed."

"Eusebius says that he overshadowed all the great men who illuminated the second century by the splendor of his name." His writings are "the most important that have come to us from the second century." McClintock and Strong's Encyclopedia, Article Justin Martyr.

Dr. Schaff says of him: "After his conversion Justin devoted himself wholly to the vindication of the Christian religion, as an *itinerant* evangelist, with no fixed abode." Church History, Vol. I, page 482. Not only were his books accepted without dispute as expressing the practice of the church, but his itinerant life, now in Palestine, then in Rome, Greece and Ephesus, enabled him to know this practice, and stamps his testimony with a force equal to demonstration. So, then, Justin is an unimpeachable witness for the faith and practice of Christians generally a few years after the death of the apostles.

Now hear what Justin says about the first day of the week: "And on the day called Sunday, all who live in cities or in the country gather together to one place, and the memoirs of the apostles or the writings of the prophets are read, as long as time permits; then, when the reader has ceased, the president verbally instructs and exhorts to the imitation of these good things. Then we all rise together and pray, and, as we before said, when our prayer is ended, bread and wine and water are brought, and the president in like manner offers prayers and thanksgivings, according to his ability, and the people assent, saying, Amen; and there is a distribution to each, and a participation of that over which thanks have been given, and to those who are absent a portion is sent by the deacons. And they who are well to do, and willing, give what each thinks fit; and what is collected is deposited with the president, who succors the orphans and widows, and those who, through sickness or any other cause, are in want, and those who are in bonds, and the strangers sojourning among us, and, in a word, takes care of all who are in need. But Sunday is the day on which we all hold our common assembly, because it is the first day on which God, having wrought a change in the darkness and matter, made the world; and Jesus Christ, our Saviour, on the same day rose from the dead. For he was crucified on the day before that of Saturn (Saturday); and on the day after that of Saturn, which is the day of the sun, having appeared to his apostles and disciples, he taught them these things, which we have submitted to you also for your consideration." *The First Apology of Justin, Chapter 67.*

Does Elder Andrews question the genuineness of this document? No, indeed. What answer does he make to it? Simply that Justin does not call Sunday the Sabbath nor the Lord's day! This is readily answered by the fact that Justin was writing to a heathen emperor who would have been wholly ignorant of the meaning of either of those terms, but who was familiar with the term "Sunday." So Justin of necessity used that term. But there the naked facts stand, clear, positive and undeniable, that within forty-four years after the book of Revelation was written Christians did not keep the seventh day, but did hold their assemblies on Sunday. And Justin says that Jesus taught these things to the apostles. With these undeniable facts before him, it is a marvel how any man can say that the Sabbath was changed to Sunday three or four hundred years after this by the apostate popes. For myself I became fully satisfied that such statements are contrary to all the plainest facts of history, as may be seen by the above unquestioned statement of Justin Martyr.

It is impossible that Sunday-keeping could have thus been universally introduced into all churches without a word of objection, unless it had started at the fountain-head, with the apostles themselves. Consider well the force of this fact: From the very earliest days, reaching almost back to the apostles themselves, the church was divided into opposing sects, and controversy between them was often very strong. Yet all agreed in keeping Sunday. So to-day: go to any part of the globe and wherever you find Christians of any sect or nation, there you find them keeping Sunday. A few Sabbatarians of late origin are the only exceptions to this. How did this universal custom come about if not started at the very foundation of the church by the apostles themselves?

DIONYSIUS, BISHOP OF CORINTH IN GREECE, A. D. 170.

But we will hear further from these fathers themselves as to whether they kept Sunday. Dionysius, Bishop of Corinth, the church which Paul raised up and to which he gave the command about Sunday collections, 1 Cor. 16: 1-2, says: "We passed this holy Lord's day, in which we read your letter, from the constant reading of which we shall be able to draw admonition." Eusebius, Eccl. History, Book 4, Chapter XXIII. That the Lord's day is the resurrection day we have seen. This term is never applied to any other than the first day. Notice that this witness is from Greece, not Rome. So the resurrection day was a "holy" day, A. D. 170.

BARDESANES OF EDESSA, SYRIA, A. D. 180.

Coming down only ten years later we have the testimony of the heretic Bardesanes, the Syrain, who flourished about

A. D. 180. He belonged to the Gnostic sect. He says: "On one day, the first day of the week, we assembled ourselves together, and on the days of the readings we abstain from [taking] sustenance." Book of the Laws of Countries. Says Elder A.: "This shows that the Gnostics used Sunday as the day for religious assemblies." Testimony, etc., page 53. Here is another good testimony for Sunday, and another good confession from Elder A. All parties, orthodox and heretic, kept Sunday as early as A. D. 180. How, then, is it that Constantine and the pope changed the Sabbath to Sunday two to four hundred years later? Elder A's own words utterly refute such an idea.

Notice here also a refutation of the idea so strongly urged by Sabbatarians, that Sunday-keeping originated at Rome, and was for a long time confined there. Elder Andrews has to admit that the Gnostics at this date used Sunday as a day of worship. But, 1. The Gnostics were emphatically an eastern sect, originating in Syria, and were most numerous in Alexandria, Asia Minor, and the East. Rome never had any influence over them. Bardesanes himself lived at Edessa, in Mesopotamia, 1,500 miles east of Rome, on another continent, under another nation. 2. This sect was numerous in the East as early as A. D. 150, or 55 years after the death of John. So we have Sunday-keeping not only at Rome but all over the east as early as A. D. 150, hundreds of years before the pope had a particle of influence there.

CLEMENT OF ALEXANDRIA, EGYPT, A. D. 194.

Clement was one of the most celebrated of the Christian fathers. He wrote about A. D. 194. He says: "He, in fulfillment of the precept, keeps the Lord's day when he abandons an evil disposition, and assumes that of the Gnostic, glorifying the Lord's resurrection in himself." Book 7,

Chapter XII. The Lord's day, it will be seen here and all along, is the resurrection day. Clement lived, not at Rome, but in Egypt. So Sunday-keeping was not simply a Roman usage as Adventists claim.

TERTULLIAN OF AFRICA, A. D. 200.

Tertullian was one of the most noted of the early fathers. Was born A. D. 160. He was highly educated, bred to the law, and very talented. Brought up a pagan, he was converted to Christ and vehemently opposed heathenism ever after. Radically severe in his principles, opposed to all conformity to the world, the laxity of the Roman church drove him to withdraw from it, which he ever after hotly opposed. So he was not a Romanist, nor did Rome have a particle of influence over him only to drive him the other way. He was strictly orthodox in faith and a lover of the scriptures. Hence if it were true that Sunday keeping, as a heathen institution, was being introduced into the church by Rome, Tertullian is just the man who would have opposed and fearlessly condemned it.

Johnson's Cyclopedia says of him: "One of the greatest men of the early church." He "joined the Puritanic sect of the Montanists. They were orthodox in doctrine, but stern in spirit and discipline." "He remained true to the faith of the Catholics, but fought them vehemently on matters of morality and discipline. He was also a representative of the African opposition to Rome." The Schaff-Herzog Cyclopedia says of him: "One of the grandest and most original characters of the ancient church." "Greek philosophy he despised." Of his great book they say: "One of the magnificent monuments of the ancient church." Authon's Classical Dictionary says of him: "He informs us more correctly than any other writer respecting the Christian doctrines of his time. * * * Tertullian was held in very high esteem by the subsequent fathers of the church." Neander says: "Tertullian is a writer of peculiar importance." Rose's Neander, page 424.

Here then is a competent and unimpeachable witness to the doctrines and practices of the universal church, A. D. 200, or only 104 years after John. Time and again he argues that the Sabbath was abolished, that Christians do not keep it, but do keep Sunday, the Lord's Day. Of the abolition of the Sabbath he says: "Let him who contends that the Sabbath is still to be observed * * * teach us that for the past time righteous men kept the Sabbath." "God originated Adam uncircumsised and inobservant of the Sabbath." So he says Abel, Noah, Enoch, etc., were "inobservant of the Sabbath." Answer to the Jews, chapter 2. Again: "The old law is demonstrated as having been consummated at its specific times, so also the observance of the Sabbath is demonstrated to have been temporary." Chapter 4. "We solemnize the day after Saturday in contradistinction to those who call this day their Sabbath, and devote it to ease and eating, deviating from the old Jewish customs, which they are now very ignorant of." Tertullian's Apology, chapter 16. Tertullian again declares that his brethren did not observe the days held sacred by the Jews: "We neither accord with the Jews in their peculiarities in regard to food, nor in their sacred days." "We, however (just as we have received), only on the day of the Lord's resurrection ought to guard not only against kneeling, but every posture and office of solicitude; deferring even our business, lest we give any place to the devil." Tertullian on Prayer, chapter 23. Sunday, then, was observed by Christians at that early date, but Saturday was not.

ORIGEN, A. D. 225.

Origen (about A. D. 225) was a man of immense learning, and his writings are numerous. "Origen may well be pronounced one of the ablest and worthiest of the church fathers." McClintock and Strong's Cyclopedia. He says: "If it be objected to us on this subject that we ourselves are accustomed to observe certain days, as, for example, the Lord's Day, the preparation, the passover, or pentecost." Origen against Celsus, book 8, chapter 22. This plainly shows that he did observe the Lord's Day. Origen's home was in Egypt, but he traveled all over the East and died at Tyre. Notice that witnesses for Sunday came from all parts of the world, not one from Rome.

THE APOSTOLICAL CONSTITUTIONS, A. D. 250.

Of the "Apostolical Constitutions" (A. D. 250) Elder Andrews says: "The so-called 'Apostolical Constitutions' were not the work of the apostles, but they were in existence as early as the third century, and were then very generally believed to express the doctrine of the apostles. They do therefore furnish important historical testimony to the practice of the church at that time. Mosheim, in his 'Historical Commentaries,' Cent. 1, section 51, speaks thus of these 'constitutions': 'The matter of this work is unquestionably ancient; since the manners and discipline of which it exhibits a view are those which prevailed among the Christians of the second and third centuries, especially those resident in Greece and the oriental regions.'" Testimony, etc., page 13. Notice again that this work was the product of the eastern church and hence shows the custom of the church in the east instead of that at Rome.

These, then, will be good witnesses to the practice of the church about A. D. 250. In section 7, paragraph 59, we read: "And on the day of our Lord's resurrection, which is the Lord's Day, meet more diligently, sending praise to God that made the universe by Jesus and sent him to us." "Otherwise what apology will he make to God who does not assemble on that day to hear the saving word concerning the resurrection." In book 7, section 2, paragraph 30, he says: "On the day of the resurrection of the Lord, that is, the Lord's Day, assemble yourselves together, without fail, giving thanks to God," etc. In the same paragraph, in speaking of the resurrection of Christ, the writer says: "On which account we solemnly assemble to celebrate the feast of the resurrection on the Lord's Day," etc.

These testimonies are decisive, and do show beyond a doubt that the Christians of those early days used Sunday just as it is used now for religious worship. Did they, then, have "the mark of the beast" at least 250 years before the beast had arisen, according to the Seventh-Day Adventists' theory? These unquestionable facts of history, taken from their own published works and admitted by them to be true, show the utter absurdity of their position that Sunday-keeping is the mark of the beast.

ANATOLIUS, A. D. 270, BISHOP OF LAODICEA, ASIA.

He was bishop of Laodicea, Asia Minor. Not a Roman, but a Greek. This church was raised up by Paul himself, and must have been well acquainted with the apostle's doctrine. In his seventh canon Anatolius says: "The obligation of the Lord's resurrection binds us to keep the paschal festival on the Lord's Day." In his tenth canon he uses this language: "The solemn festival of the resurrection of the Lord can be celebrated only on the Lord's Day." In his sixteenth canon he says: "Our regard for the Lord's resurrection which took place on the Lord's Day will lead us to celebrate it on the same principle." See how all these early Christians call the resurrection day "the Lord's Day" and how they honor it. How entirely different from our Sabbatarians who can hardly find terms mean enough by which to express their contempt for Sunday! **Why is this difference and what does it show?**

VICTORINUS, BISHOP OF PETAU, A. D. 300.

"On the former day [the sixth] we are accustomed to fast rigorously that on the Lord's Day we may go forth to our bread with giving of thanks. And let the parasceve become a rigorous fast lest we should appear to observe any Sabbath with the Jews which Christ himself, the Lord of the Sabbath, says by his prophets that his soul hateth which Sabbath he in his body abolished." Creation of the World, section 4.

PETER, BISHOP OF ALEXANDRIA, A. D. 306.

"But the Lord's day we celebrate as a day of joy, because on it he rose again, on which day we have received it for a custom not even to bow the knee." Canon 15. He gives the same reason 1581 years ago for keeping the Lord's day that Christians give now. This was more than 200 years before the pope came into power. Notice that these witnesses for Sunday are from all parts of the world, from Africa, Asia and Europe, not simply from Rome, as Seventh-Day Adventists untruthfully say. These show that Sunday-keeping was as widespread as the Christian Church itself, and that from the earliest days.

EUSEBIUS, A. D. 324.

Eusebius was born in Palestine, the very home of Christ and the apostles and the cradle of the early church. He was bishop of Cesarea where Paul abode two years. Acts 23: 33; 24: 27. He studied at Antioch where Paul labored for years. Acts 15: 1. He traveled to Egypt and over Asia Minor. He was one of the most noted men of his age. He wrote the first history of the Christian church and bears the title of "Father of Church History." The Schaff-Herzog Encyclopedia says: "As a repertory of facts and documents, his work is invaluable." Johnson's Cyclopedia says: "He was very eminent for learning, as well as talents." Horne's

Introductions says: "A man of extraordinary learning, diligence and judgment, and singularly studious in the scriptures. * * * His chief work is his Ecclesiastical History, in which he records the history of Christianity from its commencement to his own time. * * * He has delivered, not his own private opinion, but the opinion of the church, the sum of what he had found in the writings of the primitive Christians." Vol. 1, Chapter 11, Section 2, page 42.

He had every possible opportunity to know what Christians did throughout the world. Of him Justin Edwards, D. D., says: "He lived in the third century, was a man of vast reading, and was as well acquainted with the history of the church from the days of the apostles as any man of his day." At Cesarea was "a very extensive library, to which Eusebius had constant access. He was a learned and accurate historian and had the aid of the best helps for acquiring information upon all subjects connected with the Christian church." Sabbath Manual, pages 124–125. He lived right there, knew just what Christians did, and wrote about fifty years before the council of Laodicea where Adventists say the Sabbath was changed to Sunday. Hear him: Speaking of the patriarchs before the flood, he says: "They did not, therefore, regard circumcision, *nor observe the Sabbath, neither do we;* * * * because such things as these do not belong to Christians." Eccl. Hist., Book 1, Chapter 4. This is decisive. A. D. 324, Christians did not keep the Sabbath.

True, there was a small heretical sect who kept the Sabbath as Judaizers do now. Of them he says: They are "those who cherish low and mean opinions of Christ. * * * With them the observance of the law was altogether necessary [just like Seventh-Day Adventists] as if they could not be saved only by faith in Christ and a corresponding life. * * * They also observe the Sabbath and other discipline of the Jews just like them, but on the other hand they also celebrate the Lord's Days very much like us in commemoration of his resurrection." Eccl. Hist., pages 112–113. Even these Judaizers kept Sunday. On the Ninety-second Psalm he says: "The word by the new covenant translated and transferred the feast of the Sabbath to the morning light and gave us the true rest, viz., the saving Lord's Day." "On this day which is the first of light and of the true Sun, we assemble, after an interval of six days, and celebrate holy and spiritual Sabbaths, *even all nations redeemed by him throughout the world*, and do those things according to the spiritual law which were decreed for the priests to do on the Sabbath." Again: "And all things whatsoever that it was the duty to do on the Sabbath, these we have transferred to the Lord's Day as more honorable than the Jewish Sabbath." Quoted in Justin Edwards' Sabbath Manual, pages 126–127.

This testimony of the great historian of the early church is decisive. It puts it beyond doubt that Christians in all the world did then keep Sunday, the Lord's Day, and did not keep the Jewish Sabbath. It is a desperate cause which has to deny such testimony as this.

SUMMARY OF TESTIMONY FROM CYCLOPEDIAS.

As a fair, impartial and clear statement of the teachings of the early Christian fathers concerning the observance of Sunday, we refer the reader to the following from Smith's Dictionary of the Bible, article "Lord's Day." Here is a book easy of access to all anywhere, unsectarian, embodying the results of the most thorough and scholarly examination of every passage in all the fathers having any bearing upon the Sunday question. Any one who has read the fathers must confess that its statements are fair and truthful. I have only room for one short quotation:

"The results of our examination of the principle writers of the two centuries after the death of St. John, are as follows: 'The Lord's day existed during these two centuries as a part and parcel of apostolical, and so of Scriptural Christianity. It was never defended; for it was never impugned, or at least only impugned as were other things received from the apostles. It was never confounded with the Sabbath, but carefully distinguished from it. * * * * * * It was not an institution of severe Sabbatical character, but a day of joy and cheerfulness, rather encouraging than forbidding relaxation. Religiously regarded, it was a day of solemn meeting for the holy eucharist, for united prayer, for instruction, for almsgiving; and though being an institution under the law of liberty, work does not appear to have been formally interdicted, or rest formally enjoined. Tertullian seems to indicate that the character of the day was opposed to worldly business. Finally, whatever analogy may be supposed to exist between the Lord's day and the Sabbath, in no passage that has come down to us is the fourth commandment appealed to as the ground of the obligation to observe the Lord's day."

So Johnson's New Universal Cyclopaedia, Art. Sabbath, says: "For a time the Jewish converts observed both the seventh day, to which the name Sabbath continued to be given exclusively, and the first day, which came to be called the Lord's day. * * * Within a century after the death of the last of the apostles we find the observance of the first day of the week, under the name of the Lord's day, established as a universal custom of the church. * * * It was regarded not as a continuation of the Jewish Sabbath (which was denounced together with circumcision and other Jewish and anti-Christian practices), but rather as a substitute for it, and naturally its observance was based on the resurrection of Christ rather than on the creation rest day, or the Sabbath of the Decalogue."

No higher authority than this could be quoted. It states the truth exactly. So the Schaff-Herzog Encyclopedia, Art. Sunday, says: "In the second century its observance was universal. * * * The Jewish Christians ceased to observe the Sabbath after the destruction of Jerusalem."

Dr. Schaff, than whom there is no higher living authority, says: "The universal and uncontradicted Sunday observance in the second century can only be explained by the fact that it had its roots in apostolic practice." History of the Christian church, Vol. I, page 478.

The man who will shut his eyes to all this mass of testimony and still insist that Sunday-keeping is only an institution of popes of later ages, is simply held by a theory which he is bound to maintain anyway. I have had a sad experience in this matter, and know just how a seventh-day man feels in reading these historical facts. I read some of them twenty years ago. They perplexed me some, but I got over this by my strong faith in our doctrines and by believing them to be mostly forgeries. Afterwards as I read more, I saw these testimonies were reliable and very decidedly against our theory of the pope's Sunday. This disturbed me quite a little, but still I got over them by simply ceasing to think of them at all, and by dwelling upon other arguments in which I had perfect confidence. In debate I was always anxious to shut these out of the discussion. I know that Seventh-Day Adventist ministers generally feel as I did, for we often referred to these testimonies of the fathers and the effect they had in debate. Of course, the great body of the members never read these things, and are in blissful ignorance concerning them. Or, if they do read them, it is in their own books where they are all explained away. Their unbounded faith in "the message" and in their leaders carries them right over these facts as matters of no consequence.

For myself, when once I decided to look these historical facts squarely in the face and give them whatever force they fairly deserved, I soon saw the utter falsity of the claim that the "pope changed the Sabbath." The old feeling of uneasiness on this point is entirely gone. I feel that so far as the evidence of history is concerned, my feet stand on solid ground.

CHAPTER XII.

SABBATARIAN POSITIONS ON THE HISTORY OF SUNDAY REFUTED.

What answer do Sabbatarians make to all the preceding testimony? This:

1. "The Bible, the Bible only, is our rule. We don't go by history." *Reply:* Why then do they themselves appeal to history? No people depend so much upon history, none refer to it so often, none make so great claims from it as Seventh-Day Adventists. Thus Andrews' book on the Sabbath contains 512 pages. Of these 192 are on the Bible and 320 on history. Yet they don't go by history! Wherever they can find a scrap in their favor they make the most of it. Of their reliance on history Elder Smith says: "One of the grandest facts we have to present is that God has always had witnesses to his holy Sabbath from the days of Adam till now." Replies to Elder Canright, pages 41-42. Mark: One of the grandest facts they have to present in favor of Saturday is what? Bible testimony? No, but witness from history. Yet, they don't go by history! The fact is they quote history whenever they possibly can. Why, then, cry out against history when we follow them there? Because it is against them.

2. They say that "the early fathers are unreliable, fools, apostates, forgers and frauds." Listen to them: Of one of the fathers Elder Smith says: "A fraud, an impostor, a forger. * * * An old forger of the second century who wrote things too silly to be repeated and too shameful to quote." Replies to Elder Canright, page 39. Hear Elder

Waggoner: "Surely insanity could not produce any more driveling nonsense than this." "Such childish nonsense is seldom seen under the heading of reason." "It would have been a blessing to the world if they had all been lost." Fathers of the Catholic Church, pages 206, 209, 217. This is the way they dispose of all the Christian fathers who said a word in favor of Sunday. No doubt it would have been better for those who keep the Jewish Sabbath if all the Christian fathers had been lost and, better still, if the New Testament also had been lost, for both these are against them. Why this effort to break down the testimony of these early Christian writers? Because they are against them and Sabbatarians know it. Whatever crude notions those fathers might have had, they could state a simple fact of their own days as to whether they did, or did not, keep Sunday. They all agree that they did and their testimony is decisive.

But how much is there to their charge of fraud, forgery, etc.? Just this: In those days the author's name was not always signed to his book; hence it sometimes happened that a book was attributed to the wrong author by mistake. No fraud or forgery was designed or practiced by any one. Look at Hebrews. No name is signed to it. It is still a disputed point as to who wrote it, Paul, Barnabas, or some other apostle. Shall we, therefore, call it a "fraud" and throw it out of the Bible? No. So of the epistle of Barnabas for instance. No name was signed to it, yet it was generally attributed to the apostle Barnabas and was read in all the churches as authority as early as A. D. 120. Some attributed it to others; but all agree that it was written as early as A. D. 120 by some Christian and gave the opinion and customs of the church at that time. "Fraud, fraud," cry the Sabbatarians, "Barnabas never wrote it." Well, what of it? Some Christian wrote it within twenty-five years of John's death and it says that Christians then kept Sunday.

3. "None of the fathers call Sunday the Sabbath." So say the Sabbatarians. That is about right. The early church said with Paul, Col. 2:16, that the Sabbath was abolished with other Jewish rites. The first day was not the Sabbath, but "the Lord's Day," "the eighth day," "resurrection day," etc.

4. Sabbatarians say that Christians worked on Sunday during the first century or longer. Their evidence for this is very questionable as we will soon see. Yet possibly at first the day may not have been observed as strictly as later on; but still it was the day on which all Christians met for their worship according to the custom of the apostles. This is what we claim and have abundantly proved.

5. Sabbatarians say: "The Christians kept the Sabbath for centuries after Christ." Reply: All history abundantly shows that the Jewish Christians observed the Sabbath, circumcision, passover, etc., for a long time. In some churches where the Jewish element predominated, the Gentiles may have also kept the Sabbath, but all parties kept Sunday at the same time. These are the facts about Sabbath-keeping in the early church as proved above.

6. Seventh-Day Adventists quote so-called "eminent historians" to prove their assertions. With these authors they deceive the people and deceive themselves. They quote them as "reliable historians," "high authorities," "eminent divines," "all friends of Sunday," etc. But who are they? Look at Andrews' History of the Sabbath, their standard work. All others relating to the history of the Sabbath are only a re-hash of this. It is served up on all occasions and his authors are quoted over and over by writers and preachers. But the great bulk of his quotations are from such men as Heylyn, Domville, Morer, Cox, Brere-

wood, White, etc., Episcopal clergymen of England who were bitter opposers of Sunday sacredness.

1. Brerewood, in the seventeenth century, was only a college professor, not of note enough to be even named in any cyclopedia I have seen, and I have consulted many. He was a fiery erratic, and argued that the Sabbath law was given only to the master. See The Sabbath by Gilfillin, pages 122–123.

2. Coleman, an American writer of our own times, scarcely mentioned in any cyclopedia.

3. Dr. Cox, a Scottish anti-Sunday writer last century, not even named in any cyclopedia. See Gillfillin, page 168. Yet Andrews quotes him *twenty-two times*, long quotations, as a friend of Sunday! He might as well quote one of his own party. In proof of this read the following from Dr. Lewis, Seventh-Day Baptist, in his "History of Sabbath and Sunday": "A pastor of the Mill Yard Seventh-Day Baptist Church in London, Robert Cornthwaite, published five works upon the Sabbath question." Of the last book Lewis Says: "Robert Cox quotes *largely* from this work." Pages 337–339. Exactly; then Andrews calls this man a friend of Sunday!

4. Domville, another anti-Sunday writer of the nineteenth century, not in any cyclopedia. He denies that there was any authority in the Bible for observing Sunday, even as a day for meetings. Gillfillin, page 143. Yet Andrews quotes him *thirteen times* as a standard Sunday authority!

5. Heylyn was the friend of the infamous Laud of England. In 1618 Charles I. of England issued a "Book of Sports" for Sunday, allowing of dancing, wrestling and various games on Sunday. See Gilfillin, page 85. Pious people opposed the declaration as a desecration of Sunday. Laud, by the King's command, hired this Heylyn and Dr. White to write against Sunday sacredness, and in favor of

the King's book. In four months a large volume was written, printed and delivered according to order, to prove what was wanted against Sunday. The Cyclopedia of Universal Knoweledge says of Heylyn: "He was a very voluminous controversial writer, but his works are of no value now." From this man Andrews makes *thirty-six* quotations, many of them long, as his chief evidence on his main points!

6. White, the man associated with Heylyn, as the hireling of Laud in writing the above book, is quoted *eleven times* by Andrews as a reliable *defender* of Sunday! He might as well quote Elder Waggoner as a defender of Sunday.

7. Morer is a writer of the eighteenth century, mentioned in no cyclopedia. He wrote to disprove the divine origin of Sunday observance. See Gilfillan, page 142. Of one of his statements, which happened to favor Sunday, Elder Waggoner says: "Dishonest as it manifestly is," etc. Replies to Elder Canright, page 146. From this "dishonest" man Elder Andrews makes no less than *forty-seven quotations*, many of them long!

8. Jeremy Taylor, of the seventeenth century, the friend and chaplain of the villainous Laud, wrote against the divine authority of Sunday, and yet is quoted by Andrews as the friend of Sunday!

These are samples of his authors. Most of them were members of the Church of England, and that, too, during the worst period of that church; a church which permits the widest range in theological opinions, such as Unitarianism, Universalism, future probation, annihilation, rationalism, high church, low church, etc. How much then does it signify as to the soundness of one's opinion to state that he is a minister of that church?

Take from the historical part of Andrews' history his quotations and arguments from the above authors and you would hardly have a skeleton left. And even quotations from these are one-sided. Waggoner, Smith, Butler, and all the lesser lights among Seventh-Day Adventists who have come after Andrews simply use these quotations which he gathered for them. But they might as well quote Ingersoll and Tom Paine as "friends of the Bible" as to quote these men as "friends of the Sunday Sabbath." Each of them wrote on purpose to refute the claims of Sunday as a Sabbath of divine authority. Thousands of readers ignorant of history are misled, as I was once, by these quotations used by the Adventists. If they had the truth they would not be compelled to rely upon such authors.

THE PAGAN ROMANS NEVER KEPT SUNDAY.

Seventh-Day Adventists affirm that keeping Sunday was adopted from the pagan Romans by the Catholics and from the Catholics by the Protestants. This idea they industriously teach everywhere. They say that these pagans kept Sunday in worship of the sun. See Andrews' History of the Sabbath, pages 258-264. Such statements are utterly false. Each day of the week was named after some god and, in a certain sense, was devoted to the worship of that god, as Monday to the moon, Saturday to Saturn, Sunday to the sun, etc. But did they cease work on these days? No; if they had they would have kept every day in the week. Did they observe Sunday by ceasing to work? No, indeed. No such thing was taught or practiced by the Romans. They had no weekly rest day.

Prof. A. Rauschinbusch of Rochester Theological Seminary quotes Lotz thus: "'It is a vain thing to attempt to prove that the Greeks and Romans had anything resembling the Sabbath. Such opinion is refuted even by this, that the Roman writers ridicule the Sabbath as something peculiar to the Jews.' In proof he cites many passages from the

Roman poets, and one from Tacitus. Seneca also condemned the Sabbath observance of the Jews as a waste of time by which a seventh part of life was lost." Saturday or Sunday? Page 83. Herzog says: "No special religious celebration of any one day of the week can be pointed out in any one of the pagan religions." Article Sabbath. This fact is accidentally confessed by Elder Waggoner. Of Constantine's law, A. D. 321, he says: "Though the venerable day of the sun had long—very long—been venerated by them and their heathen ancestors, *the idea of rest from worldly labor in its worship was entirely new.*" Replies to Elder Canright, page 130. Mark this confession for it gives up the main pillar of their argument in their effort to prove that Sunday-keeping was taken from the pagans. *The pagans never kept Sunday.* It was a common work day like other days of the week. The idea and the custom of keeping Sunday as a day of rest from work originated with the Christians, not with pagans. So much for that falsehood. Again: Saturday was sacred to Saturn as Sunday was to the sun. So Adventists are keeping a heathen day the same as Sunday-keepers are!

CONSTANTINE DID NOT CHANGE THE SABBATH.

It has been common for Sabbatarians to point to the law of Constantine as a chief factor in changing the Sabbath to Sunday. There never was any truth in the charge; but Elder Waggoner now owns it all up and confesses that it had nothing whatever to do in changing the Sabbath. "Constantine, in his decrees, said not one word either for or against keeping the Sabbath of the Bible." "It is safe to affirm that there was nothing done in the time of Constantine, either by himself or any other, that has the least appearance of changing the Sabbath." Replies to Elder Canright, page 150. That is the truth and a good confession, though it contradicts all that they have said heretofore. Now let them revise their old books to harmonize with this truth and they will be much smaller.

CONSTANTINE'S SUNDAY LAW AND ITS OBJECT.

A. D. 321, Constantine, the first Christian emperor of Rome, issued the following edict:

"Let all the judges and town people, and the occupation of all trades, rest on the venerable day of the sun, but let those who are situated in the country, freely and at full liberty, attend to the business of agriculture; because it often happens that no other day is so fit for sowing corn and planting vines; lest, the critical moment being let slip, men should lose the commodities granted by Heaven."

The simple facts about this law are these: Christians from the days of the apostles had kept the first day of the week; but there was no civil law to protect or aid them in it. By this time they had become very numerous in the empire and their influence was rapidly gaining. The old pagan religion was falling before them. Constantine, to say the least, was favorable to Christianity. His parents were Christians. He was shrewd enough to see that it was for his interest to favor this new and rising religion. Hence, as soon as he publicly professed Christianity, he issued several edicts favoring it in various ways, this one concerning Sunday among the rest. The Schaff-Herzog Encyclopedia well says: "He was no doubt convinced of the superior claims of Christianity as the rising religion; but his conversion was a change of policy, rather than of moral character. * * * He knew Christianity well, but only as a power in the Roman Empire and he protected it as a wise and far-seeing statesman. * * * His first edict concerning the Christians (Rome, 312) is lost. By the second (Milan, 313) he granted them, not only **free religious worship** and the recognition of the state, but also reparation of previously incurred losses. * * * A series of edicts of 315, 316, 319, 321, and 323, completed the revolution. Christians were admitted to the offices of the state. * * * An edict of 321 ordered Sunday to be celebrated by cessation of all work in public."

It will be seen that this edict was only one of seven issued to favor Christians. 1. It was not made to please or favor the pagans, for, as seen above, they did not keep Sunday. 2. As we have proved, the Christians did all keep Sunday, hence this law would favor and please them. 3. The edict was not addressed to Christians for they needed no such law for themselves as they kept that day voluntarily. 4. It was not worded in Christian terms, "Lord's Day," as it was addressed to pagans. 5 It was couched in pagan terms, "day of the sun," that pagans might understand it and that it might offend them less. This law, then, made no change in the observance of Sunday on the part of Christians; but it did secure to that day a better observance by requiring everyone, pagans and all, to cease work that day. But it is said that this law of Constantine, A. D. 321, was the first law ever made prohibiting work on Sunday. Very true, but why? Because none but Christians believed it wrong to work that day; and up to that date Christians had no power to make laws and hence could not have made a law for keeping Sunday if they had desired to. It is noticeable that the first emperor who favored Christianity made, among other laws favoring Christians, a civil law prohibiting work on Sunday.

That this law was made at the request of Christians is now admitted by Adventists. Thus Elder A. T. Jones in the Battle Creek Journal, December 11, 1888, says: "It is demonstrated that the first Sunday law that ever was enacted was at the request of the church; it was in behalf of the church, and it was expressly to help the church."

Exactly, and this proves that the church kept Sunday before that law was made. It is an absurdity to say that the pagans had always kept Sunday and yet had never made a law concerning it. As Adventists all agree, the first Sunday law was made to favor Christians. This shows that Sunday observance was then regarded as an essential part of Christianity. Of this law Mosheim says: "The first day of the week, which was the ordinary and stated time for the public assemblies of the Christians, was, in consequence of a peculiar law enacted by Constantine, observed with greater solemnity than it had formerly been." Mosheim, century 4, part 2, chapter 4, section 5.

This law, addressed to pagans who had always worked on Sunday, required the cessation of business on that day and so secured to Christians a better observance of Sunday than before. The ecclesiastical historian, Sozomen, writing of Constantine, says: "He also enjoined the observance of the day termed the Lord's Day. * * * He honored the Lord's Day because on it Christ rose from the dead." Eccl. Hist., page 22. It was, then, in behalf of Sunday as a Christian day, not as a pagan festival, that this law was made.

FOUND AT LAST THE EXACT TIME AND PLACE WHEN AND WHERE THE POPE CHANGED THE SABBATH!

I pressed the Adventists to name the time and place when and where the Sabbath was changed by the pope, and to name the pope and the facts about such a change if it ever occurred. Nettled by this, Elder Waggoner undertook the Herculean task. A worse sample of assumption and perversion of facts it would be hard to find. At last he settles on the council of Laodicea, A. D. 364, as the place and time when and where the Sabbath was changed. The 29th canon of that council reads thus: "Christians ought not to Judaize and to rest in the Sabbath, but to work in that day; but preferring the Lord's Day, should rest, if possible, as Christians. Wherefore if they shall be found to Judaize, let them be accursed from Christ." On this the Elder says: "Now, if any one can imagine what would be changing the Sabbath, if this is not, I would be extremely happy to learn what it could be." "Now I claim that I have completely met his demand; I have shown the time, the place, and the power that changed the Sabbath." Replies to Canright, pages 141, 151. He claims that this was "a Catholic council" and that "historians early and late have made much mention" of this council. Now let us examine his position.

1. If the Sabbath was changed to Sunday by the pope right here, as he affirms, then certainly it was not changed before nor after nor at any other place. So if this fails their whole cause is lost. Let the reader mark the importance of this fact.

2. He admits what every scholar knows, that till after the time of Constantine the bishop of Rome had no "authority whatever above the other bishops" and so could not have changed the Sabbath before that time. He says: "It was Constantine himself that laid the foundation of the papacy." Replies to Elder Canright, page 148. Surely the papacy did not exist before its foundation was laid.

3. He admits, as above, that Constantine did nothing to change the Sabbath.

4. But we have abundantly proved in precedings pages that all Christians long before this date were unanimous in observing the Lord's Day. This one simple fact proves the utter absurdity of the claim that it was changed at Laodicea, A. D. 364, or by the papacy at any time.

5. In the year 324, or just 40 years before the council of

Laodicea, Eusebius, bishop of Cesarea, Palestine, wrote his celebrated history of Christianity. He had every possible opportunity to know what Christians did throughout the world. He says: "And all things whatsoever that it was the duty to do on the Sabbath, these we have transferred to the Lord's Day as more honorable than the Jewish Sabbath." Quoted in Sabbath Manual, page 127.

That is the way the Sabbath and Sunday stood in the church 40 years before Laodicea. They did not keep the Sabbath, but did keep the Lord's Day, had transferred all things to it. How much truth, then, can there be in the position that the Sabbath was changed to Sunday by the pope 40 years later? Shame on such brazen attempts to pervert the truth. But let us look at the real facts about the council at Laodicea. Seventh-Day Adventists claim two things, viz: that the Sabbath was changed by the Roman church, and that it was done by the authority of the pope. Then they select Laodicea as the place and time. But,

1. Laodicea is not Rome. It is situated in Asia Minor over 1,000 miles east of Rome. It was in Asia not in Europe. It was an Eastern, not a Western town, an oriental, not a Latin city.

2. It was a Greek, not a Roman city.

3. The pope of Rome did not attend this council at Laodicea, A. D. 364. Does Waggoner claim that he did? No, he does not dare to.

4. The pope did not attend, nor did he send a legate or a delegate or any one to represent him. In fact, neither the Roman Catholic church nor the pope had anything to do with the council in any way, shape or manner. It was held without even their knowledge or consent.

5. At this early date, A. D. 364, the popes, or rather bishops of Rome, had no authority over other bishops. It was 200 years later before they were invested with author-

ity over Western churches. Even then their authority was stoutly resisted for centuries in the East where this council was held. See Bower's History of the Popes, or any church history. Speaking of Sylvester, who was bishop of Rome A. D. 314 to 336, only 28 years before this council at Laodicea, Elder Waggoner says: "The bishop of Rome had not then yet attained to any authority whatever above the other bishops." Replies to Canright, page 143. This is true. Did they in the next twenty-eight years gain authority to change the keeping of the Sabbath from one day to another throughout the whole world? Preposterous!

6. Liberius was bishop of Rome at the time of this council at Laodicea. He was degraded from his office, banished, and treated with the utmost contempt. Bowers says that in order to end his exile, Liberius "wrote in a most submissive and cringing style to the eastern bishops." History of the Popes, Vol. I, page 64. And this was the pope who changed the Sabbath at a council of these same eastern bishops, 1,000 miles away, which he never attended!

7. The council of Laodicea was only a local council, a small, unimportant affair and not a general council at all. Elder Waggoner magnifies it into a great "Catholic [general] council," a claim which is utterly false. The general councils are: 1. That at Nice, A. D. 325. 2. That at Constantinople, A. D. 381. 3. That at Ephesus, A. D. 431, etc. See the list in Johnson's Cyclopedia, or any history. Bower in his extensive work, the "History of the Popes," gives an account of all the general councils, the important local councils, and all with which Rome or the popes had to do, but does not even mention this one at Laodicea. He mentions many councils held about that time, but not this one. He says: "Several other councils were held from the year 363 to 368, of which we have no particular account." Vol. I, page 79. I have searched through a number of cyclopedias

and church histories and can find no mention at all of the council at Laodicea, in most of them, and only a few lines in any. Rev. W. Armstrong, a scholar of Canton, Pa., says: "This council is not even mentioned by Mosheim, Milner, Ruter, Reeves, Socrates, Sozomen, nor by four other historians on my table." McClintock and Strong's Cyclopedia says: "Thirty-two bishops were present from different provinces in Asia." All bishops of the Eastern church, not one from the Roman church! And yet this was the time and place when and where the Roman church and the pope changed the Sabbath!

8. Now think of it: this little local council of thirty-two bishops revolutionizes the whole world on the keeping of the Sabbath!

9. The fact is that this council simply regulated in this locality an already long established institution, the Lord's Day, just the same as council after council did afterwards. If this changed the Sabbath to Sunday, then it has been changed a hundred times since! Sabbatarians point to these different regulations as so many acts in changing the Sabbath, when they have not the remotest relation to such a thing any more than have the resolutions with regard to keeping Sunday which are passed year by year now in all our religious assemblies. Elder Waggoner makes this truthful statement: "The decrees of councils have not as a general thing been arbitrary laws telling what *must be*, so much so they have been the formulation of the opinions and practices largely prevalent at the time. * * * Infallibility had been attributed to the pope hundreds of years before it became a dogma of the church." Fathers of the Catholic Church, page 333. Exactly, and just so the Lord's Day had been kept by the church hundreds of years before the council of Laodicea mentioned it.

10. The church of Laodicea where this council was held

was raised up by Paul himself, Col. 4:13, 16; 1 Tim. 6; close of the epistle. It was one of the seven churches to which John wrote. Rev. 3:14. Hence it is certain it was well instructed and grounded in the doctrines of the apostles. Between Paul and this council, that is A. D. 270, Anatolius was bishop of Loadicea. He wrote: "Our regard for the Lord's resurrection, which took place on the Lord's Day, will lead us to celebrate it on the same principle." Canon 16. Here we have that church keeping Sunday one hundred years before this council.

11. Finally, if the council of Laodicea changed the Sabbath, as Adventists say, then it was changed by the Greek church instead of the Roman church; changed by the eastern churches over which Rome had no authority; changed before the papacy was established, before the pope had any authority over the east, by a small local council which neither the pope nor any of his servants attended. The absurdity of this claim is manifest without further argument.

For many years I accepted these false statements of Sabbatarian writers as undoubted truths, as all their converts do. I had no means of knowing better. I preached strongly what I read in their books and led hundreds still more ignorant than myself to believe it. Gradually the truth dawned upon me that I was being misled, but it then took me years to learn the real facts in the case and free myself from the superstition which bound me. Now I have investigated the matter till I am fully satisfied for myself that, to sustain their false theories, they have done great violence to the plainest facts of history. The assertion that the pope changed the Sabbath is a fair sample of the rest.

CHAPTER XIII.

THE SABBATH IN THE OLD TESTAMENT.

THE SABBATH IN GENESIS.

The Sabbath is not mentioned by name in the book of Genesis, nor till the time of Moses. Gen. 2:1-3 states that God finished creation in six days and rested on the seventh day; and that he blessed and sanctified the seventh day "because that in it he had rested." On this we remark: 1. The day was not holy in itself. 2. God's rest upon that day did not make it holy. 3. God sanctified or made holy the seventh day because that in it he *had* rested. His rest was over and passed before he blessed the day. 4. As to just *when* God blessed the day the record does not clearly state. Some contend that he sanctified the day then and there in Eden. Others argue that this was not done till the exodus. Plausible arguments are used on both sides; but the simple fact that the most godly and learned men have always disagreed about the institutition of the Sabbath in Eden should teach us caution how we build a theory upon a disputed text so meager in statement and so far away in time. In all fairness it must be owned that the definite time when the Sabbath was sanctified can not certainly be determined from this text.

Smith's Dictionary of the Bible truthfully says: "It is in Ex. 16:23-29 that we find the first incontrovertible institution of the day." Art. Sabbath. Of the argument on Gen. 2:1-3 for the institution of the Sabbath in Eden it says: "The whole argument is very precarious." There is no command in Gen. 2 to keep the Sabbath. We must look elsewhere for that. The sanctification of the seventh day there mentioned is claimed by some to have been by anticipation. As Moses wrote his books after he came to Sinai, after the Sabbath had been given in the wilderness, he here mentions one reason why God thus gave them the seventh day, viz: because God himself had set the example at creation; had worked six days and rested the seventh. Such use of language is common. We say Gen. Grant was born at such a time. We do not mean that he was a general then, but we mention it by anticipation, using a title which he afterwards bore. So in Gen. 3:20, "Adam called his wife's name Eve, because she was the mother of all living." Here is a future fact stated as though it had already occurred. So 1 Sam. 4:1, the Jews "pitched beside Eben-ezer." But the place was not named Eben-ezer till years after. 1 Sam. 7:12. "Judas Iscariot, which also was the traitor." Luke 6:16. Here a future fact with regard to Judas is mentioned when he is first spoken of, though the act of betrayal did not take place till years later. Just so when the seventh day is first mentioned its sanctification is referred to, though it did not occur till afterwards. We must admit that this may have been so.

Ex. 20:8 says: "Remember the Sabbath day," etc. Sabbatarians claim that this shows that the Sabbath existed from creation. It does not prove it, because the Sabbath had been given some weeks before the decalogue was given. So this may refer back only to Ex. 16, when the Sabbath is first named. Or, which is evidently the real truth about it, it may refer to keeping the Sabbath as it comes week by week. "Remember," don't forget, to keep the Sabbath day.

Then it is now generally held by able Christian scholars that the days of creation were indefinite periods of time.

There is much to sustain this idea. Sabbatarians themselves admit this. Thus Rev. A. H. Lewis, D. D., Seventh-Day Baptist, editor and author of several critical works on the Sabbath, says: "We apprehend that the creation week was infinitely longer than our week of seven days of twenty-four hours." Sabbath and Sunday, page 8. But this fact is fatal to his definite seventh-day theory; for if God's days were not twenty-four hour days like ours, then we do not and can not rest on the same definite day He did. Hence we can only use God's week as a model—six days work, the seventh rest.

Sabbatarians think that the fourth commandment designates the identical day on which God himself rested. But this is not as clear as they claim. "The seventh day is the Sabbath of the Lord thy God." Ex. 20:10. That is, the rest day of the Lord; hence it must be the day on which he himself rested, they say. But this does not necessarily follow. The language simply claims that day as belonging to God. Take the day of the passover: "The fourteenth day of the first month is the passover of the Lord." Num. 28:16. Did the Lord keep the passover that day? Hardly. Again: "These are the feasts of the Lord." Lev. 23:4. Did the Lord feast on those days? Surely not. The language simply claims those days as sacred to God and that is all that Ex. 20:10 claims for the seventh day. The revised version gives the idea clearly: "The seventh day is a Sabbath *unto the Lord* thy God."

Away back there in the dim past, where the events of an age are covered by one line in the Bible, it is impossible now to determine exactly how it all was. Those ages before Christ are compared to shadows, Col. 2:17, and to the light of the moon, Rev. 12:1, while the gospel is compared to the sun. Rev. 12:1. Is it not the safest for us to walk in the light of the sun instead of groping our way in the moonlight and shadows of the past? But the main reliance of Sabbatarians is upon arguments drawn from those remote times of darkness, while in the New Testament they find little to support their theories, but much to explain away.

There is no statement that any of the patriarchs kept the Sabbath or knew anything about it. Sabbatarians say the record is so brief that it was omitted. Their proof then is *what was left out!*

Though the record from Adam to Moses covers a period of 2500 years; though we appear to have a full account of the religious customs and worship of the patriarchs, such as Noah, Abraham, Isaac, Jacob, Joseph, etc.; though we are told about circumcision, the altar, the sacrifices, the priests, the tithe, the oath, marriage, feast days, etc.; yet never a word is said about any one keeping the Sabbath. This does not prove positively that they did not keep it, but it does show a strong probability against it. This is the sum of what can be fairly said about the Sabbath in Genesis. When men go away back in Genesis to find their principal argument for the Sabbath, is it not going a long ways and finding little upon which to establish a Christian duty? Would it not be wiser and safer to build our faith upon the plain requirements of the New Testament?

TESTIMONY OF EMINENT MEN.

Justin Martyr, who wrote only 44 years after the death of St. John, and who was well acquainted with the doctrine of the apostles, denied that the Sabbath originated at creation. Thus after naming Adam, Abel, Enoch, Lot and Melchizedek, he says: "Moreover, all those righteous men already mentioned, though they kept no Sabbaths, were pleasing to God." Dialogue with Trypho, chapter 19.

Irenaeus says: "Abraham believed God without circumcision and the Sabbath." Adv. Hœres, lib. 4, c. 30.

Tertullian, A. D. 200, said: "Let them show me that Adam Sabbatized, or that Abel in presenting his holy offering to God pleased him by Sabbath observance, or that Enoch who was translated was an observer of the Sabbath." Against the Jews, section 4.

Eusebius, A. D. 324, the father of church history, says: "They (the patriarchs) did not, therefore, regard circumcision, nor observe the Sabbath, nor do we." Eccl. Hist., book 1, chapter 4.

From this it will be seen that the early church did not believe that the Sabbath originated at creation. The same doctrine has been maintained by such eminent men as Paley, Hessey, Bishop Bramhall, etc. Paley says: "Now, in my opinion, the transactions in the wilderness above recited were the first actual institution of the Sabbath." Quoted in Watson's Institutes, Vol. II, page 515. The great John Milton says: "Whether its institution was ever made known to Adam, or whether any commandment relative to its observance was given previous to the delivery of the law on Mt. Sinai, much less whether any such was given before the fall of man, can not be ascertained." A Treatise on Christian Doctrine, Vol. I, page 299.

John Bunyan says: "Now as to the imposing of the seventh day Sabbath upon men from Adam to Moses, of that we find nothing in holy writ, either from precept or example." Complete Works, page 892. So many of the best minds have not been able to find clear proof that the Sabbath was kept before Moses. Others, as Clarke, Barnes, Scott, Lange, etc., think that it was. We best leave it as an unsettled question.

Granting that the Sabbath was given to Adam in Eden, it does not follow that all men now must keep it. Look at what Adam was to do: 1st. Adam was only allowed to eat the fruit of trees and plants. Gen. 1: 29. The first permission to eat flesh was given to Noah. Gen. 9: 3. 2d. Adam was to tend garden. Gen. 2: 15. 3d. He was forbidden the tree of knowledge. Gen. 2: 17. 4th. He was given access to the tree of life. Gen. 2: 16. 5th. Adam was naked. Gen. 2: 25. All this was in Eden before the fall. Must all men now eat and work and dress and do just as Adam did in Eden? No one believes that. Then it would not follow that we must keep the seventh day even if Adam did. This simple fact demolishes the most confident argument of Sabbatarians.

THE SABBATH AT THE EXODUS.

The first mention of Sabbath observance is in Ex. 16. Many eminent scholars hold that God here changed the day of rest from the original seventh to the sixth day of the creation week. Others hold that the Jews, during their long slavery in Egypt, had lost the Sabbath and that it was here renewed; while others hold that it was here given for the first time. Whichever position is correct, it is clear that the keeping of the Sabbath was a new thing to the Jews. A few facts are plain. The deliverance of Israel from Egypt marked a new era in the history of the church and of Israel. This is kept prominent all through the Bible. Here God gave them a new year and a new beginning of months. "This month shall be unto you the beginning of months; it shall be the first month of the year to you." Ex. 12: 2. Hence it is very probable that he might have given them a new Sabbath day or one for the first time. The account of their first keeping the Sabbath shows plainly that they were not accustomed to it before.

Dr. H. C. Benson, the eminent M. E. editor, scholar and author, says of Ex. 16: "It is so explicit that we are not left in doubt as to the fact that the Sabbath, as observed in the wilderness of sin, had not been a day hollowed by the

Lord previous to that time." Quoted and approved by Dr. Potts and Bishop Harris in The Lord's Day Our Sabbath, page 15.

John Milton over 200 years ago said: "That the Israelites had not so much as heard of the Sabbath before this time, seems to be confirmed by several passages of the prophets." Treatise on Christian Doctrine, Vol. I, book 2, chapter 7.

John Bunyan also said: "The seventh day Sabbath, therefore, was not from paradise, nor from nature, nor from the fathers, but from the wilderness and from Sinai." Complete Works, page 895.

It was new to them. Read it: Moses said on Friday, "To-morrow is a solemn rest, a holy Sabbath unto the Lord." (R. V.) The last verse gives the conclusion of the whole matter. "So the people rested on the seventh day." That is, thus and for this reason the people here began resting on the seventh day. There is no sense in the language if this is not the meaning. Several scriptures harmonize well with this idea. Thus, Neh. 9: 13-14. "Thou camest down also upon Mount Sinai, * * * and *madest known* unto them thy holy Sabbath." This implies that it was not known before. In harmony with this, Ezek. 20: 10-12 says: "Wherefore I caused them to go forth out of the land of Egypt, and brought them into the wilderness." "Moreover also I gave them my Sabbaths, to be a sign between me and them." When did God give them the Sabbath? When he brought them out of Egypt. Where did he give it to them? In the wilderness. What for? For a sign between himself and them.

It does not say that God *restored* the Sabbath, but that he gave them the Sabbath. "I gave them my Sabbaths" implies the act of committing it to them, showing that they did not have it before. Surely all these facts are plainly stated. They show that the keeping of this day was a new thing to them and only for them. Deut. 5: 15, states that the Sabbath is to be kept as a memorial of Egypt. "Remember that thou wast a servant in the land of Egypt, and that the Lord thy God brought thee out thence; * * * therefore, the Lord thy God commanded thee to keep the Sabbath day." This indicates that the Sabbath was a Jewish institution. One reason given why they should keep it was because they had been delivered out of Egypt. Of course they would not keep it till the reason existed for keeping it. The laws regulating how it should be kept show that it was a local institution adapted only to the Jewish worship and to that warm climate. 1. No fires must be built on the Sabbath. Ex. 35: 3. 2. They must neither bake nor boil that day. Ex. 16: 23. 3. They must not go out of the house. Ex. 16: 29. 4. Their priests must offer two lambs that day. Num. 28: 9. 5. They must compel all among them, living in their land, to keep it. Ex. 20: 10. 6. They must stone all who broke it. Ex. 31: 14. 7. It must be kept from sunset to sunset. Lev. 23: 32. 8. Their cattle must rest. Ex. 20: 10. No meetings were appointed for that day. It was to be wholly a day of rest.

Seventh-Day Adventists observe none of these things. Indeed, it would be impossible for them to do most of them. They would freeze without fires and suffer without warm food. They go many miles on the Sabbath and drive their teams; they offer no lambs; they can compel no one to keep it; nor do they stone those who break it. In the extreme north and in traveling around the earth they do not go by sunset time, for they cannot. Their Sabbath-keeping is no more like that of the Old Testament, such as the law required, than darkness is like light. It shows the folly of their effort to keep an obsolete Jewish day. Nowhere are Gentiles required to keep the Sabbath except such as dwell among the Jews. They were also required to keep the other feast days. Lev. 16: 29. All through the Old Testament the Gentiles are denounced over and over for all other sins, but not once for breaking the Sabbath, though none of them kept it. The reason for this must be that it was not binding upon them. John Bunyan says: "We read not that God gave it to any but to the seed of Jacob." Complete Works, page 895.

"THE JEWISH SABBATH" A PROPER TERM FOR THE SEVENTH DAY.

Sabbatarians strongly object to our calling the seventh-day the "Jewish Sabbath." They ask, "Where does the Bible call it the Jewish Sabbath? It is 'the sabbath of the Lord thy God.'" This simple argument has great force with many. But I am satisfied it is perfectly proper to designate the seventh day as the Jewish Sabbath. Seventh-day brethren are constantly talking and writing about "the ceremonial law" and "the moral law," nor could they properly express their ideas of the "two laws" without using these terms. But neither of them is once used in all the Bible. How is this? Will they admit that their idea is unscriptural because these exact words are not used in the Bible? No. They freely use the terms "Jewish festivals," "Jewish sabbaths," "annual sabbaths," "sabbaths of the Hebrews," etc. See "History of the Sabbath," pages 82, 83, 84, etc. Yet not one of these terms is found in the Bible, though they cannot get along without them. It would be amusing to confine a Sabbatarian strictly to the Bible language and then hear him attempt to preach on the two laws and the different sabbaths. "Those who live in glass houses should not throw stones."

1. "Sabbath" is purely a Hebrew word never found till the time of Moses. Ex. 16: 23.

2. The word Sabbath is never used in the Bible except in connection with some Jewish holy time.

3. There is no record that the Sabbath was ever kept till the Jews kept it. Ex. 16.

4. The Sabbath was given to the Jews. "I gave them my Sabbaths." Ez. 20: 12. If God gave it to the Jews, was it not their Sabbath; was it not the Jewish Sabbath? I give Fred a knife. Is it not Fred's knife?

5. Notice how plain the record is that God gave the Sabbath to the Jews, but to no others. "The Lord hath given *you* the Sabbath." Ex. 16: 29. "Speak unto the *children of Israel*, saying. Verily, my Sabbaths ye shall keep." Ex. 31: 13. Who was told to keep the Sabbath? The children of Israel, the Jews. "It is a sign between me and the *children of Israel*," the Jews. Verse 17.

6. God himself calls the Sabbath "her Sabbaths." Hosea 2: 11. "I will also cause all her mirth to cease, her feast days, her new moons, and her Sabbaths, and all her solemn feasts." Isn't it the Jewish Sabbath, then?

7. The Sabbath was never given to any other nation.

8. "The children of Israel shall keep the Sabbath throughout their generation." Ex. 31: 16. To whom was it confined? To the generation of the Jews.

9. "It is a sign between me and the *children of Israel*." Ex. 31: 17. It was theirs exclusively, Jewish.

10. The Sabbath is classed right in with the other Jewish holy days and sacrifices. See Lev. 23: 1–44; Nums: 28: 2, 16; 1 Chron. 23: 29–31; 2 Chro. 2: 4; 8: 13, etc.

11. It was abolished with them. Col. 2: 14–17.

12. The Jews comprise nearly all those who keep the seventh day; hence "Jewish Sabbath" is a natural and intelligent designation for that day.

13. Christians almost unanimously keep the first day in distinction from the Jews who comprise nearly all those who keep the seventh day. Hence the Jewish Sabbath is intelligent and proper again.

14. The few Christians who keep a different day from the great body of the church keep the Sabbath which the Jews keep. Hence, again, it is significant and proper to designate them as those who keep the Jewish Sabbath.

15. But Sabbatarians say that the seventh day is called "the Sabbath of the Lord thy God." Ex. 20: 10, and "my holy day," Isa. 58: 10, therefore it is not proper to call it "the Jewish Sabbath."

Answer: Every holy season, place, person, or article was called the Lord's as "the Lord's passover." Ex. 12: 11. Yet we read, "The passover, a feast of the Jews." John 6: 4 So it is "the Sabbath of the Lord" in one place and "her Sabbaths" in another. Hosea 2: 11. Hence it is correct and scriptural to call the seventh day "the Jewish Sabbath."

EX. 31: 16–17, THE SABBATH PERPETUAL.

Here Sabbatarians find three expressions from which they argue that the Sabbath can never end. 1. "Throughout their generations." 2. "Perpetual." 3. "Forever." Thus: "Wherefore the children of Israel shall keep the Sabbath, to observe the Sabbath throughout their generations, *for* a perpetual covenant. It is a sign between me and the children of Israel for ever." They ask, when will *perpetual* and *for ever* end ? They show that the generation of the Jews still continues; hence the Sabbath is still to be kept.

But this argument would also perpetuate all the Levitical law, circumcision, incense, passover, priesthood, etc. Thus the passover: "ye shall keep it a feast to the Lord throughout your generations; ye shall keep it a feast by an ordinance forever." Ex. 12: 14. It must be kept "*throughout their generations*" and "*forever*" just like the Sabbath. So of the offering of incense. "A *perpetual* incense before the Lord *throughout your generations.*" Ex. 30: 8. Now if the Adventist argument for the Sabbath based on the terms "perpetual," "forever," and "throughout your generations," is good, then they ought to keep the passover and offer incense! This is a fair sample of the weakness of Sabbatarian arguments. The same argument will prove the perpetuity of burnt offerings, Ex. 29: 42; atonement, Ex. 30: 10; washing of hands and feet; Ex. 30: 21; first fruits, Lev. 23: 14; meat offering, Lev. 6: 18; oil for lamps, Lev. 24: 3; fringes, Num. 15: 38; pentecost, Lev. 23: 21; feast of tabernacles, Lev. 23: 41. See also Ex. 40: 15; Lev. 3: 17; 7: 36; Num. 10: 8.

The application of these terms to the keeping of the Sabbath is proof that it was to cease. Why? Because in every case where these terms are applied to the observance of any ordinance that ordinance has ceased. Adventists themselves will agree to this in everything except the Sabbath. None of these terms are ever applied to moral laws or duties. Where do you read, "you shall not kill throughout your generations?" "It shall be a perpetual statute that you shall not steal?" "It shall be a statute forever that you shall have no other gods?" This text, then, proves that the Sabbath was to cease with the other Jewish ceremonies.

"Gentile Christians must become Jews, Israelites, and so come under obligation to keep the Sabbath, for the Sabbath was given to Israel forever throughout their generations." This is a favorite Advent argument for the law and Sabbath. But see its utter fallacy: Burnt offerings, incense, washing of hands and feet, fringes, priesthood, circumcision, passover, and all the Jewish law were also given to *Israel* to keep forever throughout their generations. See above. Hence the argument proves that we must keep all these as well as the Sabbath! Do Adventists keep any of these: No.

It is argued that the Sabbath must be of perpetual obligation because it is associated in the decalogue with commandments of that nature. But it is also associated time and again with the ceremonial rites, types and shadows which were peculiarly Jewish. Thus: "Keep my Sabbaths and reverence my sanctury." Lev. 19: 30. "The Seventh day is the Sabbath." Lev. 23: 3. "At even is the Lord's passover." Verse 5. "The feast of unleavened bread." Verse 6. In verse 38 the Sabbath is named with "gifts," "vows" and "offerings." In Lev. 24: 1-8 the Sabbath is named with the offerings of oil, bread, frankincense. In Num. 28: 9, 10, it is classed with the offerings of lambs, meat and drink offerings, burnt offerings, etc. In 1 Chron. 23: 29-31, the Sabbath is classed with meat offering, sacrifices, new moons, feasts, etc. This fact offsets all the argument drawn from its place in the decalogue.

THE SABBATH IN THE HISTORICAL BOOKS.

From Joshua to Job not a word is said indicating that the Sabbath was for any one but Jews; hence no argument can be drawn from this source to bind it upon the Gentile Christians.

THE SABBATH IN THE PROPHETS.

The Sabbath is not mentioned in Job, Psalms, Proverbs, Ecclesiastes, Daniel, and most of the minor prophets. Nothing is said about it by any of the prophets which can fairly be made to apply to Christians. Several texts are applied by Adventists to our times, but it is all assumption without proof. For instance, Isa. 56 is used to prove that the Gentile Christians should keep the Sabbath. It says: The stranger, Gentile, "that keepeth the Sabbath from polluting it, and taketh hold of my covenant; even them will I bring to my holy mountain, and make them joyful in my house of prayer; their burnt offerings and their sacrifices shall be accepted upon mine altar." Verses 6, 7. If this proves that Gentiles must keep the Sabbath, it also proves that they must offer burnt offerings and sacrifices upon

God's altar in the temple on Mount Zion in Jerusalem, for all those are mentioned as plainly as the Sabbath. Either, then, this applies to the Jewish age and to those Gentile proselytes who embraced Judaism and were circumcised, Ex. 12: 48, and observed all Jewish rites; or if it applies to the Christian age, then these terms "Sabbath," "altar," "sacrifice," "my house," "my holy mountain," must be taken figuratively, for Christians do not offer sacrifices, nor have a literal altar, nor go to Jerusalem to worship in that house nor on that mountain.

So Isa 58: 12–13 is boldly applied to our days and to the work of the Adventists in urging all to keep the Jewish Sabbath. But there is not a word in all the chapter even hinting such a thing. All this they assume without any proof and then apply the words to suit their purpose. I did that a hundred times while with them, just as the rest did. I know just how they do it. At last I lost all confidence in such a reckless way of handling the word of God. Then I had to quit using the most of their proof texts on the Sabbath, this with others. Look at it. The whole chapter is addressed to the Jews, "the house of Jacob," verse 1, the "nation," verse 2, and so on. Often in the Jewish age God called them to reform their lax ways in keeping the Sabbath as well as in other things. This is one of those cases. Isa. 66: 22, 23. In the new earth "it shall come to pass *that* from one new moon to another, and from one Sabbath to another, shall all flesh come to worship before me, saith the Lord." This shows that the Sabbath will be kept in the next world, hence it is perpetual and so should be kept now. But it says just the same of the new moons and places them first before the Sabbath. So if this text proves that we should keep the Sabbath it proves we should keep the new moons also. Do Adventists keep the new moons?

Ez. 22: 26. "Her priests have violated my law, **and**

have profaned mine holy things; they have put no difference between the holy and profane, neither have they showed difference between the unclean and the clean, and have hid their eyes from my Sabbaths, and I am profaned among them." This text they also apply to their work now and to the ministers who oppose the Jewish Sabbath. But there is not a word in the whole chapter that even intimates that this applies away down here in the gospel and to Gentiles. But God himself applies it to the Jewish nation when they were overthrown by Babylon several hundred years before Christ. Read the whole chapter and compare it with Neh. 13: 17, 18. See verses 2, 6, 18, 19, etc. "Wilt thou judge the bloody city," etc. "Behold, the princes of Israel." "The house of Israel is to me become dross." "Therefore will I gather you into the midst of Jerusalem." The evidence is clear that it applies there, while no proof whatever can be given to show that it belongs away down here where Adventists apply it. I became fully convinced that it was by such groundless assumptions as these, by roundabout and far-fetched arguments, that the seventh-day theory is sustained. When you look for one plain, direct statement in all the Bible requiring Gentile Christians to keep the Sabbath, it cannot be found. It has to be *inferred* from this, *guessed* from that, and *concluded* from the other; all inference, nothing direct. So the Old Testament furnishes no evidence that Christians are to keep the Jewish Sabbath. If such proof is to be found, it must be in the New Testament itself.

CHAPTER XIV.

THE SABBATH IN THE NEW TESTAMENT.

THE SABBATH IN THE GOSPELS.

With the opening of the gospel comes the most glorious period of the church's history. The Son of God himself stands before us clothed with all the authority of heaven. Matt. 28: 18. God says, "Hear ye him." Matt. 17: 5. He came to introduce the gospel, "a new and living way," Heb. 10: 20, "the new covenant," "a better covenant" Heb. 8: 6, 8, which sets aside and supercedes the old, verse 13. Compared to the Jewish age it is a "great light," Matt. 4: 16, and the gospel church is represented as "a woman clothed with the sun, and the moon under her feet." Rev. 12: 1. Much which before was dark, shadowy and mysterious, is now light and plain. Rom. 16: 25, 26.

A great and radical change in the mode of worshipping God is now introduced. Many institutions of the Old Testament, which were once given in the most solemn manner, and by the authority of God himself, are no longer binding.

Now, where shall we look to find the clearest light upon these old institutions? Where shall we go to learn the real design of them all? Where shall we turn to obtain the necessary rules for a Christian to live by? Shall we go back to the moonlight of the Jewish law? to the starlight of the patriarchal age? or shall we come to the full sunlight of the gospel? Evidently the New Testament furnishes the clearest, and only authoritative guide for the Christian. The Old Testament can be read and rightly understood only in the light of the New. But it is a fact that Sabbatarians have to go back to the Old Testament, even clear back to the uncertain institutions of the patriarchal age, as their clearest and most certain authority for the seventh day. The evidence from the New Testament only comes in as secondary and collateral. All their strongest arguments for the Sabbath are away back among the shadows of the Old Testament. Take these from them, and the very foundation has fallen out from their theory. I know that this is so, for I have gone over the ground a thousand times. I know just how a seventh day man feels, and where he rests his confidence. It is in Genesis and the law. Of the New Testament he is a little shy. But is there any other Christian duty which is plainly laid down only in the Old Testament? I do not think of a single one, though in the past I tried hard and long to find it. On all other points the New Testament is clear and full. In it we have chapter after chapter, epistle after epistle, and book after book packed full of instruction on every Christian duty in every possible phase of it. The duty or the sin covered by each of the other nine commandments is directly named many times over in the New Testament. But the duty to keep the seventh day is not once mentioned. We arrange side by side—

THE TEN COMMANDMENTS OF THE OLD TESTAMENT.	THE TEN COMMANDMENTS OF THE NEW TESTAMENT.
1. "Thou shalt have no other Gods before me." Ex. 20: 3.	1. "We preach unto you that ye should turn from these vanities unto the living God, which made heaven and earth and the sea." Acts 14: 15.
2. "Thou shalt not make unto thee any graven image; * * * thou shalt not bow down to them nor serve them" Ex. 20: 4, 5.	2. "Little children keep yourselves from idols." John 5: 21.
3. "Thou shalt not take the name of the Lord thy God in vain." Ex. 20: 7.	3. "But above all things, my brethren, swear not, neither by heaven, neither by the earth, neither by any other oath." James 5: 12.

4. "Remember the Sabbath day to keep it holy." Ex. 20: 8.	4. There is no command in all the New Testament to keep the the seventh day
5. "Honor thy father and thy mother." Ex. 20: 12.	5. "Children, obey your parents in the Lord, for this is right." Eph. 6: 1.
6. "Thou shalt not kill." Ex. 20: 13.	6. "Thou shalt not kill." Rom. 13: 9.
7. "Thou shalt not commit adultery." Ex. 20: 14.	7. "Neither fornicators nor idolators nor adulterers * * * shall inherit the kingdom of God." 1 Cor. 6: 9, 10.
8. "Thou shalt not steal." Ex. 20: 15.	8. "Steal no more." Eph. 4: 28.
9. "Thou shalt not bear false witness." Ex. 20: 16.	9. "Lie not." Col. 3: 9.
10. "Thou shalt not covet." Ex. 20: 17.	10. "Covetousness, let it not be named among you." Eph. 5: 3.

"The duty of men to worship the Lord God only as taught in the first commandment is found no less than fifty times in the New Testament. Idolatry, which is the second commandment, is condemned twelve times. Profanity, the third commandment, is plainly condemned four times. Honor thy father and mother, which is the fifth commandment, is taught six times at least. Murder, which is the sixth prohibition, is found condemned six times. Adultery, the seventh, is condemned twelve times. Theft, the eighth, six times. False witness, the ninth, four times. Covetousness, the tenth, nine times. Now, with these facts before us, how can there be any danger that the law of God will be made void? Another remarkable fact is that the fourth commandment is not repeated in the New Testament, that no Christian was ever commanded to observe it, that no Christian was ever condemned for Sabbath breaking." Time and again, all through the New Testament long lists of sins embracing every possible shade of wickedness are given, but a disregard of the seventh day is never once included. Thus: Mark 7: 21, 22, thirteen sins; Rom. 1: 29–31, nineteen sins; Gal. 5: 19–21, seventeen sins; 2 Tim. 3: 1–4, eighteen sins, etc. How is this? Would the Sabbatarians have left it so?

Strange to say, the duty to keep the seventh day is not once mentioned in the whole New Testament. There is not one single command from either Christ or any of his apostles to keep that day. It is not once said that it is wrong to work on the seventh day, or that God will bless any one for observing it. There is no promise for keeping it, no threatening for not keeping it. No one is ever reproved for working on the seventh day, nor approved for observing it. If disregarding the seventh day is so great a crime as its advocates now claim, it is unaccountable that no warning against it should be given in all the New Testament, not even once. Is all this silence merely accidental? So Sabbatarians have to believe; but the supposition is absurd. Evidently it was left out on purpose, the same as the pentecost, passover, new moons, sacrifices and the like.

Paul, in all his fourteen epistles never even names the Sabbath but once, and that only to show its abolition. Col. 2: 16. Contrast this with Adventists' literature!

The usual answer is that the Jews were already keeping the Sabbath, even too strictly, and therefore the Jewish Christians needed no instruction on this point. But this answer is not satisfactory. The Jews were just as strictly opposed to false gods and images, and yet over and over Christians are warned against these things. Thus Paul says: "Neither be ye idolaters," and "Flee from idolatry." 1 Cor. 10: 7, 14. But where does it say, "Keep the seventh day?" or "Flee from Sabbath breaking?" Besides, the great body of the Christian converts in the latter years of the gospel, were Gentiles, who had never kept the seventh day at all. Why should they not be instructed how to keep it? Why should they be repeatedly warned against all other evil practices of their former lives, but never warned against breaking the Sabbath as they certainly had done before? This was a point which I was never able to answer satisfactorily to myself while I kept the seventh day. The simple and manifest fact is, that it was not intended to bind the Jewish Sabbath upon the Christian church. Hence it was quitely allowed to drop out with other old covenant holy days and institutions.

The arguments offered out of the New Testament for the observance of the seventh day are few and not hard to answer. Let us examine the main ones.

JESUS KEPT THE SEVENTH DAY, THEREFORE WE MUST.

With Sabbatarians this argument has more weight than all others from the New Testament. It always did with me. But now I am satisfied that, when fairly considered, there is nothing in it. Jesus was born and lived all his life under the law. Gal. 4: 4. That law was binding till his death. Col. 2: 14. Of course he ought to have kept every item of that law till the cross, just as he evidently did do. On this point Elder George I. Butler, Seventh-Day Adventist, says: "He lived under all the ceremonies and observances of the law of Moses, the same as did the other Jews. Thus he was 'born under the law' and subject to it. All his life he was careful not to break any of its provisions, and he never permitted his disciples to do it to the day of his death." "The Law in Galatians," page 59.

This is the plain truth in the case. But it shows the utter fallacy of arguing that we must keep the seventh day just because Jesus did. If we observe one institution of the old law just because Jesus did, then we should also keep all that he did; that is, live just as the Jews did under the law of Moses! For that is just what Jesus did. He instructed his disciples to offer gifts upon the altar, Matt. 5: 23, 24, sent a man to offer a gift, Matt. 8: 4, commanded his disciples to observe all that the scribes taught. Matt. 23: 2, 3, and was very particular to keep the passover just according to law only the day before his death. Luke 22: 7-15. But who thinks now of doing all these things because Jesus did? No one. Jesus was circumcised. Do Sabbatarians circumcise? No. Then why pick out the seventh day from all other holy days and rites and hold on to that while rejecting all the rest which he also observed? It seems as though a candid man must admit that this argument for the Jewish Sabbath is not a success. If that day is binding upon Christians it must be upon some other ground than because Jesus kept it while living as a Jew under the Jewish law.

MARK 2: 27, 28. THE SABBATH MADE FOR MAN.

The Sabbatarian use of this text is directly contrary to its plainest meaning. Jesus was not giving a history of the origin of the Sabbath, nor defending its sacredness against desecration, nor showing that it was made for all the race. No such thought is the subject of his remarks. He is not claiming the Jewish Sabbath as his day, as the day consecrated to himself. It was not as God, the Creator, that he claimed to be its Lord; but it was as the *Son of man*, the representative of man, that he claimed to be lord over the Sabbath.

Notice his premises and his conclusions: "The Sabbath was made for man, not man for the Sabbath: *therefore* the son of man is Lord also of the Sabbath." He says that as the Sabbath was made for man and not man for the Sabbath, *therefore* he, a son of man, was Lord of it. Why was Jesus Lord of the Sabbath? Because he was the Son of God and had made it? Not at all; but because he was the Son of man, man for whom the Sabbath was made. It is as a *man* that he claims to be its Lord. And this he said to defend his disciples against the charge of breaking the Sabbath. How did it apply? Why, the Sabbath was made for them and hence it was only their servant. They were superior to the Sabbath. Notice the cases he used to illustrate his statement. Matt. 12: 3-12.

1. David went to the priest and ate holy bread which the law forbade to any but priests. His needs were superior to that ceremonial precept.

2. "The priests in the temple profane the Sabbath and are blameless." Verse 5. They would slay cattle all the Sabbath day. Their service was superior to the Sabbath.

3. If a sheep fall into a pit on the Sabbath they would work hard to get him out. The preservation of animal life was superior to the Sabbath. I have seen Adventists work hard on the Sabbath in case of a fire to save even the goods, though the law says, "In it thou shalt not do any work." Would they dare violate the letter of any other commandment that way? No. Then, surely, Jesus himself being judge, the observance of the strict letter of the Sabbath law is not a matter of the highest importance. This is the lesson plainly taught here by Christ, the Lord of the Sabbath. It squarely condemns the rigid interpretation of the Sabbatarians who make the Sabbath more important than man himself for whom it was made.

4. The Sabbath was made for *man*, hence the necessities of men are above the Sabbath law. So, then, this text, when fairly read, gives no support to the sacredness of the Jewish Sabbath under the gospel.

MATT. 24: 20.

As this is one of their favorite texts we will examine it. Foretelling the fall of Jerusalem which occurred forty years after his death, Jesus said that when they saw the armies come around the city, they must flee immediately or be caught in the city, and perish with the others. Hence he said, "Let him which is on the housetop not come down to take anything out of his house. Neither let him which is in the field return back to take his clothes. And woe unto them that are with child, and to them that give suck in those days! But pray ye that your flight be not in the winter, neither on the Sabbath day. For then shall be great tribulation." Matt. 24: 17-21.

From this it is argued that the Sabbath would continue to be a sacred day after the resurrection. Adventists admit that it would not be a violation of the Sabbath to flee on that day in case of necessity. Then where is there any argument in the text? If their flight had occurred on the Sabbath to save their lives, would that have desecrated the day? They own that it would not. Then the sacredness of the day was not what Jesus had in view.

The context plainly shows that it was for their *safety* that he was providing, not for the keeping of the day. The proper observance of the Sabbath is not the subject at all. The dangers and tribulations of that time was the subject. Notice four points. 1. Those with child. 2. Those with nursing babes. 3. Fleeing in the winter. 4. Fleeing on the Sabbath. If they had to flee suddenly, in haste, and without any preparation, even without their ordinary clothes, women with child or with little babes, or persons in the cold of winter would be liable to suffer or die. So in all these three cases Jesus refers to the inconvenience and danger of their flight; and this is exactly why he mentions the Sabbath. On that day the gates of the city would be shut and so hinder them greatly if not detain them entirely. The gates of all the villages through which they must pass would be closed. The Jews would suspect them and arrest them as traitors. Hence it would be dangerous, almost impossible, to flee on that day. A candid person can see that this is all there is to that text. Of this I became convinced sometime before I gave up the Sabbath, and so I stopped using it.

MATT. 28: 1, MARK 16: 1, 2. "THE SABBATH" IS THE DAY BEFORE "THE FIRST DAY OF THE WEEK."

"In the end of the Sabbath as it began to dawn towards the first day of the week." "When the Sabbath was past, * * * the first day of the week." According to this the Sabbath, after the death of Christ, is still the day before the first day of the week. Hence the first day of the week on which Christ rose was not the Sabbath yet. Answer: All the days in the week, in the month, and in the year, still continued to be called by their old Jewish names for many years after Christ; but it does not follow that they continued to be sacred days, for Paul expressly states that all those feasts days, new moons, and Sabbath days were nailed to the cross. Col. 2: 14, 16; Gal. 4: 10, 11; Rom. 14: 5, 6. Take three examples: "When the day of Pentecost was fully come," Acts 2: 1; "Then were the days of unleavened bread." Acts 12: 3. "Went into the synagogue on the Sabbath day." Acts 13: 14. Here, long after the cross, we have the same old names for three of the Jewish holy days, viz: Pentecost, days of unleavened bread, and Sabbath day. Are all these days still holy days because they are still called by their former names? If so, then we ought to observe Pentecost and the days of unleavened bread as well as keep the Sabbath. So there is no force in the argument from the use of the word Sabbath after the cross. The resurrection day was not called the Sabbath in the New Testament nor by Christians for several hundred years after Christ. It was called "Lord's Day." Rev. 1: 10.

"*The Sabbath*" was the name of the Jewish rest day, "which was a shadow of things to come." Col. 2: 16, 17, but the resurrection day is another day entirely. It is called "the first day of the week," "the eighth day," or the "Lord's Day." It is only in an accommodated sense that it is called the Sabbath now as we use the words "altar," "sanctuary," "temple," "sacrifice," "Israel," etc.

LUKE 23: 56. THE WOMAN "RESTED THE SABBATH DAY ACCORDING TO THE COMMANDMENT."

This was after Christ died; hence it shows that they thought that the Sabbath was still to be kept. They were the followers of Jesus and knew what he taught. Answer: But this was before Jesus rose from the dead, before they knew anything about his resurrection, and before they had any idea of the great change which the gospel was to make in the service of God. Their old Jewish idea still blinded their minds so that they could not at once take in the nature of what Jesus had really come to do. Just before this Jesus said: "I have yet many things to say unto you, but ye cannot bear them now." John 16: 12. So he had not tried to explain all these less important matters to them; but he said that he would, after the resurrection, send them the Holy Spirit to guide them into all truth. John 16: 13. It was not till after the Holy Ghost came upon them at Pentecost that they began to comprehend the true nature of the gospel. So it is no proof that the Jewish Sabbath is binding on Gentiles because the Jewish women kept it while Jesus was dead and in his grave. Turn to Acts 1: 14, and 2: 1, and we find all these same women fifty days after the resurrection still carefully keeping "the day of Pentecost," another Jewish holy day. But do our Sabbatarians keep Pentecost because these women kept it? No, but they should if they keep the Sabbath because those women kept it. This shows how groundless that argument is.

THE SABBATH 59 TIMES IN THE NEW TESTAMENT.

They say, the fact that the Sabbath is named 59 times in the New Testament is proof that it was still of great importance and should be kept. Well, the temple is mentioned in the New Testament 115 times; circumcision, 55 times; sacrifices, 38 times; the passover, 28 times, etc. Then I suppose we ought also to have all these over in the gospel!

THE SABBATH IN THE BOOK OF ACTS.

Sabbatarians think they have a fair argument in the Acts. Here the seventh day is always called "the Sabbath," and it may be that the Jewish Christians still observed it, and met with the Jews in worship on that day. From this it is concluded that all Christians should keep that day, too. This is based upon the false assumption that whatever customs and laws of the old covenant were still observed for a few years by the Jewish Christians after the resurrection, must be binding upon the Gentile church now.

A careful examination of what the disciples did really do for many years after the resurrection will show that they kept all the Mosaic law, including feast days, the Sabbath day, sacrifices, circumcision, vows, and the whole Jewish ritual. But they did this as Jews, according to their national law and long established custom. That they did not do so as a Christian duty is manifest from the fact that Gentile Christians were not required to observe these things. Acts 15: 19-28; 21: 25. "As touching the Gentiles which believe, we have written and concluded that they observed no such thing." Every mention of the Sabbath in Acts, without a single exception, is in connection with the Jewish worship on that day. Acts 13: 14, 15, 42-45; 15: 21; 16: 13; 17: 1, 2; 18: 4. The law and the prophets were read, and Jewish worship conducted as usual. Certainly the disciples could not hold distinctively Christian meeting here under these circumstances. They must assemble by themselves to worship Jesus and have the Lord's supper, and that is just what we find them doing on the first day of the week. Acts 20: 7. There is no record of a single meeting of Gentile Christians upon the seventh day, nor of Jewish Christians, except in the Jewish worship.

Consider a few facts as to why the Jewish Christians did not immediately give up the observance of the Mosaic law.

How carefully and gradually Jesus unfolded his new doctrines, even to the chosen apostles. To the multitude he spoke only in parables "as they were able to hear it." Mark 4: 33. Had Jesus at once and plainly told the people the radical change which he had come to make in the Jewish system of worship, they would have killed him immediately. Even the apostles would doubtless have left him. During all the ministry of our Lord, nothing stands out more prominently than the fact that he was gradually, but cautiously, preparing the minds of his disciples for the great change which his gospel was destined to make in the worship of God. The great obstacles he had to contend with were their narrow views, their tenacity for the forms and ceremonies and letter of the law, and Jewish ideas of God's kingdom. That he was to take the throne of David, subjugate the world to Israel, and carry on the Jewish mode of worship with the temple service—this idea was so firmly rooted in the minds of even the apostles, that they could not understand Jesus even when he plainly told them to the contrary. Hence the Saviour simply left them to outgrow these ideas as the nature of his gospel more fully dawned upon them, after his resurrection and ascension and the descent of the Holy Spirit. Just before Jesus died, he said: "I have yet many things to say unto you, but ye cannot bear them now. Howbeit when he, the Spirit of Truth, is come, he will guide you into all truth." John 16: 12, 13. How often he had to say to them, "O fools, and slow of heart to believe." Luke 24: 25. "Are ye also yet without understanding?" Matt. 15: 16.

During all the ministry of Christ he never once stated directly that any of the Jewish rites would be abolished, not even sacrifices, the temple service, circumcision, the feast days, or anything. Yet he well knew that all these were soon to end, and designed that they should. Neither the people nor the disciples were then prepared for such an announcement. Hence he left these things for them to learn later. It is in the epistles of Paul that these changes are distinctly stated, just where we find the Jewish Sabbath abrogated.

Forty days after the resurrection still found them clinging to their old Jewish idea of the temporal reign of Jesus at Jerusalem. "Lord, wilt thou at this time restore again the kingdom to Israel?" Knowing that it was impossible to correct their wrong notions by a mere statement, Jesus left them to outgrow these errors as they learned more of the gospel. Now follow them through the book of Acts, and observe how long and tenaciously they held on to all the observances of the old Jewish law, not only the Sabbath, but all the temple service and ceremonies of the Mosaic law. On Pentecost we find them keeping the sacred day with the other Jews. Acts 2. As late as ten years after the resurrection they were "preaching the word to none but unto the Jews only." Acts 11: 19. Not a sermon had they thought of preaching to a Gentile till God, by a special miracle, sent Peter to Cornelius. Acts 10. As late as this Peter was scrupulously regarding the Mosaic law of meats. He said, "I have never eaten anything that is common or unclean." Verse 14. And he designed to keep right on observing it. And when the Holy Spirit came upon the Gentiles, the disciples were astonished "because that on the Gentiles also was poured out the gift of the Holy Ghost." Verse 45. When he returned to Jerusalem, the whole church was in an uproar over it. "And when Peter was come up to Jerusalem, they that were of the circumcision contended with him, saying, Thou wentest in to men uncircumcised, and didst eat with them." Acts 11: 2, 3.

Up to this time, then, we find the church at Jerusalem, with Peter at its head, still keeping the Jewish law concerning food, and refusing to eat with Gentiles. Now study the great council at Jerusalem, held over twenty years after the resurrection. Acts 15. Not only did the whole church in Judea keep the entire Mosaic law in all its rites, including circumcision, but some of them endeavored also to force it upon the Gentile converts. Verses 1–19. But through the influence of Paul, this move was defeated. If it had not been that, in the providence of God, Paul was raised up to oppose it, the whole Christian church would have been placed under the bondage of the Mosaic law. As it was, that council freed only the Gentile converts from obedience to Moses' law. Acts 15: 19, 23; 21: 25. All Jewish Christians still kept it.

Even as late as A. D. 60, or nearly thirty years after the cross, we still find the whole Jewish church in Judea strictly keeping the law of Moses as to circumcision, offerings, vows, shaving the head, etc. Not only did they themselves observe all these rites of the old law, but they required all Jewish Christians throughout the world to do the same. When Paul went up to Jerusalem only a few years before his death, they demanded of him a pledge that he himself also kept these rites. Read carefully Acts 21: 20-26.

These words show conclusively that the Jewish Christians observed all the rites of the laws of Moses as late as that, which was but a few years before the fall of Jerusalem. All church historians agree that the Jewish Christians continued to observe the seventh day, even for some time after the fall of Jerusalem, as we have seen.

Philip Schaff, the greatest of living authors, in his History of the Apostolical Church, page 118, says: "So far as we know, the Jewish Christians of the first generation, at least in Palestine, scripturally observed the Sabbath, the annual Jewish feasts, and the whole Mosaic ritual, and celebrated in addition to these the Christian Sunday, the death and resurrection of the Lord, and the holy supper. But this union was gradually weakened, and was at last entirely broken by the destruction of the temple. * * * The Jewish Sabbath passed into the Christian Sunday." Elder Waggoner, Adventist, says: "Dr. Schaff is justly esteemed as a man of extensive learning, and whose testimony regarding facts no one would call in question," Replies to Canright, page 132. Good. Now let them accept Dr. Schaff's statement and cease their denials.

Elder Butler, Adventist, truly says: "Indeed, it may well be doubted whether a large portion of the early church who were Jews before conversion ever fully realized the scope and extent of the gospel in setting aside those laws peculiarly Jewish. They clung to them, and were zealous for them long after they were abolished at the cross. To Paul we are indebted, through the blessing of God, for the only full explanation of the proper relation of these laws to the plan of salvation." "Law in Galatians," page 8.

How much, then, does it prove in favor of the Jewish Sabbath to find that it was still called "the Sabbath," or that it was kept by the Jewish Christians, or even by Paul himself? Just nothing at all; for by the same argument, as we have seen, we must observe the passover, pentecost, offer offerings, make vows, shave your heads, be circumcised, and keep all the rites of the Mosaic law the same as those disciples did for years.

THE APOSTLE PAUL AND THE KEEPING OF THE SABBATH DAY.

Seventh-Day Adventists try to make an argument for the Jewish Sabbath from Paul's example. They count up some 84 Sabbaths which they claim he kept, and they say that if he kept it we ought also. I used to think there was great force in this argument and have used it scores of times to convince others. But I became satisfied finally that the whole argument was a fallacy. Let us examine it.

1. Paul was a Jew, but we are Gentiles.
2. Paul was brought up in all the observances of the Jewish law. Acts 22: 3. We were not.
3. The great desire of Paul's heart was to win his Jewish brethren to Christ. To do this he was willing to die, yea even to be accursed himself. Rom. 9: 3, 4.
4. To win these Jewish brethren he was very cautious not to do anything, as far as he could possibly avoid it, which would prejudice them against him and so cut off his access to them.
5. As these Jews were very zealous in the observance of all the Jewish law, Paul knew that he must himself also keep this law if he were to obtain any access to them. Hence he says: "Unto the Jews I became as a Jew that I might gain the Jews; to them that are under the law [the Jews], as under the law, that I might gain them that are under the law." "And this I do for the gospel's sake." 1 Cor. 9: 20, 23. See what he did in the case of Timothy. "Him would Paul have to go forth with him; and took and circumcised him because of the Jews which were in those quarters; for they knew all that his father was a Greek." Acts 16: 3. Paul wanted Timothy to help him among the Jews, but he knew that the Jews would not listen to him if he were not circumcised. So he circumcised Timothy to gain the Jews, though he said, "Circumcision is nothing." 1 Cor. 7: 19. For just the same reason he kept the Pentecost, Acts 18: 21; 20: 16; shaved his head, Acts 18: 18; made offerings, Acts 21: 20-26; and lived the same as the Jews did, though he knew and taught that all these things were done away.

Now suppose it could be shown that Paul always kept the Sabbath, would that prove that he regarded it as obligatory upon all Christians, specially the Gentile Christians? Surely not. To them he wrote very plainly that they were not to keep the law concerning meats, drinks, feast days, new moons and Sabbath days. See Col. 2: 14–17; Rom. 14: 1–5; Gal. 4: 10. He taught with regard to all these just as he did about circumcision, Gal. 5: 2, that none of these were necessary, yet he himself circumcised Timothy.

We will now examine every text where Paul is said to have kept the Sabbath. Acts 13: 14, 15. "He went into the synagogue on the Sabbath day and sat down. After the reading of the law and the prophets" he was invited to preach to them, which he did. This was with the Jews in Jewish worship, in the Jewish synagogue, on the Jewish Sabbath. Paul as a Jew joined them in this, in order to preach the gospel to them. So, verses 42–46, on the next Sabbath he met with them again in the same place for the same purpose. This was two Sabbaths Paul kept. Acts 16: 13, "on the Sabbath he went out of the city by a river side where prayer was wont to be made," or rather where there was a *proseuche*, a Jewish house of prayer. So the Syriac and Greek. Here he found Jewish women at worship, and preached Jesus to them. This was the third Sabbath he kept. Acts 17: 1, 2. Paul "came to Thessalonica where was a synagogue of the Jews, * * * and three Sabbath days reasoned with them." Here again it was in the Jewish worship among the Jews in their synagogue on their Sabbath. Three more Sabbaths here, six so far. Acts 18: 1–4. Paul is again among the Jews "and he reasoned in the synagogue every Sabbath and persuaded the Jews and the Greeks." Same as before, his Sabbath keeping is every time while he is among the Jews in their Sabbath worship. But how many Sabbaths did he meet with them here? Verse 11 says: Paul remained there in Corinth one "year and six months," which would be 78 weeks. Hence Adventists say he kept 78 Sabbaths here. These added to six before make 84. But verses 6 and 7 put a different face on the matter. Instead of reasoning in the synagogue every Sabbath all this time, he withdrew from the Jews and said, "Henceforth I will go unto the Gentiles." Then he went into the house of Justus near the synagogue. So there is no evidence that he preached in the synagogue more than a few Sabbaths. So their 84 Sabbaths that Paul kept dwindled down to ten or a dozen and all these were with the Jews in Jewish worship. And this he himself explains by saying, "Unto the Jews I became as a Jew that I might gain the Jews." 1 Cor. 9: 20.

Not one single case can be found where Paul kept the Sabbath in a Christian assembly, nor is it ever mentioned in any way in connection with Christian meetings, while it is said that the disciples met on the first day of the week. Mark this: "Wherever the apostles entered the Jewish synagogues on the Sabbath to preach, it was before the Christian church was planted in such places."

PAUL DID NOTHING AGAINST THE CUSTOM OF THE JEWS, HENCE KEPT THE SABBATH.

In Acts 25: 8, Paul says he had done nothing "against the law of the Jews," and in Acts 28: 17 says, he had "committed nothing against the people or customs of our fathers." From this it is claimed that he must have kept the Sabbath, for that was the law and custom of the fathers. True, but so it was their custom to circumcise, to offer sacrifices, to keep the new moons, yearly feasts, etc. Hence Paul must have done all these. Shall we then do all these because Paul as a Jew did? Hardly. Notice that nearly every argument applies equally as well to all the Jewish law and would bind that whole system on Christians!

CHAPTER XV.

THE JEWISH SABBATH ABOLISHED. COL. 2.

1. We now come to the direct statement of Paul that the Sabbath was abolished: Col. 2:14, 16, 17. "Blotting out the handwriting of ordinances that was against us, which was contrary to us, and took it out of the way, nailing it to his cross. * * * Let no man therefore judge you in meat, or in drink, or in respect of a holy day, or of the new moon, or of the Sabbath days; which are a shadow of things to come; but the body is of Christ." With other Jewish ordinances, the Sabbath was blotted out and nailed to the cross; therefore no man is to judge us about keeping "the Sabbath days." The statement is positive and plain. When I kept the seventh day this text always perplexed me as it does my Advent brethren now, say what they will. Paul directly names "the Sabbath" or "the Sabbath days," for there is no difference, as among the shadows which have passed away.

2. It is said by some that "the Sabbath days," plural number, is not the same as "the Sabbath," singular number, hence is not the weekly Sabbath. This is a groundless objection, for both the singular and the plural numbers are used indifferently for the weekly Sabbath. Thus Greenfield's Greek N. T. Lexicon says: "Sabbaton. The Sabbath, * * * both in the singular and plural." Bagster's Greek Lexicon says: "The Jewish Sabbath both in the singular and plural." So plain is this fact that even Elder Smith, Adventist, is compelled to admit it though he tries to save his theory by excepting Col. 2, and Acts 17: 2, but without reason. He says: "When it [*Sabbaton*] is used in

the plural form [excepting Acts 17: 2 and Col. 2: 16], it means just the same as if it had been written in the singular." Greek Falsehood, page 8. Col. 2: 16, is no exception to the rule. In Acts 17: 2, the word *three* is what marks the plural. The Revised Version properly renders Col. 2: 16, in the singular, thus: "Let no man therefore judge you in respect of a Sabbath day," singular number. Sawyer's translation says: "In respect to a feast, or new moon, or Sabbath," singular. The Bible Union says: "Of a feast day, or of a new moon, or of a Sabbath," singular.

A few quotations will show that both the singular and plural numbers are used for the weekly Sabbath. "My Sabbaths [plural] shall ye keep for it [singular] is a sign between me and you." Ex. 31: 13. This is the weekly Sabbath. "Keep my Sabbaths." Lev. 19: 3. "Beside the Sabbaths of the Lord." Lev. 23: 38. Adventists argue that this is the weekly Sabbath. "Blessed is the man that * * * keepeth the Sabbath," "the eunuchs that keep my Sabbaths." Isa. 56: 2, 4. Either singular or plural, no difference. "I gave them my Sabbaths to be a sign." Ez. 20: 12. This is the weekly Sabbath, as Adventists well know. "On the Sabbath days [plural] the priests in the temple profane the Sabbath" [singular]. Matt. 12: 5. Here we have in the same verse both the plural and singular used for the weekly Sabbath. "Is it lawful to heal on the Sabbath days?" Matt. 12: 10. "Taught them on the Sabbath days." Luke 4: 31. "Three Sabbath days reasoned with them." Acts 17: 2. "Let no man therefore judge you * * * in respect of the Sabbath days." Col. 2: 16.

Who can read this list of texts and not be profoundly impressed that by "the Sabbath days" of Col. 2: 16 Paul means just what that language means in all the other cases? Of course he did, and no other reasonable application can be made of it.

3. In the Greek, in which Paul wrote Col. 2: 16, he uses not only the same word which is always used for the weekly Sabbath, but exactly the same form of the word used in the fourth commandment itself! I will give the Greek word for "Sabbath days" in Col. 2: 16 and other texts where the same word and same form of the word, letter for letter, is used for the weekly Sabbath. Col. 2: 16. "Let no man judge you in respect to the Sabbath days," Greek, $\sigma\alpha\beta\beta\acute{\alpha}\tau\omega\nu$, Sabbaton, genitive plural.

Ex. 20: 8, 10, fourth commandment, "Remember the Sabbath day [Greek, $\sigma\alpha\beta\beta\acute{\alpha}\tau\omega\nu$, Sabbaton, genitive plural] to keep it holy." "But the seventh day is the Sabbath [Greek, $\sigma\acute{\alpha}\beta\beta\alpha\tau\alpha$, Sabbate, accusative plural] of the Lord." Here it will be seen that Paul uses the same Greek word, letter for letter, that is used in the decalogue. Hence he surely meant that very Sabbath day. Notice, further, that in each case in the fourth commandment where the word "Sabbath" occurs it is plural in the Greek. So if the use of the plural in Col. 2 shows any thing, it shows that the Sabbath of the decalogue is meant. Moreover, the Revised Version renders Ex. 20: 10, and Col. 2: 16, exactly alike. Thus: "The seventh day is a Sabbath unto the Lord." "Let no man judge you in respect of 'a Sabbath.'" Plainly, then, Col. 2: 16, refers to the Sabbath of Ex. 20: 8-11.

Further, $\sigma\alpha\beta\beta\acute{\alpha}\tau\omega\nu$, Sabbaton, genitive plural, the form of the word used in Col. 2: 16, is the one often used in other texts for the weekly Sabbath. Thus: Ex. 35: 3. "Kindle no fire * * * upon the Sabbath day," $\sigma\alpha\beta\beta\acute{\alpha}\tau\omega\nu$.

Lev. 23· 38. "Beside the Sabbaths, $\sigma\alpha\beta\beta\acute{\alpha}\tau\omega\nu$, of the Lord."

Lev. 24: 8: "Every Sabbath, $\sigma\alpha\beta\beta\acute{\alpha}\tau\omega\nu$, he shall set it in order."

Num. 15: 32. "Gathered sticks upon the Sabbath day," $\sigma\alpha\beta\beta\acute{\alpha}\tau\omega\nu$.

Numbers 28: 9. "On the Sabbath, σαββάτων, day two lambs."

Deut. 5: 12. Fourth commandment again, "Keep the Sabbath, σαββάτων, day."

Isa. 58: 13. "Turn away thy foot from the Sabbath," σαββάτων.

Matt. 28: 1. "In the end of the Sabbath," σαββάτων.

Luke 4: 16. "He went into the synagogue on the Sabbath, σαββάτων, day"

Acts 13: 14. "Went into the synagogue on the Sabbath, σαββάτων, day."

Col. 2: 16. "Let no man therefore judge you * * in respect of the Sabbath, σαββάτων, days."

Unless a man is blinded by a pet theory, he must see that Col. 2: 16 does surely mean the weekly Sabbath, as in all the other texts where the same word occurs.

4. The only word ever used in the Bible for the weekly Sabbath is the very one Paul did use, σαββάτων, *Sabbaton*. So if he had meant to name that Sabbath, what else could he have said than just what he did say, the Sabbath days? Why, then, deny that he means just what he says when he could have said nothing else if he had meant the Sabbath?

5. The word Sabbath occurs in the New Testament 60 times. Seventh-Day Adventists admit that in 59 out of these 60 cases it means the weekly Sabbath; but in the 60th case, where exactly the same word is used both in Greek and English, as we have seen, they say it must mean something else! Isn't that remarkable? Hear them: "In the New Testament the Sabbath of the Lord is mentioned 59 times, and those local Sabbaths, which expired by limitation and ceased at the cross, are mentioned once." Scripture References, p. 9. Strange that the Sabbath means the Sabbath 59 times and the 60th time it don't! "Jewish feasts are often spoken of in the New Testament but, not one of them

anywhere is called a Sabbath or credited with the nature of a Sabbath." The Sabbath for Man, p. 544.

6. "The feast days and new moons" of Col. 2: 16, include all the holy days of the Jews except the weekly Sabbath; hence there was nothing else left to which it could apply but that Sabbath. The entire list is given in Num. 28 and 29.

7. But what settles it beyond a reasonable doubt that Col. 2: 16, does refer to the weekly Sabbaths is the fact that exactly the same list of holy days here given by Paul is given about a dozen times in the Old Testament, where we know it means the seventh day.

Turn to Num. 28 and 29, and you have a detailed law as to just what offerings shall be made on each day of the whole year. The first were the *daily* offerings of "two lambs," day by day, for a continual burnt offering. "The one lamb shalt thou offer in the morning, and the other lamb shalt thou offer at the even." Verses 3 and 4. The second were the offerings on the sabbath. "And on the sabbath day two lambs of the first year without spot," verses 9 and 10. None will deny that this was the weekly sabbath. Third, in the very next verse come the new moons. "And in the beginning of your months ye shall offer a burnt offering unto the Lord," verses 11–15. Fourth comes the annual feast days. "And in the fourteenth day of the first month is the passover of the Lord," verse 16. Then follows a complete list of all the annual feast days, closing with these words, "These things shall ye do unto the Lord in your set feasts," Num 29: 39.

Here we have the law for the *daily, weekly, monthly,* and *yearly* offerings; or, those on each day, on the weekly sabbaths, on the new moons, and on the yearly feast days. Now read the following texts, and notice how this list of daily offerings, offerings on the sabbaths, on the new moons, and on the set feasts, as laid down in the law of Moses, is repeatedly referred to in almost exactly the words of Col. 2: 16.

1. Chron. 23: 30, 31: "To stand every morning to thank and praise the Lord, and likewise at even; and to offer all burnt sacrifices unto to the Lord in the sabbaths, in the new moons, and on the set feasts, by number, according to the order commanded unto them." Here is a direct reference to the daily offerings, offerings on the weekly sabbaths, new moons and set feasts, just as ordered in Num. 28 and 29. Can any one doubt that "the sabbaths" here are the weekly sabbaths, the same as there? Certainly not.

2. Chron. 2: 4: "Behold, I build an house to the name of the Lord my God, to dedicate it to him, and to burn before him sweet incense, and for the continual shew bread, and for the burnt offerings morning and evening [daily], on the sabbaths [weekly], and on the new moons [monthly], and on the solemn feasts [yearly] of the Lord." Precisely the same list again, and in the same order, hence the weekly sabbaths are the ones named. Besides, it would be absurd to suppose that Solomon would name all the other and minor holy days, but say nothing about the chiefest of all days, the weekly sabbaths. Every candid man would admit that "the sabbaths" here are the weekly sabbaths, and so they are in all the passages which follow.

2. Chron. 8: 13: "Even after a certain rate every day [daily again], offering according to the commandment of Moses, on the sabbaths [weekly], and on the new moons [monthly], and on the solemn feasts [yearly], three times in the year." Same list and order as before.

2. Chron. 31: 3: "The morning and evening burnt offerings, and the burnt offerings for the sabbaths, and for the new moons, and for the set feasts, as it is written in the law of the Lord." The same list again, daily, weekly,

monthly and yearly offerings, just in the order they would naturally come, and just as given "in the law of the Lord." Num. 28 and 29. But if the sabbaths are not the weekly sabbaths, then the Lord names the daily, monthly and yearly offerings, but skips the weekly offerings. Every thinking man knows that such an interpretation is false. But it is the only way the sabbaths can be saved from Paul's list, Col. 2: 16, for that is the same as all these. As the object in these passages is to mention the service of God which must be performed on each of the holy days, it would be absurd to suppose that all the other sacred days in the whole year would be carefully mentioned time and again, while no reference whatever is made to the weekly sabbaths, the most important and the most numerous of all the sacred days.

Neh. 10: 33: "For the shew bread, and for the continual meat offering, and for the continual burnt offering, of the sabbaths, of the new moons, for the set feasts." Same list again, daily, weekly, monthly and yearly. Either the weekly sabbaths are meant here, or else reference to the worship of God on the Sabbath is always studiously avoided, while all the rest is carefully mentioned. The evidence is too plain to mistake which.

Ezek. 45: 17: "Offerings in the feasts, and in the new moons, and in the sabbaths." Here are named exactly the same days that Paul gives in Col. 2: 16, and in the same order, yearly, monthly, weekly.

Hosea 2: 11: "I will also cause all her mirth to cease, her feast days, her new moons, and her sabbaths, and all her solemn feasts." Same list of holy days that we have had over and over, where we know that sabbath meant the seventh day.

Col. 2: 16: "Let no man therefore judge you in meat, or in drink, or in respect of a feast day, (Rev. Version), or of

THE JEWISH SABBATH ABOLISHED.

the new moon, or of the sabbath days." Here, as before, are the yearly, monthly and weekly holy days just as laid down in the law where we know the weekly sabbaths are meant. It is evident that Paul had in his mind those lists of holy days so often given in the Old Testament, where the sabbath is included.

The words "the sabbath days" would certainly embrace the weekly sabbaths unless they were especially named as excepted. But no such exception is made. Hence we must apply the term as it is used in the law, to the seventh day.

Hosea 2: 11, is a plain prophecy that all these holy days should cease just as we know has happened in fact; and in Col. 2: 16, is proof that they were nailed to the cross.

8. TESTIMONY OF OTHERS ON COL. 2: 14–17.

Bunyan.—On this text, John Bunyan, than whom no man ever studied his Bible more closely, says: "Here also as he [Paul] serveth other holy days he serveth the Sabbath, he gives a liberty to believers to refuse the observation of it. Nor hath the apostle (since he saith, or of the sabbath), one would think, left any hole out at which men's inventions could get." Again: "The old seventh-day Sabbath is abolished and done away." Bunyan's Complete Works, pages 899, 900.

Dr. Scott says: "Doubtless, this last related principally to the weekly Sabbath, which, as observed on the seventh day, was now become a part of the abrogated Jewish law."

The Pulpit Commentary on this text says: "The 'Sabbath days' referred to the Jewish Sabbath which was always observed on Saturday." "If the ordinance of the Sabbath had been in any form of lasting obligation on the Christian church, it would have been quite impossible for the apostle to have used this language."

John Wesley:—"In respect of a yearly feast, the new moon, or the weekly Jewish Sabbath."

Dr. Lee, Methodist:—"The apostle refers to the seventh-day Sabbath and he gives them clearly to understand that they are not morally bound to observe it. * * * By a 'holy day' and the 'new moon,' he included all other feasts and rests which might be called Sabbaths, leaving nothing but the seventh day Sabbath to be meant by the Sabbath days." Lee's Theology, page 375.

9. That upon which Seventh-Day Adventists rely to save this text from applying to the sabbath is the assertion that there were several yearly or annual sabbath days, and that Paul's language must apply to these instead of to the weekly sabbaths. Thus Elder Andrews, in his "History of the Sabbath," says, "There were seven annual sabbaths," and then he names all the Jewish feast days, as the pentecost, day of atonement, etc., and cites Lev. 23. It is true that in our English version the word *sabbath* is applied to four of these feast days. But we turn to the Greek, in which Paul wrote, and find that the word for "sabbath" is *sabbaton*. Is that the term used where the word *sabbath* is applied to the annual feast days? No, indeed, except in just barely one instance. The day of atonement is called a sabbath (*sabbaton*) in the Greek. Lev. 23: 32. "In the Old Testament Hebrew none of those feast days are ever termed a Sabbath, save the day of atonement." Sabbath for Man, page 544.

The Hebrew word for sabbath is *shabbath*. In only this one instance is it ever applied to any of the annual festivals. But the word "sabbath" in the English version, when applied to these annual feasts, is from the Greek term *anapausis*, and in the Hebrew from *shabbathon*. These words should not be translated "sabbath," but should be rendered "rest," as they are in the Revised Version. Thus all these texts read in the New Version: "In the seventh month, in the first day of the month, there shall be a solemn *rest* unto you." Lev. 23: 24. "On the first day shall be a solemn *rest*, and on the eighth day shall be a solemn *rest*," verse 39. So also in the English version of the Hebrew used by the Jews these words are translated *rest*, not sabbath. Thus: "In the seventh month, on the first day of the month, shall ye have a *rest*," not sabbath, verse 24. "On the first day shall be a *rest*, and on the eighth day shall be a *rest*," verse 39.

Hence, except the weekly sabbaths, among all the feast days and holy days of the Old Testament only one single day in the whole year is ever called a sabbath. So it is not correct to speak of "the annnal sabbaths," much less to say that there were seven of them. There was just one, and no more, and this one was included in the annual feast days. Even Elder Andrews confesses that "the annual sabbaths, were part and parcel of these feasts and could have no existence until after the feasts to which they belonged had been instituted. Thus the first and second of these Sabbaths were the first and seventh days of the pascal feast. The third annual sabbath was identical with the feast of pentecost." History of the Sabbath, page 86. By his own confession the days he calls annual sabbaths were all included in those yearly feasts and could have no existence separate from them. Feast days (*heortes*) is the term embracing all those days, as we have seen. Hence "the sabbath days" (*sabbaton*) must apply only to the weekly sabbaths. Or, to say the least, this term being pre-emiently, almost exclusively, applied to the weekly sabbaths, must include them any way, whether it did any others or not.

10. Seventh-Day Adventists try to make a difference be-

tween "the Sabbaths of the Lord," Lev. 23: 38; Ex. 20: 10, and "her Sabbaths," Hosea 2: 11. They say that "her Sabbaths," were the Jewish Sabbaths, yearly feast days; but that the Lord's Sabbath is never called *her* Sabbaths. The assertion is contrary to facts.

Why were the yearly holy days *her* days? Did the Jews appoint them? No; the Lord appointed them just as he did the sabbath, and gave them to Israel to keep, just as he gave them the sabbath to keep. Hence, from one point of view they are the Lord's, but from another view they are her days. God's, because he commanded them; hers, because given to them. "I gave them my sabbaths." So we read of nearly every sacred institution of the Bible. In one place it is "the Lord's" and in the next it is "hers," "yours" or "theirs," but the same institution all the time. Thus we read of the temple: "Mine house," Is. 56: 7; "your house," Matt. 23: 38. Of the sacrifices: "The sacrifices of the Lord," Lev. 10: 13; "my offering, and my bread for my sacrifices," Num. 28: 2; "your burnt offerings, and your sacrifices, and your tithes," Deut. 12: 6. Of the law: "My law," Jer. 6: 19; "your law," John 10: 34. Now notice particularly that the feast days are spoken of in exactly the same manner that the sabbath is; that is, "my feasts," and "her feasts," "my sabbaths" and "her sabbaths." Thus: "The Lord's passover," Ex. 12: 11; "the feast of the Lord," Lev. 23: 4; "the sabbaths of the Lord," verse 38; "my feasts," verse 2; "my sabbaths," Ex. 31: 13; "a feast unto the Lord," Lev. 23: 41; "the holy sabbath unto the Lord," Ex. 16: 23; "*her* feast days, *her* new moons, and *her* sabbaths," Hosea 2: 11. These quotations are sufficient to show the fallacy of trying to make a distinction between "my sabbaths" and "her sabbaths." The same argument would prove that "my feasts" and "her feasts," "my sacrifices" and "your sacrifices," "my house" and "your house," etc., were entirely different. But everybody knows better. These expressions apply to the same thing from different standpoints; the sabbaths of the Lord as appointed by him; her sabbaths as kept by them; and this is the whole of it.

11. Paul represents these things as "blotted out," "nailed to the cross." Col. 2: 14. It is said that this could not apply to the Sabbath which was engraved in the stones in the decalogue, as you could not blot out nor nail up this. The answer is easy. To blot out and to nail up are only used as an illustration. Anciently a document that had been cancelled, or abolished, was rubbed or blotted out, or a nail was driven through it, as now a conductor punches a ticket to show that it has been used up. As an *illustration* it could be applied to laws written in any manner, no matter what. Such objections are unworthy a candid man. Paul says these things were *against* us; but it is said that the Sabbath was not against us; hence it cannot mean that. *Answer:* 1. Paul says it was; that ought to settle it. 2. The Jewish Sabbath was the great sign of Judaism. Ez. 20: 10–13; Deut. 5: 15. As such, it carried with it that whole system and so was against Christians.

12. It is said that the weekly Sabbath was never associated with meats, drinks, feast days, etc., as in Col. 2: 16. This is a great mistake as we have already seen. It is classed with these a score of times. See Lev. 23: 2–6; Num. 28: 3–11; 1 Chron. 23: 29–31, etc.

13. But it is argued that as "the sabbath days" of Col. 2: 16, "are a shadow of things to come," verse 17, and the weekly Sabbath is a memorial of creation, pointing back to the beginning, therefore they cannot be the same, for the sabbath could not point both ways. But is not this a mere assertion without any proof? How do we know that it cannot point both ways? The passover was a memorial of their deliverance from Egypt, and always pointed back to that

event. Ex. 12: 11-17. Yet it was also a shadow of Christ. Col. 2: 16-17. "Even Christ our passover is sacrificed for us," 1 Cor. 5: 7. So all these annual feasts were types of Christ in some way, and yet all were memorials also of past events, as all know. But who would ever have thought of this if the apostle had not said so?

If, then, these feast days could be both memorials and types, pointing both ways, so can the Sabbath. Paul says plainly that the Sabbath days are a shadow of things to come; and one plain statement of inspiration is worth a thousand of our vain reasonings. This is in harmony with Paul's argument in Heb. 4: 1-11, that the seventh day is a type. For forty years they have tried to explain away this text, and to show that it really cannot mean what it says; but there it stands and mocks all their theories. The Sabbath is a type, for inspiration says so.

Again, it is said that the Sabbath was instituted before the fall, but types could not have been instituted till after the fall. How do you know that they could not be? Where does the Bible say so? Peter says of Christ: "Who verily was foreordained before the foundation of the world, but was manifested in these last times for you," 1 Peter 1: 20. The revelator says, "The Lamb slain from the foundation of the world," Rev. 13: 8. If, then, Christ before the foundation of the world was ordained to die, then the Sabbath might have been designed even before the creation of the earth, as a type of Christ.

Dr. Watson says: "It is used as an expressive type of the heavenly and eternal rest." Theol. Inst. Vol. II, page 509. The Pulpit Commentary says: "The Sabbath of the Jews was typical." On Col. 2: 17. Dr. Adam Clarke says: "The truth is, the Sabbath is considered as a type." On Ex. 20: 8. Even Elder Andrews, Seventh-Day Adventist, says: "When the Creator gave existence to our world, did he not forsee the fall of man? And, foreseeing that fall, did he not entertain the purpose of redeeming man? And does it not follow that the purpose of redemption was entertained in that of creation?" History of the Sabbath, page 151. Exactly; and so the Sabbath as a type of that redemption might have been given in Eden according to their own showing. So, on close inspection, every argument of our Seventh-Day brethren on Col. 2 fails them.

14. By a false and ungrammatical construction of the relative pronoun *"which"* in Col. 2: 17, Adventists try to exclude the weekly Jewish Sabbath from the text. They make the pronoun *which* refer only to *"the Sabbath days,"* making it read, "Those Sabbath days which are a shadow." This they say, implies that there are other Sabbaths which are not a shadow, that is the seventh day. But the Greek word for "Sabbath days" is $\sigma\alpha\beta\beta\acute{\alpha}\tau\omega\nu$, *Sabbaton*, genitive plural, while the word for *"which"* is $\acute{\alpha}$, *ha*, nominative plural, neuter. Hence *which* cannot agree with *Sabbath days*, as any scholar knows. "Which are a shadow" relates to the whole list given in verse 16, viz., meats, drinks, feast days, new moons and Sabbaths. The revised version renders it, "a feast day, or a new moon, or a Sabbath day, which are a shadow." Not simply the Sabbath alone, but all these together were a shadow. Hence the phrase, "which are a shadow," applies to each item in verse 16. Does Paul, then, mean to say that only certain feast days, certain new moons, and certain Sabbaths were shadows, while there were other feast days, other new moons and other Sabbaths which were not shadows and so were excepted from his list? No, he makes no exception whatever, neither of feasts, moons, or Sabbaths. All were included, none were excepted. Hence as Paul included every feast day, and every new moon, so he also included every Sabbath of the Old Testament, and that took in the weekly Sabbath as the

chief of all, to say the least. So the last peg on which to hang the Jewish Sabbath goes down.

Professor A. M. Weston, President of Eureka College, Ill., says very truly: "If the Sabbath does not look to Christ for its underlying principle, then it is the one important observance of the Old and New Testament that fails to do so." The Evolution of a Shadow, page 16. We know that there was in Eden one type of Christ, that was Adam, for the Bible says so, Rom. 5: 14. "Adam * * * who is the *figure* of him that was to come." *Figure* is from the Greek τύπος, *tupos*, type. "Who was the *type* of him that was to come." Syriac, Diaglott, Sawyer, Living Oracles, and Bible Union Translations. Hence types were instituted in Eden. Therefore the Sabbath cannot be excepted from the types on that ground.

In Gal. 4: 10, 11, Paul sets aside the keeping the Jewish Sabbath and all those holy days of the law. "Ye observe days, and months, and times, and years. I am afraid of you." That this refers to the holy days of the old law is proved by his reference to that law, both before and after this text. Thus: "The law was our schoolmaster to bring us unto Christ, that we might be justified by faith. But after that faith is come we are no longer under a schoolmaster." Gal. 3: 24, 25. That law has ended at the cross as Paul said in Col. 2: 14–17. Again: "Tell me, ye that desire to be under the law, do ye not hear the law?" Gal. 4: 21. "Ye are not under the law." Gal. 5: 18. So, then, he means the holy days of the law and these included the Sabbath as the chief of all. Look at his list: *Days*, (Sabbath days, weekly), months (new moons), times (yearly feasts), and years (Sabbatical years). This is exactly the list of Jewish holy times.

To the Romans Paul taught the same doctrine: the observance of the Jewish holy days was not to be regarded.

"One man esteemeth one day above another; another esteemeth every day alike. Let every man be fully persuaded in his own mind." Rom. 14: 5.

Dr. Potts, Methodist, says: "That the Sabbath question entered into Paul's reasonings on the occasion is evident from Rom. 14: 1-6 " The Lord's Day Our Sabbath, page 27. These were the days enjoined in the law for it is of the law that he treats all through the book of Romans. He makes no exception of the Sabbath day, but says plainly "*every day.*" Only a few verses before he has quoted five of the ten commandments, Chap. 13: 9, showing that he included the days of the decalogue. It does not avail to say that Paul means only the annual Sabbaths because he mentions eating meat and herbs. I have already proved that the weekly Sabbath was associated with these time and again.

What proves that Paul did intend to set aside the Sabbath, as his words naturally mean, is the fact that nowhere does he ever in all his instructions to the churches say one word in favor of keeping the Sabbath. Time and again he enjoins every other duty, but never a word about keeping the Sabbath in all his fourteen letters. Most of those to whom he wrote were Gentiles who never had kept the Sabbath and hence needed instructions in it if they were to keep it. But not a word does he say to them about it; though he does command them about the first day of the week. 1 Cor. 16: 1, 2.

But it is said that this view of Paul's language abolishes all holy days and leaves the church without any rest day. The answer is easy and manifest. Paul was treating of the old institutions which had been nailed to the cross. Col. 2: 14. Hence his language has no reference to the new institutions of the gospel, of which there might have been a dozen holy days, so far as these texts are concerned.

CHAPTER XVI.

A HISTORY OF NUMEROUS EFFORTS TO REVIVE THE JEW-
ISH SABBATH. ALL FAIL.

WHY NOT FOUND OUT BEFORE ?

If Sabbatarians are right on the Sabbath question, then the whole Christian church has broken the Sabbath for the last 1,800 years, and has kept Sunday, "a popish institution," "the mark of the beast," in its stead. During these long ages all the holy men, martyrs, reformers, commentators, historians and Christian scholars, with all their seeking of God, searching the Bible, and studying history, never discovered this great mistake! Is it reasonable to believe that the entire church, during all its history, has been trampling upon one of God's most holy commandments? Can it be that the wrath of God is now to be poured out upon the church for keeping the same day that all others have kept for 1,800 years? Would God have blessed the reformers and his church as he has, if Sunday-keeping is such a fearful crime against God as is now claimed?

Now, just to think that the whole church of Christ, immediately after the death of the apostles, should fall into this fearful sin and error, and practice this crime without rebuke during the entire history of the church, till just a few days before Jesus comes, and then only a few find it out and change. According to the Seventh-Day Adventists, Luther, Calvin, Knox, Wesley, with all the church of Christ for hundreds of years, committed two fearful sins each week of their lives; they broke the holy Sabbath, the **most** important commandment in the decalogue, and kept

Sunday, the mark of the beast! Yet God has let the whole thing go on without any protest, till the last minute of time, and now everybody who does not acccept this "new light," is to be hopelessly damned for doing what Christians generally have always done! In all candor, this is a pretty big pill to swallow.

But Sabbatarians say that this has nothing to do with the case. "Our appeal is to the Bible alone. The Bible plainly teaches it, and we will go by that." So they say, and so they believe; but the fact is, it is only their interpretation, their explanation, of the Bible which makes it say so. Did you ever know a sect under heaven, even the wildest and most fanatical, who were not always on hand ready to "prove it all by the Bible"? Yes; they know that they are right beyond a doubt, "because the Bible just says so." They will argue you blind, and grow more confident every day, and always end by saying, "It is true, not because I say so, but because the Bible says so." Meet a Mormon, and he has the Bible at his tongue's end. He "proves it all by the Bible." So the Shaker, and the Swedenborgian, and the Universalist, and the rest of them, "prove it all by the Bible." How many persons and sects have arisen at different times with a perfect furor of enthusiasm over some new idea besides "the old, old story of Jesus and his love." No matter what harm it does to other Christians and to the gospel, "the Bible teaches it, and that is enough. When we give this up we will give up the Bible, too." So they go on till time alone demolishes their theory, and then they do indeed give up the Bible and all, while precious souls are lost.

KEEPING THE JEWISH SABBATH A FAILURE.

Sabbatarians began in England in the time of the Reformation, over three hundred years ago. They had many able men, ministers and writers. They published many books, discussed the subject widely, and made many converts. Here they had a fine field and a fair start. How did Sabbath-keeping succeed? What have they accomplished in England? Three hundred years ought to be long enough to tell whether it is a success or not. Let Elder Andrews tell the sad story: "In the seventeenth century eleven churches of Sabbatarians flourished in England, while many scattered Sabbath-keepers were to be found in various parts of the kingdom. *Now* but three of these churches are in existence! And only remnants, even of these, remain!" Hist. Sabbath, p. 491. Since he wrote the above, two more out of the three, I believe, have expired, and only one little company of less than ten members survives! Elder A. sorrowfully asks, " To what cause shall we assign this painful fact?" The cause is evident; God is not in it. It comes to naught every time it is tried. Three hundred years hence the same mournful requiem will be chanted over the grave of Seventh-day Adventism.

Now look at the history of the Sabbatarian effort in America.

In 1664, over 200 years ago, the Seventh-Day Baptists began teaching that doctrine in America at Newport, R. I. The first church was organized Dec. 23, 1671. See "Manual of the Seventh-Day Baptists," pages 39, 40. From that time on they industriously taught the observance of the seventh day, both in America and other lands, even as far as China, by preaching, by tracts, books and periodicals, till the religious world is familiar with their views. They were numerous enough to organize a general conference as early as 1802. See Hist. S. D. Bap. Gen. Conf., pages 15, 238, or any cyclopedia. They have had academies, colleges, and universities; learned men, able writers, and zealous workers. What have they accomplished? Almost nothing. They now number only about 8,000, and are not holding their own, but are losing ground every decade. They can not even hold the increase of their children. Largely their youth abandon Saturday for Sunday. For convenience they mostly colonize together, and so have little influence on the world. To their praise be it said that they are an excellent people, and free from any fanatical or other heretical notions. Here again the seventh day has had the fairest possible chance of success. Its advocates are intelligent, highly educated, respected, and live in this free land and age of investigation. Why has it not succeeded? That it has not they themselves must admit. These sober, stubborn facts should have weight with us. Sabbatarian brethren, stop and weigh these things fairly. What is the use of wasting life contending for what is a practical failure?

In 1846, nearly seventy years ago, Seventh-Day Adventists began teaching the Sabbath. They have practiced it zealously, devoted everything to it, poured out treasures by the million, and filled the land with their literature. What have they accomplished? They number only about 100,000 now. Have 4,000 workers in the field and spend $2,000,000 yearly yet gain only about 4,000 yearly, or one to each worker! Half of these are from other churches. The system lacks vitality and gospel power.

Contrast with the above the work and success of the First-Day Baptists. What a grand work they have done for Christ and souls in the last two hundred years. Instead numbering 8,000, as the Seventh-Day Baptists do, they number 5,000,000. As a body they are just as pious and devoted as the Seventh-Day Baptists. Then look at the Methodist and other Sunday-keeping churches, and see how God has blessed them all. Experience shows that keeping the Jewish Sabbath dwarfs, cripples, and unfits a church for gospel work.

If, now, keeping Saturday is so highly pleasing to God, why does he not prosper it more? If Sunday observance is such a sin in the sight of God, why does he so remarkably bless those who persist in it?

LUTHER AND THE SABBATH.

Even the Adventists acknowledge the greatness of Luther in piety and a deep knowledge of the word of God. Mrs. White says of him: "Zealous, ardent, and devoted, knowing no fear but the fear of God, and acknowledging no foundation for religious faith but the holy scriptures," etc. "Angels of heaven were by his side and rays of light from the throne of God revealed the treasures of truth to his understanding." Great Controversy, pages 94, 97. Good. Now hear Luther. Carlstadt, a zealous and learned Sabbatarian, laid his arguments for the seventh day before Luther, who examined them. Here is Luther's decision in his own words: "Indeed, if Carlstadt were to write further about the Sabbath, Sunday would have to give way, and the Sabbath—that is to say, Saturday—must be kept holy; he would truly make us Jews in all things, and we should come to be circumcised; for that is true and cannot be denied, that he who deems it necessary to keep one law of Moses, and keeps it as the law of Moses, must deem all necessary, and keep them all." Hist. Sabbath, p. 457.

So, then, the "light" on the Sabbath question was given to Luther, and he rejected it, just as the great body of Christians do now. The other leaders of the reformation were likewise familiar with the arguments for the seventh day, but, as Elder Andrews confesses, they "as a body were not friendly to such views." Hist. Sabbath, p. 460.

These facts show how untrue it is to say that people have been unacquainted with this Sabbath question before.

JOHN MILTON ON THE SABBATH.

So the great John Milton, author of "Paradise Lost," has thoroughly discussed the whole Sabbath question, using the same arguments as we use now to show the abolition of the Jewish Sabbath. I quote a few sentences from his "Treatise on Christian Doctrine," Vol. 1, Book 2, Chap. 7. "It is evident from more than one passage of scripture that the original Sabbath is abrogated." "If, then, the commandment of the Sabbath was given to those alone whom God brought out of the land of Egypt and out of the house of bondage, it is evidently inapplicable to us as Christians." He argues the question this way at considerable length.

RICHARD BAXTER ON THE SABBATH.

This great divine, the author of "Saints' Rest," "Call to the Unconverted," etc., in 1671, wrote his "Divine Appointment of the Lord's Day" against the Seventh-Day advocates of his times. Gilfillan, says: "Baxter (1671) and Bunyan (1685) wrote their interesting defences of the Lord's day for relieving the perplexities with which some good people in their time were distressed in consequence of the proselyting zeal of Saturday Sabbathists." The Sabbath, p. 144. So the Sabbatarians over 200 years ago were giving the same "light" and doing the same proselyting work as now. They were answered by such men as Baxter, Bunyan, Milton, etc.

I give a few words from Baxter: "It is also confessed, that the universal church from the days of the apostles down till now have constantly kept holy the Lord's day in the memory of Christ's resurrection, and that as by the will of Christ delivered to them by or from the apostles; insomuch that I remember not either any orthodox Christian, or heretic, that ever opposed, questioned, or scrupled it, till of late ages." Part 2, Chap. 18. Of him even Mrs. White says: Baxter, a man "of talent, education, and deep Christian experience, stood up in valiant defense of the faith once delivered to the saints." Great Controversy, page 175. Yes: such men as these stood up and opposed the Jewish Sabbath heresy.

JOHN BUNYAN.

Hear Mrs. White on Bunyan: "John Bunyan breathed the very atmosphere of heaven." Great Controversy, page 174. Well, now hear Bunyan: "As for the seventh day Sabbath, that, as we see, is gone to its grave with the signs and shadows of the Old Testament; yea, and it has such a dash left upon it by apostolical authority, that it is enough to make a Christian fly from it for ever. 2 Cor. 3." "Again the apostle smites the teachers of the law upon the mouth, saying, 'they understand neither what they say nor whereof they affirm.'" Complete Works, page 915.

If ever a man this side the apostles lived near to God, drank into his spirit, and knew the true intent of the Bible, that man was Bunyan, author of the immortal work, Pilgrim's Progress. He met these Sabbatarians and their work in his day. He studied the subject fully and wrote a book against them from which I have quoted.

He regarded them just as they are regarded now, as legalists, blind zealots, and disturbers of the church.

So all this talk that the church did not have the light on the Sabbath question till Adventists arose to give it is contrary to facts as the above proves. It is simply the old arguments of 200 years ago rehashed.

CHAPTER XVII.

THE LAW.

The foundation of the Sabbatarian error, I believe, is the idea that "the law," in all the strictness of the old letter, is binding on Christians. Hence, their constant theme is the law, law, law. They preach it ten times as much as they preach Christ. Unfortunately, a false theory of the law taught by some other churches has led them into this sad error. For twenty-eight years I was held in that "bondage." Now that I have found my way out, if I can help others, I shall rejoice.

The following simple facts with regard to the law helped me out of Adventism and I have never known anyone to get out of it any other way. I believe it to be the correct answer to the Saturday Sabbath error. I write for candid readers. They will examine my arguments fairly and allow others to do the same, even if they should not agree fully with every position. As a result of the present agitation of the Sabbath question, we ought to expect a better understanding of the whole subject than heretofore. Forty years of investigation and discussion of the question have firmly settled me on the following propositions. They are in harmony with the best men and theologians of this and past ages; hence nothing original on my part.

ANTINOMIANISM.

Antinomians, from *anti*, against and *nomos*, law, against law, is a term applied to those who maintain that Christians are under no obligation to keep the law of God or to do any good works. If they commit any kind of sin it will not hinder their salvation at all if they only believe in Jesus. Salvation is wholly of faith without any regard to a man's deeds. See any cyclopedia. This is an abominable doctrine, subversive of the gospel; yet Seventh-Day Adventists brand all as Antinomians who do not agree with them as to what is the law of God. I am as much opposed to Antinomianism as they. I believe in strict obedience to law, in keeping the commandments of God, and in the necessity of good works, as strongly as they do. Luther vehemently opposed Antinomianism and yet taught the abolition of the Mosaic law. It is unfair and unjust for Adventists to call people Antinomians who abhor that doctrine. We plead for a pure life, good works and obedience to God, as necessary to salvation. Hence it is a falsehood and a slander to represent us as Antinomians. Men who are conscious of being in the right can afford to state the position of their opponents fairly. Bunyan, Judson, and a host of such men have repudiated the Sabbatarian idea of the law, and yet have been holy men. I am not afraid to stand with them.

Even Elder Waggoner says: "As to whether the Saviour abolished the ten commandments and with them the Sabbath, is a theological question; it is only a matter of Scripture interpretation." Replies to Elder Canright, page 164. Very well; then men may differ on this question and still be honest Christians. I will now lay down a few propositions concerning the law which seem to me so plain and well supported by the Bible, that all must agree with them.

PROPOSITION 1. "THE LAW" EMBRACES THE WHOLE MOSAIC LAW, MORAL, CIVIL AND CEREMONIAL.

The term, "the law," when used with the definite article and without qualifying words, refers "in nine cases out of ten, to the Mosaic law, or to the Pentateuch." Smith's

Bible Dictionary, article Law. Largely the Adventists use the term, "the law," for the ten commandments only. They hang up a chart of the decalogue and constantly point to it as "the law," Matt. 5: 17; "the law of the Lord," Ps. 19: 7; "the law of God," Rom. 7: 22. This is their fundamental error on the law. I affirm that "the law" included the whole system of law given to the Jews at Sinai, embracing all those requirements, whether moral, civil or ceremonial, decalogue and all. Look at the term "law," in a concordance, or in any Bible lexicon, dictionary or cyclopedia. "The law" commonly included the whole of the five books of Moses. Even Elder Butler is compelled to make this confession: "The term, 'the law,' among the Jews generally included the five books of Moses, thus including the whole system, moral, ritual, typical and civil." Law in Galatians, page 70. That is the truth exactly. Dr. John Kitto, in his Cyclopedia of Religious Literature, article Law, says: "If, however, the word law alone is used it is almost invariably equivalent to the law of Moses." "The law is especially embodied in the last four books of the Pentateuch."

Now bear in mind this one simple fact, wherever you find the term "the law," and you will have no trouble with Sabbatarian arguments on "the law."

Take a few examples of the use of the term "the law." 1 Cor. 14: 34. Women "are commanded to be under obedience, as also saith *the law*." Where does the law say this? Gen. 3: 16. So Genesis is in the law. Again: "The law had said, Thou shalt not covet." Rom. 7: 7. Where? Ex. 20: 17. So Exodus is in the law. Once more: "Master, which is the great commandment in the law?" Matt. 22: 36. Jesus then makes two quotations from the law; first, "Thou shalt love the Lord with all thy heart." This is taken from Deut. 6: 5. So Deuteronomy is in the law. Second,

"Thou shalt love thy neighbor as thyself." This is from Lev. 19: 18. So Leviticus is a part of the law. And this: "Have ye not read in the law, how that on the Sabbath days the priests in the temple profane the Sabbath, and are blameless?" Matt. 12: 5. It is from Num. 28: 9. These then, embrace all the five books of Moses as *"the law."* Observe a little where the law is spoken of and you will soon see that it refers indiscriminately to each and all of the books of Moses as "the law." Of course any verse in any of these books is quoted as "the law," because it is a part of the law. So the ten commandments are quoted as the law because they are a part of the law.

Again, "the law" embraces all parts of the law, moral, civil or ceremonial. Thus the ceremonial precepts: "The parents brought in the child Jesus to do for him after the custom of the law." Luke 2: 27. That is, to offer a sacrifice. Verse 24. Moral precepts: "The law is not made for a righteous man, but for the lawless and disobedient, for the ungodly and for sinners, for unholy and profane, for murderers." 1 Tim. 1: 9. This is the decalogue. Civil precepts: "Commandest me to be smitten contrary to the law?" Acts 23: 3. Notice that every time it is simply the law. "Gamaliel, a doctor of the law." Acts 5: 34. Of what law? Was he simply a doctor of some part of the law, as the moral, or civil, or ceremonial precepts? Every intelligent man knows that "the law," of which he was doctor or teacher, was the whole Pentateuch, decalogue included. The law, then, is the whole Jewish law, in all its parts. This one point, clearly settled, destroys nine-tenths of all the Seventh-Day Adventist argument for the Jewish Sabbath.

THE TWO LAWS.

PROPOSITION 2. *There was no such thing as two separate laws given to the Jews.* To sustain their doctrine Sabbatarians have invented a theory of two laws given at Sinai; one the moral law, the other the ceremonial.

Adventists attach the utmost importance to their theory of two laws as well they may; for if this is wrong their cause is lost. Elder U. Smith says: "No question, therefore, more vital to the interest of Sabbath-keepers can be proposed." Synopsis of Present Truth, page 258. But that they are wrong on this vital question is very easily shown.

1. *"Moral law," "ceremonial law."* Adventists use these two terms as freely as though the Bible was full of them; yet, strange to say, the scriptures make no such distinctions, never speak of one law as "moral" and of another as "ceremonial." Adventists severely criticise those who happen to use an unscriptural word or phrase; yet they themselves do the very thing commonly, as in this case. It would be amusing to hear one of them try to preach on the "two laws" and confine himself to Bible language! He could not possibly do it. If there were two distinct laws given to Israel, so opposite in their nature, it is strange that there is no record of it, no reference to it in the Bible. If one was abolished and the other was not, strange that Paul should not make the distinction when he has so much to say about the law. Why did he not say, "we establish the moral law"? or, "the ceremonial law was our schoolmaster"? No, he just says "the law" and leaves it there. He seems not to have been quite as clear on that point as Adventists are! On this point Kitto's Cyclopedia of Biblical Literature, Article Law, says: "Neither Christ nor the apostles ever distinguished between the moral, the ceremonial, and the civil law, when they speak of its establishment or its abolition."

2. *The two laws contrasted.* Adventists have drawn up a long list of things which they claim are true of the "moral" law and an opposite list which can apply only

to the "ceremonial" law. These two they contrast and make out two laws. Thus Elder Smith: "Moral law:"—"Was spoken from Sinai by the voice of God and twice written upon tables of stone by his own finger." "Was deposited in the golden ark." "Related only to moral duties." Synopsis of Present Truth, page 266. Of course this was just the ten commandments, nothing more, nothing less. So here we have their "moral law." Now here is the other one: "The ceremonial law:"—"Was communicated to Moses privately and was by Moses written with a pen in a book. Deut. 31: 9." "Was put into a receptacle by the side of the ark. Deut. 31: 26." "Was wholly ceremonial." Same page.

Hence everything not found in the decalogue belongs to the ceremonial law and everything Moses himself wrote in the book of the law placed in the side of the ark is "wholly ceremonial." Deut. 31: 26, reads: "Take this book of the law and put it in the side of the ark." The decalogue was in the ark, the book of the law was by the side of the ark. We enquire, then, how much "the book of the law" contained. The answer is easy: it contained all the five books of Moses, Genesis, Exodus, Leviticus, Numbers, and Deuteronomy. Thus 2 Kings 14: 6, says it "is written in the book of the law of Moses," and then quotes Deut 24: 16, as that book of the law. 2 Chron. 35: 12, says: "It is written in the book of Moses," and refers to Lev. 3: 3. Ezra 6: 18, says: "It is written in the book of Moses," and refers to Num. 3: 6. Joshua 8: 31 quotes Ex. 20: 25, as that which "is written in the book of the law." 1 Cor. 14: 34 refers to Gen. 3: 16, as "the law." Dr. Scott on Deut. 31: 26, says: "This [book] appears to have been a correct and authentic copy of the five books of Moses."

So what they call the ceremonial law contains scores of precepts as purely moral as any in the decalogue. Read these: "Thou shalt not vex a stranger." "Ye shall not afflict any widow or fatherless child." Ex. 22: 21, 22. "Thou shalt not follow a multitude to do evil." Ex. 23: 2. "Ye shall be holy." "Thou shalt not go up and down as a tale bearer among thy people." "Thou shalt not avenge, nor bear any grudge against the children of thy people, but thou shalt love thy neighbor as thyself." Lev. 19: 2, 16,18. "Thou shalt not respect persons." "Thou shalt be perfect." Deut. 16: 19, 18, 13. Are these precepts, and scores like them, to be classed as ceremonial because God did not write them on a stone but gave them to Moses to write in a book? Surely not. Then the nature of a precept was not determined by the way it was given. God gave them all at different times as it pleased him.

As we have seen, "the law" embraces the "whole law." Gal. 5: 3. Of course, in that law, some precepts refer to moral duties, other to civil, and others to ceremonial, but all are only different parts of the same law, called, as a whole, "the law." Thus Jesus quotes from Lev. 19, as "the law." See Matt. 22: 36–40. Now read the whole chapter, Lev. 19, and you find moral, civil and ceremonial precepts all mingled together, and often in the same verse. Adventists, to sustain their theory, have to go through this chapter, as they do through the whole Bible, and cut and carve, and split hairs, and label one sentence "the moral law," another "the ceremonial law," etc. This is what is properly termed "the scrapping system." It does great violence to the Scriptures, wresting them out of their evident meaning.

In no place can they find their ceremonial law given by itself. They have to pick it out here and there in scraps. The "book of the law," which was placed in the side of the ark, Deut. 31: 24–26, is pointed to as the ceremonial law. But this "book of the law," as we see, embraced the whole five books of Moses.

It contains all of the ten commandments word for word twice repeated. Ex. 20 and Deut. 5. Elder G. I. Butler himself makes this confession: "The 'book of the law,' which was placed in the side of the ark, or at the side of it, contained both the moral and ceremonial laws." Law in Galatians, p. 39. That drops the bottom out of the theory that the moral law was "in the ark, and the ceremonial law in the side of the ark," as they usually claim. So, on close examination, every text on which they rely for two laws will fail them. That the "book of the law" did contain moral precepts is settled by Gal. 3: 10. "It is written, cursed is every one that continueth not in all things which are written in the book of the law to do them." Where in the book of the law is this written? In Deut. 27: 26. Turning there we have a curse against images, verse 15, disobedience to parents, verse 16, adultery, verse 20; murder, verse 24; bribery, verse 25; then comes the verse quoted as "the book of the law." So if the decalogue contains moral law, then the book did too. This shows the utter fallacy of their theory of two laws.

The following passage alone overturns the two law theory of Adventists: "Master, which is the great commandment in the law? Jesus said unto him, thou shalt love the Lord thy God with all thy heart, and with all thy soul, and with all thy mind. This is the first and great commandment. And the second is like unto it: Thou shalt love thy neighbor as thyself. On these two commandments hang all the law and the prophets." Matt. 22: 36–40.

1. These two great commandments were "in the law." 2. But neither of them is found in the decalogue. 3. Both of them are in what Adventists call the ceremonial law. 4. Neither of them was spoken by God, nor written by him, nor engraved on stones, nor put into the ark. Both were given by God to Moses privately and he wrote them with a

pen in the book of the law which was placed in the side of the ark. And yet these two precepts are the greatest of all. Jesus said of the first one that it is "the first of all the commandments." Of the two he said, "There is none other commandments greater than these." Mark 12: 29, 31. And on these two hang all the law. So, then, the greatest commandments are in the book of the law, not on the tables of stone. How utterly this demolishes their two law argument. It shows that the mere fact that the ten commandments were spoken by God, written on stone, and placed in the ark, is no proof that they were superior to those given through Moses in the book of the law.

We will examine a few more of their contrasts of the two laws as they arrange them. Thus:

"1. Moral: Existed in Eden before the fall. Ceremonial: Was given after the fall.

2. Moral: Was perfect. Ps. 19: 7. Ceremonial: Made nothing perfect. Heb. 7:19.

3. Moral: Contains the whole duty of man. Eccl. 12:13. Ceremonial: 'Stood only in meats and drinks, and divers washings, and carnal ordinances.' Heb. 9: 10."

1. Where do they read that the decalogue was given in Eden? Nowhere. This they assume not only without proof, but against the plain record of Ex. 19 and 20 that it was given at Sinai. So their very first comparison is a failure.

2. The law is perfect, Ps. 19: 7, and again, the law made nothing perfect. Heb. 7: 19. This they regard as one of their clearest proofs of the two laws. But where is the proof? Does it follow that if the law is perfect it will or can make sinners perfect? If it could, then, as Paul says, "righteousness should be by the law," Gal. 3: 21, and "then Christ is dead in vain." Gal. 2: 21. The law could be perfect and yet fail to make anybody perfect. So there is no proof of two laws here after all.

3. Eccl. 12: 13 is quoted as referring to the ten commandments alone and then it is asserted that these contain every duty of man. Both statements are fallacious. There are scores of duties we owe to God and men not even hinted at in the decalogue. Then there is not a particle of evidence that Eccl. 12: 13 refers alone to the decalogue. It manifestly embraces all God's commandments on all subjects. Look at the second quotation, Heb. 9: 10. It does not refer to any law whatever but is speaking of the service of the priests in the temple, which service "stood only in meats, drinks," etc. Read it. Thus their " two laws " are made out: 1. By pure assumptions. 2. By misapplications of scripture. 3. By detached phrases here and there taken out of their proper connection. So I could go through their whole list and show that it proves no such contrast as they claim.

But they assert that such opposite things are said of "the law," that it cannot be the same law all the time. This method of proving two laws by contrasting particular expressions about the law when spoken of from different standpoints, would make bad work with the Bible if urged on other subjects. Paul said he was "a Jew," Acts 21: 39, and again that he was "a Roman," Acts 22: 25; two Pauls. So Christ is "a Lion" and "a Lamb," Rev. 5: 5, 6. "The everlasting Father," Isa. 9: 6, and born of a woman, Luke, 2:7; Prince of Life, Acts, 3: 15, yet died through weakness, 2 Cor. 13: 4; a child, Isa. 9: 6 ; and yet God, Heb. 1: 1-8— two Christs. It would be much harder to reconcile the apparently opposite things said of Christ, than it would be the different things said about the law. There were different sides to Christ's nature, yet he was but one person. So there were different sides to the law, but it was only one law for all that. Viewed in the light of its ultimate design, **viz.**: to prepare the way for Christ, Rom. 10: 4; Gal. 3: 23-

25, in its spirit, Rom. 7: 6; in its righteousness, Rom. 8: 3, 4; it was "holy and just and good," Rom. 7: 12. But viewed from the side of its mere letter, Rom. 2: 29; 7:6; 2 Cor. 3: 6, 7; its numerous rites, ceremonies, penalties and rigorous exactions, it was "the ministration of death," 2 Cor. 3: 7; and a "yoke of bondage," Gal. 5: 1-3; Acts 15: 1-10. This is the true explanation of their "two laws."

Further, it is not true that there was nothing ceremonial in the decalogue. The weekly Sabbath was the chief ceremonial of all the Jewish worship. See this proved in the first part of chapter nine. Also see chapter eighteen on the decalogue. In Chapter XXI I have examined every text they use on the two laws.

PROPOSITION 3. *The ten commandments alone are never called "the law of the Lord" nor the "law of God."* Sabbatarians constantly use these two terms, applying them to the decalogue alone. With them "the law of God" and "the law of the Lord" is just the decalogue and nothing more. They are the only ones who keep God's law, as all others break the Sabbath, the seventh day. But now notice this fact which I know to be the truth, after a most thorough examination. The word law occurs in the Bible over 400 times, yet in not one single instance is the decalogue as a whole and alone called "the law." It is never in a single instance called "the law of the Lord," or "the law of God." Of course the ten commandments are a part of the law of God, but only a part, not the whole. Examine a few texts: Luke 2: 22. "The days of her purification according to the law of Moses;" verse 23, "It is written in the law of the Lord, every male that openeth the womb;" verse 24, It is "said in the law of the Lord, a pair of turtle doves;" verse 27, "To do for him after the custom of the law." Here "the law," "the law of the Lord," and "the law of Moses," all mean the same thing, viz: the law touching the birth of a son.

Again, sacrifices, offerings, Sabbaths, new moons and feasts are all required "in the law of the Lord." Thus: "He appointed also the king's portion of his substance for the burnt offerings, to-wit, for the morning and evening burnt offerings, and the burnt offerings for the Sabbaths, and for the new moons and for the set feasts, as it *is written in the law of the Lord*." 2 Chron. 31: 3. Scores of texts like these could be quoted, showing that "the law of the Lord" includes sacrifices, circumcision, feast days and all the Jewish law. So "the law of God" is not simply the decalogue, but the whole law of Moses. Read Neh. 8: 1, 2, 3, 7, 8, 14, 18. "The book of the law of Moses," "the law," "the book of the law," "they read in the book of the law of God," "the law which the Lord commanded by Moses," "the book of the law of God." The law of God, then, includes the whole law of Moses.

No Sabbatarian, therefore, keeps "the law," "the law of God," or "the law of the Lord," for if he did he would offer sacrifices, be circumcised, and live exactly as the Jews did. So all their talk about "keeping the law" amounts to nothing, for none of them do it. Moreover in their attempt to keep a part of that law they thereby bring themselves under obligation to "keep the whole law," as Paul argues in Gal. 5: 3. But as none of them keep the whole law, they bring upon themselves the curse of the law, by constantly violating one part while attempting to keep another. This is the very point which Paul made against Judaizing legalists of his day. "For as many as are of the works of the law are under the curse: For it is written, cursed is every one that continueth not in all things which are written in the book of the law to them." Gal. 3: 10. That is, the person who keeps one precept of the law just because the *law* says so, thereby acknowledges that the law is binding on him. Then if he neglects some other part of the law, he thereby becomes a transgressor of the very law he professes to keep. This is exactly what Sabbatarians do. They keep the Sabbath because the law says so and thereby become "debtors to do the whole law." Gal. 5: 3. Then they neglect many things in the same law and so are under the condemnation of the law. Gal. 3: 10. But Christians do this or that, not because the *law* says so, but because so says the New Testament.

PROPOSITION 4. "*The law*" *was given by Moses and the* "*Law of Moses*" *includes the decalogue.* Not that Moses was the author of it, but it was through him God gave it to Israel. This is stated so distinctly and so many times that it is useless to deny it. Thus: "For the law was given by Moses," John 1: 17. "Did not Moses give you the law ?" John 7: 19. "The law which the Lord had commanded by Moses," Neh. 8: 14. "God's law which was given by Moses," Neh. 10: 29. This includes the decalogue. "Moses said, Honor thy father and thy mother," Mark 7: 10. This is the fifth commandment. Again: "Did not Moses give you the law and yet none of you keepeth the law ? Why go ye about to kill me ?" John 7: 17. The law against killing is here called the law of Moses.

In Heb. 10: 28, it is said that "he that despised Moses' law died without mercy under two or three witnesses." Persons were put to death for violating the decalogue. See Deut. 17: 6. They were put to death for breaking the Sabbath, Ex. 31: 14, blasphemy, theft, and the like. Hence the decalogue is included in the "law of Moses." But in verse 24 they said ye must "keep the law." So in one verse it is "the law of Moses" and in another verse it is simply "the law": Hence there is no difference between "the law" and "the law of Moses."

In Josh. 8 : 30, 31, we read : "Then Joshua built an

altar unto the Lord God of Israel in mount Ebal, as Moses the servant of the Lord commanded the children of Israel, as it is written in the book of the law of Moses, an altar of whole stones, over which no man hath lift up any iron." It says that this about the altar was written in the "book of the law of Moses." Now turn to Ex. 20: 25, the very chapter where the decalogue is found, and there you have the text referred to. "And if thou wilt make me an altar of stone, thou shalt not build it of hewn stone; for if thou lift up thy tool upon it, thou has polluted it." This proves beyond denial that the ten commandments are in the law of Moses.

PROPOSITION 5. *"The law" was not given till the time of Moses and Sinai.* The texts above quoted prove this. Thus: "The law was given by Moses." John 1: 17. "Did not Moses give you the law?" John 7: 19. "For until the law sin was in the world; but sin is not imputed when there is no law. Nevertheless death reigned from Adam to Moses." Rom. 5: 13-14. The entrance of the law is here located at Moses. Again it is located under the Levitical priesthood. "If therefore perfection were by the Levitical priesthood, for under it the people received the law." Heb. 7: 11. So the giving of the law is located "430 years after the covenant with Abraham." "And this I say, that the covenant that was confirmed before of God in Christ, the law, which was four hundred and thirty years after, cannot disannul." Gal. 3: 17. This bring us to the very year the Jews came out of Egypt and arrived at Sinai. "And it came to pass at the end of 430 years, even the self-same day it came to pass, that all of the hosts of the Lord went out from the land of Egypt." Ex. 12: 41. Beyond dispute, then, what the Bible calls "the law" was not given till Moses, 2,500 years after Adam, or nearly half the history of the world.

PROPOSITION 6. *The law is no where found till Moses.* No copy of the law nor any reference to it can be found till Moses. Of course God's great moral and spiritual law, condemning every sin and requiring every righteous act—that existed from Adam, nay, from eternity. But what in all the Jewish Scriptures is known as "the law," as drawn out in a code on Sinai, whether in a book or on the tables of stone, this certainly did not exist till Moses. The whole dispute between Paul and the Judaizers of his day was over this law. See Romans, Galatians and Acts 15 and 21. The question was whether "the law," that which was written in "the book of the law," Gal. 3: 10, and "engraved in stones," 2 Cor. 3: 7, was to be kept under the gospel. Paul said, No; they said, Yes. Sabbatarians now stick for the law of Sinai as did the Judaizers of old. To say that the *principles* of the law existed before Sinai, does not prove that the law existed. These principles could have been taught to Adam and his descendants in a different form from the law as afterwards given at Sinai. But where do you find the law or even one of the ten commandments, as worded on Sinai, before that time? Nowhere.

The various principles and precepts, moral, ceremonial, and typical, which had previously been taught in different ways, were now gathered into one code and worded so as to adapt them, for the time being, to the circumstances of the Jewish nation. As thus worded, certainly this law had never been given before.

PROPOSITION 7. *Their fathers did not have the decalogue as worded on the tables.* This Moses directly states. Deut. 4: 12, 13, says God spoke to them from heaven, and declared to them "his covenant," "even ten commandments," Chap. 5: 2, 3, says: "The Lord our God made a covenant with us in Horeb. The Lord made not this covenant with our fathers, but with us." Then he repeats the ten commandments as spoken from heaven. Verses 4–22. That the main principles and requirements of this code were taught to the fathers in some way no one can doubt; but that the fathers had the law as worded and arranged at Sinai is directly denied by Moses, as above.

PROPOSITION 8. *The law was given only to the Jews.* This is so manifest in every item of the law, that it needs no argument to prove it. Moses says, Deut. 4: 8, that no nation has a law so good "as all this law which I set before you this day." Then he names the ten commandments as a part of it. Verses 10–13. "This is the law which Moses set before the children of Israel." Verse 44. Before whom? Israel, not the Gentiles. So again, Chap. 5: 1. "Hear, O Israel, the statutes and judgments which I speak in your ears." Then follows the decalogue. So it is a hundred times over all through the law. It is addressed to the Jews and to them only. The very wording of the law shows it was designed for them only. The decalogue is introduced thus: "I am the Lord thy God, which brought thee out of the land of Egypt, out of the house of bondage." Ex. 20:2. To whom is that applicable? Only to the Jewish nation. Neither angels, Adam, nor Gentile Christians were ever in Egyptian bondage. Then this law is not addressed to them. To whom was the law given. Let Paul answer. "Who are Israelites; to whom pertaineth the adoption, and the glory, and the covenants, and the giving of the law." Rom. 9: 4. It was given to Israel. "Remember ye the law of Moses my servant, which I commanded unto him in Horeb for all Israel, with the statutes and judgments." Malachi 4: 4. The law was "*for all Israel,*" and them only.

All these things show that this was a national law worded to fit the condition of the Jews at the time.

PROPOSITION 9. *The Gentiles did not have the law.* This has been proved already; but Paul directly says so.

Rom. 2: 14. "For when the Gentiles, which have not the law, do by nature the things contained in the law, these having not the law, are a law unto themselves." This is too plain to need arguing. The Gentiles did not have the law. Paul says so directly and that ought to settle it, and does. To understand and obey the great moral principles of that law is one thing; to be under the letter, the exact wording of the law as given in detail on Sinai, is quite another, as we will see further on.

PROPOSITION 10. *The rewards and penalties of the law were all temporal.* There are no promises of future rewards, nor threatenings of future punishments in all the Mosaic law. The learned Bishop Warburton has fully demonstrated this in his "Divine Legation of Moses." Every careful student of that law must be aware of this feature of it. The reason is evident: it was a national, temporal law, given for a national, temporal purpose. As a sample of all, see Deut. 28: 1-19. If they keep the law, they shall be blessed in children, in goods, in cattle, in health, etc. If they disobey, they shall be cursed in all these. Stoning to death was the penalty for theft, murder, etc. Hence that was "the ministration of death written and engraved in stones," 2 Cor. 3:7, and "is done away," verse 11.

Paul states that the promise of Christ and the future inheritance was made to Abraham four hundred and thirty years before the law was given. From this he argues, and forcibly, too, that the keeping of that law was not necessary in order to obtain Christ and the inheritance. Verses 16-18. "Now to Abraham and his seed were the promises made. He saith not, and to seeds, as of many; but as of one, and to thy seed, which is Christ. And this I say, that the covenant that was confirmed before of God in Christ, the law, which was four hundred and thirty years after, cannot disannul, that it should make the promise of none effect. For if the inheritance be of the law, it is no more of promise: but God gave it to Abraham by promise." So to the Romans he wrote: "For the promise, that he should be the heir of the world, was not to Abraham, or to his seed, through the law, but through the righteousness of faith. For if they which are of the law be heirs, faith is made void, and the promise made of none effect." Rom. 4: 13, 14.

This plainly teaches that the law was not given with reference to the future inheritance. Certainly Abraham did not keep a law which was not given till hundreds of years after he died. But Abraham is the father of all the faithful, and not simply of those who were "of the law." Rom. 4: 13–16. This point alone ought to open the eyes of those who contend so earnestly for the keeping of that law as necessary to salvation. We are the children of Abraham, Gal. 3: 29, and "walk in the steps of our father Abraham," who was never under the law. Rom. 4: 12–16. We are under the covenant of promise made to Abraham 430 years before the law, Gal. 2: 15–19, and not under the covenant of law from Sinai, which is bondage. Gal. 4: 21–26.

PROPOSITION 11. *God's eternal law of righteousness existed before the law of Sinai was given.* This proposition is self-evident. Surely God had a law by which to govern his creatures, both angels and men, long before Sinai. But "the law," as worded in the decalogue and in "the book of the law," was not given till Moses, 2,500 years after creation. Hence moral obligation did not begin with that law, nor would it cease if that law was abolished. "All unrighteousness is sin." 1 John 5: 17. And "sin is the transgression of the law." Chap. 3: 4. This text is used by Sabbatarians to prove that every possible sin is always a violation of the ten commandments. But, 1. "The law" is the whole Mosaic law, not merely the decalogue. 2. A correct translation entirely spoils this text for them. The word law is not in the text in the original. The revised version gives it correctly. "Sin is lawlessness." This is the true meaning of the text. Sin is lawlessness, a disregard for some law, but not necessarily always the same law. Thus: "The angels sinned." 2 Pet. 2: 4. But they did not violate the law of Sinai, for it was not given till thousands of years after they fell, and they were not under that law any way.

Adam "sinned" long before that law was given. So Paul says, Rom. 5: 12-14. Cain sinned, Gen. 4: 7. The Sodomites were "sinners," Gen. 13: 13, and vexed Lot with their "unlawful deeds," 2 Pet. 2: 8. Surely none of these violated "the law," which was not given till Moses, hundreds of years afterwards. To say that they must have violated the *principles* of that law is not to the point. When the Jews killed Stephen, Acts 7: 59, they violated the principles of the law of Michigan, which forbids murder; but did they violate the "law of Michigan"? No; for it was not given for 1800 years after. And they were not under it any way. So neither the angels, nor Adam, nor the Sodomites could have transgressed the law of Sinai, for it was not yet given. So Abraham kept God's laws, Gen. 26: 5, but surely not "the law which was four hundred and thirty years after," Gal. 3: 17. All this clearly shows that God had a law before the code of Sinai was given.

Jesus, under the gospel 1500 years later, in naming the commandments, gives them neither in the same words nor in the same order as found in the decalogue. Further, he mingles with them some precepts from the book of the law as of equal importance with the ten commandments. Thus: Do not commit adultery, do not kill, do not steal, do not bear false witness, defraud not, honor thy father and mother. Mark 10: 19. This shows that the mere form and order of the commandments is of no consequence as long as the idea is given. So the two editions of the decalogue in

Ex. 20 and Deut. 5 vary much in the wording; yet one is as good as the other. This shows that the exact wording is not essential.

In whatever form or manner God chose to communicate his will to men, this would be "his commandments, his statutes, and his laws." Gen. 26: 5. Paul says: "God, who at sundry times and in divers manners spake in time past unto the fathers by the prophets, hath in these last days spoken unto us by his Son." Heb. 1: 1, 2.

A disregard for his revealed will would be lawlessness— sin. But to claim that God gave the patriarchs his law in the exact form and words of the ten commandments is a proofless assumption, contrary to reason and all the facts in the case.

PROPOSITION 12. *This original law is superior to the law of Sinai.* When asked "Which is the great commandment in the law?" Jesus said: "Thou shalt love the Lord thy God with all thy heart, and with all thy soul, and with all thy mind. This is the first and great commandment. And the second is like unto it, Thou shalt love thy neighbor as thyself. On these two commandments hang all the law and the prophets." Matt. 22: 37–40. Neither of these is in the decalogue; but that law hangs on this higher law, and so is inferior to it. These principles, clad in the panoply of eternal immutability, lay back of the Mosaic law and existed with it throughout that dispensation as they had existed before and exist now.

In its very nature this great law of supreme love to God, and equal love to fellow creatures, must be as eternal and everlasting as God himself. This law governs angels—governed Adam, the patriarchs, the pious Jews, while under "the law," and Gentile Christians now. It is applicable to all God's creatures, in all ages and all worlds. Idolatry, murder, theft, selfishness and "all unrighteousness," 1 John

5: 17, are and always were violations of this supreme law of God. This great law might be worded in different ways at different times and yet the same essential idea be preserved. Thus Jesus stated the second great commandment in another form. "Therefore all things whatsoever ye would that men should do to you, do ye even so to them; for this is the law and the prophets." Matt. 7: 12. The idea is the same as "Thou shalt love thy neighbor as thyself." The exact words or form in which this law is stated is not material so long as the idea is made plain. Evidently this supreme law must have been made known to Adam and to the patriarchs but in just what form we are not told. To say that it was in the exact words of the decalogue is to affirm what can in no wise be proved.

PROPOSITION 13. *The Mosaic law was founded upon the higher and original law.* Jesus directly affirms this, Matt. 22: 40. "On these two commandments hangs all the law." The principles of this great law were interwoven all through the law of Sinai, being the life, "the spirit," or "the righteousness" of "the law." Rom. 2: 26-29; 8: 4. As an example, examine Lev. 19. Here you have the second great commandment, verse 18, and the principles of every one of the ten commandments. Thus: 1st commandment, verse 32; 2nd, verse 4; 3d, verse 12; 4th, verse 30; 5th, verse 3; 6th, verse 17; 7th, verse 29; 8th, verse 13; 9th, verse 11; 10th, verse 35. Mingled among these are commandments about sacrifices, verse 5; harvest, verse 9; clothing, verse 19; priests, verse 22; first fruits, verse 23; wizards, verse 31; Gentiles, verse 34, etc. All these are founded upon this higher law and can be changed to fit circumstances without affecting the supreme law, which is ever the same.

The particular wording of the law as adapted to the Jewish age was "the letter" or "form" of the law for the time being. While the spirit of the law can never change, the letter of it must change to fit the changing circumstances of God's people. If a Jew loved God with all his heart, he would have circumcised his sons, offered burnt sacrifices, paid tithes, kept the passover, the new moons, the Sabbath, and attended the temple worship, for this was "the law of the Lord." 2 Chron. 31: 3; Luke 2: 22–27. But if a Christian loves God he will be baptized, Acts 2: 38, take the Lord's supper, 1 Cor. 11: 24, attend church, Heb. 10: 25, keep "the Lord's day," Rev. 1: 10, and do many things very different from a Jew. Hence "there is made of necessity a change also of the law." Heb. 7: 12. This is both Bible and common sense. Those who make the mere letter of the Jewish law an iron rule, and contend for the exact wording under all circumstances, and in all ages, miss the spirit of the gospel, and are in bondage to a system out of date. Gal. 3: 19–25; 4: 21–25; 5: 1–3, 13, 14; 2 Cor. 3: 3–15.

PROPOSITION 14. *"The law" of Sinai was given to restrain criminals who would only obey God through fear.* Consider this proposition well. A failure to understand this simple fact is the cause of all the blunders of Sabbatarians and legalists in their extravagant and unscriptural praises of "the ministration of death written and engraven in stones." 2 Cor. 3: 7. On this point hear Paul state why that law was made and notice that it is of the moral precepts of the law that he speaks. "Knowing this, that the law is not made for a righteous man, but for the lawless and disobedient, for the ungodly and for sinners, for unholy and profane, for murderers of fathers and murderers of mothers, for manslayers, for whoremongers, for them that defile themselves with mankind, for menstealers, for liars, for perjured persons, and if there be any other thing that is contrary to sound doctrine." 1 Tim. 1: 9, 10. There can be no doubt that he refers to the code of Sinai, that which prohibited murder, theft, etc. This law he says was not made for a righteous man but for the lawless. Of this law in another place Paul says: "Wherefore then serveth the law? It was added because of transgressions." Gal. 3: 19. Again, "The law entered that the offense might abound." Rom. 5: 20, and, "until the law sin was in the world," verse 13. Hence it is manifest that sin, offense and transgression existed before "the law" was given, and that it was given to prohibit already existing crimes. Evidently God put the race on trial from Adam to Moses under the same eternal law of right and love which governed the angels and holy men. But mankind failed shamefully. They did not live by that rule. They became lawless. Disregard of God and open violence towards men were increasing, till life and property were insecure. Then God selected one nation, the Hebrews, and gave up the rest to their own ways. Rom. 1: 20-28.

Up to this time God's people had not been a nation by themselves but had dwelt among other nations and had been subject to their civil laws which prohibited open violence and protected life and property. But as soon as they became a nation by themselves, it became absolutely necessary to have a national law of their own which would prohibit and punish open crime, such as murder, theft, adultery, etc. Life and property would not have been secure without this, because many among them were wicked, lawless men, "stiffnecked and rebellious." If all had been righteous, if all had loved God and their neighbors, there would have been no need of a prohibitory law with a death penalty. We can readily see the reason why Paul says "the law was not made for a righteous man, but for the lawless." These lawless ones would have robbed and murdered the righteous ones had there been no national, temporal law to protect them, for these wicked men would have cared little about God's higher law, which pertains to the future judgment

But as the Jewish government was a theocracy, one in which God himself was ruler, the law required and regulated service to him as well as duties among themselves.

Hence to this nation God gave the law of Sinai. Ex. 20: 2. Would it have been given if men had obeyed God without? Paul has settled that point. "The law is not made for a righteous man, but for the lawless and disobedient." 1 Tim. 1: 9. Then the law was not made till man had sinned, Rom. 5: 13, offended, verse 20, transgressed, Gal. 3: 19, and became lawless. This then is not God's original law by which he prefers to govern men. It was a law largely of prohibitions, threats, pains and penalties. Its object was to restrain open crime, protect men in their natural rights and preserve the knowledge of God in the earth till Christ should come. Gal. 3: 19-25. In order to keep that nation separate from all others, many burdensome rites were incorporated into the law which made it a yoke of bondage. Acts 15: 10; Gal. 5: 1, 3.

When Christ came, and the Jewish nation was rejected and dispersed, and their national law overthrown, and the gospel went to all nations, that law had served its purpose, and so passed away as a system. Matt. 5: 17-18; Rom. 10: 4; Gal. 3: 24; Heb. 7: 12-19. Now Christians are not under the Aaronic priesthood, nor the Jewish law. Heb. 7: 11, 12; but are under the priesthood of Melchisedec, verses 14-19, as was Abraham our father, Gen. 14: 18-20, who never had "the law" of Sinai, Gal. 3: 17, but walked by the higher law which governs angels and holy men, Gen. 26: 5. The Jewish law being removed, we now come under the same law by which Enoch and Abraham "walked with God." The sermon on the mount is a beautiful elucidation of that law, the rule by which all Christians should live, and by which all sinners will be judged at the judgment.

Now, as in the days before Moses, God's people are not a

nation by themselves, but are scattered among all nations where they are governed and protected by the civil law of those nations. Hence the New Testament provides no civil law for the government of Christians, no temporal penalties for criminals. It would be directly contrary to the nature of the gospel to do either. All this is left to the rulers of nations wherever Christians happen to be. Open criminals, who will not obey from principle, the higher law, are now turned over to the civil magistrate. Paul makes this matter very plain and puts the question beyond dispute. Thus: "Let every soul be subject unto the higher powers. For there is no power but of God: the powers that be are ordained of God. Whosoever therefore resisteth the power, resisteth the ordinance of God; and they that resist shall receive to themselves damnation. For rulers are not a terror to good works, but to the evil. Wilt thou, then, not be afraid of the power? Do that which is good, and thou shalt have praise of the same: For he is the minister of God to thee for good. But if thou do that which is evil, be afraid; for he beareth not the sword in vain; for he is the minister of God, a revenger to execute wrath upon him that doeth evil. Wherefore ye must needs be subject, not only for wrath, but also for concience' sake. For, for this cause pay ye tribute also; for they are God's ministers, attending continually upon this very thing." Rom. 13: 1-6.

There is where you find prohibitory law for "the lawless;" that is, in the civil law of the land where they live. This punishes their crime against society. Their offenses against God's great law will be recompensed at the judgment, but the saints of God must be governed by the higher law, the law of supreme love to God and equal love to fellows. Such obedience can come only from a heart renewed by the Spirit of God, 2 Cor. 3: 3, and "if ye be led of the Spirit ye are not under the law." Gal. 5: 18.

Is any man a Christain who refrains from murder, theft, and adultery, simply because the law says, "Thou shalt not"? No, indeed, he must refrain from these from a higher motive than that. Then surely he must be governed by a higher law than the decalogue. "Love is the fulfilling of the law." Rom. 13: 10. The dispute between Paul and the Judaizers then was over the nature and obligation of the Jewish law. The dispute now concerning the Jewish Sabbath involves the same point, the obligation of the letter of the Jewish law.

PROPOSITION 15. *The letter of the law is not binding upon Christians as a coercive code.* Little argument ought to be needed to prove this; for if the letter of the law is binding, then we must be circumcised; offer sacrifices, keep the seventh day and all the Jewish ritual, for "the law" included the whole law, Gal. 3: 10; 5: 3.

Notice in the following text that "the righteousness of the law" and the spirit of the law is one thing, while "the letter" and outward service is quite another. Notice further that a man may "fulfill the law" without keeping the letter of it, and thus condemn the formalist who keeps the letter of the law but not the spirit of it. Paul says: "If the uncircumcision keep the righteousness of the law, shall not his uncircumcision be counted for circumcision? And shall not uncircumcision which is by nature, if it fulfill the law, judge thee, who by the letter and circumcision dost transgress the law? For he is not a Jew, which is one outwardly, neither is that circumcision, which is outward in the flesh. But he is a Jew, which is one inwardly; and circumcision is that of the heart, in the spirit, and not in the letter; whose praise is not of men, but of God." Rom. 2: 26-29.

Paul argues that Christians must be circumcised, but not "outwardly in the flesh," as formerly, but "inwardly in the spirit, not in the letter." By this he illustrates the difference between keeping the law now and formerly. So, further on: "Ye are not under the law but under grace." Rom. 6: 14. So in the next chapter he says: "But now we are delivered from the law, that being dead wherein we were held; that we should serve in newness of spirit, and not in the oldness of the letter." Rom. 7: 6.

How can one misunderstand language so plain? *Now*, under Christ, we are delivered from the law; that law is dead, and we serve Christ in the spirit, "not in the old letter." So again he says, urging this point: "That the righteousness of the law might be fulfilled in us, who walk not after the flesh, but after the spirit." Chap. 8: 4. Paul uses the word "*flesh*" for the outward "works of the law." See Gal. 3: 2, 3. We do not walk according to the outward form of the law, but we do obey the intent and spirit of it or its "righteousness," as he here calls it.

The higher law of God, supreme love to God and equal love to our neighbors, upon which the Jewish law hung, was the "spirit," "righteousness," or real intent of "the law." This "first and great" law Christians do keep, while free from the mere letter of the law, which was bondage. Hence to the Galatians who were being troubled with Judaizing legalists, Paul wrote: "For, brethren, ye have been called unto liberty; only use not liberty for an occasion to the flesh, but by love serve one another. For all the law is fulfilled in one word, even in this: Thou shalt love thy neighbor as thyself. But if ye be led of the Spirit, ye are not under the law." Gal. 5: 13, 14, 18.

How he reiterates the truth in all his letters, that Christians are not under the law; that they are called to a liberty which Jews never enjoyed. Notice how he states it over and over that all the law is fulfilled in this, Love your neighbor as yourself. "Love is the fulfilling of the law." "He that loveth another hath fulfilled the law." Rom. 13: 8, 10.

This is not a liberty to licentiousness and self-indulgence; but it is a liberty from the forms and ceremonies of the law which bound the Jews.

In Jer. 31: 31-34, it was foretold that the Lord would make a "new covenant" with Israel, "not according" to the one he made at Sinai; for he would put his laws in their hearts and minds. This clearly indicated a change from the previous formal way of governing God's people. Paul thus refers to that prophecy: "not in tables of stone, but in fleshly tables of the heart." "Who also hath made us able ministers of the New Testament; not of the letter, but of the spirit: for the letter killeth, but the spirit giveth life." 2 Cor. 3: 3, 6.

Now the law for the Christian is not that written in the book or on the tables of stone. It was not the letter but the spirit of that law which the apostles taught. So Paul says. Then he says that "the ministration of death written and engraven in stones, was" "done away." Verses 7, 11. Surely, then, Christians are free from the letter of that law; but it is still to be studied with reverence and its spirit carried out in Christian duties though in form these must differ from Jewish duties. The observance of the Lord's day meets the spirit of the fourth commandment. We are circumcised in heart, not in the flesh. Rom. 2: 26-29.

Rev. W. P. Harrison, D. D., book editor of the M. E. Church, South, truly says: "The coming of Christ did not repeal any moral law, and the ceremonial law was not repealed, but fulfilled. All that was permanent, useful, or spiritual in the Mosaic economy remains, *not in the letter of statutes*, but in the fulfilled and completed dispensation of grace." The Christian Sabbath, "The page 30. So Rev. J. H. Potts, D. D. Methodist, says: Law under the Mosaic dispensation was formulated into nine moral precepts, with a Sabbath commandment added, making ten in all. This same law under the Christian dispensation is summarized under two grand heads—love to God and love to man. Yet not one jot or one tittle of the essence of the moral law is abated. When Paul, referring to the abolishment of the law dispensation, said: 'For if that which was done away was glorious, much more that which remaineth is glorious,' he indicated the correct status of the law. The *essence* of the moral law 'remaineth.'" This is exactly what I believe.

The following, from Peter, is a fair illustration of the spiritual application of the old law which the apostles make all through the gospel: "Ye also, as lively stones, are built up a spiritual house, a holy priesthood, to offer up spiritual sacrifices, acceptable to God by Jesus Christ." 1 Peter 2: 5. The old temple, priesthood, and sacrifices of the law, now have a spiritual meaning as found in the church and its service.

PROPOSITION 16. *The law was changed.* Jeremiah predicted that under the new covenant, God's law would be written in the heart and not as it was before. "I will put my law in their inward parts and write it in their hearts." Jer. 31: 33. Paul refers to this when he says, Ye are our epistle "written not with ink, but with the spirit of the living God; not in tables of stone, but in fleshly tables of the heart." 2 Cor. 3: 3. So then God's law is not now written on tables of stone as at Sinai. This is a square contradiction to what Adventists teach. They claim that God's law is still on stones in heaven the same as of old. Paul says no, it is written by the spirit upon the heart.

This implied a radical change in the form of the law and the way it was to be taught. In Heb. 7: 12, it is expressly declared that "there is made of necessity a change also of the law." The letter of the Jewish law is wholly unfitted to the condition of the Christian church. It can only be a guide to us as modified and interpreted by the gospel. But in the gospel there is no injunction to keep the seventh day. Hence the letter of that command does not concern us.

PROPOSITION 17. *The whole Mosaic system ended at the cross.* Surely this is so plainly taught all through the New Testament that no one should deny it. But we have clearly proved that "the law" included the whole code of laws given to Israel at Sinai, moral, civil, and ceremonial precepts, decalogue and all.

That entire system of law was framed to fit the Jewish age and could not possibly be applied to Gentile Christians in all parts of the world. Hence a "new way," Heb. 10: 20, a "new covenant," Heb. 8: 13, a new "ministration," 2 Cor. 3: 8, was introduced, so there was " made of necessity a change also of the law," Heb. 7: 12.

Examine carefully a few texts to which I will refer. "The law was given by Moses but grace and truth came by Jesus Christ." John 1: 17. This implies a change. "Ye are not under the law, but under grace." Rom. 6: 14. "Under the merciful dispensation of the gospel." John Wesley. "The law was our schoolmaster to bring us unto Christ, that we might be justified by faith. But after that faith is come, we are no longer under a schoolmaster," Gal. 3: 24, 25. "Ye also are become dead to the law by the body of Christ," Rom. 7: 4. "Now we are delivered from the law," verse 6. "Christ is the end of the law," Rom. 10: 4. "The ministration of death written and engraven in stones was glorious." "That which is done away was glorious," 2 Cor. 3: 7, 10. That ends the decalogue.

"Having abolished in his flesh the enmity, even the law of commandments contained in ordinances," Eph. 2: 15. "Blotting out the handwriting of ordinances that was against us, which was contrary to us, and took it out of the way, nailing it to the cross." "Let no man therefore judge you in meat, or in drink, or in respect of a holy day, or of the new moon, or of the Sabbath days," Col. 2: 14, 16. "For the priesthood being changed, there is made of necessity change also of the law." "For there is verily a disannulling of the commandment going before for the weakness and unprofitableness thereof." "For the law made nothing perfect but the bringing in of a better hope." Heb. 7: 12, 18, 19.

Read Acts 15: 1-29 and see this whole matter of "the law" discussed by the apostles and settled in these words: "Forasmuch as we have heard that certain which went out from us have troubled you with words, subverting your souls, saying, *ye must* be circumcised, and keep the law; to whom we gave no such commandment." Verse 24. The decision is positive and clear: the apostles gave no commandment to "keep the law." It does not say *"ceremonial* law," or a part of the law, but simply *"the* law." Adventists say we must keep the law or "ye can not be saved," exactly what those Judaizers said, verse 1, and just what the council condemned. Circumcision was specially mentioned because it was the initiatory rite, the sign which represented the whole law. Thus when a Gentile would partake of the privileges of the nation, he had first to be circumcised. Ex. 12: 48. To be uncircumcised was to be a heathen, unclean, and lost; to be circumcised was to be an Israelite, a member of the holy nation. Hence circumcision represented the whole law of Moses in all its parts. Elder Butler, Adventist leader, has to confess this. He says: "The term 'the law,' among the Jews generally included the five books of Moses, thus including the *whole system*, moral, ritual, typical, and civil. This as a *system* these Judaizing teachers desired to maintain. Circumcision was a sign of the whole." Law in Galatians, page 70. Never was a truer statement. Circumcision was the sign of the whole Mosaic system, moral, typical, civil, all that was written in the five books of

Moses, of which the decalogue was a chief part. The apostles decided that Gentile believers were free from this whole system of law. Put with Butler's statement this from Elder Smith, another leading Adventist, and you have the whole truth: "That which was abolished at the cross was an entire system. God did not single out and abolish portions and pieces of some arrangement or system, and leave other parts remaining." Synopsis of Present Truth, page 259. Correct; the whole system ended at the cross.

PROPOSITION 18. *No part of God's great spiritual law was abolished, re-enacted, or changed at the cross.* Adventists make a great ado over the absurdity of the idea that God should abolish his law at the cross and then immediately re-enact nine-tenths of it. They say, as well cut off your ten fingers to get rid of one bad one and then stick nine on again. So they go on with a whole jumble of absurdities involved in the position that God's moral law was abolished at the cross and a new one given. But this is only a man of straw of their own making and hence easily demolished. We hold no such absurd position. God's great moral law is unchangeable. But the Mosaic law was only a national one founded upon the principles of God's moral law. Even while it existed it did not supercede God's higher law, and when it ended it in no way affected God's law, which continued right on unchanged and unchangeable.

To illustrate: The state law of Michigan forbids murder, theft and adultery. In these items it is founded upon God's moral law. Now abolish the law of Michigan. Does that abolish God's law? No. So with the state law of Israel. Neither its enactment on Sinai nor its abolition at the cross in any way changed God's great moral law by which he will judge the world. The Advent absurdities grew out of their own false theory, that is all. Adventists agree with us that the law of Moses, Acts 15: 5, was abolished. Well, that law contained many precepts as purely moral as anything in the decalogue. Here are some: "Thou shalt love the Lord thy God with all thy heart." Deut. 6: 5. "Love thy neighbor as thyself." "Ye shall not steal, neither deal falsely, neither lie one to another." Lev. 19: 11, 18. Scores of such precepts are all through this law which they admit was abolished. They are just as moral, spiritual, and necessary as anything in the ten commandments, and yet all this law was abolished as they admit. But did that abolish the duty enjoined in these precepts? No, because they were inherent in a higher law. Just so every moral principle involved in the decalogue existed in a higher law before that document was given, and so did not cease when that law expired. Elder White himself makes this admission: "The ten commandments are adapted to fallen beings. As worded in the sacred Scripture, they are not adapted to the condition of holy angels, nor to man in his holy estate in Eden. * * * But the two grand principles of God's moral government did exist before the fall, in the form of law. * * * These two great commandments embrace all that is required by the ten precepts of the decalogue." Law and Gospel, pages 4, 5. Good and true. Then the ten commandments are not God's primary law. They are only temporary, while that containing all that is moral in them, and much more, continues always.

"The teachings of Christianity are facts and principles, not propositions and restrictions; its institutions are simple outlines, not precise ceremonies; and its laws are moral sentiments, not minute mechanical directions." Pulpit Commentary on 2 Cor. 3: 6. This is the truth well put.

So the wicked who do not live by these principles, who do not love God nor their fellows, but who live selfish, corrupt lives, will be judged and condemned by these principles of God's eternal law, as taught in the New Testament.

CHAPTER XVIII.

THE DECALOGUE EXAMINED.

With Seventh-Day Adventists the decalogue is the one supreme moral and spiritual law of God, than which there is none higher. It is the law which governs the angels in heaven. Thus Mrs. White says: "The law of God existed before man was created. The angels were governed by it. * * * After Adam and Eve were created, God made known to them his law." "Spirit of Prophecy," Vol. I, page 261. It governs all men in all ages, and in the world to come. These ten commandments cover the whole duty of man, so that there is no sin which can be committed that is not a violation of this law, while at the same time it enjoins every virtue. "No virtue known to the moral world herein fails of approval and commendation; and no vice or crime of which man was ever guilty, escapes condemnation." Perfection of the Ten Commandments, page 4. But these claims are extravagant and unfounded. A desire to sustain the seventh-day Sabbath has led to this false position on the decalogue. Twenty-five hundred years, nearly half the entire history of the world, passed away before the decalogue was given at all, as we have proved. This is strange if the decalogue is so all important.

Let us examine it. Moses says distinctly that all the words which the Lord spoke were written on the tables of stone: "And the Lord delivered unto me two tables of stone, written with the finger of God: and on them was written according to all the words which the Lord spake with you in the Mount, out of the midst of the fire." Deut. 9: 10. This text is too decisive to be evaded. All that God spoke was written on the tables and was a part of the decalogue. Here are the first of those words: "And God spake all these words, saying, I am the Lord thy God, which have brought thee out of the land of Egypt, out of the house of bondage. Thou shalt have no other gods before me," etc. Ex. 20: 1-3. These words are as much a part of the decalogue as any of the rest of it. They were spoken by God from heaven, written by his finger, were engraven on the stone, and put in the ark. Now look at the law chart which Seventh-Day Adventists hang up as the "law of God." Are these words on there? No, indeed. Why are they left off? Because, if put on, they would spoil their whole theory of that law. They claim that this law is binding upon the angels. But how would this sound to the angels: "I am the Lord thy God, which brought thee out of the land of Egypt, out of the house of bondage"? Were the angels in bondage in Egypt? Would not that sound a little queer to Gabriel and the seraphs, to be told that they had been in bondage in Egypt? Read it to Adam. That would have been news to him to learn that he had been in bondage in Egypt! Read it to a free-born American; read it to all the redeemed hosts in heaven. To whom are the words applicable? Just to the Jewish nation and to no others. For them the decalogue was framed and to them it was given. For years I searched to find one text stating that this law was ever given to any people but the Jews. I never found it. These first words show plainly that it was addressed only to them.

Seventh-Day Adventists assert that the Sabbath precept is the only thing in the decalogue that tells who gave it. Thus: "Aside from this precept [the Sabbath] there is nothing in the decalogue to show by whose authority the law is given." Mrs. White, in Great Controversy, page 284.

This is not true. The introductory words tell plainly who gave it. It was the God who brought them out of Egypt. Here are the name, signature and seal of that law in the first words of it. Here God stands before them as their *Deliverer*, rather than as their *Creator*. Their obedience to these commands is based upon this fact. See how plain it is. I am the Lord thy God that brought thee out of Egypt, therefore thou shalt do thus and so. Egypt, not Eden, is pointed to. In the copy of the decalogue as given in Deut. 5: 6–21, there is no reference whatever to creation, while deliverance from Egypt is made prominent. "To extend it further than its own preface is to violate the rules of criticism."

What an unnatural and unheard of thing it would be, in giving an important document, to sign the name of the author in the middle of it, as Sabbatarians say the Lord did in giving the decalogue! In our time the name is signed at the close of a document; but anciently, specially among the Jews, the name of the author was always given *first*, in the first sentence of the document. Thus: "Artaxerxes, king of kings, unto Ezra," etc. Ezra 7: 12. "The vision of Isaiah," etc. Isa. 1: 1. "The words of Jeremiah," etc. Jer. 1: 1. "Paul, a servant of Jesus Christ," etc. Rom. 1: 1. "James, a servant of God," etc. Jas. 1: 1. "Peter, an apostle," etc. 1 Pet. 1: 1. So it is all through the Bible, the name and authority are given first, then follows the body of the document. Just so the Lord, according to this ancient custom then in use and familiar to all, in giving the decalogue first announces his name, "the Lord thy God," and his power, "that brought thee out of Egypt."

This he does in the opening words of that law. Here, then, in the very first words of the decalogue, and not in the Sabbath precept in the middle of the law, is the name, sign and seal of the law-giver. Jehovah, who brought them out of Egypt. This settles it that this law was not given till then, was given only to the Jews and was designed for no others. To illustrate: Opening to a law passed by the legislature of Michigan, February 16, 1882, I read: "Be it enacted by the senate and house of representatives of the state of Michigan," etc. Now suppose that some one should claim that this law was passed one thousand years ago and was designed for the whole world. Would not these opening words show that this law was not enacted till Michigan became a state and that it was designed only for the people of Michigan? Assuredly. Just so the opening words of the decalogue show that this law was not given till God brought Israel out of Egypt, that it was given to them and to no others. If any one will find a copy of the decalogue before this time, we will give up the case. All the way through it there are evidences that it was worded to fit only the Jewish nation in their peculiar circumstances.

Take the Sabbath commandment: "Thy son, nor thy daughter, thy man servant, nor thy maid servant, nor thy cattle, nor thy stranger that is within thy gates." Ex. 20: 10. Think of that commandment being given to angels in heaven! "Sons," "daughters," and "thy neighbor's wife," verse 17, when they neither marry nor are given in marriage! Again: "Cattle," "ox," "ass," etc. Do the angels own cattle and work oxen and asses in heaven? So "man servants and maid servants." This means bond servants or slaves, such as the Hebrews owned in those days. This is shown by the tenth commandment, verse 17. "Thou shalt not covet thy neighbor's * * * man servant, nor his maid servant, nor his ox, nor his ass." These were his property, servants or slaves, oxen, asses, etc. But do the angels own slaves? Did Adam have servants in Eden? Will the redeemed own them hereafter? What nonsense to apply this law to the angels and to Eden and to heaven! This wording was specially adapted to the social condition of the Jews as a nation in the land of Canaan, and to no others.

Once more: "Thy stranger that is within thy gates." Verse 10. As everybody knows, "the stranger" was the Gentile. "Within thy gates" was a common expression meaning within your cities or dwelling in your land. It has no reference to living on your farm or inside the gates that enclose your farm, as Adventists always explain it. The towns were walled in and entered by gates. Here is where the judges sat and all business was done. Thus: "All that went in at the gate of his city." Gen. 23: 10. "Judges and officers shalt thou make thee in all thy gates." Deut. 16: 18. To this custom of the Jews the Sabbath commandment refers. All the Gentiles dwelling in their cities among them must be made to keep the Sabbath. This shows it to be a national law, worded in all its parts to fit the circumstances of the Jews at the time.

This command, then, could not apply to any but the Jews there. Again, the fifth commandment: "The land which the Lord giveth them," verse 12, plainly refers to Canaan, which God gave them. The ninth precept: "Thou shalt not bear false witness against thy neighbor." This does not relate to lying in general, but only to a false oath against a neighbor in court. See Deut. 19: 15–19. A man could tell a hundred lies which would not be false witness against a neighbor. The command against lying is found in Lev. 19: 11: "Neither lie one to another." This is a moral precept much broader than the ninth commandment.

Every principle contained in the decalogue is also found time and again laid down in the law of Moses, either in the same or similar words. Thus, for example: Lev. 19 reiterates every principle found in the ten commandments, with many more besides. How erroneous, then, to call one the moral law and the other the ceremonial law, when both are of the same nature, the decalogue simply being representative precepts from the law of Moses.

But the chief argument used to prove the superior nature of the ten commandments is that they were spoken by God's voice, written by His finger on stone, and placed in the ark, while all the rest of the law was written by the hand of Moses in a book. Why were these commandments thus selected out and given in such a manner if not to exalt them above all others? The answer is easy: According to the custom of those times, any solemn contract or covenant was commemorated by selecting some object as witness or testimony of it. Thus: Jacob erected a pillar as a witness of his vow to God. Gen. 28: 18. Jacob and Laban made a heap of stones as witness of their covenant. Gen. 31: 48. Abraham set apart seven lambs as "a witness" of his covenant with Abimelech. Gen. 21: 27–30.

Just so when the solemn covenant was made between God and Israel at Sinai, the Lord gave them the tables of stone to be always kept as a witness or "testimony" of that agreement. Hence they are called "the tables of testimony," that is, witness. Ex. 31: 18. So the tabernacle was "the tabernacle of testimony," Num. 1: 53; or, "the tabernacle of witness," Num. 17: 7. These tables of stone, then, containing some of the chief items of the law, were always to be kept as "*witness*" of the covenant which Israel had made to keep that law. Evidently *this* is the reason why the decalogue was given as it was, and not because it was a perfect and eternal law in and of itself.

Manifestly it would have been impossible to carry around the whole law if written on stones; hence only a few samples out of that law could have been selected and put on stones to be kept as a witness of that covenant. So the reason why God spoke these words was not because it was a perfect law, but to impress their minds so that they never would forget it. This is just what God says himself: "I will make them hear my words, that they may learn to fear me all the days that they shall live." Deut. 4: 10. How much more simple and manifest these reasons are than the imaginary ones invented by Sabbatarians.

That the decalogue was merely the national law for the Jews and temporal in its obligation, is proved by the fact that stoning to death was the penalty for its violation. When death was thus inflicted upon a man, he had paid the penalty of that law, and all the penalty there was. But is stoning to death the penalty for God's moral law? No, that is eternal death at the judgment. A man who is hung for murder has paid the penalty of the law of our land, the same as the Jew who was stoned paid the penalty of the law of his land. Will God judge a man the second time at the judgment by the law of our land after he has once paid its penalty by hanging? No, but he will be judged by another and a higher law, the great spiritual law of God. And so it will be with the Jews. They will never be judged the second time by the decalogue, for that was only national, but by the higher law, the one that requires supreme love to God, and love to man as to himself. A law without a penalty is a nullity; but stoning, the penalty attached to the decalogue, was abolished at the cross; hence the law must have ceased there too.

Seventh-Day Adventists claim that the ten commandments are a perfect law, condemning every possible sin and requiring every possible virtue. But this is all assumption and contrary to the manifest truth. Which one of the ten commandments condemns pride, boasting, drunkenness, unthankfulness, love of pleasure, anger, filthy talk, impatience, variance, selfishness, and the like? Which one of the ten commandments requires us to feed the poor, to visit the fatherless and the widow, to suffer long and be kind, to be gentle, meek, temperate, to pray, to repent, to go to meeting, to forgive, and the like? No, the decalogue does no such thing, because it was made for no such purpose. It was merely prohibitory in its nature. The man who merely did nothing, who simply avoided crime, kept that law. But the law of God, by which a Christian must live, requires him to do, and to do much. He must love God, love his neighbor, love his enemies, visit the widow and the needy, suffer wrong, be patient, entertain strangers, and be active in every good work.

It requires unceasing activity and the consecration of all our energies to good works; but the decalogue requires nothing but to avoid open crime. The decalogue alone is never called the law of God, nor the law of the Lord, nor a perfect law, nor is it said that any one will be judged by it, or that it is binding on Christians.

THE CATHOLIC DIVISION OF THE DECALOGUE.

Seventh-Day Adventists have made a great ado over the way Catholics divide and number the ten commandments. They have gotten up a chart showing in one column the decalogue "as changed by the pope" and in another as "given by God." Here they show how "the pope has changed God's law in fulfillment of Dan. 7: 25." According to this, the Catholics included in the first commandment what we have in the first two. Then our third is their second, our fourth their third, and so on till our tenth of which they make two. Adventists claim that the pope did this to get rid of the second commandment and to change the Sabbath. But the whole thing is utterly false, as may be seen under the word decalogue in any religious encyclopedia. The Schaff-Herzog Encyclopedia says:

"There have been three arrangements of the decalogue—the Talmudic (Jewish), the Augustinian (adopted by the Roman Catholic and Lutheran churches), and the Hellenistic (Greek), the view of Philo, Josephus, Origen, the Greek and Reformed churches, etc. The following table exhibits the differences, the record in Ex. 20 being used.

TALMUDIC.	HELLENISTIC.	AUGUSTINIAN.
1. I am the Lord, etc. (v.2)	1. Against idols, (v. 3).	1. Against idols and images, (3 6).
2. Against idols and images, (3-6).	2. Against images, (4-6).	2. Blasphemy.
3. Blasphemy.	3. Blasphemy.	3. The Sabbath.
4. The Sabbath.	4. The Sabbath.	4. Filial Obedience.
5. Filial Obedience.	5. Filial Obedience.	5. Murder.
6. Murder.	6. Murder.	6. Adultery.
7. Adultery.	7. Adultery.	7. Theft.
8. Theft.	8. Theft.	8. False witness.
9. False witness.	9. False witness.	9. Thou shalt not covet thy neighbor's h. (17).
10. Coveting.	10. Coveting.	10. The rest of v. 17.

It will be seen here that the Catholics have simply followed the early fathers in this, while we have followed the Greeks. The pope had nothing to do with making this division of the commandments. It will be seen that according to the Talmudic (Jewish) division, which is the oldest of all, the first commandment is the words, "I am the Lord thy God which brought thee out of the land of Egypt," etc. The Jews, the Catholics, and the Lutherans include in their first commandment the introductory words, "I am the Lord thy God," &c., just as all should do, for these are the most important words of all, for they tell who gave that law. Adventists expunge these to save their theory.

Thus, as I learned more, I began to see on every hand how the arguments of the Adventists were fallacious and contrary to history and to facts.

EMINENT AUTHORS ON THE DECALOGUE.

Many of the most eminent, devout and learned men of the church have held that the decalogue was abolished, though they were far from being Antinomians.

Among these were the apostolical fathers, Luther, Calvin, Milton, Baxter, Bunyan, Doddridge, Whately, Grotius, Locke, Sherlock, Watts, Hessey, Judson, George Dana Boardman, and a host of such men.

Justin Martyr, A. D. 140, says: "The law promulgated on Horeb is now old and belongs to yourselves (Jews) alone: but this is for all universally. Now law placed against law has abrogated that which is before it." Dialogue with Trypho, Chap. 11. On this Elder Andrew says: "That Justin held to the abrogation of the ten commandments is also manifested." Testimony of the Fathers, page 43.

Tertullian, A. D. 200, says: "The abolition of the ancient law we fully admit." Against Marcian, Book 5. Chap. 2. On the law he quotes Col. 2: 16, and says: "The apostle here teaches clearly how it has been abolished." Ibid. Chap. 19.

Luther says: "The ten commandments do not apply to us Gentiles and Christians, but only to the Jews. If a preacher wishes to force you back to Moses, ask him whether you were brought by Moses out of Egypt. If he says no, then say: 'How, then, does Moses concern me, since he speaks (in the ten words) to the people that have been brought out of Egypt.' In the New Testament Moses comes to an end and his laws lose their force." See Kitto's Cyclopedia, Article Law.

Smith's Dictionary of the Bible, says: "In its individual, or what is usually called its 'moral' aspect, the Law bore equally the stamp of transitoriness. * * * It seems clear enough that its formal, coercive authority as a whole, ended with the close of the Jewish dispensation." Art. Law.

Kitto's Cyclopedia of Biblical Literature, says : " They [Christ and the apostles] even clearly indicate that the moral law is by no means excepted when they speak of the abolition of the law in general." Art. Law.

The recent popular commentary of Jamison, Faussett and Brown, says: "The law (including especially the moral law wherein lay the chief difficulty in obeying) is abrogated to the believer as far as it was a compulsory, accusing code." On Col. 2: 16.

The Encyclopedia Britannica says: "The ten commandments do not apply to us Gentiles and Christians, but only to the Jews." On the Ten Commandments.

Says Dr. Dobbs, Baptist: "Nor is this 'new and dangerous teaching.' It was the doctrine of the Protestant reformers of the sixteenth century. Calvin argues in this strain in his Institutes. The eminent Baptist scholar and commentator, John Gill, says, writing on Ex. 20: 1, 2: 'Verse 2 shows that this body of laws was delivered out to the people of Israel, and primarily belongs to them; for of no other people can the above things be said.' On Matt. 5: 17, and 2 Cor. 3: 7–11, Gill is emphatic in similar teaching. Read this, on the latter passage: 'The law is that which is done away; not merely the ceremonial law, or the judicial law; but the whole ministery of Moses; and particularly the law of the decalogue.' I close by citing an incident related by Mrs. Emily C. Judson, in the Life of Adoniram Judson, by his son, Dr. Edward Judson. Mrs. Judson says that her husband once reproved her for introducing some lessons from the Old Testament into her Bible classes, 'comparing it to groping among shadows when she might just as well have the noonday sun.' Mrs Judson in relating this incident, says: 'My impression, drawn from many a long talk, is that he considered the Old Testament as the Scriptures given to the Jews especially, and to them only. He did not like the distinction commonly drawn between the moral and the ceremonial law, and sometimes spoke with an earnestness amounting to severity, of the constant use made of the ten commandments by Christians. He thought the Old Testament very important as explanatory and corroborative of the New—as a portion of the inspiration which came from God, etc., but binding on Christians only so far as repeated in the New Testament. He used to speak of the Mosaic law as fulfilled in Christ, and so having no further power whatever; and to say that we have no right to pick out this as moral, and therefore obligatory, and the other as ceremonial and no longer demanding obedience. Practically we had nothing to do with the Old Testament law.'" Life of Judson, pages 411, 412.

Rev. George Dana Boardman, D. D., the eminent Baptist divine, in his recent book on " The Ten Commandments," says: "Although the decalogue, in its spirit, is for all lands and ages, yet, in its letter, it was evidently for the Jews. The very preamble proves the assertion: 'God spake all these words, saying: I am Jehovah, thy God, who brought thee out of the land of Egypt, out of the house of bondage.' Then follow the ten commandments, based on the unique fact that Jehovah was the covenant God of Israel." Pages 127–130.

John Milton says: "With regard to the doctrine of those who consider the decalogue as a code of universal morality, I am at a loss to understand how such an opinion should ever have prevailed; these commandments being evidently nothing more than a summary of the whole Mosaic law as the fourth is of the whole ceremonial law; which therefore can contain nothing applicable to the gospel worship." Treatise on Christian Doctrine, Vol. 1, Book 2, Chap. 7.

CHAPTER XIX.

THE TWO COVENANTS.

No other subject perplexes Adventists so much as the covenants. They dread to meet it. They have tried various ways to explain it away, but they are not satisfactory even to themselves. I have been there and know. "The abolition of the Sinatic covenant carries with it the abolition of the Jewish Sabbath so completely that no authoritative trace of it can be found this side of the grave of our risen Lord."

Elder Smith says: "If the ten commandments constituted the old covenant, then they are forever gone." "This, therefore, becomes a test question." Two Covenants, page 5. We will soon see the force of this. Jer. 31: 31, 32, says: "Behold the days come, saith the Lord, that I will make a new covenant with the house of Israel, and with the house of Judah: Not according to the covenant that I made with their fathers, in the day that I took them by the hand to bring them out of the land of Egypt."

Here we learn these facts about the first, or old covenant: 1. It was made between God and Israel. 2. It was made when he brought them out of Egypt. 3. A new covenant is to be made. 4. It will not be according to the old one. Adventists and all agree that this old covenant is found in Ex. 19 to 24. We all know that the ten commandments, how and why they were given, are the prominent things in those five chapters. We also know that they are called "the covenant," that was given on Sinai or Horeb. Thus: "And the Lord spake unto you out of the midst of the fire;

ye heard the voice of the words, but saw no similitude; only ye heard a voice. And he declared unto you his covenant, which he commanded you to perform, even ten commandments; and he wrote them upon two tables of stone." "The Lord our God made a covenant with us in Horeb. The Lord made not this covenant with our fathers, but with us, even us, who are all of us here alive this day." Deut. 4: 12, 13; 5: 2, 3. Then follows the ten commandments as the covenant named. Again : " The tables of stone, even the tables of the covenant which the Lord made with you." Deut. 9: 9. So also, "and he wrote upon the tables the words of the covenant, the ten commandments." Ex. 34: 28. Surely this is plain enough for a common man. What is a covenant? Webster says: "A mutual consent or agreement of two or more persons to do or forbear some act or thing; a contract." As the decalogue alone is not a mutual agreement, it must enter into, and so become a part of, some agreement, to be called the covenant as it is so frequently. Examining, we find that the decalogue was the very basis of the covenant at Sinai; the chief thing in the covenant between God and Israel. This even Elder Smith owns: " It was the basis of the whole arrangement." The Two Covenants, page 10. Being the chief thing in the covenant, it is by way of eminence put for the whole and so called " the covenant."

Opening to Ex. 19, we read: "In the third month, when the children of Israel were gone forth out of the land of Egypt, the same day came they into the wilderness of Sinai." Verse 1. It was at Sinai as they came out of Egypt. Moses was mediator. Verse 3. The Lord sends him to say to Israel: "If ye will obey my voice indeed, and keep my covenant, then ye shall be a peculiar treasure unto me above all people: for all the earth is mine." Verse 5. Moses goes and repeats this offer to the Jews: they say: " All that the Lord hath said we will do." Verse 8. Here was an agreement, a covenant, between God and Israel. They agree to obey his voice. He agrees to bless them. Next they prepare to hear his voice. Verses 9–25. In Chap. 20 God speaks the ten commandments and follows them with various precepts through Moses to the end of chapter 23, closing with a promise to bless their bread and water, to take away sickness from them, to drive out the Canaanites and give them the land. Chapter 24: 1–8, relates how Moses then rehearsed to the people "all the words of the Lord and all the judgments." Again they agree to obey. Verse 3. Then "Moses wrote all the words of the Lord" in a book. Verse 4. Assembling the people again, he read "the book of the covenant" to them, and the third time they say, "All that the Lord hath said we will do." Verse 7. "And Moses took the blood and sprinkled it on the people, and said, 'behold the blood of the covenant, which the Lord hath made with you concerning all these words.'" Verse 8. That closed the covenant. We know that this was the first, or old, covenant, for Paul, quoting this very verse, says it was. Heb. 9: 18–20. That settles it.

How much did the covenant embrace? Only one truthful answer can be given, viz. All included in the record from Ex. 19: 1 to Ex. 24: 8, for this is the covenant in detail written out. Is the decalogue included in it? As well deny that the sun shines, for there it is written out in full in the very heart of the covenant. Ex. 20: 1–17. As Smith said above, "It was the basis of the whole arrangement." It was so prominent a part of the covenant that it alone is put for the whole covenant, as we often speak of seeing a vessel, a house, or a river, when we saw only a part of it. Hence the stones on which the decalogue was written are called "the tables of the covenant," Deut. 9: 9; the book in which it was written was called "the book of the covenant," Ex. 24: 7; the ark in which it was deposited was called "the ark of the covenant," Deut. 31: 26.

But Ex. 19-24, is only an epitome of the covenant; for all the subsequent teachings of Moses are only a further explanation of it and belonged to it. Indeed, it gave its name to the whole Old Testament, that is, Old Covenant.

This covenant was only national and temporal, given only to the Jews and referred only to earthly blessings. It made no reference to the future life. Dr. Scott says: "The national covenant with Israel was here meant. * * * It was an engagement of God, to give Israel possession of Canaan," etc. "It did not refer to the final salvation of individuals." On Ex. 19: 5.

Now notice how plainly and how repeatedly the ten commandments are called "the covenant," which God gave at Sinai to Israel when he brought them out of Egypt.

"And he declared unto you his covenant, which he commanded you to perform, *even* ten commandments; and he wrote them upon two tables of stone." Deut. 4: 13.

"When I was gone up into the mount to receive the tables of stone, *even* the tables of the covenant which the Lord made with you." Deut. 9: 9. What covenant was on the tables of stone? The one the Lord made with them. Again he tells when it was made and what it was: "The Lord our God made a covenant with us in Horeb. The Lord made not this covenant with our fathers, but with us, even us, who are all of us here alive this day. The Lord talked with you face to face in the mount out of the midst of the fire (I stood between the Lord and you at that time, to shew you the word of the Lord: for ye were afraid by reason of the fire, and went not up into the mount), saying, I am the Lord thy God, which brought thee out of the land of Egypt, from the house of bondage. Thou shalt have none other gods before me." Deut. 5: 2-7. So he goes on giving the ten commandments. That ought to settle it.

"And the Lord said unto Moses, Write thou these words: for after the tenor of these words I have made a covenant with thee and with Israel. And he was there with the Lord forty days and forty nights; he did neither eat bread nor drink water. And he wrote upon the tables the words of the covenant, the ten commandments." Ex. 34: 27, 28. If that is not plain enough, what would be?

"There was nothing in the ark save the two tables of stone, which Moses put there at Horeb, when the Lord made a covenant with the children of Israel, when they came out of the land of Egypt."

"And I have set there a place for the ark, wherein is the covenant of the Lord, which he made with our fathers wnen he brought them out of the land of Egypt." 1 Kings, 8: 9-21.

"And in it have I put the ark, wherein is the covenant of the Lord, that he made with the children of Israel." 2 Chron. 6: 11.

This shuts off all possible doubt as to what the covenant was. 1. There was nothing in the ark except the tables of stone. 2. Yet in that ark was "the covenant of the Lord which he made with Israel when he brought them out of Egypt." That certainly was the ten commandments. Elder Smith says: "If the ten commandments constituted the old covenant, then they are forever gone." Two Covenants, page 5. So they are indeed as we will now see.

THAT COVENANT IS DONE AWAY.

As we have seen, Jeremiah, Chap. 31: 31-34, foretold that the Lord would make a new covenant not according to the old one. Paul quotes this in full and says it is fulfilled in the gospel, thus: "But now hath he obtained a more excellent ministry, by how much also he is the mediator of a better covenant, which was established upon better promises. For if that first covenant had been faultless, then should no place have been sought for the second. For finding fault with them, he saith, Behold, the days come, saith the Lord, when I will make a new covenant with the house of Israel and with the house of Judah: Not according to the covenant that I made with their fathers, in the day when I took them by the hand to lead them out of the land of Egypt; because they continued not in my covenant, and I regarded them not, saith the Lord. For this is the covenant that I will make with the house of Israel after those days, saith the Lord, I will put my laws into their mind, and write them in their hearts; and I will be to them a God, and they shall be to me a people. And they shall not teach every man his neighbor, and every man his brother, saying, Know the Lord, for all shall know me, from the least to the greatest. For I will be merciful to their unrighteousness, and their sins and their iniquities will I remember no more. In that he saith, a new covenant, he hath made the first old. Now that which decayeth and waxeth old is ready to vanish away." Heb. 8: 6–13.

Notice the points in this. 1. Jesus is mediator of a better covenant than the old. Verse 6. Then we have something better than the decalogue. 2. The new is established on better promises than the old, which as we have seen, were all temporal. See Ex. 23: 22–33. But the promises of the new covenant are all spiritual. They are (1) God's laws are to be in their hearts. (2.) All shall know the Lord, as only converted souls will be admitted; whereas under the old, every member of the nation, good or bad, was a citizen. (3.) God will forgive and forget all their sins, and so they will all be saints and heirs of heaven. (4.) Paul says that if the first covenant had been faultless, no place would have been sought for a second. This shows that the first covenant was always imperfect. Hence the Lord says he will make a new one, not according to the old one. Then we cannot have the old decalogue right over again unchanged. Finally, Paul says the first is made old and is ready to vanish away. That ends the old covenant, the one from Sinai, the ten commandments as we have proved.

In 2 Cor. 3 Paul makes it even plainer still that the decalogue has been removed.

Verse 3. "Ye are manifestly declared to be the epistle of Christ ministered by us, written not with ink, but with the spirit of the living God; not in tables of stone, but in fleshly tables of the heart. 6. Who also hath made us able ministers of the new testament [covenant] not of the letter, but of the spirit: for the letter killeth, but the spirit giveth life. 7. But if the ministration of death, written and engraven in stones, was glorious, so that the children of Israel could not steadfastly behold the face of Moses for the glory of his countenance; which glory was to be done away; 8. How shall not the ministration of the spirit be rather glorious? 9. For if the ministration of condemnation be glory, much more doth the ministration of righteousness exceed in glory. 11. For if that which is done away was glorious, much more that which remaineth is glorious. 13. And not as Moses, which put a vail over his face, that the children of Israel could not steadfastly look to the end of that which is abolished: 14. But their minds were blinded: for until this day remaineth the same vail untaken away in the reading of the Old Testament; which vail is done away in Christ."

Observe the following points: 1. Verse 3 refers to the prophecy of Jeremiah that a new covenant would supercede the old one on stones. Now Paul says it is not written with ink as the law of Moses was in a book, nor on stones as the decalogue was, but by the spirit in the heart. The law in the book and on stones have both gone. 2. Verse 6: he says the apostles do not minister the letter but the spirit. "The letter refers exclusively to *the law*." "The context shows that by the letter he meant the old covenant and by the spirit the new." Pulpit Commentary, pages 59–80. 3. To put it beyond all doubt, as to what he means, Paul, in verse 7, specifies "the ministration of death *written* and *engraven in stones.*" Surely we know that this was the decalogue. This he calls "the ministration of death." 4. In verses 8 and 9 he calls the gospel "the ministration of the spirit" and "the ministration of righteousness" and says that it exceeds in glory the old ministration of death. 5. To put it beyond doubt that he means the decalogue, he refers to the vail which Moses put over his face when he came down with the tables of stone in his hands. Compare verse 13 with Ex. 34: 27–35. 6. Twice Paul directly names that which was "written in stone," verses 3 and 7; once he says we do not minister the letter, verse 6; he says that that which was engraven in stones was the ministration of death, verse 7, and the "ministration of condemnation," verse 9; then he says this was "abolished," verse 13, and three times he says it "was done away," verses 7, 11, 14. 7. Compare verses 7 and 11. "The ministration of death written and engraven in stones was glorious" and "that which is done away was glorious;" the very thing which was written in stones in verse 7, is said to "be done away" in verse 11. 8. In verse 7 the ten commandments are evidently taken to represent the whole Mosaic dispensation. If these, the foundation of the whole system, are removed, then of course all the system must go with them. "The ten commandments thus written here represent the whole Mosaic economy." Notes of Am. Tract Society on verse 7.

Adventists have tried to save their theory here by saying that in verse 7, "*ministration*" was not what was "*en-*

graven" in stones; but that "*death*" is what was written there. This will not do. In the Greek the word for engraven exactly agrees with *ministration* but does not agree with *death*, hence the decalogue is what is called "the ministration," and that was done away. Dr. Clarke says on this verse: "Here the apostle evidently intends the law." "This ministration of death, the ten commandments, written on stones, a part of the Mosaic institution, being put for the whole, was glorious."

The Pulpit Commentary on this verse says: "Literally, *engraved in* letters on stones (Ex. 31: 18). The reference shows that, in speaking of 'the letter,' St. Paul was only thinking of the Mosaic Law, and indeed, specifically of the decalogue." "The ministration of death was written and engraven on stone in the form of ten commandments." Read with verse 7 Ex. 31: 18; 32: 16. "Tables of stone *written* with the finger of God." "The writing of God, *graven* upon the tables." How can a candid man deny that Paul meant this very thing, the decalogue?

To the Galatians Paul also writes that the covenant of Sinai has gone. It will be seen that he uses "covenant" and "law" as synonymous, showing that the law was the covenant.

"Tell me, ye that desire to be under the law, do ye not hear the law? For it is written, that Abraham had two sons, the one by a bondmaid, the other by a free woman. But he who was of the bondwoman was born after the flesh; but he of the free woman was by promise. Which things are an allegory: for these are the two covenants; the one from the mount Sinai, which gendereth to bondage, which is Agar." Gal. 4: 21-24.

Here the old law covenant of Sinai is declared to be "bondage" and he says "Be not entangled again with the yoke of bondage." Chap. 5: 1.

So in Heb. 12: 18-24, Paul distinctly says that Christians

do not go to Sinai and the thunders of the law, but they come to Jesus and the new covenant. Read it all. Here are a few sentences: "For ye are not come unto the mount that might be touched, and that burned with fire, nor unto blackness, and darkness, and tempest. And so terrible was the sight, that Moses said, I exceedingly fear and quake: But ye are come unto Mount Sion. And to Jesus the mediator of the new covenant."

Adventists are always dwelling upon the terrible scenes at Sinai at the giving of the law and pointing others there; but Paul says, No, do not go there; but to Mount Sion, to Jesus and the new covenant.

So Jeremiah predicted the rejection of the covenant in the ark and that instead of it, men would seek to the name of the Lord at Jerusalem where the gospel went forth.

"In those days, saith the Lord, they shall say no more, the ark of the covenant of the Lord: neither shall it come to mind; neither shall they remember it; neither shall they visit it; neither shall that be done any more. At that time they shall call Jerusalem the throne of the Lord; and all the nations shall be gathered unto it, to the name of the Lord, to Jerusalem." Jer. 3: 16, 17.

Adventists are trying to revive the very thing the Lord said should be forgotten, "the ark of the covenant." All their study and worship is centered around that just as of old with the Jews. But the effort is vain. God has said it. Since the cross Jesus and Jerusalem have been where all eyes have turned while the ark and old covenant are forgotten, just as the Lord said it would be. So Isa. 2 : 3 ; "Out of Zion shall go forth the law and the word of the Lord from Jerusalem." There is where we now go for the law, not to the ark or to Sinai.

CHAPTER XX.

WHAT LAW ARE CHRISTIANS UNDER?

When God speaks, is it not sin to disobey? Surely it is. Paul says: "God, who at sundry times and in divers manners spake in time past unto the fathers by the prophets, hath in these last days spoken unto us by his son." Heb. 1: 1, 2. This says that God hath spoken to men in various ways at different times. No matter in what way God's will was expressed, it would have been sin to disobey. "If the law of Sinai is gone, then there is no law, no sin," say Adventists. Indeed, then it is impossible for God to reveal his will to men, except in those exact words, letter for letter! Who believes such an absurdity? The whole controversy is reduced to simply this: Has God in the New Testament, plainly and fully revealed his will to men and told them what is right and what is wrong? Is the will of God revealed through his Son in the New Testament higher authority than the Old Testament, or is it not? Are the teachings of the New Testament to be modified to harmonize with the letter of the law in the Old Testament, or are the precepts of the Old Testament to be modified to harmonize with the gospel? The latter, certainly. But the gospel nowhere enjoins the seventh day.

Then is not the word of the Lord Jesus Christ law? Could there be any higher law? Said Jesus, "I and my Father are one," John 10: 30, and "All men should honor the Son even as they honor the Father." John 5: 23. Then the words of Christ are to be honored as highly as the words of God. They are law the same as God's words are. God promised to raise up Christ and put his words in his mouth, and he should speak as God commanded him, Deut. 18: 18. Jesus said his Father sent him and commanded him what to say, John 12: 49, 50. "The word that I have spoken, the same shall judge him at the last day," verse 48. Then we shall be judged by the teachings of Christ, not by the old law. Christians will be judged by the gospel. "In the day when God shall judge the secrets of men by Jesus Christ according to my gospel." Rom. 2: 16. God said, "Hear ye him," Matt. 17: 5. All authority in heaven and in earth is given to him, Matt. 28: 18. "He taught them as one having authority," Matt. 7: 29. He has a law, Gal. 6: 2. "Fulfill the law of Christ." "The isles shall wait for his law." Isa. 42: 4. We are under his law, 1 Cor. 9: 21. "Under law to Christ," Rev. Ver., "Under Christ's law," Diaglott. "Under the law of the Messiah," Syriac. The grandest summary of moral and religious truth the world ever heard was the sermon on the Mount, Matt. 5-7. It is as much superior to the decalogue as gospel is superior to Judaism. Here Christ forbids murder, verses 21, 22; adultery, verses 27, 28; swearing, verse 34; hypocrisy, 6: 1-5; covetousness, 6: 19-34; and every wrong act, 7: 12. Would it not be sin to disobey the precepts of Christ?

Jesus gave commandments to his disciples, Acts, 1: 2, and commanded them to teach them to all nations. Matt. 28: 18-20. We are to keep his commandments. John 14: 15, 21; 15: 10. Then would it not be sin to break them? Who dare deny it? "Paul, an apostle of Jesus Christ by the will of God," Eph. 1: 1, said, "Put away lying," "sin not," and "steal no more," Eph. 4: 25-28, and, "The things I write unto you are the commandments of the Lord." 1 Cor. 14: 37. And yet Adventists will say, that if the old law is gone, there are no commandments against lying, stealing, etc. We know better, as the above teaches. Indeed, Paul says, "I kept back nothing that was profitable unto you," "for I have not shunned to declare unto you all the counsel of God." Acts 20: 20, 27. Every sin of which the human heart is guilty, is plainly forbidden in the New Testament over and over by the authority of Christ and his apostles, as all know. Yet nothing condemns sin but the decalogue!

The spirit of the Mosaic law, every moral principle in it, is reiterated over and over in the gospel, with all the authority of the Son of God. Not a Christian duty can be named which is not taught in the New Testament. Not a single thing is forbidden by the Old Testament which it would be wrong for a Christian to do, which is not also forbidden in the New, in some form. Excepting the Sabbath, the other nine commandments are in the New Testament, either in the same words or in substance.

Then is the Old Testament to be thrown away? God forbid. It should be received as the inspired word of God, a mine of precious truth; but it must be studied in the light of the New Testament, and modified by it. Nothing should be required of Christians simply because it is found in the law of the Old Testament. To bind our consciences, it must be required by the New Testament. Here the seventh day fails entirely, for there is no requirement in all the New Testament to keep it; but its abrogation is plainly taught.

"THE COMMANDMENTS OF GOD" IN THE NEW TESTAMENT.

Seventh-Day Adventists have much to say about "the commandments of God," Rev. 14: 12, and claim that these are the ten commandments. With them "the commandments" always means just the decalogue, nothing more. Wherever they find this term they thus apply it. But such a position is wholly erroneous. There are over 800 texts where the phrase, "the commandments," in its various forms is used. I have carefully examined every one of them. I find that it is a general term for all the requirements of the Bible. According to my best judgment, in forty-nine cases out of fifty it means something more than the ten commandments. Let the reader examine the following texts:

Lev. 22 refers wholly to the duties of the priests and the offering of sacrifices. What the Lord commanded about these he calls his "commandments." Verse 31. In Deut. 11: 27, 28, what Moses commanded is called "the commandments of God." In Deut. 26: 12, 13, the term is used of the law of tithing. In Deut 28: 1, it is applied to all that Moses commanded them. With a concordance, any person can readily find hundreds of cases where this term means something more than the decalogue. When Jesus was questioned about the law he named as the greatest "commandments," two entirely outside of the ten. See Matt. 22: 35-40.

So the precepts of Christ and His apostles are often called commandments. Jesus says: "The Father which sent me, he gave me a commandment what I should say." John 12: 49. If God gave Christ commandments, and He gave them to His church, would they not be the commandments of God? Certainly. The old dispensation was passing away, and the Lord was proclaiming the commandments of God for the new dispensation, the gospel. So in the great commission He said, "Teach them to observe all things whatsoever I have commanded you." Matt. 28: 20.

Again Jesus said, John 14: 15, 21, "If ye love me, keep my commandments." "He that hath my commandments, and keepeth them, he it is that loveth me; and he that loveth me shall be loved of my Father, and I will love him, and will manifest myself to him." How can we, in the face of these plain texts, say that Jesus gave no commandmants? Who is it that loves Christ? He that keeps his commandments. This is what it is in the New Testament to be a commandment keeper. So again John 15: 10, 14: "If ye keep my commandments, ye shall abide in my love; even as I have kept my Father's commandments and abide in his love." "Ye are my friends, if ye do whatsoever I command you."

If, then, we do what Jesus commands us, is not that enough? and shall we not be safe and sure of his love and the love of his Father? But where did Jesus ever command to keep the seventh day? Nowhere. So Luke says he was taken up, "after that he through the Holy Ghost had given commandments unto the apostles whom he had chosen." Acts 1: 2. If Jesus gave commandments through the Holy Ghost, would they not be the commandments of God? Are not these equal to those given through Moses? Now hear Paul as to what are the commandments in the gospel: "If any man think himself to be a prophet, or spiritual, let him acknowledge that the things that I write unto you are the commandments of the Lord." 1 Cor. 14: 37.

Then all Paul's writings are "the commandments of God." And the Apostle says, Let those who are spiritual acknowledge it. Will our Seventh-day brethren acknowledge it? They may see a new meaning in "the commandments of God," Rev. 14: 12, if they will. Again Paul says, "For ye know what commandments we gave you by the Lord Jesus," 1 Thess. 4: 2. Then the Apostles did give commandments by the authority of the Lord Jesus. Peter bears a similar testimony. 2 Peter 3: 2. "That ye may be mindful of the words which were spoken before by the holy prophets and of the commandments of us the apostles of the Lord and Savior." *Entole*, the Greek word for commandment, occurs in the New Testament, in its singular and plural forms, sixty-eight times. In at least forty-eight of these cases it cannot mean the decalogue, and in over half of the others it is used in a general way. In not a single case is it certain that it means all the ten and nothing more. There is not a hint that it means the decalogue in any one of the three passages where it occurs in Revelation. To claim that it does is to assume without evidence the very point to be proved. John, who wrote the book of Revelation, also wrote the gospel of John and the three epistles of John. He uses the word "commandments," plural and singular, twenty-eight times, and in not a single case does it refer to the ten commandments; but in nearly every case, if not in all, it refers to the commandments of Jesus. See John 14: 15, 21; 15: 10; 1 John 2: 1-5; 3: 22-24; 4: 21; 5: 1-3. And naturally we would suppose that he means the same thing by commandments in Rev. 14: 12.

As Christ is our "Lord and Master," John 13: 13, the "Head" of the church, Eph. 1: 22; "All and in all," Col. 3: 11; having "all power in heaven and in earth," Matt. 28: 18; and is to judge the world, John 5: 22; at his judgment seat, Rom. 14: 10; how reasonable that he should give the laws to that church. This is just what he did do, Matt. 28, 18-20; Acts 1: 1, 2. If any one will obey the teachings of Christ he need not fear about his salvation.

CHAPTER XXI.

**FORTY-SEVEN PROMINENT TEXTS USED BY SABBATA-
RIANS EXAMINED.**

For the convenience of the reader, we will arrange here in order an examination of all the prominent texts used by Seventh-Day Adventists on the Sabbath or the law. Where the text has been fully examined in the body of the work, we will refer to the chapter where it will be found.

Gen. 2: 1-3. See Chapter XIII., page 249.

Gen. 26: 5. Abraham kept the Sabbath.

Abraham kept God's "commandments and laws." This was the ten commandments, therefore he kept the Sabbath. *Answer:* 1. They assume the very thing to be proved, viz: that this was the ten commandments. 2. This was 430 years before the decalogue was given. Gal. 3: 16, 17. How could he keep what was not yet given? 3. Anything which God commanded at any time would be "his commandments," and this would vary with circumstances. What Moses required is called "God's commandments." Deut. 28: 1, 15. Says Paul, "What I write unto you are the commandments of the Lord." 1 Cor. 14: 37. "Sacrifice to the Lord our God as he shall command us." Ex. 8: 27. The Lord's directions to Noah about the ark were God's commandments. Gen. 6: 22. To circumcise was one of the commandments of God to Abraham, which he kept. Gen. 21: 4. So Abraham obeyed all God told him to do. Hence, this text has no reference to the ten commandments, nor to the Sabbath.

Ex. 16: 23-30. See Chapter XIII., page 254.

SPECIAL TEXTS EXAMINED. 367

Ex. 20: 1-17. The decalogue. See Chapter XVIII.
Ex. 31: 13-17. The Sabbath forever. See page 259.
Lev. 23. The yearly Sabbaths. See Chapter XV.
Lev. 23: 38. "Beside the Sabbaths of the Lord."

It is claimed by Seventh-Day Adventists that the Lord here separates out the Sabbath from all other holy days, showing that it is of a different nature, in these words, verses 37, 38: "These are the feasts of the Lord: * * * beside the Sabbaths of the Lord." Yes, but read the whole verse, "Beside the Sabbaths of the Lord, and beside your gifts, and beside all your vows, and beside all your free-will offerings, which ye give unto the Lord." Not only the Sabbath, but gifts, vows and offerings are also excepted with the Sabbath in the same verse. The idea is this: the Sabbath, the gifts, vows and offerings are of regular weekly or daily occurrence, whereas the other holy days and special offerings were to come only once a year at stated seasons. When these yearly offerings and holy days came at the same time of the regular daily or weekly service they were not to take the place of the regular daily and weekly services, but must be observed besides all these. Any one can see that this is the simple meaning of the words "beside the Sabbaths of the Lord, and beside your gifts," etc. The idea is not to distinguish the Sabbath above the other feasts, but to say that these must be kept in addition to the regular service of the Sabbath and the daily offerings.

Deut. 31: 24-26. Two laws, one in the ark and another in the side of it. See Chapter XVII., page 309.

2 Kings 21: 8. Two laws. "If they will observe to do according to all that I have commanded them, and according to all the law that my servant Moses commanded them."

It is claimed that this shows two laws, one given by God, the moral law, the decalogue; the other by Moses, the ceremonial, the one written in the book. Well, Moses in the book gave the law, "Thou shalt love the Lord with all thy heart," Deut. 6: 5, and "Thou shalt love thy neighbor as thyself," Lev. 19: 18. These, then, must be ceremonial! No, there is no difference made between what God gave himself or gave by Moses. Indeed, the greatest commandments of all he gave by Moses. Matt. 22: 36-40. 2 Kings 21: 8, is loosely worded, that is all. Read the same text in 2 Chron. 33: 8. "If only they will observe to do all that I have commanded them, even all the law and the statutes and the ordinances by the hand of Moses." Revised Version. That makes it plain. God gave them all by the hand of Moses. See also Neh. 8: 14.

1 Chron. 16: 15-18. The decalogue for 1,000 generations.

Adventists claim that this covenant is the ten commandments. Hence it was given to the patriarchs and must be kept for ages yet, as less than 200 generations have passed since Adam. So this law must continue at least 800 generations yet. *Answer:* 1. The term "a thousand generations" is manifestly an expression meaning an indefinitely long time, not exactly 1000 generations, no more, no less. If the world must stand 800 generations yet, what becomes of Adventism! So they can not take it literally themselves. Hence it may have ended ages ago. 2. As this is poetry, verse 7, the license of poetry is used. 3. The "covenant" here mentioned is not the covenant of ten commandments, for Moses says expressly that the fathers did not have the covenant of the decalogue. Deut. 5: 2, 4. But this covenant was made with Abraham. 1 Chron. 16: 16. 4. The covenant here referred to is God's promise to give Canaan to Abraham, Isaac, and Jacob. See verse 18. "Saying, unto thee will I give the land of Canaan." See Gen. 15: 18, 26: 3; 28: 13. So it has no reference to the decalogue.

Neh. 9: 13, 14. Two laws.

God gave them one set of laws himself and then gave another set by Moses. Read it. *Answer*: It is true that one part of the law was given in one way and another part in another way. But this neither says nor intimates that therefore they were different laws and of a different nature. See remarks on 2 Kings 21: 8.

Ps. 19: 7. The law perfect.

Adventists constantly quote this text as proof that the ten commandments are a perfect law and hence could not be changed.

Answer: An examination of this text will answer nine-tenths of all their law texts in the Bible. So we will make the answer here and refer to this from the other texts. The grand fallacy of all their arguments is the assumption that "*the law*" is just the ten commandments, nothing more, nothing less. Hence they ring the changes on "*the law*," "*the law*," without end. But remember "the law" means the whole system of law given to the Jews on Sinai, including moral, civil and ceremonial precepts, sacrifices, priesthood, circumcision, feasts, etc. Smith's Bible Dictionary, Art. Law, says that the law refers "in nine cases out of ten to the Mosaic law, or to the Pentateuch." Elder Butler confesses, "The term 'the law,' among the Jews *generally* included the five books of Moses." Law in Galatians, page 70. Don't forget this fact and you will have little trouble with Advent arguments on "the law."

"The law," "the law of the Lord," and "the law of Moses," are all the same and include circumcision and sacrifices. Proof: Luke 2: 22, 23, 24, 27; 2 Chron. 31: 3. Again: "The law," "the law of Moses," "the book of the law," and "the law of God," are all the same. Proof: Neh. 8: 2, 3, 8, 14, 18.

Now what is meant by "the law" and "the law of the Lord" in the Psalms? It means all the law God gave Israel that which was written in the "book of the law." Proof:

David who wrote the Psalms was king of Israel. God required the king to keep a copy of "the book of the law" always by him and read in it every day of his life. Deut. 17: 15–19. The first Psalm refers to this: His "delight is in the law of the Lord; and in his law doth he meditate day and night." Verse 2. David as king read the law of Moses every day and to this he refers all through the Psalms. Adventists are constantly quoting Ps. 119 as meaning only the ten commandments. But "the law" here includes the whole law God gave Israel, moral, civil, ceremonial, all. Proof: Verse 128. "I esteem *all* thy precepts *concerning all things* to be right." David regarded God's precepts concerning tithes, sacrifices, feasts, public worship, moral duties, etc., as all right. Nine-tenths of "the law of the Lord" Seventh-Day Adventists do not pretend to keep any more than Sunday keepers do. If, then, we are law-breakers, so are they.

It is probable that Ps. 19: 7, has a wider meaning than even the Mosaic law. The marginal reading is: "The *doctrine* of the Lord is perfect." Dr. Scott on this verse says: "The word here translated 'law' may be rendered *doctrine*, and be understood as a general name for divine revelation, as then extant, the law of Moses being the principal part." Dr. Clarke, the Eclectic Commentary, and all I have consulted give the same interpretation. How narrow and unauthorized, then, is the interpretation which confines this text to simply the decalogue. It is by such unnatural methods that the seventh day is sustained.

Ps. 40: 8. The law in Jesus' heart. "Lo, I come. * * * Thy law is within my heart."

This refers to Christ. Adventists say that Jesus kept the law, the ten commandments, and therefore we should. *Answer.* 1. See how they always assume that "the law" is just the decalogue. See this answered above on Ps. 19: 7. 2. Jesus kept all the law of Moses, just as other Jews did.

SPECIAL TEXTS EXAMINED. 371

Do Adventists do it? Do they keep the law as Jesus did? No. Then their argument is a failure. 3. Jesus loved all the law and came to fulfill it. Matt. 5: 17; Luke 24: 44; and did fulfill it all at the cross. Acts 13: 29. Hence "Christ is the end of the law." Rom. 10: 4.

Ps. 89: 27-36. God will not alter his covenant

Seventh-Day Adventists claim a strong case here. The prophecy refers to Christ. If his disciples break God's law, statutes, or commandments, God will punish them. God will not break his covenant nor alter what went out of his lips, the decalogue. *Answer.* Assumptions are easy and do for the uninformed. God's law is the whole law. See above on Ps. 19: 7. The covenant and what went out of God's lips has no reference to the decalogue, but refers to God's covenant with David to give him a son to sit on his throne. See verses 3, 4, 19, 33-35. This is too plain to be denied. Thus vanishes another of their grand proof texts.

Ps. 119. The law exalted.

Every verse in this long Psalm teaches the sacredness and perpetuity of the law. *Answer.* But the law is the whole Mosaic law which the king studied daily and which Israel was to keep. See my notes on Ps. 19: 7. Are Christians to keep that law? No. Seventh-Day Adventists even don't keep it.

Prov. 28: 9. Must not turn away from the law.

He that turns away from the law, his prayer is abomination. Those who break the Sabbath do this and God does not hear their prayers. *Answer.* Seventh-Day Adventists turn away their ears from nine-tenths of that law, for it embraces sacrifices, feasts, circumcision, etc., none of which they do. See my notes on Ps. 19: 7, for proof. So this text does them no good.

Eccl. 12: 13, 14. The ten commandments cover the whole duty of man. "Keep God's commandments, for this is the whole duty of man."

These are just the ten commandments. Hence they are perfect. We need no other law. Being perfect it cannot be abrogated nor changed. All will be judged by it. Verse 14. So say Seventh-Day Adventists. *Answer.* This is a soap bubble which vanishes with a touch. 1. Does it *say* that these are the ten commandments, no more, no less? No, they assume this, for they have no proof of it. See my note on Gen. 26: 5, and Ps. 19: 7. The commandments are anything God has commanded on any subject. 2. Solomon, a king of Israel wrote this to Israel, 1,000 years before Christ. Did the decalogue cover the whole duty of a man then? Was it not a duty to pay tithes, keep the feasts, offer sacrifices, be circumcised and a hundred other things about which the ten commandments are silent? Certainly it was. Then they did not cover the whole duty of man, and this text is misapplied by Adventists. Nor does the decalogue cover all the duty of man now, nor a tithe of it. Where does it require us to visit the sick, the poor, the widow and orphans, to be sober, patient, and loving? Nowhere. It is manifest, then, that the commandments here spoken of which did cover all man's duty, embraces all that God had commanded on all subjects, moral, civil, or religious. 3. That law has been fulfilled and ended at the cross. Eph. 2: 15; Gal. 3: 19-25. Adventists themselves do not keep it.

Isa. 42: 21. Jesus magnifies the law.

"He will magnify the law and make it honorable." This is the decalogue. If Jesus magnified it he could not have abolished it; if he set it aside he would not have honored it. *Answer.* See the ready assumption again that "the law" is just the decalogue. Does it say so? No. If the reader will bear in mind once for all that "the law" is the whole Mosaic code, he will easily dispose of all their proof texts Jesus did magnify the law; first, by carefully observing every precept of that law, both moral and ceremonial;

second, by fulfilling all its predictions and types, thus accomplishing the object for which it was given. Seventh-Day Adventists themselves claim that Christ abolished the ceremonial law. Well, did he thereby belittle and dishonor that law? They dare not say so. No, he magnified and honored it, as they must admit. Then a law can be honored and magnified, and yet set aside as having fulfilled its purpose. This is just what Christ did to the law as a whole. See my notes on Rom. 3: 31.

Isa. 56, the Sabbath to be restored. See page 261.

Isa. 58: 12, 13. The Sabbath restored. See Chapter XIII., page 262.

Isa. 66: 22, 23. The Sabbath in the New Earth. See Chapter XIII., page 262.

Ez. 22: 26. The breach in the law. See page 262.

Dan. 7: 25. The pope to change the Sabbath.

"He shall think to change times and laws." This refers to the pope. He was to change God's law, the decalogue. He changed the Sabbath and thus changed times. *Answer.* 1. It does not say that it was the decalogue; this they assume. 2. To change the fourth commandment and the Sabbath would change only one law and one time; but the prophecy says laws and times, both plural. This shows that the prophecy is of much wider scope than they give it. 3. There is not a word of truth in the assertion that the pope changed the Sabbath. See Chap. XI of this book. So this application is false. 4. The old law was changed by Christ, not by the pope. Paul says: "There is made of necessity a change also of the law." Heb. 7: 12. Many other scriptures declare plainly that Jesus fulfilled the law and ended it at the cross. Gal. 3: 19–25; Rom. 10: 4; Col. 2: 14–17. This prophecy applies during the gospel age and so refers to the law of Christ, not to the old law of Sinai which ended at the cross. So their theory is wholly false. 5. In a hundred ways the pope has fulfilled this prediction outside of the Sabbath by legislating for the church in many things contrary to the laws of Christ. The Jews' translation says he shall "change the festivals and the law." See the scores of festival days which the pope has made, as Ash Wednesday, Holy Thursday, Good Friday, St. Patrick's Day, All Saint's Day, etc. This is what the prophecy means. Scott says: "Has it not multiplied its holy days till scarcely four of the six working days have been left?" Clarke says: "Appointing fasts and feasts, * * * new modes of worship, * * * new articles of faith." This is what the prophecy foretold. It has no reference to the Sabbath.

Matt. 5: 17–19. Till heaven and earth pass away.

Jesus says he did not come to destroy the law, but to fulfill it. And "Till heaven and earth pass, one jot or one tittle shall in no wise pass from the law, till all be fulfilled." Whoever breaks any one of these commandments is guilty. This law is the decalogue. Jesus says that every jot and tittle of it will stand till heaven and earth pass away. This shows that this law is unchangeable and still binding. The Sabbath is a part of it and therefore the seventh day must still be kept. *Answer.* Seventh-Day Adventists consider this the strongest text in the New Testament for the law. They are constantly quoting it. If this fails, they have no stronger fort. I am sure it teaches no such thing as they claim. 1. Seventh-Day Adventists themselves admit that Jesus fulfilled and ended what they called the ceremonial law. He abolished it at the cross. Well, did he come to destroy that law? Certainly not, and yet he did it away. So, then, it is one thing to destroy a law, and quite another to bring it to a close by fulfilling it. He says he came to fulfill the law. 2. It does not say that every jot and tittle of the law will stand till heaven and earth pass away; but it does say that it will not pass away until it is all fulfilled.

SPECIAL TEXTS EXAMINED. 375

This teaches that it would all be fulfilled and pass away sometime. The idea is that sooner would heaven and earth pass away than one letter of the law would fail of being fulfilled. Luke's words make this matter very clear. "It is easier for heaven and earth to pass, than one tittle of the law to fail," Luke 16: 17. Here we cannot mistake the meaning; the idea is not the length of time the law is to last, but the certainty that it will not fail to be fulfilled. "Fulfilled" is defined thus by Webster: "To fill up, to make full or complete; to accomplish." The Greek word is *Plarosai* and is defined by Greenfield, among other things, "To fulfill, to complete; to bring to a close, end, finish, complete." So Jesus did not come to destroy the law, but to finish it.

The translation of Campbell, Macknight and Doddridge renders it: "Heaven and earth shall sooner perish than one iota or one tittle of the law shall perish without attaining its end." That is the idea exactly. Sawyer's translation says: "I am not come to destroy, but to complete." At the beginning of his ministry Jesus said he came to fulfill the law. After his resurrection he said: "These are the words which I spake unto you, while I was yet with you, that all things must be fulfilled, which were written in the law of Moses, and in the prophets, and the psalms, concerning me." Luke 24: 44. And then Paul says: "And when they had fulfilled all that was written of him, they took him down from the tree." Acts 13: 29. So it was all fulfilled at the cross. Hence Paul says it was nailed to the cross. Col 2: 14–16. "Christ is the end of the law." Rom. 10: 4. "The law was our schoolmaster to bring us unto Christ, that we might be justified by faith. But after that faith is come, we are no longer under a schoolmaster." Gal. 3: 24, 25. What could be plainer than that the law ended at the cross?

3. The law here spoken of is not simply the decalogue, but the whole law of Moses. No candid man will deny this.

All commentators and scholars admit it. The proof is abundant. Thus: "The law and the prophets was a customary phrase for the whole Old Testament." Whedon's Commentary (Methodist) on Matt. 5: 17. "By the law or prophets are meant the writings of the Old Testament including the five books of Moses called the law, and the writing of the prophets or rest of the Old Testament." Notes on Matt. 5: 17 by George W. Clarke. "As everywhere else, so here the word *nomos* (law) refers to the whole law, and not merely to the decalogue." Lange's Com. on Matt. 5:17. "By *ton nomon* (the law) must be meant, in some sense, the law of Moses." Bloomfield's Notes on Matt. 5: 17. "The law and the prophets summarily denote the whole Old Testament revelation." Meyer's Commentary on Matt. 5: 17. "By the law and the prophets is here meant the Old Testament in general." Bible Commentary. Dr. Albert Barnes says on this text: "*The law*—the five books of Moses called the law. *The prophets*—the books which the prophets wrote. These two divisions here seem to comprehend the Old Testament." So all commentators.

The Jewish scriptures were divided into the "book of the law," which included the five books of Moses, and the "book of the prophets," which included the books written by the prophets, as the historical books, etc. Sometimes a third division was recognized, viz: the Psalms, or poetical books. I have before me the Jews' Bible which is divided that way. Portions from the book of the law and also from the prophets were read in the synagogues every Sabbath. This division of the Old Testament is often referred to in the New Testament. Paul says: "All things which are written in the book of the law." Gal. 3: 10. Again: "It is written in the book of the prophets." Acts 7: 42. Once more: "After the reading of the law and the prophets." Acts 13: 15. Hence "the law and the prophets" became a common term for the whole Old Testament. The law was the five books of Moses. Read a few texts: "This is the law and the prophets." Matt. 7: 12. "All the law and the prophets prophesied until John." Matt. 11: 13. Here the law can not mean just the decalogue, for the law prophesied. "On these two commandments hang all the law and the prophets." Matt. 22: 40. "The law and the prophets were until John." "They have Moses and the prophets." "If they hear not Moses and the prophets." Luke 16: 16, 29, 31. Here the law and the prophets is the same as Moses and the prophets. "Him of whom Moses is the law and the prophets did write." John 1: 45. "Beginning at Moses and all the prophets," "which was written in the law of Moses, and in the prophets, and in the Psalms, concerning me." Luke 24:27, 44. "All things written in the law and in the prophets." Acts 25:14. "Which the prophets and Moses did say." Acts 26: 22. Paul preached "out of the law of Moses and out of the prophets." Acts 28: 23. "Witnessed by the law and the prophets." Rom. 3: 21. See how common this phrase was then for the whole Old Testament. Hence Jesus said, "I am not come to destroy the law or the prophets." Matt. 8: 17. In the light of the above facts any one can see that Jesus here meant the whole Old Testament the same as in all the other texts.

In proof of this, notice that he mentions various parts of the law—murder, altar, gift, adultery, swearing, eye for an eye, divorce, love to enemies, etc., verses 21–43. Is all this in the decalogue? No, it is in the book of the law.

It is absurd to say that he meant only the decalogue and the prophets. This would leave out the books of Moses entirely. So, then, the law here is the whole law of Moses. Now if every jot and tittle of that law is binding till the end of the world, then we have the whole Jewish law to keep as well as the Sabbath. This shows the fallacy of the Seventh-

Day Adventists' position. The simple truth is that Christ fulfilled the law and it passed away after serving its purpose.

Matt. 19: 16–22. The commandments to be kept.

The young man asks what to do to have eternal life. Jesus said, "Keep the commandments." When asked which, he said, Do not murder, nor commit adultery, nor steal, nor bear false witness; honor father and mother and love your neighbor as yourself. Here Jesus teaches that we must keep the commandments to have life. He then quotes five of the ten showing that to be the law he meant. The Sabbath is a part of that law, hence we must keep it.

Answer: 1. It is noticeable that Jesus omits the Sabbath not only here but on all other occasions like it. 2. Of course no one could gain eternal life and break the commandments which Jesus mentioned. 3. And it is manifest he did not mention all the commandments which must be kept. 4. If it is said that in quoting a part of the decalogue, he thereby implied and endorsed the whole of it as binding, then we reply that by quoting a part of the law of Moses he thereby bound all the rest of that law upon us also. The command to love your neighbor is not in the decalogue but in "the book of the law." So in Mark 10: 19, he quotes "defraud not" from Lev. 19: 13, the law of Moses. Is then all the Levitical law binding on us because Jesus quoted a part of it? No. Then it by no means follows that the whole of a law is binding on us because Jesus quotes a part of it to a young man still under that law. We object to swallowing a whole ox because we are told that a piece of the flesh is good.

We should remember that at this time both Jesus and the young man were still under the law. Jesus often adapted his instructions to the time and circumstances. To the cleansed leper, Jesus said, "Go thy way, show thyself to the priest, and offer the gift that Moses commanded." Matt.

8: 4. Shall we apply this to Christians now and conclude that they must offer gifts according to Moses? Of course not, for he was yet under the law and we are not. Again Christ said, "The scribes and the Pharisees sit in Moses' seat. All therefore whatsoever they bid you observe, that observe and do." Matt. 23: 2, 3.

Here they were directed to observe every item of the Mosaic law just as the Pharisees taught. Why don't Adventists quote that to prove we must keep the Sabbath, for it certainly included the Sabbath? This shows that Christ's directions about keeping the Jewish law were to those still under the law and not for all time to come. It is noticeable that Jesus never stated directly that any of the old law would be abolished, not even the sacrifices, the temple-service, circumcision, etc. The time had not come; the people were not yet ready for it.

So this young Pharisee came as one looking to the law and his own deeds for righteousness. "What good thing shall I do that I may have eternal life?" Jesus answered him according to his question and according to his duty under the law, that law to which he was looking for salvation. "Thou knowest the commandments," do these, for the law said, "The man that doeth them shall live in them." Gal. 3: 12. It is evident that Jesus did this to take the conceit out of him and to show him his need of something better. He succeeded, for the young man went away sorrowful and humbled.

Matt. 24: 20. The Sabbath A. D. 70. See Chapter XIV., page 270.

Matt. 28: 1. "The Sabbath" still after the cross. See Chapter XIV., page 272.

Mark 2: 27. The Sabbath for man. See page 269.

Luke 23: 5-6. The women kept the Sabbath. See Chapter XIV., page 273.

Acts 13: 14; 18: 4, etc. Paul kept the Sabbath. See Chapter XIV., page 278.

Rom. 3: 31. The law established.

"Do we then make void the law through faith? God forbid, yea, we establish the law." The law is the ten commandments. It is not abolished but established. This is a positive statement that the law is still binding under the gospel. The Sabbath is a part of the law and therefore must be kept.

Answer: 1. A few isolated texts cannot be interpreted to conflict with the general tenor, and many direct statements of the New Testament that we are not under the law but that it ceased at the cross. 2. There is nothing in the text or context that says or intimates that it is the decalogue only of which Paul speaks. 3. Paul has argued through these three chapters that no one has ever kept the law, neither Gentiles nor Jews. So he reasons that no one can be justified by "the law of works," but all can be justified "by the law of faith." Chap. 3: 27. Then he "concludes that a man is justified by faith without the deeds of the law." Verse 28. Then he anticipates that some one will object that he is an Antinomian, setting aside all law. Verse 31. This he denies. Because the Jewish law is abrogated, it by no means follows that all law is abolished. So he says: "Do we then nullify law through the faith? By no means, but we establish law." Diaglott. This is a literal translation of the Greek and gives the idea correctly. Paul does not say *the* law, but simply *law* in general. The definite article the is not used before law in the original. Hence in this verse we understand Paul to speak of law in general and not of "the law" of Sinai. Here are other reliable translations of the text, giving the same idea. "Do we then make void law through the faith? Far be it, yea, we establish law." American Bible Union Translation. "Do we, then, make law useless through the faith ? By no means, but we establish law." Campbell, Macknight and Dodridge. "Do we, then, make law of none effect through faith? God forbid; nay, we establish law." Revised Version, marginal reading. The marginal reading in this Version where it differs from the authorized text as it does here, was supported by two-thirds of the learned translators present at the last reading. (See their preface.) This, then, is well supported.

Hence this text does not speak of the decalogue, nor even of the Mosaic law, but of law in the abstract. Paul affirms that faith in Christ does not nullify the use of law. This is exactly what I believe. God's great moral law remains unchanged through all ages, while particular expressions of that law adapted to local circumstances as was the Jewish law, may be changed.

If it be insisted that this must be the law given to the Jews, then we reply: The law would be the whole Mosaic law, not the decalogue alone. Dr. Adam Clarke gives a sufficient answer to the Adventists: "By law here we may understand the whole of the Mosaic law in its rites and ceremonies, of which Jesus Christ was the subject and the end. All that law had respect to him, and the doctrine of faith in Jesus Christ, which the Christian religion proclaimed, established the very claims and demands of that law, by showing that all was accomplished in the passion and death of Christ." On Rom. 3: 31. So this text in no way favors the Adventist idea, though it is their main hope.

Rom. 6: 14, 15. "NOT UNDER THE LAW."

Several times Paul says directly that Christians are "not under the law." See Rom. 6: 14, 15; Gal. 3: 23–25; 4: 21; 5: 18. It would seem as though that ought to settle it that Christians are not to be governed by that law: for surely if we are not under a law we are under no obligation to obey it. Living in Michigan, I am under the law of this state; but I am not under the law of England, hence it has no claim on me. So if we are not under the law it has no claims on us. In opposition to the plain meaning of this term, Seventh-Day Aventists say that it means that we are not under the curse or condemnation of the law. But Paul does not say that we are not under the curse of the law; but it is the law itself that we are not under. Every text where the term occurs shows that it means under the authority of the law.

This subject is so plain that Seventh-Day Adventists themselves are divided over it, one party writing against the other. Elder Waggoner leads one party and Elder Butler the other. I quote from Butler against Waggoner in "The Law in Galatians," pages 51, 52. "But it is thought that in this verse (Gal. 3: 23) the expression 'under the law' must refer to the sinner under the condemnation of the moral law. Lengthy arguments have been made in support of this; but we fail to see evidence to prove this position." Then he admits to the other party that "under the law" sometimes means under its condemnation though this is not its primary meaning. He had to say this to save himself on other texts, but I deny that it ever has that meaning. He continues: "We read in Matt. 8: 9, of a man under authority having soldiers under him, i. e., authority was over him and he was in authority over the soldiers, and each was to obey; not that he was under the condemnation of authority, or the soldiers under his condemnation. * * * The very nature of the expression itself signifies this, 'under the law' simply meaning the law being above or having authority over the persons who were under it. This is the primary, simplest meaning of the term; and unless strong reasons can be adduced to the contrary, we should always give the expression this signification." "Greenfield * * * gives no instance where it is used in the sense of being subject to the condemnation of the law." "We are no longer under a pedagogue [the law], i. e., no longer under his authority; his authority is no longer over us because his office ceased when the seed came." So writes Elder Butler, and he states the truth: but he tries to limit this to the ceremonial law. Here he fails, for it is "the law," not a part of it.

Here is what the lexicons say of the word under: " In relation to something that governs. In a state of subjection; subject." Webster. Under is from the Greek word "*hupo*," which is thus defined: "Of subjection to a law. Rom 6:14." Greenfield: " To express subjection;" " under his sway;" "under its guidance;" "subject to." Liddell and Scott. "Subject to." Groves Gr. and Eng Dict. "Under subjection to, Rom. 14." Bagster's Gr. Lex. So all the authorities I have consulted define "under" to mean under the authority of, subject to. Now Paul says, " Ye are not under the law," Rom. 6: 14; that is, not under its authority, not subject to it. This is plain enough.

Turning to the commentators, I read : " Under the law; in subjection to it." Clarke on Gal. 4: 4. " Subject to the law," " Bound by its requirements." Barnes on Gal. 4: 4. "Not under the law; not under a legal dispensation." American Tract Society, notes on Rom. 6:14. " Under the law, under the legal dispensation." Scott on Gal. 3: 23–25.

Thus all agree that " under the law " means subject to its authority. But we are not under the law, not under its authority. Read a few texts as to its meaning. " Edom revolted from under the hand of Judah." 2 Kings 8: 20. " Israel went out from under the hand of the Syrians." 2 Kings 13: 5. " Ye purpose to keep under the children of Judah." 2 Chron. 28:10. In every case it means under the authority of. Again : " A man under authority, having soldiers under me," Matt. 8: 9. "Ye are not under the law, but under grace." Rom. 6:14. "And unto the Jews I became as a Jew, that I might gain the Jews; to them that are under the law, as under the law, that I might gain them that are under the law." "To them that are without law, as without law (being not without law to God, but under the law to Christ), that I might gain them that are without law." 1 Cor: 9: 20–21.

This passage shows beyond a doubt what Paul means by "under the law." The Jews were under the law. When with them he did as they did to gain them. He kept the law as they did. See for proof Acts 16: 3, where he circumcised Timothy, and Acts 21: 20–26, where he shaved his head and offered offerings. Those without law were the Gentiles who were never under the Jewish law. When with them he lived as they did to gain them. He did not keep the Mosaic law. But Paul is careful to add that he was under the law to Christ, or more correctly, "Under law to Christ." Revised Version. "Under Christ's law." Diaglott. "Under the law of the Messiah." Syriac. "Under the law of Christ." Clarke. "The law enjoined of Christ." Barnes. Paul says he was under Christ's law. Does he mean that he was condemned by the law of Christ? Surely not; but he was under its authority.

Again: "But before faith came, we were kept under the law, shut up unto the faith which should afterwards be revealed. Wherefore the law was our schoolmaster to bring us unto Christ, that we might be justified by faith. But after that faith is come, we are no longer under a schoolmaster." Gal. 3: 23–25.

When were people under the law? Before Christ came. Are they under it now? No. This shows what Paul means —a change of dispensations changed their relations to the law. Before Christ, under the law; since Christ, not under it.

Before Christ came they were under the law as a teacher who was preparing them for the great Teacher. When Christ came they were no longer under that old schoolmaster, the law. Proceeding with his argument, Paul says: "But when the fullness of the time was come, God sent forth his Son, made of a woman, made under the law." Gal. 4: 4. This again is decisive as to the meaning of "under the law." Christ was born under the law, that is, subject to the law the same as any Jew. He carefully obeyed that law till it was abolished at His cross. He certainly was not born under the condemnation of the law, for he was without sin. To the Galatians who were going back to the observance of the law Paul says: "Tell me, ye that desire to be under the law, do ye not hear the law?" Gal. 4: 21. Did they desire to be under the curse of the law? Nonsense. They desired to obey the law just as Adventists do now. Finally Paul says to them, "If ye be led of the Spirit, ye are not under the law." Gal. 5: 18. If they accepted Christ, they had no further need for the old law. So, then, Christians are not under the authority of the law for it was nailed to the cross. On this point Dr. Adam Clarke forcibly says: "Under the law: In subjection to it, that in Him, all its designs might be fulfilled, and by His death, the whole might be abolished, the law dying when the son of God expired upon the cross." On Gal. 4: 4.

That "under the law" means subject to the authority of the law is plainly proven by Rom. 3: 19. "Now we know that what things soever the law saith, it saith to them who are under the law." The Jew readily admitted that all the Gentiles were sinners; but the point was to prove that the Jews themselves were also sinners. So in verses 10–18 he makes several quotations from their scripture, saying that, "There is none righteous, no, not one," etc. "Now," says Paul, "you cannot apply this to the Gentiles, for it is in your own law, and we know that a law speaks to those who are subject to it and not to those who are not. So it must mean that not one of you Jews are righteous. Hence, as all the Gentiles are sinners, and this proves that all Jews are sinners too, therefore all the world are guilty." Again Paul argues that the law speaks only to "those who are under the law." But does the law speak only to those who are condemned by it? That is false and absurd. To every man in Michigan our law says, "you shall not steal," whether they have stolen or not. So the Mosaic law was addressed to all the Jews. "Hearken, O Israel, unto the statutes and unto the judgments which I teach you." Deut. 4: 1. Who was to hearken to that law? All Israel, for it spoke to them all. This fact was so manifest that Paul said, "Now we know that what things soever the law saith, it saith to them who are under the law." What, then, does he mean by un-the law? He means under the authority of the law, subject to the law, and this is what it always means. But Paul says over and over that Christians "are not under the law."

But Adventists immediately exclaim, "Then, if we are not under the law, we can sin all we like, can steal, lie, kill, etc." They never seem to notice that this is precisely what the Judaizers, the opponents of Paul, said against his doctrine back there. He states their objection and answers it. "Ye are not under the law, but under grace. What then? shall we sin, because we are not under the law, but under grace? God forbid." Rom. 6: 14, 15.

The fact that it was objected to Paul that his doctrine of the law gave license to sin shows that he did set aside the authority of the law. If not, why was this objection made to his doctrine? The Jews believed in the pardon of sin as strongly as Paul did. So if he merely taught that the sinner was pardoned by grace so that he was no longer under the condemnation of the law, the Jew would agree with him, for they all believed in the pardon of sins. The fact that this objection was raised to Paul's position on the law the same as it is to our position now, shows that we have interpreted him correctly.

Rom. 7. The law is holy.

Verse 12. "Wherefore the law is holy and the commandment holy, and just and good." This is the decalogue as shown by verse 7. As late as A. D. 60, Paul said it was holy, just, good, and spiritual, verse 14, and that he delighted in it, verse 22. Certainly then it was not abolished.

Answer: Whoever has access to Dr. Clarke's Commentary on this chapter will find the Seventh-Day Adventist argument fully and finely answered. I will note but a few points.

Paul had just stated that we are not under the law. Chap. 6: 14. Now he illustrates it. A woman is bound to her husband as long as he lives. She is under his law, his authority. If he dies, "she is free from *that* law." Verse 3. This is not the law of the state, nor the moral law, nor the law of Moses, but it is "the law of her husband," Verse 2, as Paul distinctly says. That law under which she has been living dies with her husband and she is freed from it, no longer bound to do his will, but is free to give herself to another.

Just so the Jews had been held under the authority of the Mosaic law. That he writes this to the Jewish believers at Rome is proved by the first verse. "I speak to them that know the law."

But the law died and so the connection between them was dissolved and its authority was ended. This is Paul's conclusion as stated by himself: "But now we are delivered from the law, that being dead wherein we were held."

"Wherefore, my brethren, ye also are become dead to the law by the body of Christ; that ye should be married to another, *even* to him who is raised from the dead." Verses 4, 6. No statement could be plainer: we are delivered from the law which is dead. And we are dead to the law. Now we can be married to Christ. Says Dr. Albert Barnes on verse 4: "The idea there is, that death dissolves a connection from which obligation resulted. This is the single point of the illustration. It is an error to make everything in this illustration fit something in the case of the Roman church. Like all parables, it has just one object and that is to show the dissolution of a connection before existing, the end of an authority once in force. The Jewish believers were once under the Mosaic law. That law is dead and they are freed from its authority. Now they can accept the authority of another, the Lord Jesus." Says Dr. Clarke: "*As long as he liveth.*' Or as long as *it* liveth: law does not extend its influence to the dead, nor do abrogated laws *bind*. It is all the same whether we understand the words as speaking of a law *abrogated*, so that it cannot command; or of its objects being dead so that it has none to bind. In either case the law has no force." Surely the subject is clear enough if we want to understand it.

Viewed in the light of its many excellent precepts, the law was holy, just and good and even spiritual; yet failing to accomplish man's salvation it was superceded by a better system which does what it could not do.

Rom. 14: 5. One day above another. See page 297.

1 Cor. 7: 19. The commandments to be kept.

Paul says we must keep "the commandments of God," that is the ten commandments. *Answer:* See how they always assume just what they ought to prove, viz., that this is the decalogue. Now let Paul in the same letter explain what he means by the commandments of God. "The things that *I write* unto you *are the commandments* of *the Lord.*" 1 Cor. 14: 37. So this has no reference to the decalogue.

2 Cor. 3. The ministration of death done away. See Chapter XIX., page 356.

Galatians 3: 19. The added law.

"The law was added because of transgression." This was the ceremonial law added to the moral law. Hence the law done away in Galatians is only the ceremonial law. *Answer*. This is what one party of the Seventh-Day Adventists says, while another party says that it is all the moral law and not done away at all! So they warmly contradict each other. But, 1. There is nothing said about any such distinction as moral and ceremonial laws in all the book.

2. We have proved that there is no such distinction in all the Bible.

3. All through Galatians it is "*the*" law without an intimation that there was another law from which it was to be distinguished. *The* law was the whole law. Even Elder Butler admits this. Hear him: "The term 'the law' among the Jews generally included the five books of Moses, thus including the whole system, moral, ritual, typical and civil. This as a system these Judaizing teachers desired to maintain." Again: "There are no doubt, several references to the moral law in the epistle." Law in Galatians, pages 70, 15. Good: that ends the matter; Galatians treats of the whole law.

4. That the moral law, as they call it, is included in "the law" is easily proved. Gal. 3: 10, includes "all things which are written in the book of the law." That book contained the ten commandments. Butler admits this. "The book of the law * * * contained both the moral and ceremonial laws." Law in Galatians, page 39. Again: "Christ hath redeemed us from the curse of the law." Gal. 3: 13. This is the moral law, for there was no curse to the ceremonial law. This point is hard for them to meet. Butler makes this confession: "We are perfectly willing to ad-

mit that the curse brought to view in the text, from which Christ redeems his people, principally includes transgressions of the moral law." Law in Galatians, page 40. This gives up the whole case. In Gal. 5: 14, Paul quotes as "the law," "Thou shalt love thy neighbor." If any law is moral this is.

5. Now read carefully Gal. 3: 15-19, and see that the *law* was added to the *promise* made to Abraham. "Was added to the promise," Wesley's Notes. So all their talk about this being the ceremonial law added to the moral law is a fallacy. It is the whole law and it all ended at Christ. Gal. 3: 19-24.

Eph. 2: 14, 15. The law of ordinances.

This shows that only the ceremonial law was abolished. *Answer:* As the ceremonial precepts of the law were the greater part of it, and as it was largely on their account that the law was abolished, as a burdensome system, they are naturally mentioned as the reason why it was abolished. In giving the cause for a man's death we naturally mention the diseased parts, though the whole man died. We say that Brown died of heart disease. Then Smith reports that all that is dead of Brown is his heart! That is a fair illustration of the Adventists argument on several texts. The apostles say *that the law* is dead, died of types, shadows and carnal ordinances. Then the Adventists report that only a *part* of the law is dead, just the most diseased parts and these have been amputated! Selah! Adventists say that there are no "*ordinances*" in the ten commandments, hence this can not apply to them. But this is a mistake. What is an ordinance? Webster says: 1. "An ordaining or establishing by authority; appointment. 2. A rule established by authority; a statute, law, edict, decree." This is exactly what the decalogue was, a law established by authority. Cruden's Concordance says: "Ordinance. 1. "Any decree, statute or law, made by civil governors. 2.

The laws, statutes, and commandments of God." So then the statutes, laws and commandments of God are ordinances; specially was this true of the Sabbath to be kept on the seventh day. This depended wholly and only upon God's appointment; hence it was surely an ordinance, and so passed away with those ordinances.

Col. 2: 14–16. Nailed to the cross. See Chapter XV.

The Law in the Book of Hebrews.

It is claimed by Adventists that the law which is here so distinctly said to have been "changed," "disannulled," etc., is only the ceremonial law. *Answer:* 1. Not a word is said about a ceremonial law or that it is a particular one of two laws that is meant. It is simply "*the*" law without any qualification. If this two law doctrine was as clear to the apostles and as important as it is with Adventists, it is strange that they should not somewhere, at least once, say so plainly. But they don't. They just say "*the*" law and go right on. 2. The decalogue is distinctly referred to several times in this book, as in Chap. 8: 9, "the covenant," (See Deut. 4: 13) "the tables of the covenant," Chap. 9: 4, and the giving of the ten commandments on Mount Sinai. Chap. 12: 18–21. Hence the book does refer to the whole law.

James 2: 8–12. Every point of the law binding.

James quotes two precepts from the ten and says we must keep the whole law of which the Sabbath is a part. *Answer:* 1. Again we remind the reader that "the law" is all the law given to the Jews, of which the decalogue is only a part. So if "the law" is binding now, then we must keep it all, sacrifices, feast days, etc. 2. If all the decalogue is binding because James quotes a part of it, then all the law of Moses is binding too, because he also quotes from that, verse 8, "Thou shalt love thy neighbor." This is from Lev. 19: 18. Is that whole chapter binding now? 3. James quoted so much as was applicable to his subject, either from the decalogue or from the other books, without thereby binding either upon us. 4. "The law of liberty," verse 12, is the law of the New Testament. Wesley says: "Law of liberty —the gospel." Notes on verse 12. Adam Clarke says: "The law of liberty, the gospel of Jesus Christ." On verse 12. Every quotation in this text is taken from the words of Christ in the gospels. See Matt. 19 : 18, 19.

1 John 2: 3-6. This is the ten commandments.

So Adventists always apply it, and then make all liars who do not keep the seventh day. *Answer:* 1. Does it say that these are the ten commandments? This, as usual, is assumed. 2. The context plainly shows that the commandments of Christ are meant. Read verses 1 to 5 and notice that it is Christ who is spoken of. Hence "his commandments" are Christ's commandments. There is no reference to the decalogue.

1 John 3: 4. Sin is the transgression of the law.

From this text Seventh-Day Adventists claim that all sins of every kind are a violation of the ten commandments which is the law here meant. *Answer:* 1. Does it say that this law is the ten commandments? No, nor any hint of such a thing. Here, as ever, they assume the very thing to be proved. 2. The decalogue was not given till Moses, 2500 years after the creation. Ex. 20. Deut. 5: 2-6. But sin existed all that time. The angels sinned, 2 Pet. 2: 4; Adam sinned, Rom. 5: 12; the Sodomites sinned, Gen. 13: 13; "the Gentiles which have not the law," Rom. 2: 12-14, sinned; hence sin is something more than a violation of the decalogue. A neglect to do good is sin, James 4: 17, but that would not violate the decalogue. Unbelief is sin, Rom. 14: 23, but that is no transgression of the decalogue. So, many are damned because they neglected to feed the hungry, give drink to the thirsty, take in the stranger, clothe the naked, or visit the sick, Matt. 25: 41-43, none of which are mentioned in the decalogue. John says, "All unrighteousness [unrightness, wrong] is sin." 1 John 5: 17. There are scores of wrongs which the decalogue does not notice at all. 3. The decalogue ended at the cross, 2 Cor. 3: 7; Rom. 10: 4, so it can not condemn sin now. 4. In the original of 1 John 3: 4, the word law does not occur at all. Thus: "Sin is lawlessness," Revised Version. "Sin is iniquity," Diaglott. "All sin is iniquity," Syriac. "Sin is wickedness," Sawyer's Translation. "Sin is the lawlessness," literal Greek. This is the correct idea. So a correct translation entirely spoils this text for Adventists. It simply affirms that all sin is iniquity, wickedness or lawlessness, a disregard of law, without any necessary reference to the decalogue.

1 John 3: 22. The ten commandments again.

The same old assumption again, viz., that "the commandments" are always the ten commandments. But the next verse explodes this hobby by naming what is meant. "And this is his commandment, That we should believe on the name of his Son Jesus Christ, and love one another, as he gave us commandment." This is not the decalogue at all.

Rev. 12: 17. The remnant keep the commandments.

This text shows that the remnant, the last state of the church, will keep the ten commandments, hence the Sabbath. *Answer.* 1. This occurs under the *dragon*, which Seventh-Day Adventists say is Pagan Rome. But Pagan Rome passed away more than 1,300 years ago, as they admit. So this applies ages ago, not to the present. 2. Does it say that "the commandments" are the ten commandments? No, nor is there anything to intimate it. They assume this as usual. 3. Time and again, all through the New Testament, other things are called "the commandments." Thus the two "great commandments," Matt. 22: 36-40, the precepts of Christ: John 14: 15, 21; 15: 10; 13: 34; Acts 1: 2; the Teachings of the apostles, 1 Cor. 14: 37; 1 Thess. 4: 2; 2 Pet. 3: 2, etc. It is far more probable that these are referred to instead of the old law which was abolished.

Rev. 14: 12. See notes on Chap. 12: 17, above.

Rev. 22: 14. Do his commandments.

1. If the common version is correct, the remarks on Rev. 12: 17, will apply here the same. 2. But in the correct reading there is nothing said about the commandments. The revised version gives it thus: "Blessed are they that wash their robes." So the American Bible Union, the Diaglott, etc. Hence this text has no bearing on the subject.

Thus we have examined every text from Gensis to Revelation on which Sabbatarians rely for the perpetuity of the law and the Sabbath. 1. To say the very least, all these texts are capable of a different interpretation from what they give them; they do not necessarily mean what Adventists say. 2. I feel confident that we have fairly and conclusively proved that they do not teach what Adventists claim.

For myself, I feel profoundly impressed that the Sabbatarian theory is built all the way through upon a narrow, forced, and unnatural interpretation of the Bible, one that cannot stand the test of fair criticism. The more I study it the more apparent these facts become to me. I am devoutly thankful to God that he has led me out of that error.

CHAPTER XXII.

THE NATURE OF MAN.

On this subject I shall make only a brief argument, simply calling attention to some of the main points.

That man's spirit survives the death of his body, and lives in a conscious state, has been so generally believed by all people in all ages that we may fairly call it universal. In this, the most barbarous and the most enlightened nations have agreed. Nor has the increasing intelligence of the advancing generations lessened this belief, but rather has confirmed it. The most profound thinkers of the race have held this faith. Though this fact is not decisive, yet it does have much weight.

So this doctrine has been the universal faith of the Christian church in all ages. The exceptions to this have been few and always regarded as heretical. This fact is justly entitled to great weight. It should not be lightly regarded.

The Jews who had for so many ages enjoyed the benefits of God's revelations, also believe that the spirit lived after the death of the body.

The Apocrypha gives the views of the Jews just before the time of Christ. Here are a few verses: The wicked shall "endure eternal torture by fire " 4 Maccab. 9: 9. "The divine vengeance is reserving you for eternal fire and torments, which shall cling to you for all time." Chap. 12: 12. "Let us not fear him who thinketh he killeth; for great is the trial of soul and danger of eternal torment laid up for those who transgress." Chap. 13: 14. Of the martyrs it is said: "Through which also they now stand beside the divine throne, and live a blessed life." Chap. 17: 18. "The children of Abraham, with their victorious mother, are assembled together to the choir of their fathers, having received pure and immortal souls from God." Chap. 18: 23. "The tyrant Antiochus was both punished upon earth and is punished now he is dead." Verse 5.

These plainly show that the Jews believed in the immortality of the soul, the conscious state of the dead, and eternal punishment.

So the Jewish historian, Josephus, who lived when Paul did, plainly states that the body of the Jews believed in the immortality of souls. Of the Pharisees he says:

"They also believe that souls have an immortal vigor in them." Antiquities, Book 18, Chapter 1. Again: "They say that all souls are incorruptible: but that the souls of good men only are removed into other bodies: but that the souls of bad men are subject to eternal punishment." Wars, Book 2, Chapter 8. Of another Jewish sect, the Essens, he says: "They teach the immorality of souls." Antiq., Book 18, Chap. 1. Further: "Their doctrine is that bodies are corruptible and that the matter they are made of is not permanent; but that the souls are immortal and continue forever; and that they come out of the most subtile air, and are united to their bodies as to prisons, into which they are drawn by a certain natural enticement. But that when they are set free from the bonds of the flesh, they then, as released from a long bondage, rejoice and mount upwards." Wars, Book 2, Chap. 8. Of the Sadducees he says: "But the doctrine of the Sadducees is that souls die with the bodies." Antiq., Book 18, Chap. 1. Again: "They also take away the belief of the immortal duration of the soul and the punishments and rewards in Hades." Wars, Book 2, Chap. 8.

Josephus says much more in the same line, so that there

THE NATURE OF MAN. 397

can be no doubt as to the belief of the Jews at that time, for he was one of them and knew well their doctrines. He says that they believed in the immortality of the soul, the conscious state of the dead, and eternal punishment. The efforts of annihilationists to deny this are uncandid and futile.

THE FAITH OF THE EARLY CHURCH.

The early Christian church held to the same doctrine. The martyrs are represented at death as going immediately to heaven. "They hastened to Christ," says Eusebius, Eccl. Hist. Book 5, Chap. 1. He says that another at death "received the crown of immortality." Same chapter. Again: "With peace they departed to God." Book 5, Chap. 2. Of one who died at the same time with another he says that it was "to attach himself to the former as his companion on the way to heaven." Book of Martyrs, Chap. 11. Of the martyrs who had died he says : " Being transferred to the heavens themselves and to the paradise of celestial pleasures." Book 10, Chap. 1.

Writing of the latter part of the second century, Eusebius says: "But about this time, also, other men sprung up in Arabia as the propagators of false opinions. These asserted that the human soul, as long as the present state of the world existed, perished at death and died with the body, but that it would be raised again with the body at the time of resurrection." Book 6, Chap. 37. It will be seen that these heretics held the same doctrine as the Adventists. They were set down in those early days as " propagators of false opinions," the same as now.

ONLY A SICKLY PLANT.

Occasionally, here and there, along in the history of the church, men have arisen advocating the sleep of the soul and the annihilation of the wicked. But the doctrine has not met with favor, has been received by but few, has had a sickly existence, and has soon disappeared.

My long acquaintance with it convinced me that it does not bear the fruits which Adventists claim for it. They say that a belief in this doctrine will save men from infidelity, Spiritualism, Universalism, etc. I found it far otherwise. A larger proportion have gone into infidelity, Spiritualism, and Universalism from Seventh-Day Adventists than from any other church with which I am acquainted. The number has been fearfully large and is increasing. Where they have converted one infidel, they have made several. I often noticed that infidels and opposers of the church were greatly pleased with our attack upon the orthodox faith and that they would go away strengthened in their unbelief and hatred of the church. This created doubts in my mind as to the utility of teaching that doctrine. I noticed also that such men as Wesley, Whitefield, Edwards, Spurgeon, Moody and others who have uncompromisingly preached eternal punishment, have been the most successful in winning souls and converting skeptics to God.

I also saw that this doctrine in the hands of the Adventists led to strife, contention, discussion, and argument, to the loss of piety and devotion. It naturally catches men of that turn of mind, instead of the humble and devout. Hence, on the whole, I saw no good in it.

The Adventists assert that the doctrine of the conscious state of the dead leads into Spiritualism. But, as stated above, facts refute this, as more in proportion to their numbers go into this error from the Adventists than from the evangelical churches. These churches strongly hold other doctrines which utterly forbid their embracing Spiritualism. Further, the Bible forbids seeking to the dead and states plainly that they know nothing of things on the earth. See Deut. 18: 9-12; Job 14: 21; Eccl. 9: 5, 6; Luke 16: 19-31.

Hence, after forty years' effort, Spritualism has made no more impression upon the church than other errors have, nor is there any prospect that it will in the future.

THE CHIEF STRENGTH OF THE DOCTRINE.

That which weighs the most with believers in the sleep of the dead and annihilation is the rational argument. Many texts of scripture are decidedly against them and they feel it; but these must be explained away because the orthodox doctrine is not reasonable. So far as we can see, nothing remains alive of the man that dies. Hence Adventists assert that death ends all. But this does not necessarily follow. The most powerful agencies in the universe are invisible. God himself is "invisible." 1 Tim. 1: 17. Adventists believe that angels and devils are constantly around us; yet we never see them. Air envelops us on every side; yet we never can see it. Even water converted into steam becomes invisible. Take heat, electricity, and gravitation, the most powerful agents with which we are acquainted, and they are invisible. Who has ever seen gravitation? We see it pull the apple from the tree, the giant oak with a crash to the ground, and hold the vast earth in its place around the sun; but the thing itself we never see. What is light? None can tell.

After the study of ages, the profoundest scientists are unable to tell what life is even in its lowest form, in the simplest plant. We know it exists: we see its effects: and we see when it departs; but what it is, whence it came, and whither it has gone none can tell. Before these unsolved problems the greatest minds stand dumb and reverently acknowledge the unsearchable wisdom of God.

But of all the profound mysteries of creation, the greatest is that of the human soul, the thinking part of man. What is thought! It can not be seen, nor heard, neither weighed nor measured. We can not say, it is so high, or so wide, or so long, or round, or square. How then can we affirm that the mind or the spirit can not exist separate from the flesh and bones simply because we can not see it go away! Such reasoning is only superficial guess-work. As we have seen, it would deny the existence of God, angels, devils and the greatest forces in nature, as heat, electricity, gravitation, the principle of life, etc. God only can tell us about the soul and its nature. Hence this is a question which can only be settled by the Bible.

So the great argument for annihilation is that it is unreasonable that God should allow sin and sinners always to exist as a blot on his creation. But the same argument would prove that an Almighty God of purity and love would never have suffered sin to enter his fair creation; or having entered, that he would immediately annihilate it. But stubborn facts refute this reasoning. Sin and sinners are here. They have been here ever since the world began, age after age. God did not blot out sin nor sinners as soon as they appeared, nor has he manifested special haste to bring them to an end. Millions of sinners he suffers to live on, not only to no purpose so far as their own salvation is concerned, nor as a warning to others; but, as far as we can see, their example hardens others in sin and introduces millions more into the world as vile as themselves. Even the fallen angels, who are not on probation, whose lives can bring no good to themselves, but who live only to lead others away from God, these he has permitted to live on for thousands of years.

Who can affirm that what God has thus permitted for thousands of years, ever since creation began, so far as we know, he can not permit for ages to come, and always? We can say that it would not be according to *our* ideas of wisdom and right. Well, has the past been according to our ideas? Is the present as we would have it? No; then this explodes that argument. Till we have infinite wisdom we had best be careful how we sit in judgment on God's ways. Could we bring together and see in one place all the sinning, all the pain, suffering, woe and anguish, tears and misery in our earth to-day, it would be as horrible as hell itself. Yet God sees it all and permits it to go right on. Did we not know it to be a fact, we would pronounce it to be irreconcilable with the attributes of God. We simply and devoutly accept what we can not explain. Eternal punishment presents no harder problem, and hence may be true, all our finite reasonings to the contrary notwithstanding.

Adventists delight to picture hell with all the horrors of literal fire, roasting, torture, etc., and then represent that this is just what orthodox churches believe. But no one believes or teaches such things. Material things of earth are used to represent spiritual things of the other world. Hence it is fire in one place, outer darkness in another, worms in another, banishment in another, to be cut in two or asunder in another, etc. We do not claim to know exactly what it will be, only that it will be a fearful state of eternal punishment.

SCRIPTURE STATEMENTS.

The Bible teaches that there is an intelligent spirit in man, which exists in a conscious state after the death of the body. What is a spirit? Jesus said, "God is a spirit." John 4: 24; and, "A spirit hath not flesh and bones." Luke 24: 39. Here, then, is one intelligent, conscious, immortal spirit which has neither flesh nor bones. Paul says that he is "the Father of spirits," Heb. 12: 9, in contrast with the "fathers of our flesh." If he is the Father of spirits, then, necessarily, these must partake of his nature. Hence Jesus says:

"That which is born of the flesh is flesh; and that which is born of the Spirit is spirit." John 3: 6. Notice the marked contrast between *flesh* and *spirit*. They are of different natures. Isaiah says: "The Egyptians are men, not God; and their horses *flesh* and not *spirit*." As God is superior to man, so spirit is superior to flesh. God is the Father of our spirits but certainly not of our flesh. Hence Paul says: "We are the offspring of God." Acts 17: 29. Our spirits, then, are from a different source, and of a higher nature than our bodies.

So the Holy Spirit, the third person in the Trinity, is an intelligent, immortal spirit, without flesh or bones. He appeared at the baptism of Jesus, Matt. 3: 16, and at Pentecost, Acts 2: 2-4; he teaches and guides us, John 14: 26; 16: 10. Here, then, is another immortal spirit.

The angels are conscious, intelligent persons, yet they are spirits. "Who maketh his angels spirits." Heb. 1: 7. So the devils are spirits; yet they are intelligent persons and do not die. See Mark 5: 1-13. Here a man with an unclean spirit met Jesus and knew him. He talked with Jesus and said there were many of them in the man. Jesus sent them out of the man into the swine. This shows that they can exist in a body or out of a body and still be alive and intelligent in both cases. This shows that spirits are intelligent persons, not merely air, or breath, or an influence, as Adventists try to prove. So in 1 Kings 22: 21, 22, "There came forth a spirit and stood before the Lord and said, I will persuade him," Ahab. The Lord told him to go.

We have seen from Josephus that the Pharisees believed in the immortality of the soul; and that the spirit lived after the death of the body. On this question Paul declared he was a Pharisee. "But when Paul perceived that the one part were Sadducees, and the other Pharisees, he cried out in the council, Men and brethren, I am a Pharisee, the son of a Pharisee; of the hope and resurrection of the dead I am called in question. And when he had so said, there arose a dissension between the Pharisees and the Sadducees: and the multitude was divided. For the Sadducees say that there is no resurrection, neither angel, nor spirit: but the Pharisees confess both." Acts 23: 6-8. The Pharisees believed in the resurrection, in angels and in spirits, and so did Paul. Adventists believe the first two and deny the third. Paul enumerates several things in heaven as "Mount Sion," "the heavenly Jerusalem," the "angels," "God the judge," "Jesus," and, finally, "the spirits of just men." Heb. 12: 22-24. All these texts and many more like them, prove that a spirit is an intelligent being, without flesh or bones, living and acting the same as men in the body.

It is easy to show that man has a spirit like these. Thus: "There is a spirit in man." "The spirit within me constraineth me." Job 32: 8, 18. "The Lord * * * formeth the spirit of man within him." Zech. 12: 1. It is spoken of as a distinct entity, distinguished from the body. This spirit is not dependent upon the body for life, but rather the body is dependent upon it. "The body without the spirit is dead." James 2: 26. Everywhere the spirit is recognized as superior to the body. This spirit in man knows and thinks. "What man knoweth the things of a man, save the spirit of a man which is in him?" 1 Cor. 2: 11. Then the spirit thinks, reasons, knows. Again: "The spirit indeed is willing, but the flesh is weak." Matt. 26: 41. So it is the spirit that wills. "My spirit made diligent search." Ps. 77: 6. Then it is the thinking part of man.

The spirit does not die with the body. Not once in all the Bible is it said or intimated that the spirit ever dies, while it is distinctly stated that it does not go down to dust with the body. "Then shall the dust return to the earth as it was; and the spirit shall return unto God who gave it."

Eccl. 12: 7. This is plain enough. Again: "Who knoweth the spirit of man that goeth upward, and the spirit of the beast that goeth downward to the earth?" Eccl. 3: 21. Man's spirit, then, goes up to God. The body can be destroyed without destroying the spirit. "For the destruction of the flesh, that the spirit may be saved." 1 Cor. 5: 5. David says: "It is soon cut off and we fly away." Ps. 9:10. Yes, *we* fly away.

The case of the thief on the cross can never be fairly harmonized with the sleep of the soul at death. "And he said unto Jesus, Lord, remember me when thou comest into thy kingdom. And Jesus said unto him, 'Verily I say unto thee, to-day shalt thou be with me in paradise.'" Luke 23: 42, 43. All sorts of efforts are made to get around the plain meaning of this text. But they are futile. Jesus plainly said, "To-day shalt thou be with me in paradise." If he went to paradise that day, then all Christians go there at death. His body did not go to paradise, for it was buried. Hence his spirit did live and go there. Immediately after this Jesus said, "Father, into thy hands I commend my spirit," verse 46. His spirit went with the thief to paradise that day. So the dying Stephen said, "Lord Jesus, receive my spirit." Acts 7: 59. This doctrine of the survival of the spirit is all through the Bible.

The Bible represents the body as the tabernacle or temple in which the man lives. Jesus said, "Destroy this temple, and in three days I will raise it up." "He spake of the temple of his body." John 2: 19, 21. So Peter said, "As long as I am in this tabernacle." "I must put off this my tabernacle." 2 Pet. 1: 13, 14. Paul teaches the same doctrine. "Though our outward man perish, yet the inward man is renewed day by day." 2 Cor. 4: 16. There is, then, an inward man and an outward man. **The inward man is the substantial man**, the one that does

THE NATURE OF MAN. 405

not perish. Paul proceeds: "For we know that, if our earthly house of this tabernacle were dissolved, we have a building of God, a house not made with hands, eternal in the heavens. For in this we groan, earnestly desiring to be clothed upon with our house which is from heaven: If so be that being clothed we shall not be found naked. For we that are in this tabernacle do groan, being burdened: * * * Therefore we are always confident, knowing that, whilst we are at home in the body, we are absent from the Lord (for we walk by faith, not by sight): We are confident, I say, and willing rather to be absent from the body, and to be present with the Lord." 2 Cor. 5: 1-8. See how clear is Paul's statement: "Our earthly house," "tabernacle," "in the body," "absent from the body," etc. Adventists never talk that way. At home in the body, absent from the Lord; but absent from the body, present with the Lord. It is only by doing violence to the scriptures that this text can be made to harmonize with the idea of the sleep of the soul.

Again hear Paul. "I knew a man in Christ above fourteen years ago (whether in the body, I cannot tell; or whether out of the body, I cannot tell: God knoweth), such a one caught up to the third heaven. And I knew such a man (whether in the body, or out of the body, I cannot tell: God knoweth), how that he was caught up into paradise, and heard unspeakable words, which it is not lawful for a man to utter." 2 Cor. 12: 2-4. Then Paul believed a man could be out of his body and go to heaven and hear words there. Adventists scout such ideas.

The following text is so plain on the subject of the conscious state of the dead, that Adventists have been greatly perplexed over it. They have tried various explanations, all contradictory and none satisfactory to themselves. I have been there and know. Paul says: "For to me to live is Christ, and to die is gain. But if I live in the flesh, this is the fruit of my labor: yet what I shall choose I wot not. For I am in a strait betwixt two, having a desire to depart, and to be with Christ; which is far better: Nevertheless to abide in the flesh is more needful for you." Phil. 1: 21-24. "To die is gain," "a desire to depart and be with Christ," "I live in the flesh," "abide in the flesh"—this was Paul's faith. He was in a strait betwixt two, whether to remain in the flesh and preach Christ and aid his brethren or depart and be with Christ. How utterly contrary to Adventist ideas this is.

See the same doctrine so definitely taught in the case of the rich man and Lazarus, Luke 16: 19-31. "And it came to pass, that the beggar died, and was carried by the angels into Abraham's bosom: the rich man also died, and was buried; and in hell he lifted up his eyes, being in torments, and seeth Abraham afar off, and Lazarus in his bosom. And he cried and said, 'Father Abraham, have mercy on me, and send Lazarus, that he may dip the tip of his finger in water, and cool my tongue; for I am tormented in this flame.' But Abraham said, 'Son, remember that thou in thy lifetime receivedest thy good things, and likewise Lazarus evil things: but now he is comforted, and thou art tormented. And beside all this, between us and you there is a great gulf fixed: so that they which would pass from hence to you cannot; neither can they pass to us, that would come from thence.' Then he said, 'I pray thee therefore father, that thou wouldst send him to my father's house: for I have five brethren; that he may testify unto them, lest they also come into this place of torment.' Abraham saith unto him, 'They have Moses and the prophets; let them hear them.' And he said, 'Nay, father Abraham: but if one went unto them from the dead, they will repent.'"

1. This is Christ's own teaching. 2. As we have seen, it was what the Pharisees believed with regard to the dead. 3. Jesus accepts and confirms their doctrine. 4. These

events occured between death and the resurrection, while the brethren of the rich man were yet alive on earth. 5. Hence immediately after death and before the resurrection the rich man is in hell and Lazarus is rewarded. 6. They are both conscious. 7. Abraham is alive over there. 8. Both think and talk. Hence the dead certainly know something. Had we no other text, this alone would disprove the sleep of the dead.

Again Jesus said God is "the God of Abraham, and the God of Isaac, and the God of Jacob. God is not the God of the dead, but of the living." Matt. 22: 32. Then those patriarchs are alive and not blotted out of existence at death. Once more: "Fear not them which kill the body, but are not able to kill the soul." Matt. 10: 28. If the body is all there is of the man, if the soul is simply the life of the body, then men can kill the soul. But Jesus says they can not kill the soul. It does not, then, die with the body. How squarely these plain texts contradict the Adventist faith; yet they claim to go by the Bible. So we find Moses on the mount with Jesus, though he had died and was buried fifteen hundred years before. Deut. 32. "Behold, there appeared unto them Moses and Elias talking with him." Matt. 17: 3. But why quote more? These are decisive.

Many of the texts quoted to prove the sleep of the soul refer only to the body. Thus Gen. 3: 19, "Dust thou art, and unto dust shalt thou return." This can not refer to the spirit which has neither flesh nor bones, Luke 24: 39, but returns to God at death, Eccl. 12: 7. Read their proof texts. "David slept with his fathers, and was buried in the city of David." 1 Kings 2: 10. Was David's spirit buried? "So man lieth down, and riseth not. * * Oh, that thou wouldst hide me in the grave." Job 14: 12, 13. Did Job's spirit lie down in the grave? Was it hid in the dust? Hardly. "If I wait, the grave is mine house." Job 17:13.

Does the spirit go into the grave? "There is no work, no device, nor knowledge, nor wisdom in the grave whither thou goest." Eccl. 9: 10. "Many of them that sleep in the dust of the earth." Dan. 12: 2. "Lazarus sleepth," "Lazarus is dead." "By this time he stinketh." John 11: 11, 14, 39. Could this be said of the spirit? Did the spirit of Lazarus decay? Surely not. Take their favorite text, Acts 2: 34. "David is not ascended into the heavens." The context shows plainly that this is said of the body. "He is both dead and buried and his sepulcher is with us." "He spake of the resurrection of Christ." Verses 29, 31. So in 1 Cor. 15, the several expressions about being asleep are all explained by the subject discussed—the resurrection of the body. 1 Thess. 4:13–16, is explained the same way. Paul is referring to the resurrection. That whole class of texts refers only to the bodies which go into the grave at death. As the spirit does not go there, these texts have no reference to it, and hence prove nothing concerning it. One simple text explains them all: "The *graves* were opened and many *bodies* of the saints which *slept* arose." Matt. 27: 52. Yes, *graves, bodies, slept*—that is the whole of it. Adventists might go to our orthodox hymn-books and select expressions about our friends being asleep and in their graves and thus prove that we all believe in the sleep of the soul. But it would be false, as we know it refers only to the body.

So their main text, Eccl. 9: 5–10, "The dead know not any thing," is limited by the context to " any thing that is done under the sun," verse 6. Compare this with other texts where the same expression is used. " With Absolom went two hundred men * * * They went in their simplicity, and they *knew not any thing*." 2 Sam. 15: 11. Another: "But the lad *knew not any thing;* only Jonathan and David knew the matter." 1 Sam. 20: 39. Of a self-conceited teacher Paul says, "He is proud, *knowing nothing.*" 1 Tim. 6 : 4. Were all these absolutely without thought or consciousness ? No. It simply means that they knew nothing about the things mentioned. So of Eccl. 9 : 5. The context explains it. " Neither have they any more a portion forever in any *thing that is done under the sun.*" Verse 6.

Psalms 146 : 3, 4, " Put not your trust in princes, nor in the son of man, in whom there is no help. His breath goeth forth, he returneth to his earth; in that very day his thoughts perish." His thoughts, his *purposes.* The margin of the Revised Version reads " purposes." The Greek word for thoughts is *dialogismoi.* Greenfield defines it " reasoning, ratiocination, thought, cogitation, *purpose.*" If we rely upon earthly princes, when they die their purposes perish and we are left helpless. So this text is easily explained as are also the few remaining ones which are used to teach the sleep of the dead.

Appendixes

Appendix A

BATTLE CREEK, MICH., furnishes a good illustration of the failure of Adventism after a fair trial. Beginning in 1855, it was the headquarters of the denomination for about a half century. It was the home of Elder White and wife. For all those years it had the benefit of the labours of all their strongest men, and the influence of their great general conferences. Here were built, at immense cost, their great institutions, as their large publishing houses, their college, their great sanitarium of world renown, their large tabernacle, etc. When I withdrew in 1887, there were nearly two thousand Sabbath keepers here, all united. Often I preached in that great tabernacle when every seat, below and in the gallery, was full. In the college I taught one class of about two hundred, all young men and women preparing to work either as ministers or Bible readers. Now, 1914, the college is closed and lost to the cause; the sanitarium has revolted from the denomination, and nearly all the management, doctors, nurses and helpers are Sunday keepers; the publishing houses were burned and the remnant moved away; the church has dwindled down to about four or five hundred; the tabernacle is largely empty and an elephant on their hands; three separate companies of Sabbath keepers now meet every Sabbath, having no connection with each other. Worse still, large numbers have backslidden, lost faith in everything, and attend no where. It has been like a desolating cyclone.

About twenty years ago among the strongest men in the ranks, men of whom the whole denomination was proud, were Dr. J. H. Kellogg, head of the sanitarium; Elder A. T. Jones, editor, author, minister, orator; Elder E. J. Waggoner, editor, author, preacher; Elder Geo. Tenney editor, minister, missionary; Elder L. McCoy, minister, chaplain of sanitarium; with many persons in important positions as business managers, college professors, doctors, etc. All these are now out of the church, and all their influence is against the body.

What has happened here is constantly happening all over the field in their old churches. It is in new fields and foreign lands where their history is unknown, that their chief gains are made. I can name large numbers of churches all over the land, which were large, strong churches thirty and forty years ago. Now they are either extinct or only a little handful meeting in the corner of an old church. Such are Norridgewock, Maine, Danvers, Mass., Memphis, Wright, and Monteray, Mich.; Knoxville, Sigourney, Winterset and Osceola, Iowa, with scores of smaller churches in many of the states. The thing does not wear. If the past is any guide, twenty years hence many of their strong men now will leave and oppose them, and many of their best churches will go down. In 1912, the latest statistics available, with 4,000 workers in the field, with millions of money spent, they only gained 4,000 in membership in all the world, or only one for every labourer! The *Review and Herald,* April 23, 1914, says: "Take 1912 as a basis, and we find that it cost this denomination practically from $900 to $1,000 for every person added to the church membership."

How does this compare with the claims that theirs is the most wonderful message the world ever had and that the power of God is with them as with no other people? Cold facts are against them.

Appendix B

The system of Seventh-Day Adventism rests for its foundation on the unsupported theories of an uneducated old farmer in his last days and the reveries of a totally uneducated, unread, sickly, excitable girl. Wm. Miller, the founder of Adventism, was sixty-one years old in 1843, the year he set for the end of the world. He died six years later, disappointed and confused. He had only a limited country schooling. He rejected all Biblical helps and depended solely upon his own ideas of the Bible. See "Life of Miller," by James White, pages 46, 48, 59. He accepted as infallibly correct the dates then found in the margin of the Bible. These were arranged by Usher according to the best information then obtainable. Later investigations have shown these dates to be incorrect by many years. Miller based all his figures on these old dates and fixed by these to a year, the beginning and ending of every prophetic period in the Bible ! By this he set 1843 for the end of the world and all other periods to fit that date, such as the seventy weeks, the 2,300 days, the 1,335 days, the 1,290 days, the 1,260 days, the seven churches, seven seals, trumpets, etc. He said all were absolutely correct !

Then came the present Mrs. White, a mere girl, wholly unacquainted with history or chronology, and set her seal to all Miller's figures and dates, said not one must be altered. Hear her : "I have seen that the 1843 chart was directed by the hand of the Lord and that it should not be altered, that the figures were as he wanted them." "Early Writings," page 64, edition of 1882. By these dates the whole denomination must always abide, right or wrong ! So their whole prophetic system rests upon the figures of an old farmer and an ignorant girl made seventy years ago ! God pity them.

Appendix C

The fanatical expectations of Adventists. For about seventy years Seventh-Day Adventists have predicted that a few months, or years, before the end, the Holy Ghost would be poured out upon them like Pentecost. They call it "*the latter rain.*" Then will occur the "*Loud Cry*" to close up the work. Now, 1914, they preach and publish that all this has begun and the work is to close up quickly! Of this work Mrs. White says: "Miracles are wrought, the sick are healed, and signs and wonders follow the believers." "Great Controversy," page 430, edition of 1884. She devotes five chapters predicting the wonders to occur just before the end. Read them. I can only sketch a few items. Satan will appear personally and visibly to all, in dazzling glory, claiming that he is Christ come to earth. All the world but Adventists accept him as such. He smiles on them and blesses them. All shout "Christ has come." Then Satan tells them that Adventists are wicked blasphemers for working on Sunday and must all be killed. Pages 442, 443. Read it.

Spiritualism has taken possession of all the churches, pages 405, 422; church and state have united, pages 423, 424, not only in the United States, but "throughout all Christendom," page 444; Satan then moves all legislative bodies to issue an edict that all Sabbath keepers shall be killed and exterminated unless they recant by a certain day. "No man may buy or sell" who does not keep Sunday, page 422; whoever refuses "shall be put to death." Sabbath keepers "will be thrust into prison, some will be exiled, some will be treated as slaves." Page 426. "They are threatened with destruction." Page 427. Adventists "will then flee from the cities and villages and associate together in companies, dwelling in the most desolate and solitary places." Page 445. "Many of all nations will be cast into unjust and cruel bondage and sentenced to be slain." Page 445. "In every quarter companies of armed men, urged on by hosts of evil angels, are preparing for the work of death, with shouts of triumph, with jeers and imprecations, they are about to rush upon their prey." Page 452.

Just then Christ appears and 144,000 Seventh-Day Adventists are caught up in the clouds and saved. All the rest of mankind, worldlings, Methodists, Baptists, and all Sunday keepers, are utterly destroyed! This is what Adventists believe and teach. Read the above quoted book. Of all the wild, fanatical theories ever preached this is the climax. To bring this about the wheels of progress would have to be turned back a thousand years. It would be the most miraculous revolution the world ever saw, and all within a few short years! It is to be world-wide—"*all nations.*" Page 445. India, China, Japan, where they care nothing for Sunday, will decree that all must die who work that day! The trend of the whole world is exactly the other way,—separation of church and state, greater liberty of thought, greater toleration of all religious beliefs, and greater laxity of Sunday observance; a man is blind who cannot see this.

Appendix D

The supremacy of the pope, not Sunday, is the "*Mark*" of the papacy. The one supreme claim of the papacy, the one all essential *test* of the loyalty of every Catholic, the one thing which every Catholic must swear to when he joins that church, the one thing above all others insisted upon in all catechisms and doctrinal books, is the *supremacy of the pope of Rome*. No one can be a Catholic and deny this claim. Subscribe to this, and all else follows. During the papal supremacy tens of thousands were martyred because they would not bow to the authority of the pope. It was this that brought on the great Reformation under Luther and originated the name *Protestant.* It is what all Protestant churches have been warning against for three hundred years. The *test,* the *mark,* of the loyalty of a Mohammedan is to acknowledge the supreme authority of Mohammed as a prophet; of a Mormon, to acknowledge J. Smith as God's prophet; of a Christian Scientist, to acknowledge the authority of Mrs. Eddy; of a Catholic, to acknowledge the authority of the pope of Rome as supreme.

In this city we have several Catholic churches and scores of other churches which keep Sunday. Does anybody think of these churches as Catholic because they keep Sunday? No. Do Catholics think of them as Catholics on this account? No. Do these churches themselves ever think of themselves as Catholics because they keep Sunday? No. Is it then a *mark* of a Catholic to keep Sunday? No, because no one, either Catholic, Protestant, worldling, or any one else, ever thinks of it as the mark of a Catholic. Hence as nobody in the church or out ever regards a person as a Catholic because he keeps Sunday, that cannot be the mark of a papist.

But the moment any person acknowledges the authority of the pope as supreme, every one regards him as a Catholic, a papist. And the Catholic church so regards him. But if he simply keeps Sunday and denies the authority of the pope, will the Catholic church accept him? Emphatically no. Then what is the *test,* the *mark,* of a papist? It is to acknowledge the supremacy of the pope of Rome. That *marks* him as a Catholic.

Thus "Johnson's New Universal Encyclopædia" says: "Roman Catholic Church, that body of Christians which acknowledges the authority of the pope of Rome." The same article gives the creed to which every Catholic must swear obedience thus : " I promise and swear true obedience to the Bishop of Rome, successor of St. Peter, Prince of the apostles, and Vicar of Jesus Christ."

Here you have the *mark* of that church. It is not keeping Sunday, but the supreme authority of the Pope. Every Catholic catechism or doctrinal work has in bold letters this headline:

"MARKS OF THE CHURCH."

Sunday keeping is never given as one of them, but the supremacy of the pope is always given. Mark well this fact.

Appendix E

The following statement I drew up, and read to a leading Catholic priest of Grand Rapids, Mich., who readily signed it, as will be seen below:

"The Catholic doctrine of the change of the Sabbath is this: The apostles, by instruction from Jesus Christ, changed the Sabbath from Saturday to Sunday to commemorate the resurrection of Christ and the descent of the Holy Ghost, both of which occurred on Sunday. The change was made by the apostles themselves, and hence by divine authority, at the very beginning of the church. There are references to this change in Acts 20 : 7 ; 1 Cor. 16 : 1, 2 ; Rev. 1 : 10, etc. Yet these texts do not state positively such a change ; hence Catholics go to the statements of the early Christian Fathers, where this change by the apostles is confirmed and put beyond doubt. Catholics also rely upon the tradition of the church which says that the change was made by the apostles. Catholics never teach that the change of the day was made by the church two or three hundred years after Christ. Such a statement would be contrary to all the facts of history and the traditions of the church.

"The Holy Catholic Church began with the apostles.

St. Peter was the first pope. Hence, when they say that the church changed the Sabbath, they mean that it was done by the church in the days of the apostles. Neither the church nor the pope, two or three hundred years after the apostles, had anything whatever to do with changing the Sabbath, for the change had been made ages before. Catholics do not call the first day of the week the Sabbath, for that was Saturday; but they call it Sunday, or the Lord's Day.

"The above statement by Rev. D. M. Canright is true and pure Catholic doctrine.—Rev. James C. Pulcher, Pastor of St. James' Church, Grand Rapids, Mich."

In answer to my question Archbishop Ireland wrote me thus:

"*St. Paul, March 2, 1914.*

"MY DEAR SIR :—In answering your question I would state that the Jewish Sabbath was simply a positive precept in the Mosaic law and lapsed with that law. The apostles and early Christians instituted the Sunday as a day of special prayer in honor of the great mysteries of the Christian religion : the resurrection and the coming of the Holy Spirit, both occurring on the first day of the week.

"Very sincerely,
"JOHN IRELAND."

I have carefully examined the "Catholic Encyclopædia," the "Catholic Dictionary," a large number of Catholic catechisms, large and small, and all agree in locating the change of the Sabbath in the time of the apostles and by the apostles. This is emphatically the doctrine of the Catholic church. *Not a single Catholic authority ever locates the change anywhere else.* Adventists are unfair in omitting this fact when they quote only a part of what Catholics say. The above Catholic authorities quote Acts 20 : 7 ; 1 Cor. 16 : 2 ; Rev. 1 : 10, the same as Protestants do as evidence that the observance of the Lord's Day originated with the apostles.

www.ingramcontent.com/pod-product-compliance
Lightning Source LLC
Chambersburg PA
CBHW020346170426
43200CB00005B/59